W9-CFZ-894

AGRICULTURAL
PRODUCT PRICES

AGRICULTURAL PRODUCT PRICES

SECOND EDITION

William G. Tomek
Kenneth L. Robinson

CORNELL UNIVERSITY PRESS

Ithaca and London

First edition published 1972 by Cornell University Press.
Published in the United Kingdom by Cornell University Press Ltd.,
2–4 Brook Street, London W1Y 1AA.

Second edition 1981

International Standard Book Number 0–8014–1337–0
Library of Congress Catalog Card Number 80–16085
Printed in the United States of America
*Librarians: Library of Congress cataloging information
appears on the last page of the book.*

Preface to the
First Edition

The decision to write this book was motivated by two considerations. First, we believe that the behavior of agricultural product prices is sufficiently unusual to require special treatment. Second, we saw a need for a more up-to-date text, which would combine principles of price determination, information on pricing institutions, and an introduction to selected quantitative techniques as applied to agricultural prices.

This book is designed for an intermediate-level course in agricultural prices and marketing. Students would benefit from a prior course in microeconomic principles, although Chapters 2 through 5 provide some of the essential material. For the most part, no mathematical competence beyond ordinary algebra is assumed. The very limited use of differential calculus is confined almost exclusively to footnotes and appendixes. Some students may find the discussion of futures markets and prices (Chapters 12 and 13) at a somewhat more advanced level than the earlier chapters. Chapters 15 and 16 have been written with the assumption that students will have had an introduction to statistics, including some knowledge of regression procedures.

Students and colleagues, too numerous to mention individually, provided comments and suggestions on selected parts of the initial manuscript. Paul Farris, Richard King, Lester Manderscheid, and Ian Sturgess reviewed the entire manuscript, and we gratefully acknowledge their help. We owe a special debt to James P. Houck for an unusually thorough review and for comprehensive suggestions.

We especially appreciate the encouragement to carry through with this project given by B. F. Stanton, and we are grateful for the accurate typing and secretarial assistance of Nancy L. Brown.

WILLIAM G. TOMEK
KENNETH L. ROBINSON

Ithaca, New York

Preface to the
Second Edition

Our principal objective in preparing a second edition has been to eliminate dated material and to include the new information on agricultural product markets and prices which has appeared in the past decade. Each chapter has undergone some revisions. Major changes have been made in Chapters 10 (general level of farm prices), 11 (discovering prices), 12 and 13 (futures markets and prices), and 15 and 16 (empirical price analysis). In addition, the derivation of a demand function from indifference curves is now discussed in Chapter 2, so that the book is somewhat more self-contained.

The orientation of the book and the level at which the material is presented remain the same as in the first edition (that is, for juniors and seniors who have studied principles of economics). We are aware, however, that the book is also being used in introductory graduate-level courses, and for this reason the references at the end of each chapter have been updated to provide guides to developments in the professional literature.

We are grateful to Joseph K. Baldwin for his careful work in preparing the figures for the second as well as the first edition. Again, we would like to acknowledge the many contributions made by our secretary, Nancy L. Brown.

W G. T.
K. L. R.

Ithaca, New York

Contents

Figures

Figures

12

Tables

AGRICULTURAL
PRODUCT PRICES

CHAPTER 1

Introduction

The principal objective of this book is to provide students with an understanding of the complex array of forces that influence the level and behavior of agricultural product prices. A secondary objective is to introduce students to empirical studies and analytical techniques that are useful in predicting price changes or the economic consequences of price changes.

Agricultural product prices are important both economically and politically since they strongly influence the level of farm incomes, the welfare of consumers, and, in many countries, the amount of export earnings. The incomes of nearly half the world's population are determined principally by the prices received for agricultural commodities. A decline of only a few cents per pound in the prices of such internationally traded commodities as sugar, coffee, and cocoa can have serious political and economic repercussions in such countries as Mauritius, Colombia, and Ghana. Even in the United States, where agriculture accounts for only a small part of the Gross National Product, farm and food prices are politically sensitive. Boycotts of meat purchases by consumers in the mid-1970s and tractor marches on Washington by farmers attest to this fact.

Distinguishing Characteristics of Agricultural Prices

Agricultural commodities provide an exceptionally interesting vehicle for the study of price-making forces. The manner in which commodity prices are determined ranges over the entire spectrum from almost complete government regulation to perhaps the closest approximation that now exists to the textbook example of pricing under freely competitive market conditions. Thus, in examining agricultural prices, one is

17

inevitably led to a study of a wide range of models of price determination and of pricing institutions.

Agricultural commodity prices are much more volatile than are the prices of most nonfarm goods and services. It is not unknown for the price of a commodity like eggs or pork to drop by as much as 50 per cent within a period of twelve to eighteen months. The international price of coffee has been particularly unstable since the early 1970s. It more than doubled between 1975 and 1977 and then, within a period of eighteen months, fell about 50 per cent. Nonferrous metals and ship charter rates are among the few nonfarm prices that exhibit short-run changes of similar magnitude.

The biological nature of agricultural production is, of course, a principal cause of price instability. Unlike most nonfarm industries, actual production in agriculture may exceed or fall short of planned production by a considerable margin. Yields vary from year to year because of unusually favorable or unfavorable weather and the presence or absence of disease or insect infestations (e.g., the failure of the monsoon in Asia or the occurrence of corn blight in the United States). Seasonal variations in production likewise contribute to price instability from month to month.

Substantial time lags exist between a decision to produce and the realization of the final output. These lagged relationships are especially important in agriculture. Relatively high or low prices may persist for considerable periods because of the inability of farmers to respond promptly to a change in price signals. At least a year is required for producers to change hog production, three years to change the supply of beef, and five to ten years for growers to change production plans for tree crops, such as apples. In the case of livestock, an increase in price may lead to a reduction in supply in the short run as farmers cut back the number of animals sent to market and hold female stock for breeding.

The nature of the demand for farm products is also a factor in price instability. For many foods, price changes tend to have a small effect on consumer purchases, or, what amounts to the same thing, a change in supply induces a relatively large price change for many farm products.

Moreover, price determination at the first handler level tends to be more competitive and more decentralized in agriculture than in other industries. There are a relatively large number of producing units, and they are geographically dispersed. While farms are becoming larger, their concentration is still far less than in most manufacturing and service industries. In many nonfarm industries, such as automobiles, tires, TV sets, and petroleum refining, a few firms dominate the market

(Caves, 1977); in contrast, for many farm products thousands of firms are needed to account for 80 per cent of sales (United States Senate Committee on Agriculture, Nutrition, and Forestry, 1979). Both the large number and spatial dispersion of farm firms make it difficult to estimate supplies and still more difficult to control total output.

Price-making forces in agriculture are not confined to national boundaries. For many commodities, a world view is essential to understanding why prices change. An increase in the price of soybeans, for example, may be due to drought in Brazil or to an early frost which cuts sunflower production in the USSR. Grain prices in the United States are strongly influenced by what happens to production in Canada, Argentina, Australia, and, increasingly, the Soviet Union.

Role of Prices

Prices play a central role in economic theory in guiding production and consumption. The authors are under no illusion, however, that either the production decisions of farmers or the buying decisions of consumers are governed solely by prices. Government programs, including land-retirement or acreage-control measures, as well as personal preferences, the limits of climate and soils, and the availability of equipment, obviously exert a strong influence on what farmers plant each year. Consumers are likewise influenced in their decisions by advertising, the display space given to foods in supermarkets, personal whims, packaging, and convenience, as well as by prices.

Some economists argue that prices no longer serve the function they once did of coordinating production and consumption (Breimyer, 1962; Collins, 1959). This view has been challenged by others (e.g., Gray, 1964). We take an intermediate position. Prices, especially relative prices, influence human behavior. Consumers do respond to changes in the price of beef relative to the prices of pork and chicken. Farmers, likewise, have demonstrated repeatedly that they will produce more onions, potatoes, cabbage, or pork in response to relatively favorable prices. Thus, an understanding of the concepts of economic theory does provide valuable insight into human behavior and to the way prices are determined.

Neither consumers nor producers respond to price changes in a consistent or mechanical way; that is, the responsiveness of quantity to a given size price change may itself change with the passage of time. As consumers become more affluent, their purchases of individual food

19

products may become less responsive to changes in prices, and as farmers become more specialized and incur large fixed investments, their output also may become less responsive to price changes.[1]

National governments have played an increasingly important role in pricing farm products since the 1930s. Agricultural price-support policies now strongly influence the prices of commodities which make up about half the value of all farm products sold by farmers in the United States. Government programs also influence the prices of about 90 per cent of all agricultural commodities produced in the European Common Market. The prices of such internationally traded commodities as coffee and sugar may be influenced by international commodity agreements or the joint decisions of several governments. The prices of still other commodities are influenced by marketing boards (for example, the Canadian and Australian wheat boards). In the United States, federal and state marketing orders have been used to divert supplies and to fix minimum prices for such commodities as raisins and milk. Clearly, many agricultural prices are no longer determined by the free play of market forces. But pricing decisions, whether made on the basis of market forces or political considerations, have important economic consequences. For this reason, tools of analysis that will help one to anticipate the economic effects of pricing decisions are still important.

Farmers, marketing and supply firms, and government officials have to make many decisions which require a knowledge of what will happen if the price of a particular commodity rises or falls. Meat packers, for example, want to know how much the production of hogs will change in response to the price of hogs or, more importantly, to the price of hogs relative to corn. Government officials need to know how much domestic use, exports, and production will be affected if the support price for wheat or cotton is raised 10 per cent. Those firms storing apples would like to anticipate the consequences for late-season prices of putting more apples in controlled atmosphere storage, which lengthens the storage life of fruit. Students of prices can help answer these questions.

Plan of the Book

The first section of this book is devoted to a review of the economic concepts that underlie price determination, particularly as they apply to

[1]These statements illustrate possible changes in the degree of responsiveness of producers and consumers to price, and they should be treated as hypotheses subject to empirical verification. Since economic growth has been associated with the development of new substitutes and since increases in the number and importance of substitutes imply greater sensitivity of quantity to price, increased affluence could lead to greater rather than less responsiveness by consumers to price changes.

agricultural commodities. This is followed by a section dealing with price variation and the linkage between prices at the retail, wholesale, and farm levels, at different points in time, and in different locations. The third section is devoted to a description and analysis of alternative pricing arrangements for agricultural commodities, such as commodity exchanges, auctions, pricing formulas, collective bargaining, and government-support programs. The final section provides an introduction to analytical methods and empirical studies of demand and supply relationships for agricultural commodities.

References

Breimyer, Harold F. 1962. "The Three Economies of Agriculture," *J. Farm Econ.*, 44:679–699.

Caves, Richard. 1977. *American Industry: Structure, Conduct, Performance.* 4th ed. Englewood Cliffs, N.J.: Prentice-Hall. Chapter 2.

Collins, Norman R. 1959. "Changing Role of Price in Agricultural Marketing," *J. Farm Econ.*, 41:528–534.

Gray, Roger W. 1964. "Some Thoughts on the Changing Role of Price," *J. Farm Econ.*, 46:117–127.

United States Senate Committee on Agriculture, Nutrition, and Forestry. 1979. *Status of the Family Farm.* Committee print, 96th Congress, 1st Session (June 18).

I

PRINCIPLES OF
PRICE DETERMINATION

Selected elements of the principles of price determination are reviewed in this section. In addition, some topics not ordinarily discussed in introductory economics courses are considered. Principles of demand theory and their application to the demand for agricultural products are discussed in Chapter 2, and elasticity and flexibility concepts are described in Chapter 3. Principles of supply theory with special reference to the supply of farm products are discussed in Chapter 4. Principles of demand and supply are combined in selected models of price determination in Chapter 5; models of particular interest in agricultural economics are stressed.

Demand for
Agricultural Products

An objective of this chapter is to review elements of demand theory, relating these principles to the demand for agricultural commodities. An understanding of demand theory is essential, not only because it helps to explain price behavior, but also because it provides the framework for empirical studies of demand.

Logical Basis of Demand Theory[1]

The basic unit of demand theory is the individual consumer or household. Each consumer is confronted by a problem of choice. A large number of wants arise from basic needs (e.g., food and shelter), personal characteristics, and the social and physical environment. On the other hand, the consumer usually has a limited income. Thus, the problem is to choose the specific goods and services that "best" satisfy his or her wants within the limits imposed by income.

Economists usually define "best" in terms of the consumer's attempt to maximize utility (well-being). The utility approach to the theory of demand can be stated mathematically. This involves the maximization of a utility function subject to an income constraint. The theoretical concept of a utility function could be given empirical content *if* we knew the algebraic form and the coefficients of the function. Then, the classical mathematics of constrained optimization could be used to derive explicit demand relations for the consumer. In practice, this is not done, and the utility function is used mainly as a conceptual device.

---

[1]This section presents an intuitive, rather than rigorous, argument. The student may wish to consult an intermediate price–theory text for more detail and alternative approaches (e.g., Leftwich, 1973).

Principles of Price Determination

On the basis of such theory, we can conclude that a consumer tends to prefer more to less of a commodity but that he or she will buy more only at a lower price. That is, there is an inverse relationship between quantity demanded and price. Also, a number of useful, general theorems about relationships among elasticities have been derived from the idea of maximizing a utility function subject to a constraint. These topics are discussed in Chapter 3.

Consumer and Market Demand

Consumer demand is defined as the various quantities of a particular commodity which a consumer is willing and able to buy as the price of that commodity varies, with all other factors affecting demand held constant. The consumer demand relation can be described in two ways: as a table of prices and quantities (a demand schedule) and as a graph or algebraic function of prices and quantities (a demand curve). The demand relation simply defines the pure relationship between price and the quantity purchased per unit of time while holding other factors constant.

Price and quantity vary inversely; that is, the demand curve has a negative slope. This inverse relationship is sometimes called the law of demand, and it can be explained in terms of the substitution and income effects of a price change.

The substitution and income effects of a change in price can be illustrated by constructing an "indifference map," which is a graphical method of describing a consumer's preferences. In Figure 2–1, the quantity of X (say, food) is shown on the horizontal axis and the aggregate quantity of all other commodities (Y) is shown on the vertical axis. Each indifference curve or isoquant (U_1, U_2, and U_3) identifies the various combinations of X and Y that will give the consumer equal satisfaction or utility. For example, the consumer depicted in Figure 2–1 will be equally as well off on U_1 with 20 units of X and 65 units of Y as with 55 units of X and 20 units of Y. The higher the indifference curve, the greater is the consumer's utility.[2]

Assuming that the consumer has $500 to spend each month and that the price of Y is $5 per unit, the maximum amount of Y that can be purchased per month is 100 units. Likewise, if the price of X is $10, the consumer can purchase a maximum of 50 units per month. Based on the

---

[2]To simplify discussion, economists assume that the commodities are continuously divisible and that the consumer finds both commodities desirable. Thus, the indifference curves are continuous and have a negative slope.

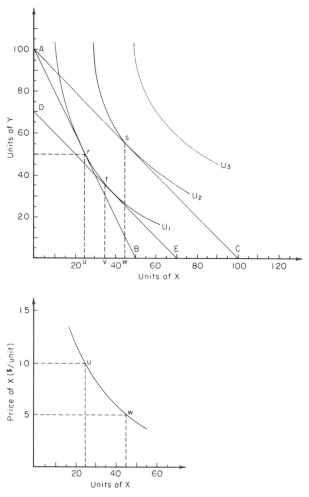

Figure 2-1. Relationship of consumer preferences to demand

foregoing price and income assumptions, a line *AB* can be constructed showing the maximum quantities of *X* and *Y* that can be purchased per unit of time with $500. This "budget" or "price-ratio" line establishes the upper boundary for purchases of *X* and *Y*. Any combination of *X* and *Y* on or below line *AB* represents a feasible purchase plan; any combination above and to the right is not feasible. The slope of *AB* is determined by the price of *Y* relative to *X*, and the distance of the line from the origin—its level—is dictated by the income constraint.

27

Principles of Price Determination

The consumer's total utility is maximized by selecting the combination of X and Y that enables the individual to reach the highest feasible point on the utility surface. This is the point at which the budget line just touches the highest indifference curve, i.e., the point of tangency r in Figure 2-1. The precise quantity of X that should be purchased to maximize utility is determined by dropping a line from the point of tangency (r) to the horizontal axis. A corresponding line can be drawn parallel to the horizontal axis through r to determine the optimum quantity of Y. Thus, in Figure 2-1, the combination which maximizes utility within the income constraint of $500 is 25 units of X and 50 units of Y (25 units of X times $10 per unit plus 50 units of Y times $5 per unit equals $500, the total income available).

A decrease in the price of X will enable the consumer to purchase more of X with the same income. The change in the price of X will also influence purchases of Y. The price-ratio line pivots away from the origin as the price of X declines, given that the price of Y and income remain constant. For example, if the price of X falls to $5 per unit, 100 units can now be purchased, and the new price line is AC. Since the prices of Y and X are both $5, the slope of the line is -1.0. The new point of tangency which maximizes utility is at s on U_2. The new optimum purchase plan consists of 45 units of X and 55 units of Y ($5X + 5Y = 5(45) + 5(55) = 500$). With the fall in the price of X, the consumer maximizes utility by purchasing 20 additional units of X and still has sufficient income left over to purchase an additional 5 units of Y. In other instances, the consumption of Y could decrease as a result of a decline in the price of X.[3] Clearly, a change in the price of one commodity can have important secondary effects on the consumption of other commodities.

A decrease in the price of any commodity is equivalent to an increase in real income; more can be purchased with the same amount of money. In general, income effects are positive; that is, an increase in income leads consumers to purchase more of any given commodity.[4] Assuming the income response is positive, the consumption of X will benefit from

---

[3]If a decrease in the price of X results in an increase in the consumption of Y, then the demand for X is price inelastic. The percentage increase in the quantity of X is less than the percentage decrease in the price of X, and as a consequence the total expenditure on X declines with the decrease in price. This inelasticity is a function of the preference map. The demand for X could be price elastic, and in this case the decline in the price of X would result in a decrease in the consumption of Y. The concept of elasticity is explored in greater depth in Chapter 3.

[4]At high-income levels, further increases in income may reduce demand, such as the demand for dry beans in the United States.

a fall in price due to the income effect as well as the substitution effect. If the commodity in question accounts for a large proportion of total expenditures by the consumer, then clearly the income effect of a fall in the price of that commodity is substantial. It will be less important for a commodity which accounts for a small percentage of total expenditures. The substitution effect is always inversely related to prices; that is, a consumer will tend to buy more as the price declines.

The income effect can be separated from the substitution effect of a price change using the analytical apparatus of indifference curves. In the example given earlier, a decrease in the price of X from \$10 to \$5 led to an increase in consumption of X from 25 to 45 units. To separate the income and substitution effects, one can draw a line DE parallel to line AC which just touches the original indifference curve for the initial price (Figure 2–1). This represents the change in income required to offset or compensate for the real income effect of the fall in the price of X. With the lower price of X and the level of income represented by line DE, the consumer is just as well off (on the same indifference curve) as with the higher price and higher money income. The point t represents the optimum expenditures pattern with the new prices and the lower level of money income. The move along indifference curve U_1 from r to t is attributable to the substitution effect of lowering the price of X. The change from t to s is the result of the increase in real income arising from the fall in the price of X. By dropping vertical lines from points r, s, and t, the total increase in consumption (uw on the horizontal axis) can be partitioned into the substitution effect (uv) and the income effect (vw).

In the preceding illustration, the income effect served to reinforce the substitution effect, but this need not be the case. The substitution effect of a price change is always negative (Wold and Jureen, 1953, p. 103); that is, an increase in price invariably results in a fall in consumption if there is an offsetting change in money income, thus keeping real income constant. The income effect also is generally negative; an increase in price results in a decrease in real income and hence a decrease in demand. For a few commodities the relationship is just the reverse; real income and demand are inversely related. This is the case of so-called "inferior goods." For such goods, the income effect offsets part or all of the substitution effect.

At the extreme, the income effect of a price change could outweigh the substitution effect. Then, a price increase would result in an increase in the quantity demanded—a positively sloped demand curve. This situation is called "Giffen's Paradox." It might occur when a staple commodity, like rice, constitutes a large portion of a consumer's expenditures and has a low price. A price increase would cause a large decline in real income, and if few or no close substitutes exist at prevailing prices, the substitution effect would be overwhelmed by the decline in real income.

Normally, of course, price and the quantity demanded have an inverse relationship. In theory, the magnitude of the change in quantity in response to a change in price can be determined from the preference map and the underlying assumption that consumers maximize utility. In Figure 2–1, the optimum quantity of X that the consumer would purchase at a price of $10 per unit of X was 25 units. When price declined to $5 per unit, the quantity demanded increased to 45 units (holding the price of Y and income constant). Thus, two points on the demand function for X have been derived from the indifference curves, and they are plotted in the lower half of Figure 2–1 as points u and w. The nature of the demand function is suggested by the line connecting the two points. Actual intermediate points on the demand function could be determined by rotating the price-ratio line and noting the points of tangency with successive indifference curves. The resulting demand curve for X represents the demand of an individual consumer in a particular time period; the individual's tastes and preferences, as measured by indifference curves, are assumed constant over the time period.

Market demand is defined in terms of the alternative quantities of a commodity which all consumers in a particular market are willing and able to buy as price varies and as all other factors are held constant. A market demand curve can be thought of as a summation of individual demand relations. This includes consumers who enter the market as price declines or drop out at high prices. Thus, a change in price influences the number of consumers as well as the quantity each consumes. Of course, since utility functions or indifference maps of individual consumers are not observable, it is not feasible to build up a market demand curve from this approach.

Data are often available on total sales and average prices by time periods such as a month, a quarter, or a year, and such data can be used to approximate a theoretical market demand curve. Invariably, with the passage of time, numerous factors which affect consumption will change. Thus, strictly speaking, it is almost impossible to ascertain the true, *ceteris paribus* relationship between price and quantity demanded. But time-series data can be used to estimate demand relations which are useful for forecasting and for policy analyses. This topic is introduced in Chapter 15.

The results of a relatively simple analysis of the demand for beef in the

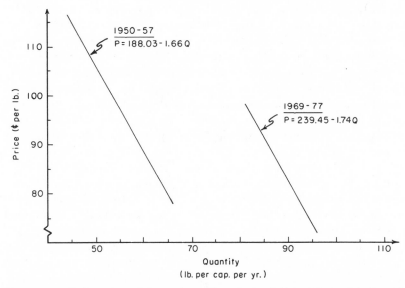

Figure 2-2. Estimated retail demand equations for beef, United States, 1950–1957 and 1969–1977. Quantity data are: retail weight of beef disappearance divided by U.S. population, and annual retail prices of choice beef as divided by the Consumer Price Index (1967 = 1.0). Intercepts of the equations are adjusted to the average level of incomes for the two periods, and the length of each line reflects the range of consumption in each period.

United States are shown in Figure 2–2. Conventionally, price is placed on the vertical axis and quantity on the horizontal axis, though theory usually expresses quantity as a function of price. The equations in Figure 2–2 are based on annual observations, and they represent average relationships for two different time periods. Clearly the demand for beef has shifted to the right between the 1950–1957 period and the 1969–1977 period. The question of shifts in demand is discussed in the next section.

Static and Dynamic Aspects of Demand

The static concept of demand refers to movements along a demand curve; this is called a change in the quantity demanded. It is static in the sense that we are looking only at quantity response to price, and all other factors (e.g., incomes and the prices of competing products) are assumed constant. With the passage of time, however, other things do not remain constant. Thus, the strictly defined demand curve of economic theory shows how much consumers stand ready to purchase at alternative prices at a particular moment in time. It is also assumed that consumers can and will respond instantaneously to a change in price.

The response to a given change in price will depend on the assumptions consumers make about future price changes. If a fall in price leads consumers to expect a further decline, the change in quantity will be smaller than if consumers think the price decline is only temporary. Strictly speaking, a static demand curve does not permit expectations about forthcoming prices to influence current demand, but empirical models have been proposed which attempt to take changing expectations into account.

The static concept as outlined in the preceding paragraphs may seem artificial, but it is useful nevertheless. It enables one to separate price changes from other variables and provides a guide to thinking logically about the factors that influence prices. The *ceteris paribus* assumption permits one to ascertain the effect of one variable at a time.

The term "dynamic" is used in two ways in demand theory. First, it may refer to changes in demand which are usually associated with changes in income, population, or other variables influencing demand and which occur with the passage of time. Second, it may refer to lags in adjustment. Quantity adjustments do not take place instantaneously because of imperfect knowledge, the time required to make changes, and so on. The concept of delayed adjustments associated with the passage of time leads to differentiating between short-run and long-run demand. The latter is sometimes defined as the quantity that will be purchased after sufficient time has been allowed for all adjustments to be completed.

Changes in Demand

It is important to distinguish between a change in quantity demanded and a change in demand (i.e., between movements along a demand curve and shifts in the level of the curve). The major factors influencing the level of demand may be grouped under four headings:
  (1) population size and its distribution by age, geographic area, etc.,
  (2) consumer income and its distribution,
  (3) prices and availability of other commodities and services,
  (4) consumer tastes and preferences.
These factors are sometimes called determinants of demand. As emphasized previously, these factors are assumed constant for a given level of a demand function, but with the passage of time, changes in demand are an important aspect of price changes.

Demand for Agricultural Products

Before discussing the specific effects of various determinants of demand, a distinction also needs to be made between simple or "parallel" shifts in the demand curve and "structural changes" in demand.[5] The difference in the concepts is most easily demonstrated by an example. For this purpose, we assume a simple demand equation in which quantity (Q) is a straight-line function of its price (P) and of consumer income (Y).

$$Q = \alpha - \beta P + \gamma Y,$$

and α, β, and γ are parameters which indicate how the variables are related.

A graph (demand curve) of Q and P can be plotted for a fixed level of Y. If the level of Y changes, then the P-Q function shifts to a new level. This illustrates a parallel shift in the demand function. However, it is also possible that the parameters—α, β, and γ—may change; that is, the coefficients relating the variables may change. A change in one or more of the parameters is a structural change. In addition, a structural change may result in a change in the algebraic form of the equation, say from a straight line to a curve.

A demand curve assumes a given set of tastes and preferences. As long as tastes and preferences remain unchanged, relationships between price and income and quantity also remain unchanged (in the simplified case where these are the only relevant variables). For a consumer demand curve, the obvious source of a structural change is a change in the individual's tastes and preferences. The individual's demand curves, as pointed out previously, are derived from the individual's own utility function or indifference map. If preferences change, the demand curves change. For a market demand curve, other sources of structural change include changes in the distribution of income and the introduction of new products.

A simple shift in demand is illustrated in Figure 2-2; for all practical purposes the slope coefficients of the demand functions are the same in the two time periods. The function has simply shifted to the right with the passage of time. If the slope of the relation had changed as well, this would be an example of a structural change. For simplicity of exposition, we will sometimes refer to both as a "change in demand" or a "shift in demand."

[5]The term "parallel" is used in a loose way, since demand relations need not be straight lines.

Principles of Price Determination

An increase in demand means that the demand curve has moved to the right (Figure 2–2). Consumers are willing to buy more of the commodity at the same price, or they are willing to buy the same quantity at a higher price. A decrease in demand (shift to the left) has the opposite effect.

Increases in demand both for food in the aggregate and for individual products are closely linked to the rate of population growth. The age distribution of the population also influences total demand as well as the demand for different commodities. A teen-age population obviously consumes more calories than one made up of a high proportion of persons over sixty-five. Baby food manufacturers gain relative to those selling soft drinks during the early stages of a population boom, but as the population grows older, suppliers of the latter gain relative to the former. Changes in the regional distribution of the population or the proportion living in urban areas likewise may influence the demand for certain types of food. For instance, rural families tend to consume more milk than those living in urban areas. A shift in the demand for commodities such as rice or pork also may occur as a result of changes in the racial composition of the population.

For most agricultural commodities, income and demand are positively related; that is, an increase in income shifts demand to the right. But for a few commodities the reverse is true. Bread and dry beans are among the commodities for which demand in the United States is likely to decline as incomes rise. Thus, in principle, the relationship between income and demand can range from positive through zero to negative.

Changes in demand also can occur as a result of redistributing income from the rich to the poor. It is possible to increase the demand for meat and citrus fruit by transferring income to families near or below the poverty line without changing the total or average level of income. In most cases, very little of the marginal tax dollar collected from upper-income families would have been used for food, while a substantial proportion of the increase in income going to lower-income families in the form of welfare payments or "food stamps" is likely to be used to purchase more food or to upgrade diets. However, an income redistribution scheme may reduce the demand for certain farm products such as high-quality wines or avocados.

In general, the quantity purchased of a commodity (other than inferior goods) rises with increases in income, but at a decreasing rate. Total expenditures usually rise even more rapidly because families shift to higher grades or buy foods with more built-in services. The relationship between total income and the quantity purchased or the amount spent

34

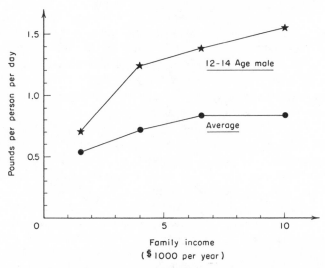

Figure 2-3. Consumption of milk and milk drinks by income groups, sample house-holds, United States, one day in spring 1965. The observation on the highest income category represents the range $8,000 and over. Data from Robert R. Miller, "Milk Consumption by Age, Sex, and Income, Including Away-from-Home Use," *Dairy Situation,* DS-331 (July 1970), pp. 25-31.

on a particular food or commodity group is sometimes referred to as an Engel curve.[6] Such curves are also called consumption functions; consumption, as measured by quantity or expenditure, is a function of income. An empirical relationship of this type is shown in Figure 2-3. Average per capita daily milk consumption for the U.S. population as a whole (based on a household survey conducted in 1965) rose from about 0.5 pounds for the lowest income group to approximately 0.8 pounds for the highest income group (Miller, 1970). Note that the level and the rate of increase was much greater for twelve- to fourteen-year-old males than for the population as a whole. Both relationships are curvilinear, and this is typical of most foods.

Changes in tastes and preferences obviously contribute to shifts in the demand for agricultural commodities, although their effects are often

[6]The German statistician Ernst Engel was among the first to undertake empirical studies of the proportion of income spent on food and other items such as clothing and housing as incomes rise (Burk, 1962). One relationship, which he observed, has persisted and has become known as Engel's law. Essentially, it states that as consumer incomes increase the proportion of income spent for food decreases. This implicitly assumes other things remain constant. With the passage of time, services are added to food; food prices change; and so forth.

difficult to isolate because they appear to be associated with changes in income or other variables. For example, the demand for table wine seems to have risen markedly in the United States during recent years, but it is not clear whether this is the result of changes in tastes or income or both. Long-run trends in per capita consumption are sometimes used as an indicator of changes in preferences; however, such trends are not necessarily a reliable guide to shifts in demand. A downward trend in per capita consumption may simply reflect changes in per capita production. For instance, if growers produce fewer apples, per capita consumption will decline, regardless of what happens to demand. Thus, per capita consumption figures for agricultural commodities can reflect availability rather than changes in demand.

The demand for each commodity is a function, not only of its own price, but of the prices of every other commodity and service. All prices, in theory at least, are linked together in an interdependent system. A change in the price of one commodity brings about shifts in the demand for other commodities. The direction of change in demand depends on the direction of change in the price of the related commodity and on whether the related commodity is a substitute or a complement. For substitutes, the change in the price of the substitute and the change in demand are usually positively related.[7] If, for instance, the price of beef decreases, then the demand for pork can be expected to decrease. Consumers tend to shift from pork to the relatively cheaper beef. Most agricultural products are substitutes, some much more so than others.

For complements, the change in the price of the related commodity and the change in demand are usually inversely related. Assuming cranberries and turkeys are complementary commodities, an increase in the price of turkeys would decrease the demand for cranberries. The price of turkeys and the quantity of cranberries move in opposite directions. While all prices in an economy are technically interrelated, some commodities can be treated as being independent. Presumably, there is no measurable influence on the demand for beef of a change in the price of cranberries.

An important shifter of demand for some agricultural products has been the development and introduction of new products. Artificial fibers have substituted for natural fibers such as cotton and wool. Detergents have tended to replace soap, which is produced from animal fats, thereby causing a decline in demand for this animal by-product. The

---

[7]We say "usually" because there are exceptions to the statement. For an explanation see the discussion of cross elasticities in Chapter 3.

demand for natural rubber and sugar also has been influenced by the development of synthetic products. On the other hand, the total demand for oranges has risen as a result of technical improvements in the process of concentrating and freezing juice.

Speculative Demand

The reader perhaps has thought of demand concepts only in terms of demand by consumers for current use. Speculative demand represents a type of demand related to anticipated use and prices (relative to current prices). Since numerous agricultural products are produced seasonally but are consumed throughout the year, the concept of storage or speculative demand is of particular interest to agricultural economists. Inventory holders, for example, provide the service of carrying stocks from harvest throughout the marketing season. They anticipate that price will rise from harvest through the year by enough to provide them with a profit.[8]

A demand function can be interpreted as including both demand for current use and for speculative purposes. Assuming speculative demand is incorporated in the demand function, additional factors may contribute to shifts in demand (hence, to changes in prices). For instance, the prospect of a small crop for next year would increase speculative demand for current inventories. Crop prospects for substitutes, the expectation of war, and the possibility of a dock strike, which would restrict imports and exports, are other examples of factors that could change speculative demand.

The current price of a commodity may be strongly influenced by expected future events as well as current conditions. Changes in factors that influence expectations tend to occur randomly and are unpredictable. For instance, a natural disaster may damage the grain crop in another country, and hence the demand for U.S. grain to be exported in the forthcoming year would increase. The disaster causes an unanticipated rise in current prices; these price adjustments usually occur in a matter of hours or days; the adjustments are not deferred until the actual exports occur nor till orders are placed. (The question of short-run price behavior is discussed further in Chapters 5 and 12.)

---

[8]Inventory positions can be hedged through the use of futures contracts for some commodities (discussed in Chapters 12 and 13). This transfers risk to speculators who do not have physical control of the inventory. Also, inventories are carried for purposes other than speculation. Thus, one cannot classify all inventories as speculative positions.

Principles of Price Determination

Speculation is sometimes viewed only as increasing the amplitude and frequency of price fluctuations. If speculators add to total demand, this, of course, contributes to an increase in price, and if the speculator's expectations are not realized, the price fluctuation was unnecessary. But this is an *ex post* judgment. At the time the purchase was initiated, it no doubt appeared justified. For example, a "war scare" is likely to produce a rise in commodity prices; if the forecast of war turns out to be correct, the price rise will have been justified; but if a war does not occur, prices will subsequently decline. In this case, speculation increased the amplitude of price fluctuations based on what turned out to be an erroneous forecast.

Speculation which correctly anticipates future events can have a moderating effect on price fluctuations. The purchase of stocks by warehousemen at harvest time increases price over the level that would otherwise have prevailed. Likewise, the sale of stocks during the year keeps prices below levels that would have prevailed with little or no inventory. Hence, the amplitude of the seasonal price pattern is reduced. In an analogous way, if speculators correctly anticipate a relatively small crop for the next crop year, carrying additional inventory into the new year helps ameliorate the price effects of the small crop.

In sum, total demand is influenced by speculative demand. Speculation that incorrectly anticipates future events may increase price variability, but speculation that correctly anticipates the future reduces price variability.

Lengths of Run in Demand Theory

We turn now to a second aspect of the dynamics of demand theory—namely, the concept of length of run. Simple, static theory assumes instantaneous adjustments to price changes. In the real world, however, there are a number of reasons why we do not expect instantaneous adjustments; the quantity demanded at a given price is likely to change gradually over time. The impediments to quick adjustments in the quantity demanded in response to a price change include such factors as imperfect knowledge, consumer uncertainty, technological and institutional barriers to changes in use, and rigidities in consumer habits.

The consumer cannot be expected to react to price changes of which he or she is not aware. Thus, lack of knowledge can prevent rapid adjustments. Uncertainty or anticipated changes in prices also may affect consumer behavior. If the consumer is uncertain about future price changes, purchases may be postponed or accelerated. If the price of an item falls, the consumer may even defer purchases anticipating a still further price decline.

Technological impediments cover several related ideas. Consumers tend to wear our durable goods before replacing them. A consumer is not likely to buy a new refrigerator simply on the basis of a price change if his current refrigerator is relatively new.

A second type of technical impediment is the lack of complementary goods needed to take advantage of a relative price change. A farmer cannot instantaneously adjust the fuel used in a tractor in response to a price change; nor is a homeowner likely to change the furnace immediately to take advantage of price changes for various types of fuel.

In the short run, consumers' incomes are largely committed. They have installments due, rent, insurance premiums, electric and other utility bills to pay. Thus, the consumer's discretionary income (i.e., the income remaining after deducting all cash commitments including debt repayment) may be small, and consequently he or she cannot take advantage of a price change. For example, a consumer may observe a decline in the price of carpeting, but will not be able to act if he does not have the income or is not able to borrow at the moment to take advantage of the lower price. After some time lag, the consumer's discretionary income may increase and the purchase can be made.

Consumers may continue to make purchases on the basis of habit even though price has changed; that is, it is impractical for a consumer to remake all consumption decisions every day, and consequently response to a price change may be delayed. Houthakker and Taylor (1970, p. 62) report that food consumed in the home is subject to some habit formation but that habit wears off quite rapidly.

A distinction is made in demand theory between the "short run" and the "long run." The long run is usually defined as the time required for a complete quantity adjustment to occur in response to a "one-time" price change. The long-run time period corresponds to the adjustment period for each commodity, but since the time required for adjustment (because of the lags or impediments outlined above) is likely to vary among commodities, the long-run time period will necessarily differ for different items purchased by consumers. For example, the time required to complete the adjustment process is likely to be greater for durable goods which are purchased infrequently than for food items which are purchased daily or weekly.

The estimation of long-run demand relationships from empirical observations is difficult because prices and other factors affecting demand do not remain constant for a long enough period of time for the full effects of a given combination of variables to work themselves out. Further changes in prices or other variables are likely to occur before the adjustment to the initial price change is completed.

In addition, price changes may induce changes in the structure of demand which are difficult to separate from the other delays in the adjustment of quantity. If the price of a product remains at a relatively high level, new substitutes are likely to be developed. Moreover, consumers learn new ways to economize in the use of a high-priced commodity, and even if prices decline subsequently, these economizing techniques are retained. High coffee prices led consumers to brew more cups of coffee per pound; this structural change apparently was not reversed when the price of coffee declined (Hogarty and Mackay, 1975). A persistent low price may induce a shift in preferences toward a commodity which is maintained in the face of a subsequent price increase.

The short-run demand schedule is simply a "snapshot" of demand at a given point in time, before complete adjustment has occurred. Since the short run may refer to any time period of shorter duration than the one required for full adjustment to occur, it cannot be uniquely defined.

Pasour and Schrimper (1965) suggest that adjustments in the very short run should be distinguished from those that occur over a longer period of time for commodities that can be stored. In the very short run, the response to a price decrease may be somewhat greater than in the intermediate run simply because some buyers are willing to purchase a commodity in order to hold it for speculative or other purposes (as discussed in the previous section). The demand for use may change very little, but when the demand for storage is superimposed on the demand for use, the response to a short-run price change may be substantial. The householder, for example, may buy additional cuts of meat to place in the freezer if the local supermarket announces a "special" on beef. Thus, in the very short run, storage demand must be considered in addition to purchases for consumption, while, in the long run, demand will be determined almost entirely by use. During the intervening period, the response to price changes may be very difficult to predict because of the possible liquidation of stocks previously acquired.

Concept of a Distributed Lag

The idea of a delayed adjustment to a price change leads rather naturally to the concept of a distributed lag. The lapse of time between a cause and its effect is called a lag. In demand theory, the price change is specified as the "cause" and the quantity change as the "effect." The effect is likely to be spread through time rather than occurring instantaneously at a point in time. Hence, the term distributed lag arises from a delayed response which is spread over time.

Given a change in the causal variable (e.g., price), there are many alternative paths of adjustment that the other variable (quantity demanded) might follow through time. For example, adjustment might follow a smooth, geometric path. Alternatively, there may be a large initial adjustment followed by a lower rate of adjustment. One of the problems of empirical analysis is that many alternative paths of adjustment are theoretically possible. The price analyst has little basis on which to select one in preference to another unless special knowledge is available about the product.

Nonetheless, econometric models have been developed to estimate economic relationships for which distributed lags are thought to exist (Nerlove, 1958; Tomek and Cochrane, 1962). Their intent is to take account of possible lagged responses in economic relationships. Distributed lag models often, though not always, assume a geometric form for the lag. In empirical work, distributed lag models have been used more frequently in estimating supply relations in agriculture than demand relations.

Derived Demand

The ultimate consumer is the one who determines the shape and position of the demand function. For this reason, consumer demand relationships are often referred to as "primary demand." In empirical analysis, retail price and quantity data are customarily used to determine primary demand relationships.

The term "derived demand" is used to denote demand schedules for inputs which are used to produce the final products. Corn, for example, is an important input in the livestock industry, while wheat is used to make a variety of bakery goods. Thus, the demand for wheat and corn is derived from the demand for end products. Similarly, one can say that the demand for soybeans is derived from the demand for soybean meal and soybean oil, the major products produced from crushing soybeans. Demand schedules for inputs such as labor and land, likewise, can be derived indirectly from the demand for commodities which are produced with these inputs.

The idea of derived demand can be carried a step further to include

41

the demand for characteristics of the commodity (Lancaster, 1971; Ladd and Suvannunt, 1976). The potential buyer may be viewed as demanding nutrients, such as protein, and not just rice, wheat, or some other commodity. A feed manufacturer, for example, is interested in the least-cost set of ingredients to make, say, a dairy feed with particular protein, energy, fiber, and other components. The idea is perhaps less apparent for individual households, but Lancaster and others suggest that households should be treated both as producing and consuming units. The consumer is buying foods (inputs) to produce meals that are nutritious, have variety, are tasty, and so forth, and the demand for the inputs may be viewed as being derived from the demand for a nutritious meal.

The term "derived demand" also may be extended to most wholesale- or farm-level demand functions. Derived demand differs from primary demand by the amount of marketing and processing charges per unit of product. The demand for meat animals at the farm, for example, is based on the retail-level demand function for meat, minus marketing costs such as slaughtering, processing, and transporting meat. The concept of derived demand can be carried even further. For example, the demand for feeder calves on the part of feed-lot operators is ultimately derived from the retail-level demand for beef.

A derived demand curve can change either because the primary demand curve shifts or because marketing margins change. Empirically, derived demand relationships can be estimated, either indirectly by subtracting appropriate margins from the primary demand schedule, or directly by using price and quantity data which apply to the appropriate stage of marketing (e.g., wholesale prices and quantities can be used to approximate the derived demand at an intermediate level, while farm prices and sales data may be used to estimate the demand curve confronting producers). The relationship between primary and derived functions is discussed more fully in Chapter 6.

References

Burk, Marguerite C. 1962. "Ramifications of the Relationship between Income and Food," *J. Farm Econ.*, 44:115–125.

Hogarty, Thomas F., and Robert J. Mackay. 1975. "Some Implications of the 'New Theory of Consumer Behavior' for Interpreting Estimated Demand Elasticities," *Am. J. Ag. Econ.*, 57:340–343.

Houthakker, H. S., and L. D. Taylor. 1970. *Consumer Demand in the United States: Analyses and Projections.* 2d ed. Cambridge, Mass.: Harvard Univ. Press.

Ladd, George W., and Veraphol Suvannunt. 1976. "A Model of Consumer Goods Characteristics," *Am. J. Ag. Econ.*, 58: 504–510.

Lancaster, Kelvin. 1971. *Consumer Demand: A New Approach.* New York: Columbia University Press.

Leftwich, Richard H. 1973. *The Price System and Resource Allocation.* 5th ed. Hinsdale, Illinois: The Dryden Press. Chapters 5 and 6.

Miller, Robert R. 1970. "Milk Consumption by Age, Sex, and Income, Including Away-from-Home Use," *Dairy Situation.* USDA, DS-331 (July). Pp. 25–31.

Nerlove, Marc. 1958. *Distributed Lags and Demand Analysis.* USDA Ag. Hb. 141. Pp. 1–20.

Pasour, E. C., and R. A. Schrimper. 1965. "The Effect of Length of Run on Measured Demand Elasticities," *J. Farm Econ.*, 47:774–788.

Tomek, William G., and Willard W. Cochrane. 1962. "Long-Run Demand: A Concept, and Elasticity Estimates for Meats," *J. Farm. Econ.*, 44:717–730.

Wold, Herman, and Lars Jureen. 1953. *Demand Analysis.* New York: John Wiley and Sons. Chapter 5.

CHAPTER 3

Demand Elasticities
and Related Coefficients

One objective of this chapter is to review the concepts of own-price, cross-price, and income elasticities of demand. Interrelationships among these coefficients as implied by theory are described. In addition, the relationship between own-price elasticities at different market levels is discussed. Two additional concepts, total elasticity and price flexibility, are introduced.

Price Elasticity

Definition

The concept of a demand schedule or a demand curve has been defined. It provides a description of the relationship between price and the quantity buyers are willing and able to buy, other factors remaining constant. Price theory suggests an inverse relationship between price and quantity, but the inverse relationship by itself says nothing about the responsiveness of quantity demanded to a price change for a commodity. This responsiveness is likely to vary from commodity to commodity.

An explicit demand curve is defined by its algebraic equation, assuming it is known. The quantity variable is normally expressed in physical units while price is expressed in monetary terms per physical unit. But since different units of measurement are often employed (bushels, pounds, kilograms), it is difficult to make direct comparisons from algebraic equations of the impact which a given change in price will have on different commodities. To facilitate comparisons, economists frequently make use of percentage relationships which are independent of the size of units used to measure price and quantity. The most common of these relationships is the concept of own-price elasticity of demand. This is simply a ratio which expresses the percentage change in quantity associated with a given percentage change in price.

Price elasticity is defined for a point on the demand curve, and hence for most demand curves the magnitude of the elasticity coefficient varies along the curve. Let Δ equal a very small change, then a mathematical definition of price elasticity is

$$E_P = \frac{\dfrac{\Delta Q}{Q}}{\dfrac{\Delta P}{P}} = \left(\frac{\Delta Q}{\Delta P} \right) \left(\frac{P}{Q} \right).[1]$$

An alternative equation for defining price elasticity is the arc formula

$$E_P = \frac{\dfrac{Q_0 - Q_1}{Q_0 + Q_1}}{\dfrac{P_0 - P_1}{P_0 + P_1}} = \left(\frac{Q_0 - Q_1}{Q_0 + Q_1} \right) \left(\frac{P_0 + P_1}{P_0 - P_1} \right).$$

The subscripts represent two different points on a demand curve. The arc equation is mainly a device for computing an elasticity at an average between the two points—not the average of the elasticities on the arc between the points. The smaller the arc or segment the more nearly the elasticities computed from the arc and point formulas approach each other. Remember, elasticity is strictly defined only with respect to a particular point.

Interpretation

The own-price elasticity-of-demand coefficient for any commodity can be interpreted as the percentage change in quantity demanded given a very small percentage change in the price of that commodity, other factors held constant. A convenient way to think of a price elasticity is as the percentage change in quantity corresponding to a one per cent change in price. Since the slopes of demand curves are negative, price-elasticity-of-demand coefficients have a negative sign.

[1]If the demand function is written as $Q = f(P)$, then the slope of the function is dQ/dP, and the price elasticity at a point $(\bar{Q}, \bar{P})$ is $E_P = \dfrac{dQ}{dP} \left(\dfrac{\bar{P}}{\bar{Q}} \right)$. Since graphs of demand functions have price on the vertical axis, the equation may be written $P = f(Q)$. In this case, the slope is dP/dQ, and $E_P = \dfrac{1}{dP/dQ} \left(\dfrac{\bar{P}}{\bar{Q}} \right)$.

The range of the price-elasticity coefficient is from zero to minus infinity. This range is traditionally divided into three parts. (1) If the absolute value (neglecting sign) of the coefficient is greater than one, demand is said to be *elastic*. The percentage change in quantity demanded is greater than the corresponding percentage change in price. The limiting case is the horizontal demand curve—demand is perfectly elastic (coefficient is infinite). (2) If the absolute value of the coefficient is less than one, demand is *inelastic*. The percentage change in quantity is less than the corresponding percentage change in price. Quantity demanded is relatively unresponsive to price changes. The limiting case is an elasticity of zero—demand is perfectly inelastic. (3) A coefficient of -1 represents the case of *unitary elasticity*. The percentage change in quantity equals the percentage change in price.

The elasticity coefficient varies along the demand curve for most functional forms of the curve. If a straight-line demand function is extended to the two axes, the elasticity varies from infinity on the price axis through various (negative) values to zero at the point on the quantity axis. This may be verified by referring to the definition of price elasticity (point equation) and noting that price is zero when the demand function intersects the quantity axis and that quantity is zero when the function intersects the price axis. A few special cases exist where the elasticity is a constant over the range of the curve. These cases include a straight horizontal line, a straight vertical line, a power function, and a rectangular hyperbola.[2]

Since in general the elasticity coefficient varies in magnitude along the demand curve, it is not technically correct to say that the demand for a commodity is elastic or inelastic. Demand is elastic (or inelastic) only within some range of prices. However, it is convenient to categorize and speak of the demand for a commodity as being either elastic or inelastic. This shorthand reference should be interpreted as referring to the elasticity within the *usual* range of prices. In making empirical estimates, a common procedure is to compute the elasticity at the mean of the observations.

Price Elasticities and Total Revenue

Total revenue is defined as price multiplied by quantity; it has two components. Since these two components are inversely related, it is not obvious how changes in price will influence total revenue. For example, the question whether a given percentage increase in price will increase

[2]Letting Q = quantity demanded and P = price, the power function is $Q = \alpha P^{\beta}$. A rectangular or equilateral hyperbola is $QP = \beta$, or $Q = \beta (1/P)$; in this case $E = -1$.

or decrease total revenue depends on the magnitude of the corresponding percentage change in quantity. The question is answered by the magnitude of the price-elasticity-of-demand coefficient.

If demand is elastic in the relevant range of prices, then price and total revenue vary inversely. A price increase will decrease total revenue, and a price decrease will increase total revenue. This follows from the definition of an elastic demand, which means that the percentage change in quantity demanded is greater than the percentage change in price. A decrease in price, for example, results in a more than offsetting percentage increase in quantity taken. Hence, total revenue increases as price decreases. However, it does not follow that total revenue will increase indefinitely as price decreases. At some point, price would presumably move into an inelastic range of the demand relation.

If demand is inelastic in the relevant range of prices, then price and total revenue vary directly. A price increase will increase total revenue and vice versa. The reader should reason out why this is true based on the definition of an inelastic demand.

The demand for hogs at the farm level in the United States is inelastic. Thus, other things being equal, we would expect farm price and total revenue to vary directly. When hog production increases and consequently prices decline, total revenue falls. In 1974, for example, 20.3 billion pounds of hogs were marketed, and cash receipts were $6.9 billion. The next year hog marketings declined to 17.0 billion pounds, but cash receipts increased to $7.8 billion. Since the demand for pork is not constant from one year to the next and since the elasticity relates to a point on the demand function, the change in revenue cannot be entirely related to a particular elasticity. Nonetheless, the example suggests the approximate effect of volume changes on total revenue for a commodity with an inelastic demand, and it is a phenomenon common to many agricultural commodities. This was recognized at least as early as 1915 when Henry A. Wallace wrote, "The Demand Laws . . . indicate to me that the farming class as a whole is penalized for over-production and rewarded for under-production" (as cited in Stigler, 1962, p. 17).

Farm policy measures which attempt to limit supply assume that the demand for the commodity is inelastic. Otherwise, reducing volume would lower the total revenue received by farmers. Also, reducing production reduces total costs.

The price-elasticity concept measures responsiveness *along* a demand curve. This, of course, is implicit in the discussion of elasticities and total revenue. If, for example, demand increases, then total revenue and quantity may increase even though demand is inelastic. This is a function of the shift in demand and not of the elasticity of one demand

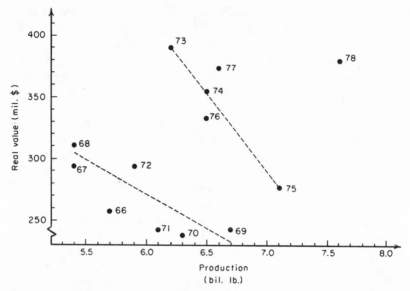

Figure 3-1. Apples: production and value of production, United States, 1966-1978 crop years. Values deflated by the Consumer Price Index, 1967 = 1.0. Data from USDA, *Noncitrus Fruits & Nuts: Production, Use, and Value,* Crop Reporting Board, ESCS, FrNt 1-3(79) (July 1979), and prior issues.

relation. The effect of an increasing demand for apples on the total value of apple production in the United States is illustrated in Figure 3-1. The size of crop and value of the crop are inversely related within a period of a few years, but with the passage of time, the value of a given size crop has increased.

Income Elasticity

Income elasticity of demand is a measure of the responsiveness of quantity to changes in income, other factors held constant. The income-quantity relationship, of course, can be expressed algebraically. This relation is sometimes called a consumption, or Engel, function. The income elasticity is defined at a point on the function and typically varies along the range of the curve.

Let Y represent income, then the definition of income elasticity at a point is

$$E_Y = \frac{\frac{\Delta Q}{Q}}{\frac{\Delta Y}{Y}} = \left(\frac{\Delta Q}{\Delta Y} \right) \left(\frac{Y}{Q} \right).$$

It may be interpreted as the percentage change in quantity corresponding to a one per cent change in income, other factors held constant.

In most cases, the coefficient is positive. This is consistent with the idea that as income increases, a consumer buys more of most products, and when income decreases the opposite occurs. The income elasticity for food in the aggregate in the United States is about 0.2 (Mann and St. George, 1978). A few commodities like dry beans have negative income elasticities at the average level of incomes in the United States.

For individual foods, income elasticities are thought to decline as incomes increase.[3] Households with high incomes will generally have smaller income elasticities for foods than households with low incomes. Since income elasticities are used in making demand projections (i.e., to estimate the impact of increasing income on the demands for specific commodities) and since the elasticity itself can change as incomes increase, the researcher must exercise great caution in making projections using a single coefficient.

In empirical analyses, "income elasticities" are sometimes estimated from observations on expenditures rather than observations on physical quantities and on incomes. Expenditure on a particular commodity is made a function of total expenditures. Observations on income obtained in sample surveys often contain errors and do not correspond to the economic concept of income. For instance, evidence exists that income earned by household members other than the respondent in the survey is frequently overlooked. Also, observations on expenditures are sometimes more easily obtained than observations on physical quantities. This elasticity represents the percentage response of expenditure on an individual commodity to a one per cent change in total expenditures. Occasionally, individual expenditure is made a function of household income. Coefficients which measure the responsiveness of expenditures to a change in income (total expenditure or other measure) are sometimes called expenditure elasticities. These elasticities generally are larger than those based on physical quantities. Expenditures are usually more responsive than quantities to changes in income. This is reasonable since consumers with higher incomes probably buy higher-quality items (hence higher-priced items) as well as larger quantities. Thus, the expenditure change in response to an income change includes a price effect due to quality as well as the quantity effect (Klein, 1962).

Estimated expenditure elasticities for two commodity groups plus

---

[3]This implies that, in empirical analyses, the consumption function for foods should be in a form that permits a declining income elasticity as income increases (for further discussion see Leser, 1963).

total food are plotted in Figure 3-2. This figure illustrates how elasticities may vary with income levels. In these examples, the expenditure elasticities rise and then decline as household incomes increase. This is related, in part, to the quadratic functional form used by the analysts (Salathe and Buse, 1979).

Cross Elasticity

Cross-price elasticities of demand are measures of how the quantity purchased of one commodity responds to changes in the price of another commodity. More precisely, the cross elasticity of commodity i with respect to commodity j is defined as

$$E_{ij} = \frac{\frac{\Delta Q_i}{Q_i}}{\frac{\Delta P_j}{P_j}} = \left(\frac{\Delta Q_i}{\Delta P_j} \right) \left(\frac{P_j}{Q_i} \right).$$

This may be interpreted as the percentage change in the quantity of i given a one per cent change in the price of j, other factors held constant.

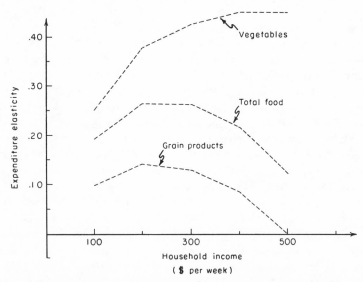

Figure 3-2. Estimated expenditure elasticities by household income level, United States, 1965. Elasticities are computed from coefficients presented in Larry E. Salathe and Rueben C. Buse, *Household Food Consumption Patterns in the United States,* USDA Tech. Bul. 1587 (1979), table 3. The elasticities are computed for households with two adult equivalents ($A = 2$ in table 3).

Demand Elasticities and Coefficients

In practice, three types of cross relationships can be identified: the commodities may be substitutes, complements, or independent. The definition of the three types of relationships is based on the *substitution effect* of the price change of j (see Kuhlman and Thompson, 1965).

The substitution effect is positive for substitute commodities; the price of j and the quantity of i move in the same direction. If the price of j increases, then consumers tend to substitute i for j. If the price of j decreases, then consumers tend to substitute the relatively cheaper j for i. In both cases, there is a positive relationship between the price of j and the quantity of i.

The substitution effect is negative for complementary commodities such as cranberries and turkeys. In this case, the price of j and the quantity i move in opposite directions. An increase in the price of j (turkeys) means that the quantity demanded of j decreases and hence the quantity of the complementary commodity i (cranberries) also decreases. A similar argument can be made for a decrease in the price of j, and in both cases there is a negative relationship between the price of j and the quantity of i.

The substitution effect is zero for independent commodities. Independence means that no substitution or complementary relationship exists between the two commodities.

On the basis of the reasoning outlined above, economists generally say that substitute commodities have positive cross elasticities; complementary commodities have negative cross elasticities; and independent commodities have zero cross elasticities. However, from a technical mathematical viewpoint, these generalizations need not be true. There is also the *income effect* of the price change for j. The income effect on the demand for i is generally, but not always, negative for cross elasticities. A decrease in price increases real income and hence tends to increase quantities purchased. An increase in price decreases real income and tends to decrease quantity.

The income effect may "outweigh" the substitution effect resulting in a net reduction in the demand for commodity i when the price of commodity j increases. Consumers will normally substitute i for j if the price of j increases; but an increase in the price of j is equivalent to a reduction in real income. This will adversely affect consumption of both i and j. Thus, the real income effect on consumption of i will be negative, while the substitution effect will be positive. If the former exceeds the latter, the net effect may be negative even though the two commodities are substitutes.

The income effect usually tends to reinforce the substitution effect for complementary commodities. However, two commodities could be independent from the viewpoint of substitution and still have a negative cross elasticity from the income effect of the price change. The interpretation of cross elasticities is further complicated by the fact that the income effect is not always inversely related to price. There are inferior commodities, which means some commodities have negative income elasticities. This implies a positive income effect which would reinforce or add to the substitution effect for some commodities.

The importance of the income effect depends on the size of expenditure on the commodity relative to total expenditures. Typically, the expenditure on one commodity is a small fraction of total expenditures, and hence the income effect usually does not "outweigh" the substitution effect. Thus, the generalizations economists make about the signs of cross elasticities usually hold, that is, a positive cross elasticity implies that the commodities are substitutes while a negative cross elasticity implies the commodities are complements; and a coefficient near or equal to zero implies the commodities are independent.

Butter and margarine are examples of substitute commodities. Hot dogs and buns are complementary. In practice, economists have found the measurement of cross elasticities very difficult. Substitution relationships have been somewhat easier to identify than complementary relationships.

Reversing the commodities in the cross-elasticity equation does not necessarily give the same coefficient. The cross elasticity of sugar with respect to coffee probably is not the same as the cross elasticity of coffee with respect to sugar. A change in the price of coffee is likely to have a modest influence on the use of sugar, but a change in the price of sugar probably will have very little influence on the use of coffee.

The explicit relationship between cross elasticities can be spelled out mathematically. The substitution effect (whether for complements or substitutes) is symmetric, but the income effect is not. The exact relationship is given in the next section.

Relationships among Elasticities
Consumer Demand

A great deal of effort has been devoted in recent years to the implications of demand theory for relationships among elasticities and to the application of these concepts to the estimation of elasticities for food products (Brandow, 1961; George and King, 1971; Wetmore, *et al.*, 1959; Wold and Jureen, 1953). The important relationships include the homogeneity condition, the Slutsky condition, and the Engel aggregation condition; each of these conditions is discussed in this section.

The theory from which these interrelationships are derived makes certain assumptions regarding individual consumer behavior. Thus, the elasticity conditions hold for an individual consumer with a given utility function, which satisfies certain assumptions including the assumption that the individual's tastes and preferences are in some sense reasonable.[4]

While the theory has been developed in terms of the individual consumer, the empirical uses of the elasticity conditions have been for market (aggregate) elasticities. A limited number of studies, such as one by Barten (1967), make this type of application. In any case, the elasticity conditions provide a theoretical basis for the intuitive arguments about differences in elasticities for different products.

Homogeneity condition. Equation (1) states that the sum of the own- and cross-price elasticities and the income elasticity for a particular commodity is, taking account of signs, zero.

$$\text{(1)} \qquad E_{ii} + E_{i1} + E_{i2} + \ldots + E_{iy} = 0,$$

where E_{ii} = own- (or direct-) price elasticity

$\begin{matrix} E_{i1} \\ E_{i2} \end{matrix}$ = cross-price elasticities

$\quad\cdot$

$\quad\cdot$

$\quad\cdot$

E_{iy} = income elasticity.

Wold (1953) calls this equation the Slutsky-Schultz relation; it has also been called the row constraint.

The meaning of the homogeneity condition is that the substitution effect and the income effect of an own-price change must be consistent with the cross and income elasticities for the commodity. A large income elasticity tends to imply a large (in absolute value) own-price elasticity. A large number of substitutes (hence a large number of significant cross elasticities) and/or some very close substitutes (implying large positive

---

[4]To be precise, the axioms must be stated in mathematical terms. Roughly, the consumer is assumed to be able to rank commodity bundles in an order of preference, and the ranking must avoid ambiguity and be consistent (transitivity). Moreover, the consumer is assumed not satiated and prefers more to less. A further assumption is required about the nature of the utility function to assure that the usual conditions for a constrained maximum (from the calculus) are necessary and sufficient. The reader may refer to George and King (1971, pp. 33 ff.), Phlips (1974), or Wold and Jureen (1953, esp. pp. 82 f.) for careful discussions of the assumptions.

cross elasticities) also suggests a relatively large own-price elasticity for the commodity.

The relation is illustrated using estimated retail-level elasticities for beef (Brandow, 1961, p. 17).

own-price elasticity	-0.95
cross-price with veal	0.06
cross-price with pork	0.10
cross-price with lamb	0.04
cross-price with chicken	0.07
all other cross elasticities	0.21
income elasticity	0.47
sum	0

Economists argue that commodities with many substitutes or some close substitutes have price elastic demands. This is implied in equation (1) which says that if E_{i1}, E_{i2}, etc. are collectively large and positive then E_{ii} must be large and negative (i.e., elastic). Viewed in another way, the sum of the cross elasticities is equal to the difference between the price and income elasticity (assuming income elasticity is positive and price elasticity is negative). If this difference is small, then the "cross effects" are collectively small. This suggests few substitutes. If the difference is large, then the reverse reasoning would apply. Thus, given information on the own-price and income elasticities for a commodity, some inferences can be made about the cross elasticities.

The commodity salt has commonly been used as an example of a product with an inelastic demand. The intuitive argument is that it has few substitutes and it constitutes a very small proportion of a consumer's total expenditure. From equation (1), we can observe that if the cross elasticities and income elasticities are near zero, then the own-price elasticity will also be near zero (i.e., inelastic).

The homogeneity condition combined with two reasonable assumptions suggests that the absolute value of the own-price elasticity is likely to be greater than the values of the cross-price elasticities. The assumptions are (1) that the income elasticity is positive and (2) that most of the cross relationships are substitute relations and hence the cross elasticities are mostly positive numbers. Consequently, for the sum of the elasticities to be zero, the commodity's own-price elasticity must be large relative to the cross elasticities and negative.

The homogeneity condition also can be used to set a lower limit on the price elasticity and an upper limit on the income elasticity. We again use the reasonable assumption that the sum of the cross elasticities is positive and that the lower limit of this sum is zero. If the sum of the cross elasticities were about zero, then $|E_{ii}| \approx |E_{iy}|$. If the sum of the cross elasticities were positive, then the price elasticity would be larger (in absolute value) than the income elasticity. Thus, the magnitude of the income elasticity tends to set the lower limit of the own-price elasticity. In a similar way, we can argue that the price elasticity, if known, sets an upper limit for the commodity's income elasticity.

For example, suppose previous research indicates that the income elasticity for food grains in India is 0.7, then the price elasticity of demand is implied to be at least −0.7 and because of substitutes is probably slightly higher. Thus, the estimate of one elasticity can provide a general guide to another elasticity.

Slutsky condition. Equation (2) specifies the relationship between the cross elasticities E_{ij} and E_{ji}. Namely,

$$(2) \qquad E_{ij} = \frac{R_j}{R_i}E_{ji} + R_j\,(E_{jy} - E_{iy}),$$

where R_i = expenditure on i as a proportion of total expenditures

R_j = expenditure on j as a proportion of total expenditures

E_{ij}, E_{ji} = cross elasticities

E_{iy}, E_{jy} = income elasticities.

This is also called the symmetry relation.

Assuming (1) that the consumer's expenditure on commodity j is a small fraction of total income and/or (2) that the income elasticities for the two commodities are approximately equal, then

$$(2') \qquad E_{ij} \approx \frac{R_j}{R_i}\,E_{ji}.$$

This relation has been called the Hotelling-Jureen relation; it is an approximation of the Slutsky relation.

The Slutsky (or Hotelling-Jureen) relation indicates how cross elasticities are related. If E_{ij} is known, then E_{ji} can be estimated and vice versa. This relation has also been used in applied research in combination with another restriction to place a limit on the maximum admissible values for cross elasticities (Wetmore, *et al.*, 1959, p. 69). This is of interest because cross elasticities have proven difficult to estimate directly from available data. Thus, economists have attempted to combine estimates of a few elasticities with their knowledge of interrelationships among elasticities to infer estimates of other elasticities.

The substitution effect of a price change is in a sense symmetric, but the income effect is not.[5] The income effect of a price change will be larger for the commodity which takes a larger proportion of total expenditures. We know, for example, that a much smaller proportion of the average consumer's income is spent on lamb than on beef in the United States. Thus, a one per cent change in the price of lamb has much less effect on the consumption of beef (smaller cross elasticity) than the reverse.

Assuming the average consumer spends 2 per cent of total expenditures on beef (b) and 0.1 per cent on lamb (a) and assuming the cross elasticity of lamb with respect to beef (E_{ab}) is 0.6, then from equation $(2')$

$$E_{ba} \approx \frac{R_a}{R_b} E_{ab} = \left(\frac{.001}{.02} \right) (.6) = (.05)(.6) = .03.$$

With the assumed conditions, a one per cent change in the price of lamb will result in only a 0.03 per cent change in the consumption of beef. This is true even though a one per cent change in the price of beef will result in a 0.6 per cent change in the consumption of lamb.

Engel aggregation condition. Equation (3) states that the weighted sum of the income elasticities for all items in a consumer's budget is one.

---

[5]The "absolute" response of the quantity of i to a price change in j is defined by the partial derivative $\partial Q_i/\partial P_j$. This partial derivative can be divided into the substitution effect and the income effect.

$$\frac{\partial Q_i}{\partial P_j} = K_{ij} - Q_j \frac{\partial Q_i}{\partial Y} \ ,$$

where K_{ij} = substitution effect,

Y = income, and the last term defines the income effect. The partial derivative $\frac{\partial Q_j}{\partial P_i}$ can be partitioned in an analogous way. The symmetry is between the substitution effect components of the two partial derivatives. Namely,

$$K_{ij} = K_{ji};$$

and this implies

$$\frac{\partial Q_i}{\partial P_j} + Q_j \frac{\partial Q_i}{\partial Y} = \frac{\partial Q_j}{\partial P_i} + Q_i \frac{\partial Q_j}{\partial Y} \ .$$

Using the commodity's own price, the substitution and income effects are defined by $\partial Q_i/\partial P_i = K_{ii} + Q_i(\partial Q_i/\partial Y)$. $\partial Q_i/\partial P_i$ is also defined as the effect of the "uncompensated" price change while K_{ii} may be defined as the "compensated" price effect (Phlips, 1974, pp. 41 f.). Uncompensated and compensated price elasticities have analogous definitions.

Demand Elasticities and Coefficients

The weights are the expenditures on the respective commodities as a proportion of total expenditures (the R_i's). The equation for n items is

$$(3) \qquad R_1 E_{1y} + R_2 E_{2y} + \ldots + R_n E_{ny} = 1.$$

The readers should not interpret relation (3) as meaning that all income elasticities need to be small. The weights are fractions (less than one). A hypothetical example for three commodities with assumed elasticities of 5, 1, and 0.2 illustrates the point:

$$(.1)\,(5) + (.4)\,(1) + (.5)\,(.2) =$$
$$.5 \quad + \quad .4 \quad + \quad .1 \quad = 1.0.$$

Wetmore (1959) describes a method of estimating cross elasticities for food groups when estimates of own-price elasticities and the expenditures on each food group as a proportion of total expenditures on food are available. The own-price elasticities are the diagonal coefficients in Table 3–1, and the expenditure proportions are shown in the last column of this table. The sum of any row of elasticities in Table 3–1, excepting the "all foods" column, which is the sum, represents the net percentage change in quantity of the product group heading the row (e.g., meat)

Table 3-1. Own-price and cross-price elasticities for six food groups in the United States, 1957

Demand for	Effect of one per cent change in the price of							R
	Meat	Dairy products	Eggs	Fruits	Vege-tables	Other	All foods*	
Meat	−.60	.10	.04	.08	.06	.03	−.29	.363†
Dairy products	.21	−.50	.02	0	.06	.03	−.18	.171
Eggs	.29	.08	−.58	0	0	.05	−.16	.045
Fruits	.33	0	0	−1.00	.20	.03	−.44	.088
Vegetables	.22	.10	0	.18	−.70	.02	−.18	.098
Other	.05	.02	.01	.01	.01	−.10	0	.235

Source: John M. Wetmore *et al., Policies for Expanding the Demand for Farm Food Products in the United States,* Part I: *History and Potentials,* Univ. of Minn. Tech. Bul. 231 (April 1959), p. 71, table 18.

*This column contains the sum of the elasticities in each row. The weighted average of the column equals −0.2, the assumed price elasticity for all food.

†R is the proportion of total food expenditures spent on each group. The sum is 1.0.

resulting from a one per cent change in all food prices. Thus, the weighted average of the row sums is the price elasticity of demand for all food, which is given as −0.2 (Wetmore, *et al.*, 1959, p. 68). Consequently, the admissible values for the cross elasticities (the off-diagonal elements of Table 3–1, which were unknown) are restricted to those which combined with the known own-price elasticities give row sums whose weighted average is −0.2.[6]

Three additional restrictions were used. (1) The cross elasticities are assumed to be nonnegative, that is, zero or positive. This is reasonable since the analysis is restricted to food groups which are presumably substitutes. (2) The sum of the cross elasticities for a specific group (say, meat) may not exceed the absolute value of the own-price elasticity (in the case of meat, −0.6). This means that the sum of the own-price elasticity and the cross elasticities for, say, meat must be zero or negative. It also follows from restriction (1) that none of the individual cross elasticities may exceed the absolute value of the own-price elasticity for the commodity group. (3) The cross elasticities are assumed to be interrelated as specified by the Hotelling-Jureen conditions (equation 2′). This equation in effect reduces the unknowns by one-half and helps place maximum admissible limits on the cross elasticities.

These restrictions limit the number of admissible sets of cross elasticities, but they do not provide a rigorous mathematical means of computing the cross elasticities. Restriction (1) provides the minimum values which may be taken by the cross elasticities (zero). Restrictions (2) and (3) help determine maximum admissible values. However, the final specification of cross elasticities is based on the judgments of the analysts. The final outcome of such a procedure is illustrated in Table 3–1.

Since the Wetmore study was published in 1959, contributions in demand theory have provided additional conceptual bases for computing a complete set (matrix) of elasticities.[7] Frisch's (1959) concept of

[6]Another condition used in applied research (e.g., Brandow, 1961) is the Cournot aggregation or column restriction. If a column of price elasticities is viewed as containing the price elasticity of the *i*th commodity and the cross elasticities of the response of all other commodities to a price change of *i*, then the restriction states that the expenditure weighted sum of any *i*th column of the complete set of price elasticities equals the negative expenditure weight of the *i*th column. For commodity 1 (column 1), this restriction is $R_1 E_{11} + R_2 E_{21} + \ldots + R_n E_{n1} = -R_1$.

[7]In an economy with n goods, there will be n price elasticities for each commodity plus an income elasticity. This gives $n (n + 1)$ total elasticities to be estimated. The symmetry condition, the homogeneity condition, and the Engel aggregation provide restrictions that reduce the elasticities to be estimated to $\frac{1}{2} (n^2 + n - 2)$, still a large number (George and King, 1971).

"want independence" gives a base for computing cross-price elasticities given estimates of income and own-price elasticities and expenditure weights as well as some assumptions about utility functions. Related concepts such as separability in the utility function also help provide a basis for reducing the number of demand coefficients to be estimated directly from data.

If a limited number of commodity groups is used, then it is practicable to estimate a complete system of demand equations statistically from data rather than by the more "ad hoc" approach illustrated by the Wetmore study. Elasticity estimates consistent with the theoretical restrictions (discussed above) are obtained, but the estimates are limited to the commodity groups in the system such as food and clothing. Income elasticities for food are typically larger than 0.4 (see Green *et al.*, 1978, for a useful summary), which seem high relative to elasticities obtained in conventional studies. Barten (1977) and King (1979) provide useful critiques of the empirical implementation of demand systems. A detailed discussion of demand systems is beyond the scope of this book.

Derived Demand

Relationships between price elasticities of demand for primary and derived demand relations for the same commodity are discussed in this section. This discussion is applicable to market demand relations. The idea of derived demand is broadly interpreted to include the relationships (1) between elasticities at various market levels and (2) between elasticities for joint products and the commodity from which they are derived.

Market levels. In empirical work, it is sometimes difficult to estimate directly price elasticities of demand for a product at different points in the marketing chain, and the elasticities are likely to be different at the retail than at the farm level. It is possible, however, provided knowledge of marketing margins and of the elasticity at one level (say, at retail) exist to estimate the elasticity at another level (say, at farm). Thus, we turn to relationships between elasticities at two market levels. The comparison is for a given quantity moving through the marketing system (see Figure 3–3).

The exact relationship between elasticities depends on how the primary and derived demand curves are related. Since the two curves are separated by a schedule of marketing margins, the problem reduces to one of how the marketing margin behaves. A simple, but somewhat unrealistic, alternative is that the margin is a constant, absolute amount. That is, the margin is a constant regardless of the amount marketed. The

Principles of Price Determination

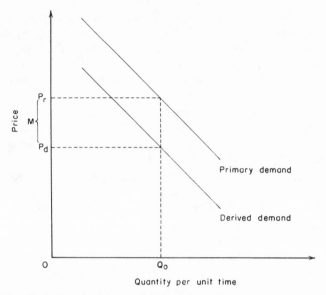

Figure 3-3. Illustration of primary and derived demand curves

two demand curves would be "parallel." In this case, the elasticity at one level can be estimated from the elasticity at the other level from

$$E_d = E_r \left(\frac{P_d}{P_r} \right),$$

where subscript d = derived (say, farm) level
                            r = primary (say, retail) level.[8]

Let c stand for the constant margin; $c = P_r - P_d$. The primary- (retail-) level price will always be greater than the derived-level price. Thus, the price ratio P_d/P_r will always be less than one. This ratio is analogous to the farmer's share of the consumer's food dollar (see Chap-

---

[8]Under the assumptions, the only thing that differs between the two elasticities is the price.

$$E_r = \left(\frac{\Delta Q}{\Delta P} \right) \left(\frac{P_r}{Q} \right) \text{ and } E_d = \left(\frac{\Delta Q}{\Delta P} \right) \left(\frac{P_d}{Q} \right).$$

Thus, if E_r is known, E_d can be computed.

$$E_d = E_r \left(\frac{P_d}{P_r} \right) = \left(\frac{\Delta Q}{\Delta P} \right) \left(\frac{P_r}{Q} \right) \left(\frac{P_d}{P_r} \right).$$

60

ter 6). When a constant absolute margin is assumed, the derived-level elasticity will always be smaller in absolute value than the primary-level elasticity. A large margin results in a large difference in the elasticities at the two levels. For instance, if the farm value of a commodity is 50 per cent of the retail price, the farm-level elasticity is one-half of the retail elasticity. Thus, the primary demand for bananas in the United States could be price elastic while the derived demand in Central America is inelastic. The two market levels are separated by a large transportation cost, implying a large marketing margin.

A second alternative is a fixed-percentage marketing margin. This means the margin is a constant percentage of the purchase or sale price. It is highly unlikely that the entire margin would be of this nature, although some marketing firms use percentage mark-ups. Assuming a constant percentage margin regardless of the quantity marketed, the price elasticities at the two market levels would be the same for a given quantity marketed.

In practice, a marketing margin is likely to be a combination of absolute and percentage markups. A further complication is that these absolute and percentage figures may not be constant but may vary with the quantity marketed. The exact relationship between elasticities depends on the nature of the marketing margin. Thus, the economist must have some knowledge of the behavior of the margin to specify the relationship between elasticities.

One fairly simple specification of a margin (M) is the linear combination of a constant absolute amount (c) and a constant percentage (a) of the retail price.

$$M = c + aP_r$$

$$\text{where } 0 \leq c$$
$$0 \leq a < 1.$$

This specification indicates that the per unit margins decrease with lower prices as the quantity marketed increases. Actual margins, of course, may not change in this precise way although some margins behave in a manner consistent with this hypothesis (see Chapter 6).

Using previous notation, the derived-level elasticity is

$$E_d = E_r \left[1 - \frac{c}{(1 - a) P_r} \right].$$

61

The constant absolute component in the margin means that the derived-level elasticity is less elastic or more inelastic than the respective primary-level elasticity.

As an example, assume $M = .40 + .20\ P_r$. If $P_r = \$1.00$ and if the primary-level elasticity is -0.8, then the derived-level elasticity is

$$E_d = -.8 \left[1 - \frac{.40}{(.8)(\$1.00)} \right]$$

$$= -.8\ [1 - .5] = -.4.$$

The price at the derived level is

$$P_d = P_r - M$$
$$= \$1.00 - (.40 + .20\ (\$1))$$
$$= \$.40.$$

If $a = 0$, then the equation reduces to the case of the constant absolute margin.

$$E_d = E_r \left[1 - \frac{c}{P_r} \right] = E_r \left(\frac{P_d}{P_r} \right)$$

since $c = P_r - P_d$.

If $c = 0$, then $E_d = E_r$. This is the case of the constant percentage margin.

Joint products. If joint products are obtained in fixed proportions from the basic commodity and if the elasticities are all computed at the same market level, then the price elasticity of the basic commodity (E_x) is a weighted harmonic average of the price elasticities of the joint products (say, E_1 and E_2) (Houck, 1964).[9]

---

[9]A simple harmonic mean is defined

$$\tilde{X} = \frac{1}{\dfrac{\dfrac{1}{X_1} + \dfrac{1}{X_2} + \ldots + \dfrac{1}{X_n}}{n}} = \frac{n}{\dfrac{1}{X_1} + \dfrac{1}{X_2} + \ldots + \dfrac{1}{X_n}}.$$

For a weighted average, each member $\frac{1}{X}$ is multiplied by the appropriate weight and n is replaced by the sum of the weights.

Let $\qquad X =$ the basic commodity

$\qquad X_1$ and $X_2 =$ the joint products (an example of two)

$\qquad w_1$ and $w_2 =$ the fixed yields per unit of X

$\qquad P_1$ and $P_2 =$ price per unit of the joint products.

Hence, $\qquad X_1 = w_1 X$, and

$\qquad\qquad X_2 = w_2 W.$

Then, the mathematical relationship among the three elasticities is

$$E_x = \frac{P_1 \, w_1 + P_2 \, w_2}{\dfrac{1}{E_1} \, (P_1 \, w_1) + \dfrac{1}{E_2} \, (P_2 \, w_2)} \ .$$

The example can be generalized to the case of n joint products (see Houck, 1964).

The weights in the expression are the proportions of X's average value (per unit) attributable to the sales of the joint products. Thus, taking E_1 and E_2 as constants, E_x will vary as the value weights vary. The extreme cases would be $P_1 w_1$ or $P_2 w_2$ equal zero; that is, X_2 or X_1 represents the entire value of X and the remaining component is, say, thrown away. If X_1 is discarded and $P_1 w_1 = 0$, then $E_x = E_2$. Or, in a more realistic case, if X_2 represents the major proportion of the value of X, then $E_x \approx E_2$. An example is the division of beef animal into the joint products beef and hide. The hide represents a relatively small proportion of the total value of the animal. Hence, the farm-level elasticity for the animal and for beef would be similar.

Soybeans provide an example. They are processed into the joint products meal and oil. In this case, X is a bushel of soybeans; X_1 is soybean meal; and X_2 is soybean oil. Hence, w_1 equals 47.8 pounds and w_2 equals 10.4 pounds. Meal and oil are obtained in the relatively fixed proportion of 47.8 pounds and 10.4 pounds, respectively, from a bushel of soybeans. Assume for the purposes of this example that the price of meal is 9 cents per pound and the price of oil is 30 cents per pound at wholesale. If the respective price elasticities are -0.9 and -2.5, then the wholesale-level elasticity for whole soybeans can be computed as follows:

$$E_x = \frac{(9)(47.8) + (30)(10.4)}{\dfrac{1}{-.9} \, (9)(47.8) + \dfrac{1}{-2.5} \, (30)(10.4)} = -1.23.$$

Principles of Price Determination

Total Elasticity[10]

Price elasticity of demand provides a measure of the percentage change in quantity demanded in response to a one per cent change in price, assuming all other factors are held constant. However, if the price for one commodity changes, the prices of its substitutes will change as well (unless they are fixed, say by a government support program). The prices of competing products tend to move in the same direction, but by varying amounts. Thus, a change in the price of one commodity sets in motion forces which ultimately result in establishing a new structure of prices. For example, if the price of beef declines, the demand for pork (a substitute) also declines. Given a constant supply of pork, the price of pork decreases, and the change in the price of pork will in turn influence the demand (and hence the price) for beef.

Consequently, one needs to consider more than the price elasticity of demand for beef in order to forecast the net final effect on the consumption of beef of a change in the price of beef. The foregoing discussion assumes that the quantities of the substitutes (in our example, pork) are constant within the period of analysis. The relationship becomes even more complex if one takes account of the possible effects of changes in the relative prices of competing commodities on quantities supplied. To predict the full effect of one initial price change, one needs a knowledge of all own-price and cross-price elasticities of demand and supply for the set of competing products including the commodity in question.

The interrelationship among prices leads to the idea of a total demand response curve and total elasticities. The total demand response curve is defined as the price-quantity relationship resulting when all other important demand variables are "allowed to act and interact as the market structure requires to reach a new equilibrium level" (Buse, 1958, p. 882). The elasticity of total demand response or simply total elasticity is defined as the *net* percentage change in quantity resulting from a one per cent change in own price, taking account of the interactions of related variables.

Assuming the main interrelationships are substitute relations, then Figure 3–4 depicts the idea of the total response relation and hence illustrates the total elasticity concept. The prices of substitutes are likely to decline as the commodity's own price declines. This would appear as a decrease in demand for the commodity under consideration. The total

[10]This section is largely based on Buse (1958). As Buse indicates, J. R. Hicks provided the basic concepts in 1939.

Demand Elasticities and Coefficients

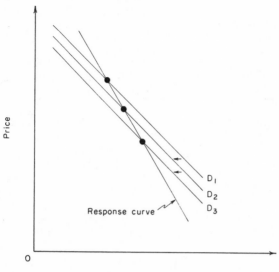

Figure 3-4. Hypothetical total demand response curve

response curve is less elastic or more inelastic than the *ceteris paribus* demand curve. That is, the net quantity response is less than that indicated by the own-price elasticity of demand. Thus, if the main interrelationships are substitute relations, the total elasticity is smaller in absolute value than the corresponding price elasticity.

Assuming just one substitute (j) for the commodity i, the total elasticity for i is

$$T_i = E_i + E_{ij}S_{ji}$$

where E_i = own-price elasticity

E_{ij} = cross-price elasticity

S_{ji} = the percentage change in the price of j given a one per cent change in the price of i.

Conceptually, the total elasticity coefficient can be viewed as the sum of two terms: the own-price elasticity and a cross elasticity multiplied by the elasticity of the price of j with respect to changes in the price of i. The own-price elasticity is adjusted for the cross effects.

E_{ij} and S_{ji} are usually positive and less than one for substitute commodities (Buse, 1958, p. 889). E_i is, of course, negative and larger in absolute value than the cross elasticities. Thus, T_i is negative but smaller in absolute value than E_i.

65

Principles of Price Determination

For example, if beef is the main substitute for pork, then the approximate total elasticity for pork is

$$T_p = E_p + E_{pb}S_{bp},$$

where the subscript p = pork and b = beef.

Buse (1958, pp. 886 f.) gives the following numerical illustration:

$$T_p = -.94 + (.72)(.29) = -.73.$$

The own-price elasticity of demand for pork was estimated to be -0.94, but the *net* percentage change in the quantity of pork that buyers would be willing to purchase in response to a one per cent change in the price of pork after taking account of the cross effects with beef is -0.73.

Price Flexibility Coefficients

Price flexibility is often treated as the inverse of price elasticity. The flexibility coefficient gives the percentage change in price associated with a one per cent change in quantity, other factors constant.

The price flexibility concept is particularly important for agricultural products. The biological nature of the production process results in many crops being produced annually or only at regular time intervals. Further, some of these commodities are perishable or semiperishable; they cannot be stored for long periods. For such commodities, the quantity available for consumption is largely fixed by the size of production, and the entire quantity must be consumed within a period of months after harvest. Hence, the situation is one of a fixed supply and a given level of demand for a specific time period. Within the time period, the level of production cannot be changed. The remaining question is what price will clear the market of the given supply. The direction of causation is from quantity to price.

Apples produced for fresh use illustrate the point. They are produced annually, and they cannot be stored from one crop year to the next. The level of production is the main factor determining average price for the year. Variations of price within the year have very little influence on the size of production in that year.[11]

---

[11] Price may have a small influence on the level of imports and exports and, in some years, on the quantity harvested.

Demand Elasticities and Coefficients

The price flexibility coefficient (F_i) is defined as

$$F_i = \frac{\frac{\Delta P}{P}}{\frac{\Delta Q}{Q}} = \left(\frac{\Delta P}{\Delta Q} \right) \left(\frac{Q}{P} \right).$$

Under some conditions it is approximately equal to the reciprocal of the corresponding price elasticity, and like the price elasticity of demand, the direct price flexibility coefficient has a negative sign. A price flexibility of -3.0 means that there is a 3 per cent price response to a one per cent quantity change.

Thus, if demand is inelastic, then the price flexibility coefficient is likely to be greater than one in absolute value. A flexible price is consistent with an inelastic demand; that is, a small change in quantity has a relatively large impact on price. If demand is elastic, then the price flexibility coefficient is likely to be less than one in absolute value. An inflexible price is consistent with an elastic demand.

The price flexibility coefficient implies that price is a function of the quantity of the particular product as well as the quantities of substitutes. In contrast, the usual demand function makes quantity a function of the price of the product as well as other product prices. Since different variables are held constant in the two equations, the reciprocal of the flexibility is not always a good approximation of the elasticity.[12]

Mathematically,

$$|E_{ii}| \geqq \left| \frac{1}{F_{ii}} \right|.$$

The reciprocal of the price flexibility sets the lower limit of the price elasticity of demand. If the cross effects are zero (essentially no substitutes), then the reciprocal of the flexibility is a good approximation of the

---

[12]The derivative dP/dQ from $P=f_1(Q)$ is the reciprocal of dQ/dP from $Q=f_2(P)$. However, demand functions are more complex than this, and we must compare the partial derivatives, say from

$$P_i = f_3 (Q_i, Q_j, Y) \text{ and}$$
$$Q_i = f_4 (P_i, P_j, Y).$$

Since we are holding different variables constant, we can no longer assume that the partial derivative $\partial P_i/\partial Q_i$ is the reciprocal of $\partial Q_i/\partial P_i$. Houck (1965) provides more details but assumes the reader is familiar with matrix algebra.

elasticity. If significant cross effects exist, then the reciprocal of the flexibility is less than the elasticity.

Flexibility coefficients that are analogous to the concepts of income elasticity and cross elasticity also may be defined. The price flexibility of income is the percentage change in price in response to a one per cent change in income, other factors remaining constant. It is calculated as follows:

$$F_{iy} = \left(\frac{\Delta P}{\Delta Y} \right) \left(\frac{Y}{P} \right).$$

The flexibility of income is typically expected to be positive. Price moves directly with the shift in demand. A higher income implies a larger demand, and this suggests a higher price for any given level of quantity.

The cross flexibility of i with respect to j is the percentage change in the price of commodity i in response to a one per cent change in the quantity of commodity j, other factors remaining constant. The algebraic relationship is as follows:

$$F_{ij} = \left(\frac{\Delta P_i}{\Delta Q_j} \right) \left(\frac{Q_j}{P_i} \right).$$

The cross flexibility based on the quantity variable of a substitute is expected to be negative. This is in contrast to cross elasticities for substitutes which usually are positive. A larger supply of a substitute results in a lower price for the substitute, which in turn results in a decline in demand for the first commodity. The lower demand implies a reduction in price. Hence, a larger supply of the substitute (commodity j) reduces the price of the commodity under consideration (commodity i).

Houck (1966) has worked out the relationships among flexibility coefficients similar to those developed for elasticities, such as the symmetry relation. His results are derived from equations in which quantity is a function of price, i.e., "normal" demand equations. (If one starts with price-dependent equations, some of the results are different [Waugh, 1964].) It follows that the assumptions which underlie Houck's work are the same as those made for the relationships among elasticities.

Empirical Elasticities

The theoretical concept of a commodity's own-price elasticity is rigidly defined. Economists have attempted to estimate elasticities using empirical data, but these do not always conform to the rigid definition specified by economic theory. An examination of these measured coefficients reveals that there is no such thing as "the" price elasticity of demand for a commodity. The question of why estimates are not unique is discussed in Chapter 16 (see also Manderscheid, 1964), but some examples of empirical elasticities are presented here.

Despite numerous difficulties, reasonably consistent estimates of elasticities have been obtained from a number of studies. The degree of consistency, of course, varies among commodities. There is probably more agreement among price analysts about the price elasticity of demand for beef, for example, than for cotton. One cannot escape making judgments where different estimates have been obtained. Widely used elasticity estimates include those from Brandow's study of demand interrelationships among farm products (1961) and from George and King (1971). Some examples are given in Table 3-2. Both the Brandow and the George and King studies use a variety of devices to arrive at a comprehensive set of elasticity estimates. Some coefficients are estimated by statistical procedures; other coefficients are inferred from economic theory based on the relationships discussed earlier. Judgment is an important factor in making the estimates.

The demand for most agricultural commodities is price inelastic— certainly in the short run and often in the long run as well. But it is important to keep in mind that empirical estimates are usually made for a point on the demand curve and that elasticities are likely to vary at different points along a demand curve; hence estimates made for one point may not hold for other ranges of prices and quantities.

Table 3-2. Estimated elasticities of demand, selected foods, United States, 1946–1967

Commodity	Price elasticities		Income elasticities at retail
	Retail	Farm	
Beef	−0.64	−0.42	0.29
Chicken	−0.77	−0.60	0.18
Fluid milk	−0.35	−0.32	0.20
Ice cream	−0.53	−0.45	0.33
Potatoes	−0.31	−0.15	0.12
Apples, fresh use	−0.72	−0.68	0.14

Source: P. S. George and G. A. King, *Consumer Demand for Food Commodities in the United States with Projections for 1980,* Giannini Foundation Monograph 26, Univ. of Calif., Div. of Ag. Sciences (March 1971), tables 5 and 11.

Principles of Price Determination

References

Barten, A. P. 1967. "Evidence on the Slutsky Conditions," *Rev. Econ. Stat.*, 49:77–84.

———. 1977. "The Systems of Demand Functions Approach: A Review," *Econometrica*, 45:23–52.

Brandow, G. E. 1961. *Interrelations among Demands for Farm Products and Implications for Control of Market Supply*. Penn. State Univ. Ag. Exp. Sta. Bul. 680.

Buse, Rueben C. 1958. "Total Elasticities—A Predictive Device," *J. Farm Econ.*, 40:881–891.

Frisch, Ragnar. 1959. "A Complete Scheme for Computing All Direct and Cross-Demand Elasticities in a Model with Many Sectors," *Econometrica*, 27:177–196.

George, P. S., and G. A. King. 1971. *Consumer Demand for Food Commodities in the United States with Projections for 1980*. Giannini Foundation Monograph 26, Univ. of Calif., Div. of Ag. Sciences.

Green, Richard, Zuhair A. Hassan, and S. R. Johnson. 1978. "Alternative Estimates of Static and Dynamic Demand Systems for Canada," *Am. J. Ag. Econ.*, 60:93–107.

Houck, James P. 1964. "Price Elasticities and Joint Products," *J. Farm Econ.*, 46:652–656.

———. 1965. "The Relationship of Direct Price Flexibilities to Direct Price Elasticities," *J. Farm Econ.*, 47:789–792.

———. 1966. "A Look at Flexibilities and Elasticities," *J. Farm Econ.*, 48:225–232.

King, Richard A. 1979. "Choices and Consequences," *Am. J. Ag. Econ.*, 61:839–848.

Klein, Lawrence R. 1962. *An Introduction to Econometrics*. Englewood Cliffs, N.J.: Prentice-Hall. Pp. 52–60.

Kuhlman, J. M., and R. G. Thompson. 1965. "Substitution and Values of Elasticities," *Am. Econ. Rev.*, 55:506–509.

Leser, C. E. V. 1963. "Forms of Engel Functions," *Econometrica*, 31:694–703.

Manderscheid, Lester V. 1964. "Some Observations in Interpreting Measured Demand Elasticities," *J. Farm Econ.*, 46:128–136.

Mann, Jitendar S., and George E. St. George. 1978. *Estimates of Elasticities for Food Demand in the United States*. USDA Tech. Bul. 1580.

Phlips, Louis. 1974. *Applied Consumption Analysis*. New York: American Elsevier Publishing Co. Inc.

Salathe, Larry E., and Rueben C. Buse. 1979. *Household Food Consumption Patterns in the United States*. USDA Tech. Bul. 1587.

Stigler, George J. 1962. "Henry L. Moore and Statistical Economics," *Econometrica*, 30:1–21.

Waugh, Frederick V. 1964. *Demand and Price Analysis: Some Examples from Agriculture*. USDA Tech. Bul. 1316.

Demand Elasticities and Coefficients

Wetmore, John M., *et al.* 1959. *Policies for Expanding the Demand for Farm Food Products in the United States,* Part I: *History and Potentials.* Univ. of Minn. Tech. Bul. 231.

Wold, Herman, and Lars Jureen. 1953. *Demand Analysis.* New York: John Wiley and Sons. Chapters 5 and 6.

CHAPTER **4**

Supply Relationships
in Agriculture

In this chapter, we are concerned with supply concepts and especially with the role prices play in determining the production decisions of farmers. For this reason, attention is focused first on supply-price relationships. This is followed by a review of the factors which bring about shifts in the supply curve. These and additional concepts are then used to identify the factors that are most important in determining changes in aggregate farm output as well as the production of individual commodities.

Theoretical Basis of Supply Functions

A static supply schedule shows how much of a given commodity will be offered for sale per unit of time as its price varies, other factors held constant. In theory a static supply function can be derived from a knowledge of the underlying input-output relationship (or cost functions) in a manner analogous to deriving a demand curve from an individual utility function or an indifference map. Demand theory assumes the consumer wants to maximize utility. A theoretical supply curve is based on the assumption that producers seek to maximize net returns. Producers have control over the kinds and quantities of inputs (seed, fertilizer, land, labor, and machinery) they employ in production, but not over output. In a biologically based production process, output is also influenced by weather, disease, or damage due to pests.

Technology is assumed constant in deriving a static supply curve. This determines the shape of the production function (the relationship between inputs and output) under normal or average conditions. The marginal productivity curve for a particular input or factor is, in turn, derived from the production function. A producer who wants to maximize profits employs factors up to the point where the cost of the last unit of input is equal to the value of the added output. In the short-hand of economics, profits are maximized by equating marginal cost and marginal revenue. Stated another way, the rule for determining optimum factor use is to set the marginal physical product of the factor equal to the factor/product price ratio and solve for the quantity of input which satisfies this equality. Algebraically,

$$MP_x = P_x/P_Q,$$

where MP_x = the marginal product of input x
         P_x = the price of x, and
         P_Q = the price of a unit of output, Q.

If the price of the product (Q) increases, the factor/product price ratio becomes smaller. This implies a greater use of the factor to achieve optimal factor use, assuming a constant price of x. As long as the marginal product of the input is positive, output will increase as inputs are increased, given normal weather, no disease, and so forth. A supply curve can be derived by altering product prices, computing the optimal factor use, and then inserting these factors into the production function to compute the output (supply) that one would expect based on optimum factor use.[1]

One can immediately derive some useful conclusions about what affects supply from the foregoing theory. Planned output (but not necessarily actual output) will change if any one of three things changes: the marginal productivity of one or more inputs, the prices of inputs, or the price of output. The *ceteris paribus* supply function, as pointed out previously, assumes that the production function (hence the marginal productivity of each factor) and the price of each factor are constants. Changes in quantity supplied are a function of changes in the price of a unit of output.

Optimum factor use and hence planned output will not change if both factor and product prices increase or decrease by the same percentage. If the price of the product rises by 10 per cent but at the same time the

---

[1]For simplicity, assume output is a quadratic function of a single input. Then the production function is $Q = a + bx + cx^2$ and the marginal product is $dQ/dx = b + 2cx$. For optimal factor use, $b + 2cx = P_x/P_Q$. Given P_x, one can compute alternate levels of x for alternate P_Q's. These x's can be inserted into the production function to compute corresponding Q's.

price of a factor rises by 10 per cent, the factor/product price ratio remains unchanged, and consequently the solution for the optimal use of the factor does not change.

An individual firm's supply schedule also can be derived from cost functions. The shape of these functions is dictated by the same underlying production function, and the price of each factor is assumed to be constant. Rising marginal cost is simply another way of expressing diminishing marginal productivity to the use of additional units of a factor. Under the usual profit-maximizing assumptions of economic theory, the optimum level of output on a particular farm is determined by the point at which marginal cost and marginal revenue are equated. Marginal cost is defined as the addition to total cost of producing one more unit of product, and marginal revenue is the added revenue from selling one more unit of product. Clearly, if a firm produced output beyond the point at which marginal cost and marginal revenue are equated, then by definition the added cost of producing the product exceeds the added revenue from its sale.

Hypothetical marginal cost and corresponding average variable and average total cost curves are shown in Figure 4–1. As discussed above, these curves are determined by physical production possibilities (the production function) and the cost of factors of production (inputs).[2] Since the individual farmer is assumed to be a price taker, his marginal revenue is equal to the price received for the product; the sales of an individual farmer do not influence price and additional units can be sold at the prevailing price. (Technically, a supply curve can be defined only for the case when individual sellers cannot influence price.) Hence, at price P_1 (Figure 4–1) profits are maximized by producing Q_1 units; at price P_2, the profit maximizing output increases to Q_2.

As long as the price of the product exceeds average variable costs, the supply curve for the individual farm will be determined by the shape of the marginal cost curve. At any point above the low point on the average variable cost curve, the supply schedule coincides with the marginal cost schedule—the steeper the marginal cost curve, the more inelastic the supply curve. Assuming profit-maximizing behavior on the part of each producer, the aggregate supply curve for any commodity can be obtained simply by summing the marginal cost curves for all farms.

A farmer will cease to produce a commodity if the price falls below

---

[2]If the production function and the costs of inputs are known, then the various cost curves can be constructed (see, for example, Leftwich, 1973). In practice, empirical production functions sometimes are difficult to estimate. Nerlove and Bachman (1960) provide a summary of alternative approaches to the analysis of agricultural supply.

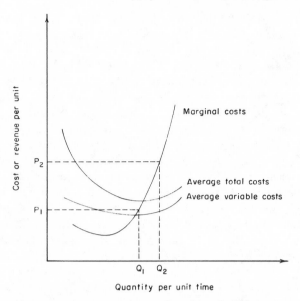

Figure 4-1.   Cost curves and optimum output at alternative prices

average variable costs of production. Variable costs are those that can be avoided by not producing or not harvesting the commodity. It does not pay a poultryman, for example, to produce eggs if income is not sufficient to cover feed costs; however, in the short run it does pay to remain in production at prices exceeding average variable costs, even if all fixed or overhead costs are not covered. In the long run, of course, a producer will continue to produce only if all costs are covered.

The concept of "opportunity cost" is important in determining the point at which farmers will switch from the production of one commodity to another. The opportunity cost of producing commodity A is the income foregone by not producing commodity B. Thus, if the income foregone (the opportunity cost) of producing A exceeds the revenue from that crop, it does not pay to continue to produce A. The opportunity cost of continuing to produce a particular commodity such as wheat may include revenue foregone from working off the farm as well as the earnings from commodities that could have been produced with the same resources such as barley or grain sorghum.

Market Supply Curves

For forecasting or policy analysis, we want to know the shapes and the position of market supply curves which express the relationship between price and the aggregate quantity offered for sale by all producers within a given region or country. Logic dictates that, under normal circumstances, the supply curve should slope upward and to the right. The additional output which producers are prepared to offer at higher prices depends, among other things, on the time allowed for adjustments to take place. In general, the longer the time allowed for adjustments to occur, the greater the response to a given change in price.

In the very short run, once the crop is produced and harvested (assuming no reserve stocks or imports and that the current crop cannot be stored), the supply function is a vertical line. The quantity offered for sale can neither be increased nor decreased, regardless of the price offered, until the next harvest comes in. Prior to harvest, the supply can be adjusted by deciding not to harvest a part of the crop if the price is too low. As more time is allowed for farmers to respond to price changes, production can be altered. In the short run, the amount of inputs such as fertilizer applied to crops or feeding rates for livestock can be varied, and in the longer run, the area sown to crops and the number of livestock units can be changed. The tendency for supply curves to become more responsive (flatter) as more time is allowed for adjustments is illustrated schematically in Figure 4-2.

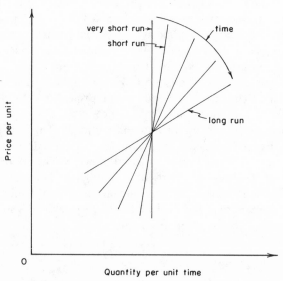

Figure 4-2. Changing supply-price relationships through time

The time dimension obviously is important in specifying supply relationships in agriculture, but it is difficult to define precisely and unambiguously what is meant by the very short run, the short run, the intermediate run, and the long run as applied to supply. The time required for a production response varies from commodity to commodity. It takes more time for production decisions to be altered with tree crops, for example, than for poultry products.

Short-run supply schedules are of particular interest in agriculture, and they assume that some factors of production are fixed, while others can be varied in response to prices. This means a short-run period of one or two years for many farm commodities. The long run is usually defined as that period of time required for all factors of production to become variable: the acreage can be increased, buildings can be altered, additional labor and new machinery can be acquired. In the real world, there is continuous change; hence, the full effect of a particular price change can seldom be observed since additional price changes will often occur before the consequences of the first change are fully worked out.

Price Elasticity of Supply

The price elasticity of supply is defined in a manner analogous to the price elasticity of demand. It expresses the percentage change in quantity supplied in response to a one per cent change in price, other factors held constant. In algebraic terms, it is expressed as follows:

$$E_s = \frac{\frac{\Delta Q}{Q}}{\frac{\Delta P}{P}} = \left(\frac{\Delta Q}{\Delta P} \right) \left(\frac{P}{Q} \right),$$

where Q refers to the quantity supplied. Since an increase in quantity supplied is normally associated with a rise in price, the sign of the coefficient usually is positive. A zero elasticity means that supply is fixed; there is no quantity response to a price change. This is called a perfectly inelastic supply. An *inelastic* supply refers to the range of elasticities between zero and one. Quantity supplied is relatively unresponsive to price changes. An *elastic* supply refers to coefficients greater than one. The percentage change in quantity is larger than the corresponding percentage change in price.

As is the case with demand functions, the elasticity coefficient typically varies in magnitude along the supply function. It is convenient to speak of "the" price elasticity of supply, but such a coefficient usually is measured at the arithmetic mean of prices and quantities. In empirical research, supply equations are often specified as straight lines, but this particular specification places special restrictions on the magnitude of the elasticity (Houck, 1967). As the quantity supplied is increased along the function (that is, as output approaches infinity), the price elasticity of supply approaches one. Specifically, if the linear supply function with a positive slope intersects the origin (intercept equals zero), then the elasticity is a constant equaling one. If the quantity dependent function intersects the price axis first (horizontal intercept negative), the elasticity is always greater than one but approaches one as quantity supplied becomes large. If the function intersects the quantity axis first (horizontal intercept positive), the elasticity is always less than one but approaches one as quantity supplied becomes large.

There are logical reasons to expect that the supply function for a farm product will exhibit changes in elasticity at particular prices. Changes in elasticity—more precisely changes in the slope of the function—are likely to occur at a price that just covers variable or "out of pocket" costs or at a price at which returns from alternative enterprises are approximately equal. At prices below variable costs, farmers will not be able to cover harvesting and marketing costs and hence will not offer anything for sale. As prices rise above variable costs, the quantity supplied of product A will increase, but at varying rates, depending on the profitability of switching resources from other farm enterprises to enterprise A. Thus, for example, at low prices little or no land may be switched to A, and increases in output would be limited to the profitability of adding more inputs such as fertilizer to the area planted to A. However, at some price it will become profitable to switch land formerly planted to other crops to A. At this price, supply is likely to become more elastic. Finally, the supply function may become very steep again if no additional land is available for producing product A and the application of other inputs is subject to sharply diminishing marginal returns.

Empirical estimates of the price elasticity of supply are useful to those who have the responsibility of forecasting future supplies or making policy decisions. If the supply schedule for a commodity is relatively elastic, a modest reduction in the support price, for example, may be sufficient to solve a surplus problem, but this would not be true if the supply is price inelastic. The problems of obtaining reliable empirical estimates of supply elasticities are similar to, although somewhat more complex than, those discussed in connection with demand elasticities.

Learn and Cochrane (1961), Nerlove and Bachman (1960), and Tomek and Robinson (1977) provide useful references and background information about empirical supply analysis.

It is sometimes difficult to isolate the effect of a change in the product price from other factors, such as changes in the prices of inputs or alternative crops which compete for the same resources. Time lags compound the problem of obtaining reliable estimates. Usually an attempt is made in empirical analysis to distinguish between short-run elasticities (based on responses which occur within one or two production periods) and long-run elasticities (based on the full effects of a price change allowing whatever time is necessary for all adjustments to occur).

Empirical estimates of short-run elasticities of supply for selected agricultural commodities produced in the United States are shown in Table 4–1. The elasticity estimates are highest for livestock products with short production cycles such as eggs and broilers. The production of these commodities can be altered quite readily within a few months. Elasticity coefficients also tend to be higher for crops which are produced as a sideline enterprise on many farms and planted on only a small portion of total acreage. Potatoes are commonly cited as an example of such a crop although, because of increasing specialization, fewer farmers are now in a position to expand or contract potato acreage as compared with a generation ago. Short-run elasticities tend to be lower for crops such as wheat, which occupy a large proportion of the cropland and are grown in areas where alternatives are limited, and for commodities such as beef and fruit, which have long production periods. Price elasticities

Table 4-1. Estimated short-run elasticities of supply for selected commodities

Crops	Elasticity	Livestock products	Elasticity
Potatoes	.8	Eggs	1.2
Soybeans	.5	Poultry meat	.9
Feed grains	.4	Hogs	.6
Cotton	.4	Beef	.5
Tobacco	.4	Milk	.3
Wheat	.3		
Fruits	.2		

Source: Reprinted from Luther G. Tweeten, *Foundations of Farm Policy,* by permission of University of Nebraska Press. Copyright © 1970 by the University of Nebraska Press. The elasticities are derived by the author from numerous sources and are based on an adjustment period of about two years.

of supply also tend to be lower for subsistence crops grown in less developed countries than for cash crops such as cotton.[3]

Changes in Supply

Empirical studies of supply relationships for farm products, both in the United States and in other countries, indicate that changes in product prices typically (but not always) explain a relatively small proportion of the total variation in output which has occurred over a period of years. Short-run changes in output are often influenced by the weather and pests, while long-run changes in supply are attributable to such factors as improvements in technology which result in higher yields. These and other factors which lead farmers to produce more at the same price are frequently referred to as "supply shifters." It is important to know whether changes in output occur as a result of movements along a static supply schedule (change in quantity supplied) or because of shifts in the supply curve (changes in supply).

A shift in the supply curve to the right (an increase in supply) means that a larger quantity will be offered at a given price; a shift to the left has the opposite effect. The principal causes of shifts in the supply curve are

(1) changes in input (or factor) prices,

(2) changes in the returns from commodities that compete for the same resources,

(3) changes in technology which influence both yields and costs of production or efficiency,

(4) changes in the prices of joint products (i.e., commodities which are produced together such as wool and mutton), and

(5) institutional constraints such as government acreage control programs.

Changes in production resulting from "unusual" weather and insect or disease damage also can be treated as temporary shifts in supply. Oury (1965), for instance, has considered the problem of explicitly incorporating the effects of weather in a supply model. These effects are generally treated as random shifts in the supply function.

---

[3]According to a summary prepared by Krishna (1967) price elasticities of supply (as measured by acreage response) tend to cluster around 0.1 for subsistence crops and to range as high as 0.7 for cotton and jute. Askari and Cummings (1977) summarize the results of additional studies. While they found wide differences in supply elasticities among commodities and regions, their conclusion is consistent with that drawn by Krishna, namely acreage response elasticities are larger for cash crops than for subsistence crops.

As with demand relationships, it is useful to distinguish between a parallel shift in the curve and a structural change (Learn and Cochrane, 1961).[4] To illustrate, a hypothetical supply function may be written as follows:

$$Q = \alpha + \beta P - \gamma X,$$

where Q = quantity
          P = price of product (output)
          X = price of input (measure of cost)
and α, β, and γ are parameters of the equation.

The output (Q) is a function of the price of the product (P) and costs (X). The static supply function assumes a fixed level of X. A change in the magnitude of X shifts the level of the equation by a constant amount and hence leads to a parallel shift in supply. However, if the parameters or the functional form of the equation change, this is a structural change. Changes in technology, such as the development of a new variety of a commodity, are an important source of structural changes. Structural change may also arise from changes in management skills, changes in the number and size distribution of firms, development of new areas capable of producing the commodity, and changes in government programs influencing supply. Clearly, changes in shift variables (like X) and structural changes may be related.

Input Prices

As pointed out earlier, an increase in the use of inputs (and hence an increase in output of a commodity) may occur as a result of either an increase in the price of the product or a decrease in the price of inputs. Conceptually, a change in the price of a factor is treated as a supply shifter. An increase in factor prices, other variables constant, shifts the cost curves of each firm, and hence the supply curve, to the left; a decrease in the price of a factor has the opposite effect.

A given percentage decrease in the price of all factors accompanied by an equal percentage decrease in the price of the product results in the same use of quantities of inputs. Analytically, this can be viewed as a downward movement along the static supply curve in response to a reduction in the price of the product and a shift to the right in the supply curve as a result of a corresponding decline in the price of factors. This

---

[4]This is analogous to the distinction made on the demand side, although the sources of structural change are different.

situation is illustrated schematically in Figure 4–3. Production will remain at Q_1 despite the decline in the product price from P_1 to P_2 if factor prices decrease by an amount sufficient to shift the supply curve from S_1 to S_2.

Relative price changes are usually expressed as a price ratio. One of the best-known ratios in agriculture is the hog/corn price ratio which shows the number of bushels of corn required to equal in value the farm price of hogs per hundredweight. It is calculated as follows:

$$\text{Hog/corn ratio} = \frac{\text{price of hogs (\$ per cwt.)}}{\text{price of corn (\$ per bu.)}}$$

For example, when the price of hogs is \$30 per hundredweight and the price of corn is \$2 per bushel the ratio is equal to \$30/\$2 or 15.

A ratio of 20 or higher is usually followed by an expansion in hog production, while a ratio of 15 or less generally leads to a cut in production the following year. The relationship between the hog/corn price ratio and subsequent changes in the number of sows farrowing for the period 1964 to 1979 is shown in Figure 4–4. Note that there have been exceptions to the general rule. A ratio of approximately 15 led to an expansion in the number of sows farrowing in 1967 and 1968, whereas a much higher ratio led to a slight reduction in 1973 and 1978.

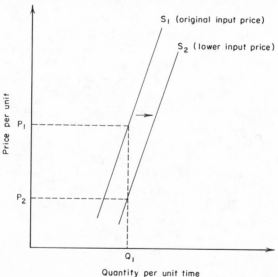

Figure 4-3. Changes in supply associated with a decrease in input prices and a corresponding decline in the price of the product

Supply Relationships in Agriculture

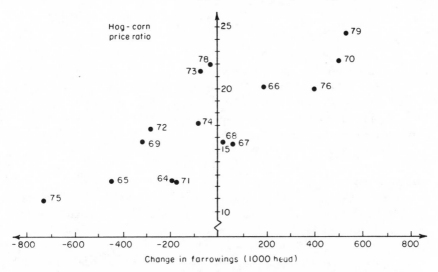

Figure 4-4. Relationship between September-December hog-corn price ratio (Omaha basis) and change in number of sows farrowing subsequent March-May, 10 states, 1964-1979. Data from *Livestock and Meat Statistics,* USDA Stat. Bul. 522, 1973 and supplements.

The hog/corn ratio has become less reliable as a predictor of changes in hog production in recent years, partly because a higher proportion of the total supply now originates on specialized farms that are less inclined to vary production from year to year, and partly because the cost of feed, represented by the price of corn, now makes up a smaller proportion of total costs. But the data presented in Figure 4-4 indicate that there is still a positive relationship between farrowings and the hog/corn ratio. The principle which the scatter diagram illustrates is important, namely that production does respond to changes in the price of the product relative to the price of one of the principal inputs.[5]

In statistical analyses of supply, using separate variables for the price of hogs and the price of each of the principal feed ingredients may yield more satisfactory results than using the hog/corn price ratio as the single explanatory variable. Meilke (1977) developed an improved forecasting equation by introducing the price of hogs, the price of corn, and the price of soybean meal as separate variables.

[5]Factor/product price ratios also help to explain changes in crop yields. Houck and Gallagher (1976) found a statistically significant relationship between the fertilizer/corn price ratio and yields of corn in the United States over the period from 1951 to 1971.

Profitability of Competing Commodities

The supply curve for a given commodity will shift to the left if competing or alternative commodities become more profitable; it will shift to the right if other commodities become less profitable. Competing commodities are ones that can be produced with the same resources. A competing commodity B can become more profitable because the price of that commodity rises relative to the first commodity A or because costs of producing B decline relative to A. Thus, relative changes in product prices, yields, or efficiency can change the relative profitability of different commodities.

Corn and soybeans are important alternative crops over much of the central and southern part of the United States. In the 1960s, an increase in the average yield of corn relative to soybeans in the midwestern area made corn more profitable than soybeans at prices which prevailed at the time. In southern areas, the yield disadvantage of soybeans was less than in the Corn Belt. Consequently, soybean acreage increased in the South relative to the Corn Belt (Brown, 1971). Over time, of course, an initial yield advantage may be offset by a subsequent change in relative product prices. Soybean prices have risen relative to corn since the 1960s, tending to offset the yield disadvantage.

In empirical analysis of supply, the prices of products which compete for the same resources are usually included as one of the explanatory variables. Other things remaining the same, a rise in the price of commodity B can be expected to lead to a decrease in the area planted to commodity A.

Technology

Improvements in technology are important causes of long-term shifts in agricultural supply functions. An improvement in technology is defined as something that enables firms to produce more output with the same quantity of inputs as previously. In technical terms, it shifts the production function upward so that producers will find it profitable to increase output at the same ratio of product to factor prices.

Among the more important technical changes which have increased agricultural supply are the development of high-yielding varieties of crops and improved breeds of livestock; better methods of insect, disease, and weed control; mechanization which makes it possible to plant and harvest more promptly; and better tillage techniques. The effects of these changes are well known, but it is often difficult to identify and measure precisely how much of a given change in output is due to technical improvements and how much is due to changes in factor or product prices. Rapid technical changes in agriculture during the 1950s and 1960s in the United States, for example, were accompanied by a substantial decline in the price of nitrogen fertilizer. Both shifted the supply schedule to the right; however, it is difficult to determine how much of the shift was due to technology and how much to the lower price of fertilizer (which, in turn, was the result of rapid technological changes in the fertilizer industry).

Because of the definitional and measurement problems involved, there has been a tendency in empirical analysis of supply to use time or some simple trend variable as a measure of technological improvements without specifically identifying and measuring those factors responsible for shifts in supply. A few economists, however, such as Griliches (1957, 1963) have sought to determine the important causes of technical change in agriculture, including the contributions of public expenditures for research, and to measure the rate of adoption of improved production practices.

Joint Product Relationships

Supplies of a number of agricultural commodities are determined in part by joint relationships. Joint products are those that are produced in approximately fixed proportions, such as soybean oil and soybean meal from soybeans. The supply of wool, for example, is determined by the price of lamb as well as the price of wool. In some cases, crop rotations or particular combinations of enterprises may be fixed largely by technological considerations. This, in turn, leads to the production of joint products. Under such circumstances, an increase in the price of one product can cause the supply curve of the other (joint) product to shift to the right. Such relationships are important for commodities like vegetable oils, wool, or butterfat.

Institutional Factors Affecting Supply

The supply schedule for an agricultural commodity is often influenced by institutional factors such as increases or decreases in acreage allotments, incentive payments to keep land idle, zoning or land-use regulations, and bases or quotas. Government programs obviously have had a marked influence on the production of such commodities as wheat, corn, cotton, rice, and tobacco in the United States since the depression years of the 1930s (Houck, et al., 1976).

85

Principles of Price Determination

Supply Response Relation[6]

A distinction is sometimes made between the traditional supply function of economic theory and a "response relation." The traditional supply curve specifies a price-quantity relation, all other factors held constant. The response relation is more general; it specifies the output response to a price change not holding other factors constant. Thus, the response may involve both movements along a supply curve and shifts in supply.

The response relation is not a reversible function in the sense that a supply curve is reversible. In fact, the supply response elasticity is likely to be different for an increase in price than for a subsequent reduction in price.[7] The traditional supply curve specifies that if price increases and then decreases, the quantity supplied will return to its original level. It is reversible.

The response concept is based on the hypothesis that when price changes, there are likely to be correlated changes in supply shifters. In particular, when prices increase, new techniques of production are more likely to be introduced. This presupposes a backlog of new technologies which may be adopted by the producer. Under conditions of rising prices, firms may be induced to adopt new techniques at a somewhat faster rate than with constant or declining prices. Also, a large proportion of agricultural capital comes from retained earnings, and consequently higher prices may make it possible to finance the adoption of new techniques more rapidly. Under these circumstances, an increase in price can be expected to have two effects. First, it will cause farmers to increase output along the static supply curve; and second, it will lead them to shift to a new supply curve. The resulting increase in supply will thus be greater than one might have anticipated if the forecast were based solely on the static concept of supply.

Once adopted, improved production practices usually are retained even though the price of the product subsequently declines. Farmers are not likely to discard new technologies and thereby shift the supply function to the left once it has moved to the right. Hence, the supply

---

[6]This section is based on Cochrane (1955).

[7]Various statistical models have been developed in an attempt to test whether or not the response of output to an increase in price differs from the response to a decrease in price. The evidence suggests differences do exist; the percentage response to a given price increase generally exceeds the response to a corresponding decrease in price. Empirical results from the application of alternative asymmetric supply functions are reported by Traill, Colman, and Young (1978).

response to a subsequent decline in price is likely to be less than to the previous increase in price. Under these circumstances, the response elasticity is higher for a price increase than for a price decline. A hypothetical response relation of this type is shown in Figure 4-5. At a price of P_1, producers offer an output of Q_1, but as the price increases to P_2, output expands along the diagonal between S_1 and S_2, ultimately reaching Q_2. If the price thereafter declines to P_3, output declines along the new supply curve S_2, resulting in the production of Q_3.

Favorable or unfavorable agricultural prices obviously can have a marked influence on the rate at which new technology is adopted, and hence on the rate of change of farm output. Farmers must have an incentive to use new techniques and access to sufficient capital to make the necessary investments. During the 1940s, farmers in the United States experienced these conditions. In contrast, price relationships were unfavorable to agriculture in many of the less developed countries in the 1950s and early 1960s. T. W. Schultz attributes the lag in farm production during this period among the less developed countries to "widespread underpricing of agricultural products and overpricing of agricultural inputs" (1965, p. 51).

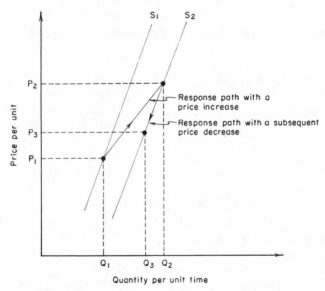

Figure 4-5. Hypothetical supply response paths

Principles of Price Determination

Aggregate Farm Output

Changes in aggregate farm output over time have been associated mainly with shifts in the aggregate supply function rather than movements along a static supply curve. The aggregate supply relationship in agriculture in most countries is highly price inelastic in the short run. This is due mainly to the fact that resources once committed to agriculture tend to remain in use, especially when alternative opportunities for employment are limited. This phenomenon is sometimes referred to as "asset fixity" (Edwards, 1959). Land, buildings, family labor, and machinery often have low salvage or alternative use value outside of agriculture. Even when agricultural prices are relatively low, a farmer will find it more profitable to use his labor and equipment to produce another crop when nearby alternative employment opportunities are unavailable or intermittent, rather than to attempt to work off the farm and to sell his equipment at second-hand prices. Stated in another way, the salvage value of such resources frequently is below their value in use. Hence, it pays to continue farming, at least until the resources are "used up" or need to be replaced.

The unresponsiveness of aggregate farm output to a fall in product prices was dramatically demonstrated in the United States in the early 1930s. Total farm output remained about the same between 1929 and 1932 despite the fact that farm prices fell about 50 per cent during this period. Farmers continued to produce because they had no better alternatives. Their behavior was consistent with profit-maximizing principles as D. Gale Johnson (1950) has pointed out. The optimum use of factors, as emphasized earlier, is a function, not of product prices alone, but of the ratio of product to factor prices. In the early 1930s, feed prices, land rents, and eventually even the wages of hired labor in agriculture fell almost as much as farm product prices. This meant that product/factor price ratios remained approximately constant, and consequently farmers used about as much of these factors after the decline in product prices as before.

The experience of the 1930s is not likely to be repeated in precisely the same way, but it illustrates a very important principle: namely, that input prices in agriculture, especially for land and those items produced by some farmers and sold to others such as seed, feed, and livestock, are likely to decline along with product prices. When this occurs, output will remain relatively stable in the face of a severe agricultural depression. This is less likely to occur as more inputs with inflexible or administratively determined prices are used in agriculture.

Because of the rigidities which exist in agriculture, including "asset fixity" and the difficulty of changing production plans in the short run, it is not surprising to find that empirical estimates of the aggregate elasticity of supply are quite low. Tweeten and Quance (1969) estimate the aggregate short-run elasticity of farm production in the United States to be no more than about 0.15. This estimate is based on historical data. Their analysis suggests further that the aggregate quantity supplied is less responsive to a price decrease than to a price increase. The elasticity estimate for periods of falling prices is 0.07, while for periods of rising prices it is 0.17.

Understanding Changes in Agricultural Product Supply

Supply relationships for individual farm commodities are often complex. One reason for this is that yields are subject to unpredictable elements. Too much or too little rain, an early frost, or disease damage may cause actual production to deviate substantially from planned production. The biological nature of agricultural production also means that supply cannot respond immediately to a change in prices. Moreover, production decisions, unlike those in many nonfarm industries, are highly decentralized and are made by thousands or even millions of individuals managing small units.

In attempting to predict changes in domestic production, it is important to distinguish between those factors of production that can be altered within a short period of time and those that cannot. With increasing specialization in both equipment and skills, many farmers find it difficult to change production plans very significantly in a short period of time. In order to forecast changes in supply one needs to identify those regions and types of farms which have the capacity to alter production plans and to estimate the relative returns from alternative enterprises on such farms. One also needs to keep in mind that changes in supplies of livestock products are limited by the availability of female stock and the time required to produce a new generation.

Feeding rates are important and can be adjusted more quickly than the number of female animals. Rates of grain feeding are determined mainly by the ratio of the price of the product to the price of feed or the price of feed ingredients such as corn and soybean meal. Crop yields are influenced by such factors as the amount of irrigation water applied during the growing season (which in turn is related to pumping costs or water allotment rights), rates of fertilizer application, and the kinds of pest control measures adopted. Empirical analysis is required to determine how much the use of each factor is likely to change in response to changes in the relationship between factor and product prices.

Switches between enterprises also must be considered. The production of milk, for example, is influenced in some areas by the price of beef relative to milk, and in other areas by the price of hogs relative to milk. In Australia, the production of wool or lambs in some regions is influenced principally by the relationship between the prices of these (joint) products and the price of wheat. The relevant price ratio to consider in attempting to forecast the supply of a particular commodity obviously varies from commodity to commodity and region to region, but again it is relative prices that are critical, not the price of one commodity alone.

In forecasting production, an understanding of the prices to which farmers respond is important. For most commodities, except those grown under contract, product prices are uncertain at planting time or when breeding plans must be made. Expected future prices may be based on recent past prices, average prices over a period of years, current prices for the distant delivery of a commodity as observed on an organized futures market, government price-support levels, or outlook statements. For some commodities there is considerable empirical evidence to suggest that future production plans are based on current prices. If this relationship persists, a cycle of alternating high and low production may develop, with corresponding changes in prices. High prices in one year will lead to high production and low prices in the following year, which will then induce a cut-back in production the next year. The economic implications of this type of response, sometimes called the "cobweb model," are explored more fully in Chapter 9.

A closely related question, as previously mentioned, is the role of time lags in agricultural supply. The biological nature of farm production precludes rapid adjustments of output. A time period ranging up to eight years or more for some tree crops is required for a complete quantity adjustment to a change in expected prices.

Weather during the planting season also can have a significant influence on the acreage planted to certain crops. Unusually wet weather may make it impossible to plant the desired acreage of the crop which is expected to be the most profitable, thereby forcing farmers to plant an alternative crop with a shorter growing season. In the Corn Belt, for example, a late spring may lead farmers to cut down on the acreage planted to corn and to increase the area planted to soybeans.

Off-farm employment opportunities can affect the supply of some commodities. A rapid increase in employment opportunities off the farm during a period of business expansion, for example, may encourage some dairymen to cease production, especially in areas such as the northeastern region of the United States. High unemployment, on the other hand, may slow up the exodus from agriculture.

In sum, the most important economic factor affecting production of an individual commodity in the short run is the availability of alternatives. The supply relation is much more likely to be price-elastic for a particular commodity when alternative opportunities are available, including work off the farm as well as the production of other commodities. With the passage of time, changes in the supply of farm products are determined principally by shifts in the supply schedule most often associated with improvements in technology and changes in the availability and cost of inputs.

References

Askari, Hossein, and John Thomas Cummings. 1977. "Estimating Agricultural Supply Response with the Nerlove Model: A Survey," *Internat. Econ. Rev.*, 18:257–292.

Brown, W. Herbert. 1971. *Soybeans: Acreage Response to Price and Farm Program Changes.* USDA, ERS-473.

Cochrane, Willard W. 1955. "Conceptualizing the Supply Relation in Agriculture," *J. Farm Econ.*, 37:1161–1176.

Edwards, Clark. 1959. "Resource Fixity and Farm Organization," *J. Farm Econ.*, 41:747–759.

Griliches, Zvi. 1957. "Hybrid Corn: An Exploration in the Economics of Technological Change," *Econometrica*, 25:501–522.

———. 1963. "The Sources of Measured Productivity Growth: U.S. Agriculture, 1940–1960," *J. Pol. Econ.*, 71:331–346.

Houck, James P. 1967. "Price Elasticity and Linear Supply Curves," *Am. Econ. Rev.*, 57:905–908.

———. 1977. "An Approach to Specifying and Estimating Nonreversible Functions," *Am. J. Ag. Econ.*, 59:570–572.

———, et al. 1976. *Analyzing the Impact of Government Programs on Crop Acreage.* USDA Tech. Bul. 1548.

———, and Paul W. Gallagher. 1976. "The Price Responsiveness of U.S. Corn Yields," *Am. J. Ag. Econ.*, 58:731–734.

Johnson, D. Gale. 1950. "The Nature of the Supply Function for Agricultural Products," *Am. Econ. Rev.*, 40:539–564.

Krishna, Raj. 1967. "Agricultural Price Policy and Economic Development," in *Agricultural Development and Economic Growth.* Ed. H. M. Southworth and B. F. Johnston. Ithaca, N.Y.: Cornell Univ. Press.

Learn, Elmer W., and Willard W. Cochrane. 1961. "Regression Analysis of Supply Functions Undergoing Structural Change," in *Agricultural Supply*

Principles of Price Determination

Functions. Ed. Earl O. Heady *et al.* Ames, Iowa: Iowa State Univ. Press.

Leftwich, Richard H. 1973. *The Price System and Resource Allocation.* 5th ed. Hinsdale, Ill.: The Dryden Press. Chapters 8 and 9.

Meilke, Karl D. 1977. "Another Look at the Hog-Corn Ratio," *Am. J. Ag. Econ.,* 59:216–219.

Nerlove, Marc, and Kenneth L. Bachman. 1960. "The Analysis of Changes in Agricultural Supply: Problems and Approaches," *J. Farm Econ.,* 42:531–554.

Oury, Bernard. 1965. "Allowing for Weather in Crop Production Model Building," *J. Farm Econ.,* 47:270–283.

Schultz, Theodore W. 1965. *Economic Crises in World Agriculture.* Ann Arbor: Univ. of Michigan Press.

Tomek, William G., and Kenneth L. Robinson. 1977. "Agricultural Price Analysis and Outlook," in *A Survey of Agricultural Economics Literature.* Volume 1. Ed. Lee R. Martin. Minneapolis: Univ. of Minnesota Press. Pp. 328–409.

Traill, Bruce, David Colman, and Trevor Young. 1978. "Estimating Irreversible Supply Functions," *Am. J. Ag. Econ.,* 60:528–531.

Tweeten, Luther G. 1970. *Foundations of Farm Policy.* Lincoln: Univ. of Nebraska Press.

———, and C. Leroy Quance. 1969. "Positivistic Measures of Aggregate Supply Elasticities: Some New Approaches," *Am. J. Ag. Econ.,* 51:342–352.

CHAPTER 5

Price Determination:
Theory and Practice

This chapter is concerned with the determination of prices within alternate market structures. The term "market structure" refers to the number and size distribution of buyers and sellers, the degree of product differentiation, and the ease of entry of new firms into an industry.[1] These "structural characteristics" may be used as a basis for classifying markets. Price behavior, in terms of level and frequency of change, varies with the type of market structure.

Classification of Markets

Markets may be classified as competitive (many buyers and sellers), oligopolistic (few firms), or monopolistic (a single firm). Another category, which is sometimes used, is monopolistic competition (many firms selling similar but differentiated products). In this section, we outline the characteristics of some types of markets.

A *purely competitive market* is one in which the following conditions prevail:[2]

(1) The number of buyers and sellers is sufficiently large so that no individual can perceptibly influence price by his or her decision to buy or sell.

---

[1]Other market or product characteristics besides these which may affect pricing decisions include the durability of the commodity, the adequacy of grade descriptions (where relevant), bulkiness of the product relative to its value, the ratio of fixed to variable costs in the industry, and the continuity and length of the production process. Additional comments on market characteristics and market structure in agriculture are contained in Breimyer (1976).

[2]These conditions lead to what is sometimes referred to, alternatively, as atomistic competition (Dorfman, 1964, p. 78).

(2) The product is sufficiently homogeneous so that the product of one firm is essentially a perfect substitute for that of another firm.

(3) There are no artificial restrictions on demand, supply, or prices such as government intervention or collusion among firms.

(4) Mobility of resources and products exist in the economy; e.g., a new firm should be free to enter the industry.

In a purely competitive market, it is assumed that every producer-seller seeks to maximize profits by selling at as high a price as possible, and that every buyer seeks to maximize utility by obtaining the product at as low a price as possible. The collective actions of buyers and sellers determine prices.

To simplify theoretical analysis, economists use the concept of a *perfectly competitive* market. In addition to large numbers and product homogeneity, the term "perfect" implies perfect knowledge by buyers and sellers, complete divisibility of the product, and perfect mobility of the product within the market. With these assumptions, we can talk about "the" price for a product in a market.

Under competitive conditions, the supply and demand relations faced by the individual differ greatly from the market supply and demand functions. Since each buyer and seller cannot perceptibly influence price, the demand and supply relations appear horizontal to the respective individuals. For instance, the individual farmer typically views the (derived) demand function for his product as being perfectly horizontal. A farmer cannot influence price by the quantity he offers for sale; he is a price taker.

A second type of market, at the opposite extreme from perfect competition, is that designated as *absolute monopoly*. The distinguishing characteristic of this type of market structure is a single seller. The firm's demand schedule coincides with the industry demand schedule. Product differentiation is implicit in this definition, since a monopoly could not exist unless the firm's product were substantially different from the products of other firms.

Monopolistic competition refers to a market in which a large number of sellers offer a differentiated product. These products are presumably close substitutes, but the individual sellers are able to differentiate their product on the basis of a trade name, style, quality, service, location, or other factors. Consequently, the firm has some influence on price, but the number of substitutes is likely to limit the firm's discretion in pricing. The demand relation faced by the individual firms, while not perfectly elastic, is likely to be quite elastic in the prevailing range of prices.

Oligopoly refers to a market with a few large sellers. Each firm produces a large fraction of the industry's total product, and consequently the action of one firm in the industry can greatly influence other firms. In a *pure oligopoly*, the sellers are producing a homogeneous product. The steel industry is an example. In a *differentiated oligopoly*, the firms are producing a similar but not identical product. The automobile industry is an example. Because each oligopolistic industry tends to develop unique interrelationships among firms, this type of market structure is the least susceptible to generalizations about price and output policies.

This classification of markets emphasizes the number of sellers and implicitly assumes a large number of buyers. Other classifications may be devised with emphasis on the number of buyers in the market. For instance, a market with a single large buyer is referred to as a *monopsony*. A market with a single buyer and a single seller is called a *bilateral monopoly*. Obviously, a large number of market structures could be devised, each involving different combinations of numbers of buyers and sellers and degree of product differentiation.

Many markets do not fit neatly into the categories just described. It is not easy to define an industry or to determine the number of firms which should be included, especially with the growth of large conglomerate enterprises. Measuring the degree of concentration also is difficult. One common measure of concentration is the proportion of total industry sales made by, say, the four largest firms in the industry. If the four largest firms in the industry account for 90 per cent of total sales, then the market may be classified as an oligopoly. Of course, such a single measure does not take account of the degree of product differentiation or other possible monopoly elements. In addition, a global or industrywide measure does not reflect the possible high levels of concentration in a local market area, and conversely a firm may have a large share of the total market but only a small share of some local markets.[3]

Price Determination under Pure Competition

Models of agricultural product price behavior often assume a purely or perfectly competitive market structure. Prices of perhaps one-half of

[3]Economists have made some attempts to classify firms on the basis of the direct-price elasticity of demand faced by the firm and by the cross-price elasticities between firms. For instance, we argued above that the individual firm in a competitive market faces a perfectly elastic (horizontal) demand function. Hence, evidence that a firm faced a perfectly elastic demand schedule for its product would be evidence that the firm was part of a competitive market. Bishop (1952) shows, however, that a classification system based on elasticities involves great subtlety and does not give a completely mutually exclusive classification of markets.

the farm products in the United States are determined under conditions approximating pure competition. Even if the number of firms producing the commodity is fairly small, price behavior may still approach that expected under pure competition. This occurs when relatively free entry of other firms is possible. Thus, one can argue that the prices of many fruits and vegetables, poultry, eggs, and meat animals are determined under competitive conditions. The trading of commodity futures contracts also takes place under conditions of pure competition (see Chapters 12 and 13), although price manipulation or an "imbalance" of use by buyers or by sellers may create conditions that deviate from the competitive model.

The federal government, of course, intervenes in the pricing of grains, cotton, rice, tobacco, peanuts, and dairy products in the United States. But models which assume competitive behavior are still useful as a norm against which actual behavior under government intervention can be checked or evaluated. Hence, price determination in the very short run and in the short run under pure competition is discussed in this section. The objective, however, is not to provide an exhaustive discussion of the theory of price determination (this may be found in, for example, Leftwich, 1973).

One of the important concepts in economics is that of an equilibrium price. This is simply the price at which quantity demanded and quantity supplied are equated. If the demand function has a negative slope and the supply function a positive slope, then the two curves will intersect at some price. At prices above equlibrium, the quantity consumers are willing to buy is less than the quantity producers are willing to sell, while at prices below equilibrium, quantity demanded exceeds the quantity that will be supplied. Thus, statements such as "demand exceeds supply" are meaningless unless specified in relation to a particular price. Quantity demanded exceeds quantity supplied at relatively low prices, is equal to quantity supplied at another price, and falls short of quantity supplied at still higher prices.

Actual market prices approximate equilibrium prices in a purely competitive market. However, with imperfect information about current and expected economic conditions, actual transactions prices may deviate from the equilibrium level. There are at least two "models" of the relationship of transactions prices to the theoretical equilibrium price. One view is that prices within a particular time period (say, a day) are distributed about the true equilibrium for that time period. Thus, the average of transactions prices is taken as equal to the equilibrium price. This is the implicit assumption of most empirical studies which use average prices for a month, quarter, or year in the analyses. In essence, the reported average price is treated as an unbiased estimate of the true equilibrium price.

A second model views successive transactions as tending toward equilibrium. Given a certain set of supply-demand conditions, prices are "discovered" in a search or *tatonnement* process.[4] In theory, prices and quantities are revised until an equilibrium is reached. Presumably prices would tend to stabilize at the equilibrium level, and the last price in the sequence (for the specific period with fixed economic conditions) is the equilibrium price.

In practice, however, neither of the foregoing models is necessarily correct. In real markets, sequential, binding trades are made with the passage of time based on imperfect information. The average of these prices may not equal the true equilibrium or even tend toward the equilibrium. Since true equilibrium prices are unobservable, it is difficult to test for the relationship between them and transactions prices. Some experiments have been conducted in an attempt to simulate reality. Hess (1972) and others found that under a few experimental situations, the average of transaction prices was a biased estimate of the equilibrium.

Nonetheless, an equilibrium price probably does represent a norm toward which transaction prices tend to converge under competitive conditions. Of course, acting on incomplete or poor information is different from acting irrationally. Also, as we shall see, valid economic reasons exist for differences in prices for different lots of the same commodity (e.g., due to quality or location differences).

Very Short Run

The slopes of demand and supply schedules, as pointed out in earlier chapters, tend to become more elastic as additional time is permitted for adjustments to occur. In the very short run, the supply function is by definition a vertical line; i.e., supply is perfectly inelastic. For nonstorable commodities, supply consists only of the current season's production. The vertical supply function also implies that additional quantities cannot be imported within the time period in response to a price change. The intersection of the vertical supply curve with a sloping demand curve determines the equilibrium price, designated as P_1 in Figure 5-1. This price exactly clears the market of the available supply.

---

[4]A distinction is sometimes made between the theory of price determination and "price discovery." Price discovery refers to the actual institutional method of arriving at prices and is discussed in Chapter 11.

Principles of Price Determination

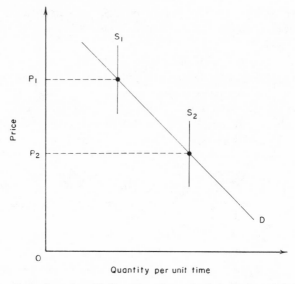

Figure 5-1. Illustration of equilibrium prices for perfectly inelastic supply functions

The level of the very-short-run supply function, of course, can shift from one harvest period to the next. Poor growing conditions in one year would result in a small quantity available for sale, such as S_1 in Figure 5-1, while good growing conditions would result in a large quantity for sale, such as S_2 in Figure 5-1. Total production could be so large that if the entire crop were harvested and marketed, the resulting price would be below harvesting and marketing costs. In this case (not shown in Figure 5-1) a part of the crop would be abandoned.

The real world is obviously more complex than the simple model depicted in Figure 5-1. Demand functions also shift, and a farm-level price would be related to derived, rather than primary, demand. Nonetheless, an elementary model can be a useful first step in understanding agricultural product price behavior.

For example, the production of pecans in any given year is fixed and independent of price in that year (see Fowler, 1963). Typically few pecans have been stored from year to year, and few are imported. Thus, domestic production each year is approximately the same as a perfectly inelastic supply function for the year (as in Figure 5-1). Production, however, is highly variable so that the vertical supply schedule shifts from year to year.

The dots in Figure 5-2 may be viewed as points of equilibrium between a fixed supply and the derived, farm-level demand for pecans. The wide scatter of observations reflects both shifts in demand and supply. Since supply has been more variable than demand, the dots form a negative slope. A careful study of Figure 5–2 indicates also that demand has been increasing. For instance, the production of 200 million pounds of pecans in 1978 would have sold for about 45 cents per pound more than in the early 1960s.

The points in Figure 5–2 do not necessarily represent the theoretical equilibria. First, although production is fixed, there is uncertainty about the actual crop size at the time growers are harvesting and selling pecans. Errors may be made in estimating crop size or other variables influencing price, and actual prices reflect these errors. Second, pecan growers have the option of not harvesting a part of their crop; harvest-time prices in some years may not be sufficient to cover harvesting and marketing costs (note the price "floor" of about 18 cents a pound in Figure 5–2). In such years, the quantity sold and price are simultaneously determined; that is, the quantity supplied is not fixed and independent of current price.

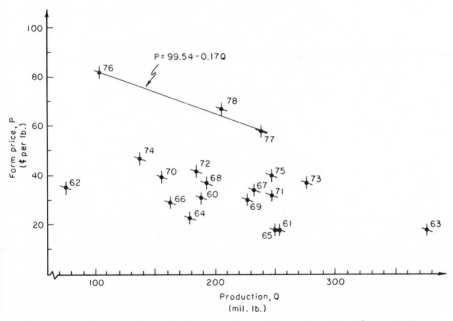

Figure 5-2. Pecans in the shell: total production and farm price, United States, 1960–1978. Data are from USDA, *Agricultural Statistics, 1978,* Government Printing Office.

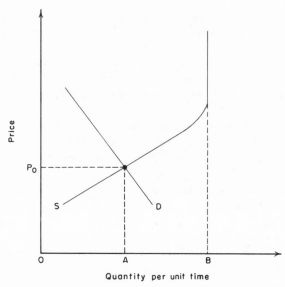

Figure 5-3. Illustration of equilibrium price for storable commodity with fixed available supply OB

If a commodity is storable, then the supply curve is no longer vertical (perfectly inelastic) over its entire range. Supplies may be drawn from stocks at high prices, or certain quantities may be withheld from current sale for storage at low prices. In this case, the supply curve reflects an estimate of the quantities suppliers desire to hold (or supply) at alternative prices (Figure 5-3). The demand curve D illustrates the demand in a particular time period, say a month. The equilibrium price (P_0) is the price at which the quantity buyers want to purchase exactly equals the quantity suppliers (producers and stock holders) want to offer. In Figure 5-3, the total supply available is OB, and the quantity sold within a particular time period is OA. Alternatively, the quantity AB may be viewed as a measure of the sellers' demand to hold that quantity at price P_0. Shifts in either function would, in general, change the level of the equilibrium price.

Short Run

The short run in conventional price theory is a situation in which some factors of production are variable. Hence, as previously discussed, the short-run supply curve includes production costs. The short-run equilibrium price is depicted as being determined by sloping supply and demand schedules similar to those illustrated in Figure 5–4. It is an equilibrium for a given set of short-run demand and supply conditions.

For reasons described in previous chapters, the supply and demand schedules are likely to become more elastic the greater the time allowed for adjustment to price changes. Thus, in the longer run, the equilibrium price may differ substantially from the one in the short run. The equilibrium price represents that price at which producers will find it just profitable to make the investments necessary to continue producing the marginal unit which will satisfy the quantity demanded at that price.

The conventional supply-demand diagram depicting an equilibrium does *not* imply that price and quantity are constant in a purely competitive market. An equilibrium price is defined for given (static) supply and demand functions. In a dynamic economy, the forces which influence both the level and slope of demand and supply schedules are changing. Hence, the equilibrium price generally changes through time. An increase in income or population typically shifts the demand curve to the right. Changes in the prices and available supplies of inputs or the prices of products competing for the same resources, for instance, cause the supply curve to shift either to the right or to the left. Structural changes in demand and supply may occur as well.

If shifts in demand and supply are equal and in the same direction, the equilibrium price will remain constant. If the demand schedule shifts to

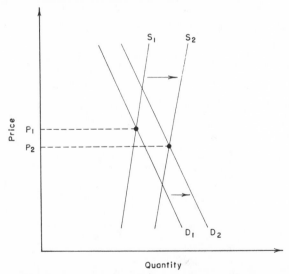

Figure 5–4. Illustration of increase in supply relative to increase in demand

101

the right more rapidly than the supply schedule, the equilibrium price increases; however, if supply increases relative to demand, then the equilibrium price falls (Figure 5-4).

The frequency and magnitude of price changes under purely competitive market conditions depend (1) on the frequency and magnitude of shifts in demand and supply and (2) on the elasticities (more specifically, the slopes) of the demand and supply functions. Wide price fluctuations over short periods of time can be expected if both demand and supply schedules have steep slopes (are relatively inelastic) and if either demand or supply changes sharply from period to period. The typical agricultural commodity has an inelastic demand and a supply which shifts from season to season. As a result, equilibrium prices for commodities like potatoes are highly variable from year to year.

Price changes will be relatively modest if the demand or supply functions are flat (relatively elastic) and do not shift greatly from one time period to the next. However, even if the demand schedule has a steep slope and shifts from period to period, as long as the supply schedule is relatively flat, price changes will be relatively small. Various combinations of shifts in supply and demand and differences in slopes are possible. This helps explain why different commodities have different degrees of price variability.

The short-run economic model just discussed is most directly applicable in explaining the annual variation of prices and quantities of many farm commodities. (The quantity variable would be represented by an annual total and the price variable by an annual average.) The principal fluctuations in supply often occur from year to year. The reader also should recall that supply may be related to past or lagged prices, not to current ones.

Of course, prices also may vary from day to day (or week to week) under competitive conditions. This occurs with changes in transient factors, which may be viewed as day-to-day changes in demand and supply, and with changing evaluation of information about economic forces by buyers and sellers. Such price changes through time are more fully discussed in several subsequent chapters.[5]

Prices established under purely competitive market conditions should

---

[5]In formal economic theory, change in price is made a continuous function of excess demand: $dP_t/dt = f(D_t - S_t) = f(E_t)$, where D = demand, S = supply, E = excess demand $(D - S)$, P = price, and t = time. Henderson and Quandt (1971) discuss the conditions necessary to produce a stable equilibrium. McCallum (1974) provides an illustration of using competitive price adjustment equations in empirical analysis. Instability in prices resulting from basing production decisions on last year's price is discussed more formally in Chapter 9.

not be considered as inherently superior and therefore sacrosanct. For a variety of reasons, society may prefer to maintain prices above or below those that would prevail with competition. A particular price can be judged "good" or "bad" only insofar as society as a whole considers the consequences of that price desirable or undesirable. Prices established under competitive market conditions do have desirable properties, not the least of which is the avoidance of problems associated with programs to limit production or to ration available supplies. Also, if prices approximate those that prevail under perfectly competitive conditions, the total social product is maximized (resources are optimally allocated). The marginal social benefit of the last unit purchased is just equal to the marginal social cost of producing that unit of output. However, the social product is maximized only if *all* industries operate under competitive conditions. For a more detailed explanation of the conditions necessary to maximize gains to society as a whole see Lerner (1946, pp. 72–88).

If society chooses to use the pricing system, not to allocate resources in a particular way, but to influence the distribution of income, it may do so, provided it is also willing to use nonprice mechanisms to restrain production or to subsidize consumption. Prices may be maintained above equilibrium by such devices as acreage-control programs, land-retirement schemes, or marketing quotas. Likewise, society may choose to keep prices below equilibrium and then use ration cards or other devices to limit consumption. This is frequently done during major wars. Thus, for social or political reasons, actual market prices may be established and maintained above or below equilibrium prices, but this does not make a study of demand and supply relationships irrelevant. It is still essential to know something about the position and slopes of the demand and supply functions in order to ascertain the amount of surplus or deficit that is likely to exist at whatever level prices are established.

Price Determination under Monopoly

Pure, unrestricted monopoly is, in practice, a relatively rare phenomenon. Under the antitrust laws in the United States, monopolies are illegal with exceptions such as public utilities (telephone and electric service). In such instances, rates are regulated by public agencies. Thus, the discussion of pricing under conditions of pure monopoly may seem somewhat academic. However, there are situations in which the theory of pricing under monopoly helps to explain price behavior. A firm, for example, may develop a new product which has few substitutes. In the short run, it may price the product in a manner similar to that of a pure monopolist. There also may be local areas in which the size of the market

Principles of Price Determination

is such that one firm can operate profitably, but two could not. The existing firm then has a local monopoly, although there are limits to the ability of a firm in this position to raise prices since customers may go elsewhere, or if the price is too high, another firm may find it profitable to enter the market despite the limited scale. Finally, and most important for our purposes, governments sometimes permit monopoly-type pricing by groups or organizations in some sectors of agriculture. Examples include marketing orders in the United States and marketing boards in Commonwealth countries.

The distinguishing feature of a pure monopoly market structure is that the demand schedule facing the individual firm or monopoly organization is sloping rather than horizontal and coincides with the industry demand schedule. Although the monopolist has some discretion in pricing, he must consider the effect of his price policy on sales and net revenue. The more *potential* substitutes available for the product he or she sells, the more elastic is the long-run demand schedule facing the monopolist. In such cases, raising prices will result in a substantial loss of sales. Thus, the greatest protection society has against the possibility of undue exercise of monopoly power is the potential availability of substitutes, including imported products.

A monopolist can choose any price he or she likes, but consumers have the final choice of accepting or rejecting the article or service at the stated price. The willingness of buyers to purchase varying quantities at alternative prices is, of course, reflected in the demand schedule facing the firm. The monopolist can establish a price and sell whatever quantities consumers will buy at that price, or, alternatively, the monopolist can produce a certain volume and place it on the market. The demand schedule then dictates at what price this volume can be sold. Thus, a monopolist can determine price or the volume of sales but cannot simultaneously determine both unless they are consistent with the aggregate demands of consumers.

The monopolist, like all firms, is assumed to maximize profits. This is done by choosing the volume of production (or price) at which marginal costs and marginal revenue are equated. Under monopoly conditions, price does not equal marginal revenue, whereas in perfectly competitive markets, price and marginal revenue are the same. Price is higher than marginal revenue whenever the demand curve facing the individual firm is sloping rather than horizontal. The relationship between marginal revenue and price is expressed by the following equation:

$$MR = P \left(1 + \frac{1}{E} \right),$$

where E is the price elasticity of demand (a negative coefficient).

If elasticity is infinite (horizontal demand curve), the last term $(\frac{1}{E})$ approaches zero as a limit and the equation becomes $MR = P\ (1 + 0)$ or $MR = P$. The more inelastic the demand curve (i.e., the steeper the slope), the greater the difference between price and marginal revenue. Marginal revenue is positive only if the elasticity of demand is greater than unity. If the elasticity is -1.0 (unit elasticity), the marginal revenue becomes zero, regardless of the price, $MR = P\ (1 + \frac{1}{-1}) = P\ (1 - 1) = 0$; while if the demand schedule is price inelastic (less than -1.0), marginal revenue becomes negative. For example, if elasticity equals -0.2, then $MR = P\ (1 + \frac{1}{-.2}) = P\ (1 - 5)$ or $-4P$. It follows that a "rational" monopolist would not set a price in the range of demand that was inelastic.

The profit-maximizing price and volume of output for a monopolist (or for a group of agricultural producers if they were to combine and operate as a single seller) are illustrated in Figure 5-5. In this case, it would never be profitable to sell more than OB units, even if costs of production were zero, since beyond that point the marginal revenue becomes negative. If one takes account of costs, then the optimum level of output

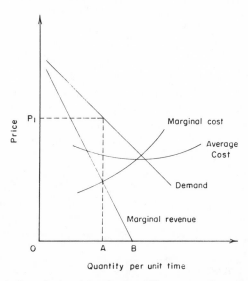

Figure 5-5. Illustration of price determination with a monopoly market structure

105

is at OA, that is, the volume at which the marginal cost curve intersects the marginal revenue curve. The price at which this output would sell (determined by the average revenue or demand schedule) is P_1.

The volume of output that will maximize profits for the monopolist obviously will change if either the demand or cost curves change. Prices, however, are less likely to change in the short run under conditions approaching pure monopoly than under purely competitive conditions. The monopolist is more likely to establish a price with long-run rather than short-run profits in mind and to maintain that price for a considerable period of time. If the initial price is high, this may encourage potential competitors to develop new products, or the government may seek to break up the firm or to regulate it. Thus, the monopolist may price below the short-run equilibrium position in an attempt to perpetuate or maintain his long-run profits. However, the firm which has developed a new product (e.g., nylon) may price the product relatively high initially when manufacturing capacity is small, and then reduce the price over time in order to encourage sales as capacity expands. Consequently, at any one point in time, the monopolist's price may vary substantially from that suggested by the pure theory of monopoly pricing.

Price Discrimination

Under some circumstances, it is possible for a monopolist (whether an individual firm or a farm cooperative that has control over a high proportion of the total supply of a particular commodity) to increase its revenue by charging some buyers higher prices for its product than others. The conditions that must exist for a monopolist or a monopoly-type organization to gain from discriminatory pricing are as follows:

(1) It must be possible to identify two or more separate groups of buyers (markets) with different price elasticities of demand.

(2) The markets must be effectively separated to prevent a flow of the commodity among markets; it should not be possible to buy the product in the low-priced market and sell it profitably in the high-priced market.

If these conditions exist, it is possible to increase revenue by charging a higher price in the market with the more inelastic (or less elastic) demand and a lower price in the market with a less inelastic (or more elastic) demand.[6]

The principles involved in maximizing returns by practicing dis-

[6]Economists sometimes define three degrees of price discrimination (see Pigou, 1952, p. 279). We discuss "third degree" discrimination, the only degree of practical importance.

criminatory pricing can be simply illustrated by assuming just two groups of buyers with different price elasticities of demand. Initially, assuming a fixed supply of the commodity to be sold and that the cost of allocating the supply between markets is zero, marginal costs are zero and can be ignored. The profit-maximizing rule is to shift quantities between markets up to the point where the marginal revenue (MR) obtained from the sale of the last unit in each market is equal. This may be done (provided there is sufficient quantity) up to the point that $MR_1 = MR_2 = 0$. It would not, of course, pay to sell quantities such that the marginal revenue becomes negative in either market.

Successful price discrimination requires differences in price elasticities, which implies different demand relations and hence different marginal revenue curves. If the same price were charged to the two groups of buyers, then the marginal revenues would be different. The equalization of marginal revenues increases total revenue by transferring part of the available supply from the market with the lower marginal revenue (raising price in this market) to the market with the higher marginal revenue (lowering price in this market). For example, if reducing sales by one unit in the primary market increased revenue 25 cents per unit and if the added quantity in the secondary market decreases revenue only 8 cents per unit, there is a gain of 17 cents from the transfer. It would pay to continue transferring units until the gain in revenue in one market equals the loss in the other market, that is, until marginal revenues are equal.

In the longer run, where production costs must be considered, the optimum level of output and the quantity sold in each market may change since the monopolist must take account of marginal costs as well as the marginal revenue in each market (Figure 5–6). The optimum level of output is that at which the added cost to the firm (or to the monopoly selling organization) of producing the last unit of product just equals the combined marginal revenue from sales in both markets. The optimum level of output is then allocated between markets in such a way that marginal revenue is equal in all markets and also is equal to marginal costs, that is, $MC = MR_1 = MR_2$.

Under the Robinson-Patman Act it is illegal for firms to charge buyers different prices unless they can prove that the differences in prices are accounted for by differences in costs.[7] Nevertheless, there are cases

---

[7]The courts have held in some cases, however, that a firm may charge buyers lower prices for a particular commodity or service in one market than in other markets provided the lower price is maintained simply "to meet competition" (for additional discussion see Papandreau and Wheeler, 1954).

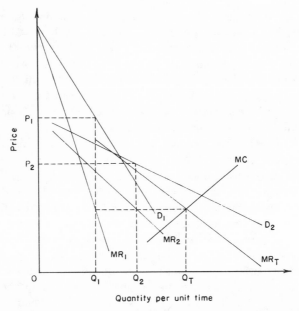

Figure 5-6. A two-market price discrimination model. In this diagram, a monopolist is assumed to be able to divide his market into two parts with demands D_1 and D_2, and his marginal costs are given by *MC*. The profit-maximizing output is Q_T of which Q_1 should be sold in Market 1 at price P_1 and Q_2 should be sold in Market 2 at price P_2. MR_T is the horizontal sum of MR_1 and MR_2.

where discriminatory pricing practices are adopted. In agriculture, this is frequently done with the assistance of the government.

To profit from discriminatory pricing, as pointed out earlier, it must be possible to maintain separate markets. Markets may be differentiated on the basis of

(1) place or location, e.g., domestic and export markets;
(2) time, e.g., seasonal differences in resort hotel prices and higher first-run movie prices;
(3) form or use of the commodity, e.g., price differences between fresh and processed use of a raw material;
(4) type of consumer, e.g., residential versus industrial use of a service, charging different fees for medical services by income groups, or different prices for theatre tickets by age groups;
(5) a combination of the above.

Even if separate markets can be established, gains will be small or nonexistent unless elasticities also differ significantly in the separate markets and a relatively large fraction of the total output is sold in the higher-priced market. The potential methods of separating markets are suggestive of reasons for differences in elasticities. In Chapter 3, we noted that income elasticities may vary with the level of income; the homogeneity condition implies that price elasticities vary with income elasticities, the magnitude of cross elasticities held constant. Thus, it is not surprising that different income groups may have different price elasticities of demand for a particular commodity. Elasticities also may differ among markets because of differences in the availability of substitutes, differences in age level or age distribution of the population, and differences in tastes and preferences. Even if retail demand functions are identical, derived demands faced by the discriminator may still be different.

A large literature has developed dealing with the application of price-discrimination concepts in agriculture (Tomek and Robinson, 1977; Waugh, 1964). To illustrate, a part of the apple crop is sold at harvest, part in the winter, and part in the spring. These seasonal markets are naturally separated by time, though they are not necessarily independent of each other. If the demand for apples differs seasonally, then the principles of price discrimination could be used to determine the allocation of sales through time in order to maximize revenue to sellers. The implementation of such a scheme, however, would require apple growers to organize and act as a monopoly.

Federal and state marketing orders make it possible for producers of some products to practice price discrimination. Under milk-marketing orders, for example, handlers of milk are required to pay higher prices for milk which is bottled for fluid use than for milk of equal quality which is converted into cheese, ice cream, and so forth. Such regulations clearly assume that the demand for fluid milk is more price inelastic than the demand for manufactured dairy products.

Some farm products are exported at lower prices than those prevailing in the domestic market. The demand in the export market is assumed to be more elastic than in the domestic market. The government provides the power for separating markets, subsidizing exports, and maintaining price differences by imposing import quotas or tariffs. Most such schemes probably have increased total revenue, but prices have not necessarily been established at levels which will maximize returns to producers. The possibilities of extracting more revenue from consumers have not been fully exploited. For example, it has been suggested that wheat exporters should sell wheat to developed countries such as the United Kingdom, Japan, and Germany (with high internal price supports and price inelastic demands) at relatively high prices and sell the remainder to developing countries (with more elastic demands) at relatively low prices (Abel, 1966).

The analytics of a price-discrimination scheme require a knowledge of the calculus of constrained optimization, which is beyond the scope of this book. The interested student, however, may wish to study Waugh (1964, appendix 6) or a similar reference. We provide here the first steps in setting up the problem.

The simplest problem involves two markets, an unlimited quantity to allocate between the markets, and zero costs of allocation. In this simple case, no constraints exist, and the algebra is relatively simple.

An essential first step is to have reliable estimates of the demand functions for the separate markets. Assuming such functions are available and further assuming they are straight lines, we write them in the form of price (P) as a function of quantity (Q). The subscripts represent the two markets.

$$P_1 = a - b\,Q_1, \text{ and}$$
$$P_2 = c - d\,Q_2.$$

The total revenues (R) for the two markets are

$$R_1 = P_1 Q_1 = (a - bQ_1)Q_1$$
$$= aQ_1 - bQ_1^2.$$
$$R_2 = cQ_2 - dQ_2^2.$$

In this simple case, the optimum point is for the allocation in which the marginal revenues are zero. Readers familiar with calculus will also recall that a necessary condition for a maximum is that the first derivatives equal zero.

The marginal revenues (MR) are defined as the first derivatives of the total revenue functions.

$$MR_1 = \frac{d\,R_1}{d\,Q_1} = a - 2bQ_1 \text{ and}$$

$$MR_2 = \frac{d\,R_2}{d\,Q_2} = c - 2dQ_2.$$

Setting these equations equal to zero and solving for the respective Q's gives

$$\hat{Q}_1 = \frac{a}{2b} \text{ and } \hat{Q}_2 = \frac{c}{2d}.$$

The total quantity sold would be $\hat{Q}_1 + \hat{Q}_2$ with the respective quantities allocated to the two markets. The optimizing prices for the two markets are computed from the demand equations.

A somewhat more realistic problem in agriculture is the allocation of a fixed supply to the alternate markets. At harvest, for example, the quantity of apples to be allocated to the alternate seasonal markets is a fixed amount. In terms of an example using two markets, the problem is to maximize total revenue (R) subject to the constraint that the quantities allocated equal the total quantity (Q_T) available. That is,

$$\text{maximize } R = R_1 + R_2,$$
$$\text{subject to } Q_T = Q_1 + Q_2.$$

As previously, the definitions of R_1 and R_2 can be substituted so that R becomes a function of the Q's.

The allocation problem also can be made more realistic by taking account of allocation costs. In the apple example, a seasonal allocation of the crop must take account of the costs of storage. Thus, we could adjust gross revenue for storage costs in such a way as to maximize revenue net of these costs.

It is important to note that—even in the simplest case—the derivation of an appropriate solution is dependent on the quality of the underlying information. Thus, good estimates of the demand functions and cost functions are essential. If the allocation is to be made among four markets, then estimates of four demand functions are required. This is not necessarily a trivial task. The lack of precise estimates may explain why policy programs often use the principles of price discrimination as general guides to allocations among markets but not to find specific optimum points.

Most elementary discussions of price discrimination assume that the various markets are independent, but it is not easy to maintain separate markets, even if they can be differentiated initially. Cheaper processed products, for example, may gradually reduce sales in the higher-priced fresh-use market. Products made from raw materials sold at lower prices in export markets also may eventually undercut sales of domestically manufactured products. This happened in the United States during the late 1950s when cotton was sold abroad at prices substantially lower than those paid by domestic cotton mills. Eventually the textile products manufactured from lower-priced U.S. cotton in Japan, Hong Kong, and Taiwan found their way back into the United States and reduced the sales of domestic mills.

With lack of independence, the profit-maximizing discriminatory prices can *not* be based on the marginal revenues of demand functions that assume independence. Rather, these functions (and the corresponding marginal revenues) must be adjusted for the net effect of possible substitutability among the markets, or more likely, the demand functions must be estimated in such a way as to take account of the interrelatedness (Hoos and Seltzer, 1952).

Finally, one must keep in mind the effect of higher prices on supply of the farm product involved. If discrimination succeeds in raising total revenue, and the additional revenue is paid out to producers, this will encourage expansion. The net effect then may be simply to add to the quantities going into the secondary market, which will subsequently cause average returns to decline. This explains why multiple-price schemes in agriculture may increase returns to producers in the short run, but not in the long run, unless the lower marginal price is reflected back to producers so that there is less incentive to increase output. Monopoly power is required to control allocations of supply to various markets; it also may be necessary to use such power to control or influence production.

In sum, the use of price-discrimination concepts to allocate a product among markets assumes some monopoly power, and the resulting allocations tend to equalize *net marginal revenues* in the markets. This allocation, in general, can be quite different from the allocation that would occur under perfectly competitive conditions. The allocations under competitive conditions tend to equalize *net prices* in the alternate markets. This topic is discussed more fully in subsequent chapters. For example, the relationship of spatial prices under competitive conditions is discussed in Chapter 8.

Price Behavior with Monopolistic Competition and Oligopoly

Monopolistic competition, as previously discussed, is essentially a competitive market structure but with product differentiation. Many variants of a product are involved which are close but imperfect substitutes. Thus, the demand curve faced by the firm operating in an industry characterized by monopolistic competition is likely to be very elastic.

It is usually assumed that the firms have similar cost structures. Firms with high costs relative to others in the industry presumably could not exist in the long run in a relatively competitive industry. The equilibrium price (and output) is based on equating marginal revenue and marginal cost. Since the products are good substitutes and since similar cost structures are assumed, the prices of the various firms are expected to be similar but not necessarily identical.

Firms operating under conditions of monopolistic competition tend to avoid price competition because of the threat of retaliation by other firms. An individual firm, of course, would gain if it reduced its own price (since its own demand schedule is reasonably elastic), provided other firms did not. But if competing firms also lower their prices to meet the competition, each would gain relatively little. This explains why such firms prefer to avoid price wars. Since price cutting often leads to retaliation, the profit-maximizing price is likely to be similar among firms in the industry and relatively stable as long as costs remain constant.

Similar pressures to avoid direct price competition prevail in industries where a few firms produce or market identical or similar products, i.e., where oligopolistic conditions prevail. In making pricing decisions, each firm must take account of the possible reactions of its competitors. If, for instance, other firms do not follow a price increase, the firm initiating the increase would lose sales and profits. Hence, there is often a "price leader" in the industry, and competition for sales may take the form of offering more favorable credit terms, advertising or promotion allowances, or even secret discounts or rebates.

It is difficult to generalize about price performance under oligopolistic conditions without specific knowledge of individual industries and firms. One principle of long-term pricing is to set price at a level which is sufficient to earn a target rate of return on capital when production is at a "normal" level. Price is altered primarily when the cost of producing this standard output changes, but not in response to temporary changes in demand. If demand falls, inventories are built up and production is lowered, but prices are not reduced. If demand rises, the response, at least in the short run, is to draw down inventories and increase order backlogs rather than to raise price.[8]

An aggressive firm seeking to enlarge its market share may establish a price very close to that which would prevail under purely competitive conditions. On the other hand, if a tacit agreement exists to maintain

[8]Eckstein and Fromm (1968) have drawn on these ideas to formulate price adjustment equations under disequilibrium. They recognize formally that reported prices may be above (or below) equilibrium levels with economic adjustments occurring through such variables as inventory build-up and drawdown of unfilled orders (or the reverse for prices below equilibrium). More recently, the concept of price adjustments under disequilibrium conditions has appeared in the agricultural economics literature (Heien, 1977). However, a model based on a competitive equilibrium framework seemed to be a better predictor of prices in the crop sector than a model based on the disequilibrium framework (Baumes and Womack, 1979).

market shares and to avoid open price competition, the price established may approximate that which would prevail under conditions of pure monopoly.

Marketing margins for some farm products are determined under conditions which more nearly conform to the oligopolistic or monopolistic competition model than the purely competitive model. A high proportion of the fluid milk sold on retail routes or through chain stores in most cities is processed and distributed by a small number of firms. While these firms usually are compelled to pay producers certain minimum prices under federal or state marketing orders, the distributors are free to establish retail prices (except in a few states which also regulate retail prices). Thus, the behavior of individual firms is an extremely important factor affecting fluid-milk marketing margins. Retail prices (hence margins) are likely to be low in cities where there are one or more aggressive firms seeking to increase their market share; they are more likely to be high in cities where a "live and let live" policy prevails among distributors.

Small processors such as those canning or freezing fruits and vegetables often face a situation best characterized as oligopsony (many sellers and a few buyers). Each produces a small part of the total supply, which must then be sold in competition with similar products offered by other processors to a small number of retail-chain buyers. When supplies of processed products are large, the temptation is for each processor to shave the price to avoid carrying large inventories. Chain-store buyers are then in a position to play off one supplier against another. This can lead to depressed prices for processors, low profits, and little capital for investment in more modern equipment or facilities.

Among agricultural commodities, the breakfast cereal industry offers perhaps the best illustration of what may occur under an oligopolistic structure. Each of the small number of firms which dominates the industry seeks to capture a larger share of the market, not so much through price competition, but by developing new products, by offering coupons or prizes, and through increased expenditures for packaging, promotion, and advertising.

Retail food stores also may seek to increase their sales by building more elegant stores, offering trading stamps, or providing additional services. The net effect of this form of competition is to increase the number and variety of products and services available and perhaps consumer satisfactions as well, but at the same time marketing costs are increased. While prices are still determined mainly by competitive forces, nonprice competition obviously now plays a significant role in the marketing strategies of food retailers (Nelson, 1966; Padberg, 1968).

114

Price competition apparently can be enhanced by providing comparative price information to consumers. Devine and Marion (1979) found that provision of such information by a public agency significantly reduced the average level of prices and the dispersion of prices in one market relative to a control market.

Concluding Remarks

Price performance under alternate market structures is difficult to appraise. Prices established under competitive conditions are likely to be somewhat lower than those that would prevail under monopolistic or oligopolistic conditions. Competitive prices also are likely to vary more frequently and with wider amplitude, especially where demand and supply schedules are inelastic and where either supply or demand shifts abruptly from year to year or season to season.

Economists tend to prefer competitive pricing to monopoly pricing. There is a greater possibility of farmers being exploited when only a single buyer or a few outlets are available in a local area. But it is difficult to determine empirically whether or not farmers are being charged higher prices for the things they buy or are being offered lower prices for what they sell than would prevail with a larger number of sellers and buyers.

The economies of scale may be sufficiently large that marketing costs may be lower with a small number of large firms than with a large number of small competitors. Galbraith (1952, pp. 90–99) also calls attention to the fact that where pricing is very competitive, profit margins may be so thin as to limit expenditures for research or capital improvements. He maintains that the most innovative firms have been those that have had sufficient market power to maintain prices above average costs in the short run. By investing in research, they were able to develop improved products and increase efficiency. A substantial share of the benefits of these innovations was subsequently passed on to consumers. In sum, the issue is whether or not the benefits of economies of size, improved products, and so forth when they exist for large firms are more or less offset by higher profits, excessive product differentiation, larger advertising expenses, and other costs.

References

Abel, Martin E. 1966. "Price Discrimination in the World Trade of Agricultural Commodities," *J. Farm Econ.*, 48:194–208.

Baumes, Harry S., Jr., and Abner W. Womack. 1979. "Price Equilibrium or

Principles of Price Determination

Price Disequilibrium in the Crop Sector," *J. Northeastern Agr. Econ. Council,* 8:forthcoming.

Bishop, Robert L. 1952. "Elasticities, Cross-Elasticities, and Market Relationships," *Am. Econ. Rev.,* 42:779–803.

Breimyer, Harold F. 1976. *Economics of the Product Markets of Agriculture.* Ames, Ia: Iowa State Univ. Press. Chapters 4 and 5.

Devine, D. Grant, and Bruce W. Marion. 1979. "The Influence of Consumer Price Information on Retail Pricing and Consumer Behavior," *Am. J. Ag. Econ.,* 61:228–237.

Dorfman, Robert. 1964. *The Price System.* Englewood Cliffs, N.J.: Prentice-Hall.

Eckstein, Otto, and Gary Fromm. 1968. "The Price Equation," *Am. Econ. Rev.,* 58:1159–1183.

Fowler, Mark L. 1963. *Factors Affecting Pecan Prices and Price Relationships in the United States.* Okl. St. Univ. Tech. Bul. T-100 (May).

Galbraith, J. K. 1952. *American Capitalism: The Concept of Countervailing Power.* Boston: Houghton Mifflin.

Heien, Dale. 1977. "Price Determination Processes for the Agricultural Sector Models," *Am. J. Ag. Econ.,* 59:126–132.

Henderson, James M., and Richard E. Quandt. 1971. *Microeconomic Theory: A Mathematical Approach.* 2d ed. New York: McGraw-Hill Book Co. Chapter 4.

Hess, Alan C. 1972. "Experimental Evidence on Price Formation in Competitive Markets," *J. Pol. Econ.,* 80:375–385.

Hoos, Sidney, and R. E. Seltzer. 1952. *Lemons and Lemon Products: Changing Economic Relationships.* Calif. Ag. Exp. Sta. Bul. 729.

Leftwich, Richard H. 1973. *The Price System and Resource Allocation.* 5th ed. Hinsdale, Ill.: The Dryden Press, Chapters 7, 10, 11, 12, 13.

Lerner, Abba P. 1946. *The Economics of Control.* New York: Macmillan.

McCallum, B. T. 1974. "Competitive Price Adjustments: An Empirical Study," *Am. Econ. Rev.,* 64:56–65.

Nelson, Paul E., Jr. 1966. "Price Competition among Retail Food Stores," *J. Farm Econ.,* 48, No. 3 (Part II):172–187 (Aug.).

Padberg, Daniel I. 1968. *Economics of Food Retailing.* Ithaca, N.Y.: Cornell Univ. Food Distribution Program.

Papandreau, Andreas G., and John T. Wheeler. 1954. *Competition and Its Regulation.* Englewood Cliffs, N.J.: Prentice-Hall. Chapters 6 and 21.

Pigou, A. C. 1952. *The Economics of Welfare.* 4th ed. London: Macmillan.

Tomek, William G., and Kenneth L. Robinson. 1977. "Agricultural Price Analysis and Outlook," in *A Survey of Agricultural Economics Literature.* Volume 1. Ed. Lee R. Martin. Minneapolis: Univ. of Minnesota Press. Pp. 368–370.

Waugh, Frederick V. 1964. *Demand and Price Analysis: Some Examples from Agriculture.* USDA Tech. Bul. 1316.

II

PRICE DIFFERENCES AND VARIABILITY

This section focuses on those factors which help to explain price differences associated with the provision of marketing services, with grade or quality, with location, and with the passage of time. Price differences between those paid to the farmer and those paid by the consumer are commonly referred to as marketing margins, and these differences are analyzed in Chapter 6. In the following two chapters, price differences based on quality and on region or location are discussed. Price changes that occur through time are discussed in Chapter 9; particular emphasis is placed on seasonal and cyclical (cobweb-like models) variation. In Chapter 10, changes in the terms of trade of farm products (i.e., in the relationship between farm and nonfarm prices) and changes in the general level of all farm prices are considered.

CHAPTER 6

Marketing Margins
for Farm Products

Price theory in its simplest form assumes that buyers and sellers meet directly. Equilibrium prices are determined by the aggregate demand and supply schedules of these buyers and sellers. Elementary textbooks in price theory generally say little or nothing about price differences between producers and final consumers. However, substantial research has been done in agricultural economics on questions related to price differences between farmers and consumers. Nonetheless, unanswered questions remain.

The difference between the price received by producers and that paid by consumers is a marketing margin. Both producers and consumers are concerned about the size of marketing margins, changes in marketing margins, and the incidence of changes in margins. Among the questions frequently asked are the following: Are marketing margins too large? Why do margins differ among products? How have they changed with the passage of time? Are margins larger for small-sized crops than for large-sized crops? If marketing costs increase, does this result in a higher consumer price or a lower farm price, or both?

A principal objective of this chapter is to provide tools of analysis and evidence that will help the student to answer such questions as those posed above. Attention is focused exclusively on marketing margins and not on price differences due to quality, space, or time. Most of the analysis is based on the marketing margin for a single product and assumes a purely competitive market structure. Some comments are made in the next to last section of this chapter on the potential effects of imperfect competition on marketing margins.

119

Defining Marketing Margins
Theoretical Concepts

A marketing margin may be defined alternatively as (1) a difference between the price paid by consumers and that obtained by producers, or as (2) the price of a collection of marketing services which is the outcome of the demand for and the supply of such services.

Under the first definition, a marketing margin is simply a difference between the primary and derived demand curves for a particular product. These concepts were explained in Chapter 2. Primary demand is determined by the response of the ultimate consumers. Empirical estimates of primary demand functions are usually based on retail price and quantity data. Derived demand is based on price-quantity relations which exist either at the point where products leave the farm or at intermediate points where they are purchased by wholesalers or processors (see, for example, Daly, 1958).

Primary demand is in some sense a joint demand for all of the inputs in the final product. Thus, a food product at retail may be divided (conceptually) into two inputs: the farm-based components and the processing-marketing components. Given several simplifying assumptions, the derived demand for the farm product is obtained by subtracting the per unit costs (prices) of all marketing components from the primary demand function. Thus, the farm-level function represents the derived demand for the farm component of the final product, and in empirical analyses the farm price usually must be adjusted so that comparable components are being priced at each level. The assumptions are that the final product is made from fixed proportions of the inputs (e.g., one unit of final product is always obtained from one unit of farm product and two marketing units) and that the supply function of marketing inputs is fixed (static) at a particular level (Friedman, 1962).[1]

Under some conditions, marketing margins can be expected to remain constant as the quantity of a commodity marketed is changing, while under other conditions, margins will vary. The manner in which they respond to changes in the volume marketed depends on the assumptions made with respect to the supply function for marketing services. If this supply function is perfectly elastic (horizontal), the margin remains

---

[1]This "fixed proportions" assumption implies that the elasticity of substitution between the farm and marketing inputs is zero. The assumption seems fairly realistic, although a high price for the farm input would, for example, provide an incentive to use more labor to reduce wastage and spoilage. Gardner (1975) provides a mathematical analysis of marketing margin behavior for the more general case when the elasticity of substitution is not zero.

constant as the demand for services (associated with increasing volume) increases. The same marketing margin is subtracted from the primary demand function at all levels of quantity, and hence the derived demand function is parallel to the primary demand function when they are straight lines. This is the situation assumed in Figure 6-1.

Assuming the supply function for marketing services has a positive slope, then the price of such services would increase as demand increases; hence margins would be higher with larger quantities produced and marketed. But empirical evidence is not always consistent with this assumption (Buse and Brandow, 1960). It may be more realistic to assume that economies of scale in providing marketing services exist. If so, this could lead to a negatively shaped supply curve for marketing services, at least over some range. Under these circumstances, one would expect to find lower margins associated with a larger volume of production. For instance, a small crop may result in an underutilization of marketing facilities while a large crop *may* lead to increased efficiency and hence to lower unit costs. Since many food products undergo a complex transformation from the farm to the consumer, the actual nature of the marketing margins is often difficult to determine.

The concepts of primary and derived supply are analogous to those for demand. Primary supply, however, refers to the relationship at the

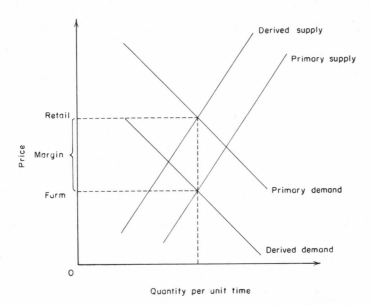

Figure 6-1. Illustration of primary and derived functions and marketing margins

121

producer level (Chapter 4). Empirical estimates are based on farm-level data. The supply relation at retail is derived from the primary relation by adding an appropriate margin.

Thus, a retail price is established at the point where the primary demand and the derived supply relation intersect (Figure 6-1). The farm-level price is based on derived demand and primary supply. The difference in the two prices is the marketing margin. The situation depicted in Figure 6-1 is, of course, static; possible changes in these functions are discussed in a subsequent section.

A marketing margin also may be defined as the price of a collection of services. This price is a function of the demand for and supply of all such services. Marketing services include such items as assembly, processing, transportation, and retailing. These services are sometimes classified by time, form, and place utilities (see Waite and Trelogan, 1951). The supply relation for marketing services (mentioned above) is defined in terms of the marginal cost curve for the services, which in turn depends on input prices, etc. In principle, a demand relation for marketing services also may be defined. A particular marketing margin would thus depend on the particular demand and supply relations for services. An attempt has been made to obtain empirical estimates of aggregate service relationships for food (Waldorf, 1966).

Margins differ among products because marketing services differ. Changes in margins may be depicted as resulting from shifts in the supply or demand relations for services. For example, higher input prices for a service with other things the same would result in a decrease in supply and a higher margin (Figure 6-2). Of course, if the supply curve were perfectly elastic, shifts in the demand for marketing services would not change the margin.

In practice, there are many marketing services, and hence empirical analysis requires substantial aggregation. Demand and supply concepts, however, can be useful in categorizing variables influencing margins. In the remainder of this chapter, the marketing margin will be defined as the difference between retail and producer prices.

Empirical Measures

The USDA (1979) publishes two commonly used measures of marketing costs: farm-retail price spreads for individual foods and the food-marketing bill. In addition, an aggregate measure of farm-retail price spreads is computed for a fixed market basket of foods, and estimates of the cost components of price spreads are made.

Marketing Margins for Farm Products

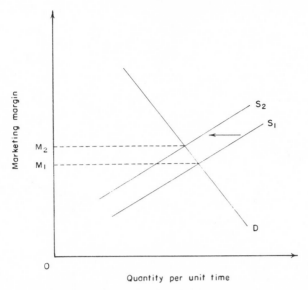

Figure 6-2. Hypothetical demand and supply relations for marketing services

The farm-retail price spread is calculated by deducting the farm value of the raw product (adjusted for the value of any by-products) from the retail price of a commonly purchased unit such as a pound of beef, a dozen eggs, or a one-pound loaf of bread. The quantity of raw product embodied in the typical consumer unit is estimated and valued at the average farm price prevailing at approximately the same time as the reported retail price. This procedure does not take account of possible time lags between changes in farm prices and adjustments in retail prices. For relatively unprocessed commodities such as a dozen eggs, the calculation of a marketing margin is straightforward; estimates of marketing margins perhaps are more difficult to make and certainly more difficult to interpret for retail products which embody numerous inputs as is the case with breakfast cereals or a loaf of bread.

Marketing margins for meat present special problems. The reported retail price of beef, for example, is a weighted average of the prices of 30 cuts of choice beef with the weights based on the average proportion each cut makes up of the total carcass weight. The farm value of a pound of beef sold at retail is based on the average price received by farmers for choice steers multiplied by a factor of 2.4, since about 2.4 pounds of live animal are required to obtain one pound of retail weight. The estimated

Price Differences and Variability

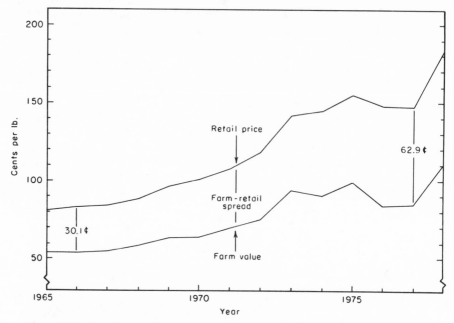

Figure 6-3. Retail price, farm-retail spread, and net farm value per pound, choice beef, United States, 1965-1978. See text for discussion of computing price spreads for beef. Data from Lawrence A. Duewer, "Changes in Price Spread Measurements for Beef and Pork," *Livestock and Meat Situation,* USDA, LMS-222 (Aug. 1978), pp. 30-40.

gross margin is adjusted for a by-product allowance to obtain the net farm-retail price spread (Duewer, 1978).[2] The spread for choice beef is illustrated in Figure 6-3.

Price spreads, such as those for beef, have been used to analyze public policy questions. Hence, their construction has been the subject of controversy. Some critics claim that the USDA's procedures for obtaining the weighted average retail price of beef do not take adequate account of the effects of price specials at retail. Another problem is that retail prices have been collected early in the month while farm prices are collected at mid-month or are an average for the month. Of course, the time lag in the physical flow of product is just the opposite with the raw farm product being priced first and then processed and sold at retail.

[2]In mid-1978, the Bureau of Labor Statistics discontinued the publication of retail prices. Estimates of price spreads for beef and pork have been continued using USDA retail price surveys. Price spreads for other commodities will be published again when BLS makes retail price information available.

The average conversion factors from live animal to retail cuts of beef also can be subjected to criticism.

Price spreads are less meaningful for interpreting retail and farm price movements when the farm value is a small proportion of the retail price. For products that are greatly differentiated from the farm commodity (e.g., a frozen TV dinner or bread), it is difficult to define the marketing margin. In any event, changes in farm prices have little impact on changes in retail prices. Published data on marketing margins obviously need to be interpreted with these limitations in mind (USDA, 1976).

The familiar "farmer's share of the consumer's dollar" statistic is based on the aggregate market-basket data. Retail cost and the farm value of the total market basket are computed. The market basket is based on the purchasing patterns of urban consumers for domestically produced farm foods which were bought in food stores during the period from July 1972 through June 1974. Thus, the weights of the items in the market basket are fixed. The farmer's share statistic is the percentage computed by dividing the farm value by the aggregate retail cost (Table 6-1). The percentage is sometimes interpreted as the cents received by farmers per dollar spent on food by consumers.

The USDA also computes an aggregate food-marketing bill based on the cost of all marketing services. This figure reflects changes in the volume of food marketed, changes in the services provided, changes in product-mix marketed, as well as changes in costs of existing services. Consumer expenditures at retail, the marketing bill, and the farm value of domestic farm-food products in a recent period are depicted in Figure 6-4.

The per unit margin (farm-retail spread) statistics and especially the

Table 6-1. Farmer's share of retail cost of a market basket of farm-food products, selected years

Year	Share (%)	Year	Share (%)
1918	51	1960	39
1933	32	1965	40
1945	53	1970	38
1950	47	1975	41
1955	41	1978	39

Source: USDA, *Farm-Retail Spreads for Food Products, 1947–1964*, ERS-226 (1965), and USDA, *Developments in Marketing Spreads for Food Products in 1978*, Ag. Econ. Rep. 420 (March 1979).

Price Differences and Variability

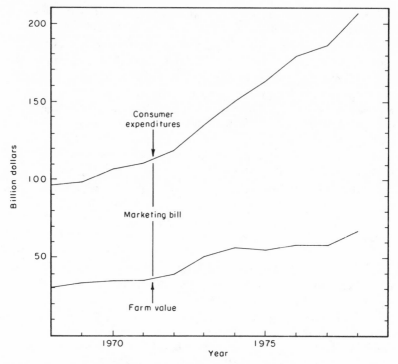

Figure 6-4. Consumer expenditures, marketing bill, and farm value for U.S. farm foods, 1968-1978. Data from USDA, *Developments in Marketing Spreads for Food Products in 1978,* Ag. Econ. Rep. 420 (March 1979).

related concept of the farmer's share of the consumer's dollar are subject to misinterpretation. This concept is a frequently quoted, but often misused, number. There is a tendency to use the number to indicate the "well-being" of farmers or to indicate that marketing costs are "too high." In fact, the farmer's share statistic has little to say about either problem. For example, poultry farmers have received about 55 per cent of the consumer's dollar in recent years, apple growers about 33 per cent, and wheat producers about 12 per cent of the price of white bread. But poultry farmers have not been better off in general than wheat producers.

Farm prices and the farmer's share statistic have tended to move up and down together (Table 6-1). That is, the farmer's share was high when farm prices were high as in the war years 1918 and 1945. However, this is a function of the relative flexibility of farm prices and the relative inflexibility of the margin, at least in the short run. Hence, when farm prices decrease, they tend to become a smaller percentage of retail prices.

The farmer's share statistic remained relatively constant at about 39 per cent throughout the 1960s and 1970s. As pointed out earlier, this tells very little about the welfare of farmers. Producers will be better off, regardless of what happens to the farmer's share statistic, if farm costs decline relative to farm prices. Nor does a decline in the share of the consumer's dollar going to farmers necessarily mean that marketing firms are performing poorly. The decline may simply reflect the increased cost of marketing inputs such as labor. Price spreads provide only a starting point in an attempt to evaluate the performance of the food industry. Measures of efficiency and profits earned by marketing firms also must be examined to determine whether or not margins are excessive (National Commission on Food Marketing, 1966, p. 19).

Changes and Incidence of Changes in Margins

Margin Changes

A margin per unit of product marketed has been defined as the difference between a retail-level and a producer-level (or an intermediate-level) price. These prices, as previously indicated, are determined by particular primary and derived demand and supply relations (review Figure 6–1). Thus, a margin changes because certain of these functions shift relative to others. Of course, the fundamental questions are: What functions shift? and why do they shift?

The derived demand and supply curves shift because the costs of providing existing marketing services embodied in the final product change. Stated another way, the supply function of marketing inputs shifts. Thus, the farm-level (derived) demand for a product may change as the usual determinants of demand change and as the costs of marketing services change. Larger per unit costs, for example, would result in a decrease in derived demand and in derived supply. Marketing costs include waste, loss, and spoilage in the marketing process as well as the more "typical" costs.

Changes in per unit marketing costs (i.e., shifts in the supply curve for marketing inputs), of course, mean changes in marketing margins. The derived demand and supply curves shift relative to the primary curves. A technological improvement in providing marketing services implies a possible structural change in the supply curve of such services. Consequently, the shift in the derived demand curve for the farm product may not be "parallel" to the original level. For instance, the technical change may favor a large volume marketed relative to smaller quantities; the per unit margin may decline more at the larger volumes than at the smaller volumes.

The nature of margins obviously varies among products, and the magnitude of a change in margin depends on the magnitude of the change in per unit costs. There are differences among products in the services provided, such as the amount of processing or transportation included in the product. The degree of perishability also affects margins. Technical improvements may influence the cost of marketing services for one product much more than another.

The primary demand curve shifts with the adoption of new services. When marketing services change, then the product definition at the retail level changes. New inputs or combinations of inputs are used in the final product. Thus, in effect, a new demand curve exists for the new or at least slightly different product. The addition of new services generally has the effect of shifting the primary demand relation up and to the right (increasing demand). The new service probably means increased costs. In the transition, consumers probably have the alternative of buying the old product or the new higher priced one (with added service). If they are willing to buy the same units of the new product at the higher price, then primary demand has increased. In principle, the demand for certain services also may decline and certain services might be removed, which would result in a decrease in primary demand and a decrease in the margin.

The net effect of an entirely new product on the primary and derived demand relationships for related, substitute products is often very complex. In some instances, the development of a new product, say frozen orange juice, may increase total demand, say for orange products in the aggregate. Primary demand may increase by more than enough to cover additional processing and handling costs, thereby increasing the derived demand for the farm component. In other instances, the demand for the new product may not offset the decline in demand for existing products, at least so that the total derived demand for the farm components is smaller. A consumer in buying a frozen dinner in place of similar products in less processed form is perhaps buying less farm product (and is clearly buying more service). The net effect of this substitution on the derived demand for the farm products is thus difficult to ascertain. In addition, the per unit marketing costs for existing products may increase as the volume sold declines.

In sum, changes in factor prices, efficiency, and services embodied in farm products change marketing margins. Hence, over the longer run, average margins tend to parallel changes in costs (as broadly defined). These costs tend to be "sticky," especially relative to farm prices. Thus, while marketing costs can decrease, the usual tendency is to remain the same or to increase (see Scott and Badger, 1972).

In the short run, there may be temporary changes in margins due to lagged responses in the marketing system to changes in primary supply or demand. Meat margins "have exhibited a persistent short-run tendency to widen when supplies increase and narrow when supplies decrease" (Breimyer, 1957, p. 691). Some have also charged that wholesale and retail prices respond more rapidly to increases than to decreases in farm product costs. The Council on Wage and Price Stability (1976) found little evidence to support this charge, but the concern has persisted.

Numerous hypotheses have been advanced to explain the sticky response of retail prices to changes in farm prices. An obvious reason is the time it takes for farm products to be processed and to move through the marketing system. Marketing firms also prefer price stability (Breimyer, 1957). Thus, the relative stability of retail compared with farm prices can be explained, in part, by the desire of supermarket managers to avoid price changes. It is costly to reprice products (Parish, 1967), and consumers may react adversely to frequent price changes or to seeing remarked goods on the grocery shelves.

The nature of demand, where only a few firms are competing, can lead to a preference for price stability. If a single firm attempts to raise prices and others do not follow, that firm will lose sales and total revenues; demand is elastic. On the other hand, if the firm seeks to increase its share of the market by reducing prices, this may lead competing firms to cut their prices as well. Thus, all firms may end up selling very little more at lower prices; in short, the demand associated with a price decrease is inelastic. This is often called a "kinked" demand curve; i.e., individual firms face a relatively flat demand curve above the prevailing price and steep demand curve below that price. Revenue is maximized for each firm under such conditions by maintaining the existing price.

Finally, the failure of retail prices to respond promptly to changes in farm prices may be related to market imperfections. One type of imperfection is poor information. A second type of imperfection is the absence of competition. If a firm possesses monopoly power, it may fail to pass on to consumers any reduction in farm prices, keeping the difference as a larger profit. However, in this situation, the incentive may be to pass higher farm prices along rapidly, and such firms presumably have the power to raise retail prices even if there is no change in farm prices.

Price Differences and Variability

Incidence of Margin Changes

The question of incidence of changes in marketing margins has traditionally been divided into two parts (Waite and Trelogan, 1951): incidence of changes due to the introduction of new service and incidence of changes related to existing services. With a new service and other things the same, the margin is likely to be larger, and the hypothesis is that this change is reflected primarily as a higher retail price. Consumers presumably have the choice of the old product at the old price or the product with new service at a higher price. If they accept the new product, then this appears as a new primary demand at a higher level. Hence, the retail price and the margin are higher, but derived demand and the farm price have not necessarily changed. If consumers do not accept the new service, then primary demand, retail price, and the margin remain unchanged. The incidence of the higher cost of a new service is mainly at the retail level.[3] However, as discussed above, the new service may increase retail demand by more than the cost of the service, thereby increasing derived demand.

If the cost of providing an existing set of services changes, the effect is generally to change *both* retail and producer prices. The change in margin appears as a shift in the derived demand and the derived supply relations for the product. An *increase* in the margin means a decline in derived demand (downward shift) and derived supply (upward shift) with a consequent *increase* in retail price and *decrease* in farm price. Of course, a decrease in margin would have the opposite effect. A competitive market structure is assumed in these statements so that margin changes are reflected through the marketing system.

The magnitude of the price changes at the retail and farm levels, with a given margin change, depends on the slopes of the demand and supply curves. For linear relations, equal slopes (in absolute value) would mean equal, but opposite, changes in retail and farm prices (Waite and Trelogan, 1951). If the slope of the demand relation is steeper than that for the supply relation, then the magnitude of the price change at the consumer level will be greater than at the producer level (Figure 6-5). If the slope of the supply relation is steeper than that for the demand relation,[4] then the magnitude of the price change at the producer level

---

[3]If farm price is constant and retail price increases, then the farm price as a percentage of the retail price declines.

[4]To be precise, the slope of a function in a price (P)-quantity (Q) diagram is defined as dP/dQ, and the slope of a demand function is negative. Consequently, to say one slope is steeper than another means that the absolute value of dP/dQ for one function is larger than for the other. Let b and c be the absolute values of the slopes of the demand and supply functions, respectively, then if $b>c$, demand is steeper than supply. Conversely, if $b<c$, then supply is steeper than demand.

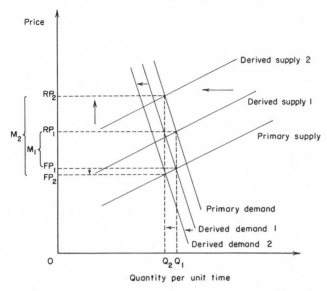

Figure 6-5. An example of a change in margin and the incidence of change on retail and farm prices

will be larger than at the consumer level. For many agricultural products, the supply relation is thought to be more price inelastic than the demand relation. In these cases, to the extent the theory is appropriate, the incidence of a given margin change would be greater at the farm level than at the retail level. Note that, if supply were perfectly price inelastic (a limiting case), then the entire incidence of a margin change would fall on the farm price (Figure 6-6).

A farm price depends on primary supply and derived demand. From the foregoing, we may observe that derived demand changes with changes in primary demand or with changes in the marketing margin. Thus, a lower farm price may be the result of a larger supply or a smaller derived demand, and the latter may be due to a decline in primary demand or to a larger marketing margin. Some attempts have been made to attribute various proportions of declining farm prices to each of these factors (Freeman, 1966; Waldorf, 1966).

The theoretical analysis presented in this section is an example of partial-equilibrium theory. An equilibrium situation for a single product is depicted; one variable—the marketing margin—is changed; other factors are assumed constant; and the new equilibrium position is observed. This method is useful in illustrating the influence of a margin change on farm and retail prices, but it may be somewhat misleading

131

Price Differences and Variability

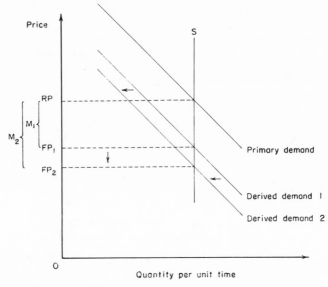

Figure 6-6. Incidence of a margin change with perfectly inelastic supply

when applied to a "real world" situation, because other factors are not constant. Under a competitive market structure, the prices of substitutes will not remain constant, as pointed out in Chapter 3. In addition, the assumption of a competitive market structure may not be appropriate.

For example, an analyst could demonstrate that a smaller transportation cost for apples produced in the Far West would result in higher prices to growers in that area and lower prices to eastern consumers. However, the analysis would be incomplete unless it took into account the substitutability between western and eastern apples. A lower retail price for western apples in eastern markets would result in a sympathetic price decrease in substitutes. Thus, the net effect on price, while it may be in the direction indicated, may not be as large when secondary effects are considered.

The incidence of changes in marketing margins, as described above, has to be modified as assumptions underlying the model are modified. For example, some agricultural products have floor prices established by a price-support program. Thus, when the farm price is at the support level, an increase in the margin and the concurrent decrease in farm-level demand would not decrease farm prices. The margin is, in effect, added to the farm-level support price. An increase in margin would result in a higher retail price and hence in a smaller quantity purchased at retail. A smaller quantity would move through the marketing system to the retail level, but farm prices would not decrease. (This implies added government activity to support prices.)

The analysis also assumes a competitive market structure. Imperfect competition may result in a different incidence of changes in the margin. This situation is discussed briefly in the next section.

Market Structure, Margins, and Prices

Assumed Conditions

The preceding discussion of the theory of margin changes has been based on the assumption of a competitive market structure. Price is the integrating force between market levels. If primary demand increases relative to supply, then retail price increases. The higher price is reflected through the marketing system to producers, and the eventual result, other factors remaining the same, is a larger quantity supplied.

A change in the marketing margin would be reflected through the marketing system in an analogous way. Prices both at retail and at the farm would generally be affected.

As an example, let us assume that a transportation rate is reduced. For simplicity, we also assume that one type of middleman assembles the product and pays the cost of transportation from the farm to the stores. The lower transportation rate initially accrues to the benefit of these middlemen. However, the assumption of a purely competitive market structure implies that the lower rate will be passed on to producers as higher prices, to retailers as lower prices, or in general as a combination of the two effects. The lower cost (hence higher profit) will induce existing middlemen to do more business and perhaps attract the entry of new middlemen. However, as they compete with each other for more of the farm product, the result would be higher farm prices, and as they compete to sell more to retailers, the result would be lower retail prices. Competition among retailers would imply that the lower price is passed on to consumers. Thus, the lower marketing cost affects both farm and consumer prices (depending, of course, on the slopes of functions, the effect of price support, etc.).

In practice, the structure of the food-marketing system does not fulfill all of the requirements of a purely competitive model. With some monopolistic power, marketing firms may retain all or a part of the benefits of cost decreases as added profits while passing on higher costs to consumers and producers. This suspicion of monopoly power and "unnecessarily" large marketing margins has resulted in studies such as those conducted by the National Commission of Food Marketing (1966).

Some results from studies of the food industry are summarized in the next subsection. However, the incidence of changes in marketing costs remains a controversial question. That is, are marketing margins too large? And, if so, is the impact mainly on consumers or producers?

Current Conditions

Food retailing may be characterized as monopolistically competitive (Holdren, 1964). There are a large number of firms, and price is used as a competitive tool (Padberg, 1968). But food retailing is local in character; competition for customers is limited to small geographic areas (Marion, *et al.*, 1979). Thus, the level of concentration in local markets is probably important in measuring the level of competition and in appraising the behavior of prices. Possible monopoly-like behavior in local markets may not be obvious in national data.

Two recent studies suggest that retail prices are indeed influenced by the level of concentration in particular metropolitan areas. Marion *et al.* (1979) analyzed factors influencing the cost of a "basket" of 94 comparable grocery items across 35 metropolitan areas. They conclude (p. 432) that "consumers pay substantially more in highly concentrated markets dominated by one or two firms than in less concentrated markets without a dominant firm. However, ... many independents and small chains, as well as large chains in many of their markets, do not have significant market power." Hall *et al.* (1979) found the wholesale-retail marketing margin for beef to be significantly related to the level of concentration of food chains. Thus, both the price of a single product and the prices of an aggregate basket of products appear to be influenced by the level of concentration in local markets.

Some food-manufacturing industries are highly concentrated, while others are not.[5] The breakfast cereal industry is highly concentrated; fluid-milk processing is relatively unconcentrated. Moreover, the trends in concentration have not been uniform across industries. In the 1950s, meat packing was concentrated in four firms, but subsequently the level of concentration declined with the entry of new firms. In the 1970s, the trend appears to have reversed with four-firm concentration in meat packing again growing. But this is not true for all food industries.

[5]The National Commission on Food Marketing (1966) defined "high concentration" as a situation in which the four largest firms have more than 50 per cent of the business, say, as measured by sales or value of shipments. Parker and Connor (1979) take a concentration ratio of 40 per cent or below as the norm for effective competition.

Concentration in food processing appears to give a mixture of results. The report of the National Commission on Food Marketing (1966) was generally favorable to the food-marketing system from the viewpoint of physical efficiency and progressiveness. But selling costs could be reduced without reducing the inherent value of the final product. Nonprice competition based on product differentiation exists in food processing. Brands of a particular type of product may proliferate and compete for a limited amount of shelf space, and advertising and promotion expenses for these brands add to marketing costs. Thus, imperfect competition may result in higher selling costs through advertising and promotion expenses, packaging costs, and potentially inefficient delivery and service systems—all designed to differentiate products and to attract and hold customers. In addition, monopoly power may result in profits above competitive levels, excess manufacturing capacity, and unusually large compensation for executives.

Parker and Connor (1979) studied the relationship between concentration and net margins in food-manufacturing industries, where the net margin is defined as the sum of returns to capital, executive salaries, and expenditures for advertising and other contract services. They found a positive and statistically significant relationship, and they estimate that concentration in food manufacturing is associated with at least a $10 billion aggregate loss to consumers in 1975. Imel and Helmberger (1971) also found that profits adjusted for taxes and a return on capital were positively related to the level of concentration in food processing.

The degree of competition may differ by marketing level, adding complexity to the analysis of marketing margins. To illustrate, a retail chain may have more market power than the processors of a particular commodity, while competition among processors results in purely competitive pricing at the farm level. Thus, the farm-wholesale margin would be at a competitive level, but the retail chain may be able to maintain a noncompetitive margin. For another commodity, processors may have monopoly power, and a long-standing concern in agriculture is whether buyers of farm products can depress prices below competitive levels.

Given the differences in market structure among food industries and among markets or regions, one can draw few generalizations about the behavior of marketing margins for food. On balance, the evidence suggests that farm-retail spreads can be reduced not so much by cutting profits as by reducing the amount of packaging, product differentiation, advertising, and other promotional expenses. Since a large part of total marketing costs consists of labor, packaging, and transportation, major

Price Differences and Variability

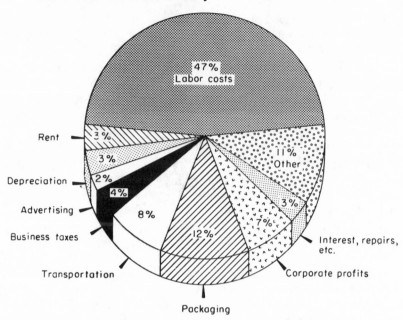

Figure 6-7. Components of the farm-food marketing bill in the United States, 1978. From USDA, *1979 Handbook of Agricultural Charts,* Ag. Handbook No. 561 (October 1979).

reductions in prices paid by consumers can be made only if these costs are reduced. Labor costs alone now account for around half of the total marketing bill (Figure 6-7). Corporate profits average only about 7 per cent of the farm-food marketing bill. Hence, on the average, a reduction in profits could have only a small percentage effect on retail food prices.[6]

Vertical Integration

One change in the structure of marketing services that occurs in some parts of the food industry is vertical integration. Vertical integration occurs when successive stages of marketing or of production and marketing are linked together. The usual meaning is that of nonprice linkage through direct ownership or by contract. That is, successive stages of

[6]Two *caveats* need to be made. First, although the per unit reduction for one commodity may be small, the aggregate effect over products and consumers may be large (Marion *et al.*, 1979 and Parker and Connor, 1979). Second, since an increase in competition might reduce marketing costs as well as monopoly profits, the amount of this reduction could be large even on a per unit basis for certain commodities.

marketing are tied together in some formal way other than by the price system.

An important reason for integration is the inefficiency or inadequacy of market exchange as a coordination mechanism. The price system may not have assured the retailer or processor of a flow of product with the desired attributes. Further, integration may reduce marketing costs, especially those involved in transferring products from one marketing stage to another. Moreover, integration can reduce price or procurement risks.

Thus, in principle, vertical integration can reduce marketing costs, but in practice there is no assurance that these cost savings will be passed on to consumers as lower retail prices or to producers as higher farm prices. Indeed, vertical integration may also be motivated by a desire for increased market power. For example, a retailer who is integrated back to the processing level probably can reduce marketing costs. In addition, the retailer may be able to exert more leverage on suppliers in negotiating prices. In this circumstance, the retailer rather than consumers will gain.

Another interesting aspect of vertical integration, from the viewpoint of economists, is the changing nature of the price system. Vertical integration has changed the locus of price formation, and has reduced the number of points in the marketing chain at which prices are established. Price coordination has been partially replaced by administrative coordination.

This change has several implications. Published prices (from the USDA and other sources) may become less meaningful as a larger volume of a product moves through integrated channels. Thus, the empirical definition of marketing margins between the producer and the retail level becomes more difficult. For example, what is the margin between the retail and farm price of broilers or eggs when the producers are mainly part of an integrated operation?

Information available to nonintegrated producers is reduced, and they may have fewer alternative markets. Naturally, such producers are concerned when buyers disappear. Producers believe that the lack of buyers may lead to lower prices as the remaining nonintegrated producers compete for a smaller share of the market.

Gray (1964, p. 122) argues that vertical integration has eliminated price as a coordinator between market levels when markets were informal or weak. Administrative or engineering coordination, in these cases, does a better job of assuring a given flow of product with a given specification. However, Gray believes that price competition has been strengthened at the remaining price junctures. For example, he argues that price competition is vigorous among retail food stores. Thus, while the role of price is declining in one sense, Gray (p. 126) believes that its role as an allocator at the remaining junctures is strengthened.

Summary

The marketing margin may be defined as the difference between prices at two market levels. But the margin for a particular commodity, like wheat, is often difficult to determine since the form of the commodity changes drastically as it is combined with other products and services in the marketing system. Farm-retail price spreads are computed by the USDA for selected products and for a market basket of farm-food products. These spreads measure the cost of providing a mix of marketing services. They do not measure the effect of adding new products, nor do they indicate the well-being of farmers.

Marketing margins change with changes in factor prices, the efficiency of providing services, and the quantity and quality of services embodied in the final product. Margins obviously vary greatly among commodities. The effect of changes in margins on retail and farm prices under purely competitive conditions depends on the relative slopes of demand and supply relations, when the source of change is in the cost of providing existing services. The incidence of change is more complex when a new service or product is added, though under some circumstances the incidence is primarily at retail. The consequences of changes in margins become even more complicated when the assumption of pure competition is relaxed.

Vertical integration and other forms of concentration in the food industry can result in cost savings, especially for the firms involved. However, the added costs of advertising or other promotional devices related to nonprice competition may increase total marketing costs. Even if there are cost savings associated with concentration, it is not clear that they are passed on to consumers in the form of lower prices. Thus, the net effects of changes in concentration in the food industry on consumer and producer prices are not always clear.

References

Breimyer, Harold F. 1957. "On Price Determination and Aggregate Price Theory," *J. Farm Econ.*, 39:678–694.

Buse, Rueben C., and G. E. Brandow. 1960. "The Relationship of Volume, Prices and Costs to Marketing Margins for Farm Foods," *J. Farm Econ.*, 42:362–370.

Council on Wage and Price Stability. 1976. *The Responsiveness of Wholesale and Retail Food Prices to Changes in the Costs of Food Production and Distribution.* Washington, D.C.: Staff Report (November).

Daly, Rex F. 1958. "Demand for Farm Products at Retail and the Farm Level," *J. Am. Stat. Assoc.*, 53:656–668.

Duewer, Lawrence A. 1978. "Changes in Price Spread Measurements for Beef and Pork," *Livestock and Meat Situation.* USDA, LMS-222 (Aug.). Pp. 33–37.

Freeman, Robert E. 1966. "Roles of Farm Productivity and Marketing Margins in Postwar Decline in Farm Prices," *J. Farm Econ.*, 48:31–41.

Friedman, Milton. 1962. *Price Theory: A Provisional Text.* Chicago: Aldine Publishing Co. Chapter 7.

Gardner, Bruce L. 1975. "The Farm-Retail Price Spread in a Competitive Food Industry," *Am. J. Ag. Econ.*, 57:399–409.

Gray, Roger W. 1964. "The Changing Role of Price," *J. Farm Econ.*, 46:117–127.

Hall, Lana, Andrew Schmitz, and James Cothern. 1979. "Beef Wholesale-Retail Marketing Margins and Concentration," *Economica*, 46:295–300.

Holdren, Bob R. 1964. "The Nature of Competition among Food Retailers in Local Markets," *J. Farm Econ.*, 46:1306–1314.

Imel, Blake, and Peter Helmberger. 1971. "Estimation of Structure-Profit Relationships with Application to the Food Processing Sector," *Am. Econ. Rev.*, 61:614–627.

Marion, Bruce W., *et al.* 1979. "The Price and Profit Performance of Leading Food Chains," *Am. J. Ag. Econ.*, 61:420–433.

National Commission on Food Marketing. 1966. *Food from Farmer to Consumer.* Commission Report. Washington, D.C.: U.S. Govt. Printing Office.

Padberg, Daniel I. 1968. *Economics of Food Retailing.* Ithaca, N.Y.: Cornell Univ. Food Distribution Program. Chapter 9.

Parish, R. M. 1967. "Price 'Levelling' and 'Averaging,'" *The Farm Economist*, 11:187–198.

Parker, Russell C., and John M. Connor. 1979. "Estimates of Consumer Loss Due to Monopoly in the U.S. Food-Manufacturing Industries," *Am. J. Ag. Econ.*, 61:626–639.

Scott, Forrest E., and Henry T. Badger. 1972. *Farm-Retail Spreads for Food Products.* USDA Misc. Pub. No. 741 (revised).

USDA. 1979. *Developments in Marketing Spreads for Food Products in 1978.* Ag. Econ. Rep. 420 (March).

USDA. 1976. *Review and Evaluation of Price Spread Data for Foods.* ERS and AAEA Task Force Report (January).

Waite, Warren C., and Harry C. Trelogan. 1951. *Agricultural Market Prices.* 2d ed. New York: John Wiley and Sons. Chapter 8.

Waldorf, William H. 1966. "The Demand for and Supply of Food Marketing Services: An Aggregate View," *J. Farm Econ.*, 48:42–60.

CHAPTER 7

Price Differences

Associated with Quality

The specific lots of an agricultural product differ in terms of such attributes as size, color, moisture level, protein content, and the proportion of defects or impurities, and prices often vary depending on alternate grades, classes, and varieties. Price differences based on quality are sometimes referred to as premiums or discounts. These price differences may change through time, but such variations are usually small relative to changes in the average level of prices for the commodity. The prices of all grades of a commodity tend to move up and down together, although price premiums and discounts between grades often change from season to season and may exhibit trends over time. The economic meaning and justification for price differences related to quality variation are explored in this chapter.

To simplify exposition, the term "grade" is used interchangeably with quality differences. The analysis of relationships among prices of different grades is, for the most part, simply a special case of price relationships among substitutes. The prices of close substitutes are highly related except where market imperfections exist.

Defining Grades

Grade standards are usually established by governmental agencies in consultation with producers, consumers, and marketing firms. Occasionally, grades are informally established by members of the trade.

Two important decisions are required in establishing a grading system. One is to determine the attributes of the product to use as a basis for defining grades. A second question is, given information on the attributes, how should it be used and reported? A grading system is

140

usually based on numerous characteristics. Moreover, these attributes often vary continuously, but a relatively small number of classes must be established for practical use. What attributes should be used to define grades, and how should boundaries between grades be established (e.g., see Zusman, 1967)?

The attributes used to define grades should be related to the demand for the product. As discussed in Chapter 2, consumer demand for a product can be visualized as a demand for certain characteristics of the product such as the protein or starch content. A problem arises, however, when a product has multiple end uses, and buyers place different economic values on particular attributes. A particular grading system, for example, may be based on attributes like moisture content, weight, and proportion of damaged kernels, and this may be suitable for a certain group of buyers. Other buyers, however, may be interested in the protein content of the grain and find the grading system unsuitable for their use. A second problem arises from the potential costs of alternative grading systems. Some characteristics like size and weight are easier and less costly to incorporate into the standards than other characteristics like taste or protein content.

The principal objective of a grading system is to make the market work more efficiently. Grades should improve information. Contracts can be based on grade specifications, and buyers need not personally inspect each lot of product (which may be graded by an official inspector). Standardization reduces uncertainty between buyers and sellers, and this helps reduce marketing costs (Mehren, 1961).

Assuming grades do accurately reflect attributes desired by buyers, then, of course, price premiums and discounts reflect existing demands and supplies for the different attributes. Under these circumstances, the price system serves to better direct production relative to consumers' preferences. For example, if premiums are sufficient, farmers will respond by producing leaner hogs. But grading systems can also result in confusing price signals. Hyslop (1970) shows that it is possible for a particular lot of U.S. Number 3 hard red spring wheat to sell for a higher price than Number 2 wheat even though grade 2 is supposed to be more desirable than grade 3. Since confusing price signals can result in the wrong "mix" of qualities, it is important that grades reflect the preferences of consumers. The revised grading system for beef, which was instituted in February 1976, apparently has succeeded in more nearly identifying what buyers want; price differentials which prevailed after the new grading system was established were more consistent with carcass values than under the previous grading system (Nelson, 1977).

Price Differences and Variability

The grading and sorting of commodities is not costless. Thus, the question arises as to whether or not the gains from grading, in terms of improved economic efficiency, justify the added cost (Dalrymple, 1968). Grading schemes may not always be justified, at least on purely economic grounds. Moreover, the grading system simply may not be based on attributes relevant to buyers' decisions. The discussion in subsequent sections assumes that grading is economically justified.

We also need to note that grades and price differentials sometimes contribute to market imperfections. If monopoly power exists, grades may make it possible to practice price discrimination, and as noted in Chapter 5, price differences between grades with discriminatory pricing exceed those that would prevail under competitive conditions. Also, prices are a part of the information system; consumers may use price as one guide to quality. When sellers have discretion in setting prices, the resulting prices may convey incorrect information about quality as measured by the inherent physical characteristics.

Demands by Grades

If grades have economic significance, then it follows that a separate demand schedule exists for each grade. Each such schedule has the usual determinants. Shifts in each demand curve associated with income changes probably differ by grades. The income elasticity of demand is thought to be highest for the best or preferred grade and smaller for lower grades. The reasoning is by analogy with the superior-inferior product concept. In fact, one method of defining grades is on the basis of the relative income elasticities. However, little empirical knowledge exists about quality differences and income elasticities, and for this reason it is difficult to implement such a concept.

In general, there is great substitutability among grades of the same commodity, even though each has some unique characteristics. Thus, the main demand shifter for a particular grade is the change in price of its closest substitutes, and these are typically other grades of the same product.[1] The various grades typically have large positive cross-price elasticities of demand with each other; hence, the demand for each grade is usually more price elastic than that for the entire product.

Wheat provides one example of the price relationships that exist between grades. Since there is considerable substitutability among grades,

[1]This explains the high positive correlation in price changes for various grades, but the unique characteristics of each grade explain why this correlation is not perfect.

Price Differences Associated with Quality

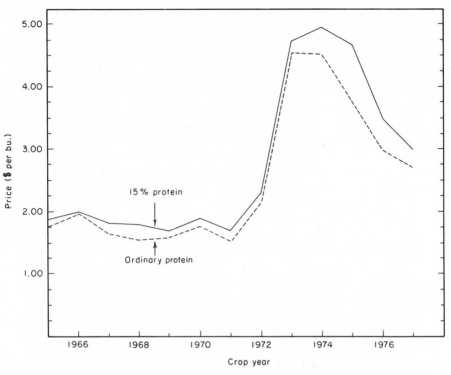

Figure 7-1. Prices of Number 1 Dark Northern Spring Wheat, two protein levels, Minneapolis, 1965-1977. Data from various issues of *Wheat Situation,* USDA, ESCS.

their prices tend to move together (Figure 7-1). High-protein hard spring wheat is preferred in making the flour that is used in most of the commercial bread in the United States. For this reason, high-protein spring wheat customarily sells at a premium over other wheats, but the size of the premium varies from season to season and sometimes even within a season.[2] The domestic farm-level demand for wheat in the aggregate in the United States is highly price inelastic, perhaps −0.2. The demand for separate grades is much more elastic because of the substitutability among grades. Taplin (1969) estimates that the world demand for commercial wheat exports of all grades has a price elasticity of −1.0; the corresponding elasticity for soft wheat is −7.4 and for hard wheat is −3.6.

[2]Variability in premiums and discounts through time is of more than academic interest. For instance, a grain merchant storing grade-one grain and hedging this inventory in a futures contract specifying delivery of grade-two grain is assuming that the prices of the two grades are closely correlated in using the futures market for hedging (see Chapter 13).

143

Price Differences and Variability

The separate demand functions for different qualities probably exhibit sharp changes in slope over a range of quantities and prices, at least for some commodities. Demand for a particular quality or variety may be quite price inelastic for relatively small quantities but become elastic for larger quantities. This occurs when a specified amount or a fixed proportion of a particular quality or variety is desired, say, by a processor for a product mix. The flour miller needs a certain proportion of high-protein wheat to achieve a desired protein level in flour (although milling techniques have changed so that this is less true today). When supplies are more than adequate to meet these special uses (i.e., uses for which no good substitutes exist), then price drops into a range where the high-quality product becomes competitive with lower quality products. In this range, demand is likely to be more price elastic.

Logic does not provide a clear guide as to whether the demand for high grades is, on the average, more or less price-elastic than for lower grades. If one assumes that (1) the best grade has the largest income elasticity, (2) the sum of the cross elasticities is the same for all grades, and (3) the homogeneity condition with respect to elasticities prevails, then the demand for the best grades would tend to be more price elastic. But Waite and Trelogan (1951) argue that the best grade typically has fewer substitutes and hence has the smaller (in absolute terms) price elasticity of demand. The critical question in this case is whether the sum of the cross elasticities is equal for all grades.

Generalizations about empirical elasticities must await additional research, and, in any event, the relationship among elasticities for various grades may not be uniform among commodities. Research by Arzac and Wilkinson (1979) and Taplin (1969) are illustrative of estimates of demand for different grades or classes within a commodity group.[3]

Further, one may argue that estimates of own-price elasticities for separate grades are misleading, or at least subject to misuse. The own-price elasticity, of course, is a measure of responsiveness of quantity to own price, *other factors constant.* But we know that prices of the various grades are likely to be highly related. Other factors are not constant; there are high positive cross elasticities. Thus, the *net* percentage change in a particular quantity depends on the relative movements of a

[3]Arzac and Wilkinson obtain price elasticities of −1.86 and −2.97 for fed and nonfed beef, respectively; the estimated income elasticities are 1.02 and 0.45. The smaller income elasticity for nonfed beef is consistent with this product being inferior to grain-fed beef. As the authors point out, however, elasticities estimated for fed and nonfed beef by various studies have been rather different. It is difficult to disaggregate the available data into the fed and nonfed components and to obtain appropriate measures of variables. Also, there are some difficult statistical questions in this type of analysis.

constellation of prices. The net result of these interrelated changes is embodied in the concept of total elasticity (Chapter 3).

Supplies by Grades

While demands for alternate grades can and do change, most year-to-year variations in price premiums are the result of changes in relative supplies. The proportion of various grades produced in any one season is influenced partly by chance factors such as the weather or insect and disease damage. Good weather in the northern Great Plains and excessively wet weather in eastern states, for example, can increase the proportion of hard wheat to soft wheat produced and hence influence the price difference between the two types of wheat. Hail or insect damage may increase the quantity of cull fruit relative to the higher grades.

Through time, the changing profitability of growing alternate varieties or grades also can influence relative supplies. Expected profitability is influenced by price premiums and by relative per unit costs of production. Clearly, other things being equal, a price premium for a particular variety should tend to shift resources toward the production of that variety. But the variety may be more costly to produce and market. Changes in relative yields may in some cases offset the effects of price premiums. For example, some of the earlier varieties of rice developed by the International Rice Research Institute sold at a discount relative to the local or traditional varieties because of their inferior quality, but the yield advantage of the new varieties was sufficient to make it profitable for rice producers to adopt them despite the discount.[4]

The relative supplies of different grades of a particular commodity also may vary within a year. For example, the proportion of cattle marketed which grade "good" is likely to increase relative to the proportion which grade "choice" in the fall of the year as cattle are sold directly off pasture without going through feed lots. The proportion of eggs in various size categories likewise varies within the year. Young pullets coming into production tend to produce smaller eggs than older hens, and historically substantial seasonality has existed in the placement of laying flocks and hence in the proportion of various sized eggs marketed. However, seasonality in the placement of young chicks has declined sharply. Commodities in storage also may decline in quality over the storage

[4]Producers sometimes face difficult economic decisions in determining what particular varieties to grow (see Burt, 1965). Such decisions are complicated by questions like timing of harvest for alternate varieties—hence the impact of the variety on distribution of labor requirements.

period. Seasonality in the supplies of various qualities, sizes, or varieties of a product can result in seasonal patterns in quality premiums or discounts.

Price Differentials

Price differentials between grades at a point in time are, of course, the result of particular levels of demand and supply for the various grades. With the passage of time, price differentials change with shifts in the supply and demand functions. The size of the changes in quality discounts and premiums depends on the size of shifts in functions and on the algebraic form and consequent slopes of these functions.

Generalizations about price relationships among grades are difficult to make because of the many possible combinations of changes in relative supplies and demands by grades and of different slopes for the various functions. For instance, an increase in the supply of one grade depresses the price of that grade and thereby reduces the premium or widens the discount of that grade relative to others. However, the lower price for one grade leads to reduced demands for the other related grades and hence tends to lower prices of these other grades. These lower prices, in turn, influence the demand for the grade with the initial price change. The larger supply for one grade, then, tends to lower all prices as well as change the price difference between grades. The precise size of the changes depends on the size of the increase in supply, the size of the relevant own-price elasticity of demand, and the sizes of the relevant cross-price elasticities with the other grades.

The nature of changes in demands and supplies by grades, as discussed in previous sections, is suggestive of the nature of changes in price differentials. For instance, a small supply of a grade that is required by processors to make a particular product can push the price premium for this grade to a high level. We have also stated elsewhere (Chapter 5) that in years of large production the price of some products may be so low that a part of the crop is not harvested. Under competitive conditions, the lower quality component of the total crop is the quantity typically abandoned. The poorer quality has the lowest price, and this price may not cover harvesting and marketing costs.

The greater the substitutability among products, the more closely prices of the products are likely to be related. Price relationships among vegetable oils illustrate this principle. Coconut oil and palm oil are both lauric oils; their primary uses are in the manufacture of soap and in fillings and coatings for confectionary products (Nyberg, 1970, p. 97). Other oils commonly used in cooking or in the manufacture of margarine

Table 7-1. Correlation coefficients between prices of selected oils, United States, 1952-1967

	Coconut	Soybean	Cottonseed	Peanut	Palm kernel
Coconut	1.0	0.30	0.21	0.34	0.94
Soybean		1.0	0.89	0.58	0.10
Cottonseed			1.0	0.60	0.25
Peanut				1.0	−0.52
Palm kernel					1.0

Source: Adapted from Albert J. Nyberg, "The Demand for Lauric Oils in the United States," *Am. J. Ag. Econ.,* 52 (1970):98, table 1.

are not as satisfactory for these special uses. Thus, one would expect to find the prices of coconut and palm oil highly correlated with each other, but not necessarily with the prices of other vegetable oils. Empirical evidence for the 1952-1967 period was consistent with these logical expectations (Table 7-1).[5] The correlation between the prices of coconut and palm kernel oil was 0.94, while the correlations between coconut and soybean, cottonseed, and peanut oils ranged from only 0.21 to 0.34.

Certain attributes of the lauric oils mean that no close substitutes exist for particular uses with current technology. However, if the supplies of lauric oils exceed the demand for oils in these special uses, then the prices of lauric oils decline, and these oils become more competitive with other oils such as in making margarine. Consequently, the demand for lauric oils becomes more price elastic (less inelastic) at lower prices. This is consistent with the point made previously, that the demand for one grade may be quite inelastic at high prices when that grade is a "required" component of a particular product but that, if the special demand is filled, the additional supply of that grade leads to a decline in price to where demand is more elastic.

Imperfect Competition and Price Differences

Price differences between grades or qualities of products are often determined administratively by sellers of industrial products (e.g.,

[5]The correlation coefficients used in Table 7-1 are measures of the linear association between two variables. A coefficient of one indicates a perfect linear association, and of course the coefficients of one on the diagonal of the table indicate that a price series is perfectly correlated with itself. Coefficients near one show high degrees of association; coefficients near zero imply a small degree of association; negative coefficients suggest an inverse relationship.

prices for a line of refrigerators) or by those marketing "branded" commodities. This situation usually occurs where the number of sellers is limited and/or firms have successfully differentiated their product from other products. Premiums or discounts in such cases may be based on quality or cost differences, but they also may simply reflect the ability of the seller to exploit consumer ignorance.

Premiums or discounts for "quality" are not always determined on the basis of competitive supply-demand relationships as outlined earlier. A meat packer, for example, may sell his brand-name bacon at a price premium over a "standard" brand which more than covers the additional cost of the brand-name item. The seller conveys the impression that his product is superior in quality; on the basis of its physical attributes, it may not be superior. However, the seller in such cases is able to exercise some degree of market power in pricing.

The ability of producers or sellers of farm products to extract more money from consumers by such pricing practices depends on their ability to differentiate their product and to create a favorable "image" (including quality) with consumers. For many food products, it is difficult to do this because of the high degree of substitutability among different grades or brands. The demand, even for a branded agricultural product, is likely to be quite price elastic. In such cases, an attempt to increase the price premium for a particular commodity or brand would result in a substantial loss in sales.

Differences in demand among grades may provide the basis for a price-discrimination scheme. This assumes, of course, that the seller or sellers have the monopoly power to make price discrimination work. Agricultural cooperatives have occasionally been able to do this. For instance, marketings to the higher-priced fresh fruit sector may be restricted with the remaining fruit going to a processing sector (presumably with a more elastic demand). Marketing orders permit the culling of low-quality fruit. David Price (1967) points out that total returns may be increased by culling out low-quality produce even though the demand for it is elastic. The price increase from the higher quality sold may be large enough to offset the effect of the reduced quantity sold, even after the costs of culling are covered. Mr. Price considers in detail the question of optimum (profit-maximizing) culling rates. Of course, returns are not automatically increased by culling low-quality produce (Waugh, 1971). Correct allocations under a price discrimination program depend on the demand functions for the different grades.

Price differentials serve an important function provided that they reflect the relative demands of buyers for different grades or qualities.

Price Differences Associated with Quality

Premiums or discounts for certain grades do not perform this function effectively if they are arbitrarily maintained on the basis of historical relationships such as may occur under government price-support programs. Thus, price-support programs are another type of "imperfection" for some agricultural commodities. At times, lower grades of tobacco, cotton, and wheat have been overpriced relative to higher grades (i.e., the discount on such grades has not been sufficiently wide). As a result, the lower grades have ended up in government warehouses while the higher grades have moved into consumption. By overpricing lower grades, the government also provides an incentive for farmers to continue producing excess quantities of the inferior grades of the product.

References

Arzac, Enrique R., and Maurice Wilkinson. 1979. "A Quarterly Econometric Model of United States Livestock and Feed Grain Markets and Some of Its Policy Implications," *Am. J. Ag. Econ.*, 61:297–308.

Burt, Oscar R. 1965. "Optimal Replacement under Risk," *J. Farm Econ.*, 47:324–346.

Dalrymple, Dana G. 1968. "On the Economics of Produce Grading," *Am. J. Ag. Econ.*, 50:157–159.

Hyslop, John D. 1970. *Price-Quality Relationships in Spring Wheat.* Univ. Minn. Ag. Exp. Sta. Tech. Bul. 267.

Mehren, G. L. 1961. "The Functions of Grades in an Affluent, Standardized-Quality Economy," *J. Farm Econ.*, 43:1371–1383.

Nelson, Kenneth E. 1977. *Economic Effects of the 1976 Beef Grade Changes.* USDA Tech. Bul. 1570.

Nyberg, Albert J. 1970. "The Demand for Lauric Oils in the United States," *Am. J. Ag. Econ.*, 52:97–102.

Price, David W. 1967. "Discarding Low Quality Produce with an Elastic Demand," *J. Farm Econ.*, 49:622–632.

Taplin, John H. E. 1969. "Demand in the World Wheat Market and the Export Policies of the United States, Canada, and Australia." Cornell Univ. Ph.D. thesis.

Waite, Warren C., and Harry C. Trelogan. 1951. *Agricultural Market Prices.* 2d ed. New York: John Wiley and Sons. Chapter 12.

Waugh, Frederick V. 1971. "Withholding by Grade," *Am. J. Ag. Econ.*, 53:500–501.

Zusman, Pinhas. 1967. "A Theoretical Basis for Determination of Grading and Sorting Schemes," *J. Farm Econ.*, 49:89–106.

CHAPTER **8**

Spatial Price
Relationships

This chapter deals with factors which cause prices to differ between regions and particularly with the economic forces that are likely to cause prices in one region to change in relation to those in another. A simple model is presented to illustrate the impact of shifts in demand or supply or changes in transfer costs on price differentials between regions. The spatial price equilibrium model also provides a convenient analytical framework which may be used to determine the indirect as well as the direct effects of changes in production in one or more regions on the volume and direction of trade. In addition, such an analytical model may be used to ascertain the price effects of relaxing or increasing trade barriers between countries or regions.

Spatial price relationships are determined largely by transfer costs between regions provided competitive conditions prevail. Transfer costs, which include loading or handling as well as transportation charges, are often high in relation to the farm value of agricultural commodities, especially perishable products. Hence, farm prices differ depending on whether the production area is near or far from the principal market areas. Farmers in more distant areas frequently refer to themselves as being "out on the end of a whip." Even modest changes in central market prices when combined with high and fixed transportation costs can result in wide swings in producer prices.

The principles that determine spatial price differences within a country apply equally well to international prices, provided no barriers exist to the movement of commodities between countries. For many agricultural commodities, of course, the conditions necessary for free trade do not exist. There is no longer a single world market for grains, sugar, or dairy products. On the other hand, prices for cocoa, bananas, rubber,

150

soybeans, palm oil, and tea are still determined under relatively competitive conditions.

The principles which underlie price differences between regions (assuming a competitive market structure including homogeneous commodities, perfect knowledge, and no barriers inhibiting trade) can be summarized as follows:

(1) price differences between any two regions (or markets) that trade with each other will just equal transfer costs;

(2) price differences between any two regions (or markets) that do not engage in trade with each other will be less than or equal to transfer costs.

Price differences between regions cannot exceed transfer costs. The reason for this should be obvious: any time the price difference is greater than transfer costs, buyers will purchase commodities from the low-priced market and ship them to the higher-priced market, thereby raising prices in the former and reducing them in the latter. This form of arbitrage will continue until it is no loger profitable to ship commodities between markets—that is, until the price difference between them no longer exceeds transfer costs.

Using these principles, theoretical spatial price relationships, sometimes called the "structure of prices," can be determined. The structure of prices is a function of the pattern of trade (i.e., who ships to whom) and transfer costs per unit of product between regions that engage in trade. Where no trade exists between regions, an upper, but not a lower, price boundary can be established since, as pointed out above, the difference in price cannot exceed transfer costs between any two regions. In the absence of trade, the precise structure of prices cannot be determined solely on the basis of transfer costs. They are easily determined, however, if all surplus-producing areas ship to one central market. In this case, the price in each surplus area will differ by the cost of transporting the commodity to the central market. The determination of spatial price relationships becomes more complicated when there are several markets to which producers may ship their product and more than two surplus-producing areas. The optimum pattern of trade in that case may not be intuitively obvious, and until the pattern of trade is identified, the structure of prices cannot be determined.

Determining Transfer Costs

Transfer costs are the most important single variable determining spatial price relationships. The transfer cost between any two points

Price Differences and Variability

cannot be determined simply on the basis of an average transportation rate. It normally includes a fixed charge which is independent of the distance traveled (usually associated with loading or unloading) and a variable charge related to the distance over which the commodity is moved. Transportation costs *per mile* often decline as the distance traveled increases; thus, the cost of moving commodities between two points is not necessarily a linear function of the mileage. In most cases, however, the transfer cost *per unit of product* rises as distance increases, but less than proportionately.[1] Calculation of total transfer costs is further complicated by the fact that transportation rates are frequently regulated by public authorities. In the United States, rail and truck rates (with certain exceptions for agricultural commodities) have been regulated by the Interstate Commerce Commission. The rate structure established for different commodities and methods of transportation becomes extremely complex as amendments and exemptions are granted in response to petitions submitted by railroads and truckers. As a result, transfer costs between any two points often are not identical for different forms of the same product, nor do these costs necessarily bear a close relationship to the distance separating markets.

Interregional price differences presumably are based on the least-cost method of moving commodities between points. But it may not be possible for every handler or shipper to use the least-cost system, especially where new handling methods are being introduced. Considerable time may elapse before firms are reorganized or sufficient equipment becomes available to take advantage of the more efficient system. For example, in the early 1960s, differences in butter prices between markets in the United States exceeded transfer costs using the most efficient method of transporting butter. It cost less per pound to ship butter in large, mechanically refrigerated railroad cars than in smaller, traditional iced cars; however, some shippers did not have sufficient production at any one time to make effective use of the larger cars or were not able to obtain them at the time they were ready to make a shipment. For this reason they were forced to use the more expensive transfer system, and price differences did not fully reflect the potential economies which existed at that time.

---

[1]The total transfer cost increases with distance, and consequently the cost per unit of product moved increases. Since the transfer cost contains a fixed component regardless of volume and distance traveled, the cost per unit increases but at a decreasing rate.

152

Geographical Price Relationships for Commodities Originating
in Many Areas and Sold in One or a Few Central Markets

If all producers ship homogeneous units of the same commodity to a
single central market, the price each producer receives under perfectly
competitive conditions is the central market price less the cost of transferring a unit of that commodity to the central market. This is based on the
reasonable assumption that buyers are indifferent as to the source of
supply of a homogeneous product and would not therefore pay more for
a unit of product from one area than from another. If producers in a
particular region offered their product for less, this would cause prices
for the same commodity produced in other regions to fall by an equal
amount. Such price adjustments would be necessary for producers to
remain competitive.

The impetus for price changes can come either from producing regions or from central markets. For some agricultural commodities,
forces of demand and supply are brought together in central markets.
Prices at the farm are usually closely linked to central-market price
quotations. For example, the price which a country elevator offers farmers for grain is normally based on price quotations at a central market
such as Kansas City or Minneapolis less total transfer and handling costs.
Butter and egg prices in producing regions, likewise, have customarily
been tied to prices established at Chicago or New York less the cost of
moving commodities to these markets.

Central markets play a less important role in pricing some commodities, such as fruits and vegetables sold to processors, than in pricing
grains. But even where price-making forces are dispersed, prices in
different regions are closely interrelated. Interregional price differences, as pointed out earlier, cannot for very long exceed the cost of
moving commodities between regions.

Observed vs. Theoretical Price Differentials

Observed price differences between regions within the United States
for such commodities as wheat, corn, and soybeans are generally consistent with those suggested by theory. Producer prices for grains decline
as one moves inland from grain-deficit areas or from major ports through
which the commodity is exported. Average prices received by farmers
for corn and oats, for example, tend to be highest in the New England
and South Atlantic states and lowest in the Great Plains (Waite and
Trelogan, 1951, pp. 173–175). Quoted prices for flour and wheat in

Price Differences and Variability

Buffalo differ from those in Chicago or Minneapolis by an amount that is approximately equal to the cost of transferring these commodities from one area to the other. Similar relationships prevail between wholesale prices paid for butter in New York and Chicago. Prices paid farmers for milk which is sold for fluid use are imperfectly but positively correlated with the distances from the major surplus-producing area in Wisconsin (Lasley, 1977, p. 8). The degree of correlation is surprising in view of the presence of many separate marketing orders and of the attempts of producer groups or, in some instances, state or local officials to restrict the movement of milk between markets.

While the general structure of prices in the absence of trade barriers, such as tariffs, conforms to what would be expected based on transfer costs, there are important exceptions. Differences may exceed transfer costs, even for extended periods, because of incomplete or inaccurate information, preferences on the part of buyers for produce grown in a particular area, and institutional or legal barriers to the movement of commodities between regions. Temporary factors, such as a shortage of railroad cars, elevator space, or barge transporation also can lead to price differences between regions that at times exceed normal transfer costs.

Preferences of buyers are important in determining spatial price relationships. Products which appear to be homogeneous may not, in fact, be substitutable in the minds of buyers. Trading patterns are often dictated by traditional arrangements or personal contacts among sellers and buyers. This may lead a firm to continue purchasing commodities from a certain region or particular producers even though it might be able to obtain supplies of the same quality at a lower price from a different area.

Institutional and legal barriers to the movement of commodities between regions also contribute to distortions in spatial price relationships. Inspection requirements, sanitary codes, tolerance limits for chemical residues, tariffs, import quotas, and licensing requirements are typical of the devices used to restrict interregional or international trade.

Government price-support activities, likewise, can cause price differences between markets to exceed or fall short of those that would prevail if transfer costs alone were the major determinant of spatial price relationships. At times, prices of grain have been depressed in certain areas of the United States as a result of the government's decision to unload surplus stocks at a particular location. In addition, regional differences in price-support purchase and loan rates have, in some cases, exceeded transfer costs. For example, the price at which the government offered to buy butter was higher in New York at one time than in

Chicago or at country shipping points in Wisconsin by more than the cost of moving butter to New York. This distortion of price relationships led to excessive movement of butter from the Midwest to New York and consequently higher government acquisition costs.

Market Boundaries

If producers have the option of shipping to different markets, the boundary between supply areas is determined by the price at each destination less the cost of transferring the product from each point of origin to each destination. Natural barriers such as rivers or mountain ranges, man-made barriers such as a major highway, or political boundaries frequently determine the dividing line between supply areas for different markets; but where such barriers do not exist and prices paid to producers decline continuously as the distance from each market increases, the boundary between supply areas can be determined by drawing concentric circles around each market and noting the points at which producer prices (net of transfer costs) are the same. Given free choice, producers will always ship to the market offering the highest net price. But some producers may be located at points where the price is the same whether they ship to one market or another. The locus of these points determines the market boundary.

The boundary between two markets will shift if the price rises in one market relative to the other or if transfer costs change. Differential rates of growth in population or income or the introduction of a more efficient processing system, for instance, may cause producer prices to rise in one market relative to another. This will tend to widen the market area serving the higher-priced market and reduce the area serving the other market.

The effect of changes in relative market prices and transfer costs on the location of a boundary point between hypothetical markets is illustrated in Figure 8–1. The downward sloping lines originating at each vertical axis show the net price that would be paid to a producer located at varying distances from markets A and B. At the initial price of $6 per unit in Market A and $5 per unit in Market B, and with transfer costs equal to 50 cents for each 100 miles in both markets, the boundary point would be located 400 miles from Market A and 200 miles from Market B. The price at this location would be $4 per unit.

If the price in Market B rises to $6 per unit, and if at the same time a more efficient transfer system is introduced in that market but not in the other, thereby reducing transportation costs to Market B by 20 per cent

Price Differences and Variability

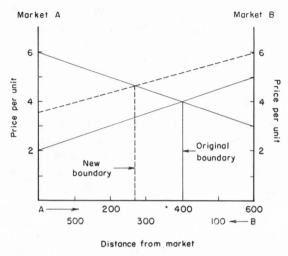

Figure 8-1. Effect of changes in market prices and transfer costs on the boundary between markets

(i.e., to 40 cents per 100 miles), the new net price line for Market B would be shifted upward and would be less steeply inclined. The new position is indicated by the dashed line in Figure 8–1. Some producers located along the axis joining the two markets would shift from Market A to Market B; hence, the new boundary point would be located to the left of the old boundary.

The preceding illustration shows how *one point* on a boundary line between markets may be established. Prices, of course, will vary along the boundary line, depending on the distance from each market. Boundary lines between markets may be linear under some conditions and curved under others. When more than two markets are involved, the location of boundaries becomes very complex.

A market-area boundary line can be identified by noting the points at which prices paid to producers, net of transfer costs, are the same whether they ship to one market or another.[2] The manner in which theoretical boundary lines are established between adjacent markets is illustrated in Figure 8–2. In this illustration, the price at Market A is $6 per unit and at Market B, $5. Prices paid to farmers shipping to these two markets are assumed to decline uniformly in direct relation to the

[2]This statement can be formalized algebraically. Let P_A = price at Market Center A, P_B = price at Market Center B, T_A = transfer cost from farm to Market A, and T_B = transfer cost from farm to Market B; then the boundary is defined by the points where $P_A - T_A = P_B - T_B$.

156

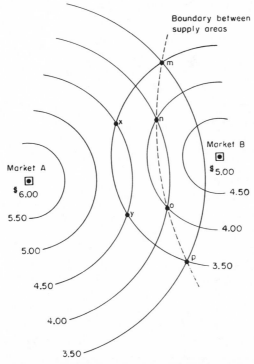

Figure 8-2. Location of boundary between areas supplying alternative markets

distances from each market; that is, the transfer cost is a linear function of distance, increasing 50 cents each unit of distance. Under these assumed conditions, the boundary is represented by a curved line passing through the points m, n, o, p. These are points at which producers are indifferent as to which market they supply.

Returns from shipping to alternative markets are the same at each point on the boundary but the net price varies along the boundary. Farmers located at points m and p receive $3.50 per unit regardless of where they send their product, while producers at points n and o receive $4. In this example, the boundary is a curved line because the price is higher in one market center than in the other.[3] The boundary, of course, is closer to the lower-priced market center.

[3]Given the assumption that transfer costs are a linear function of distance, the market boundary line is a hyperbola. Bressler and King (1970, pp. 126–129, 189–195) provide a much more complete discussion of the theory and practice of establishing boundaries between markets under various conditions including those associated with differences in product forms.

Price Differences and Variability

If the price in Market B equaled the price in A (i.e., $6 per unit), the boundary would be a straight line bisecting and perpendicular to a line joining the two market centers. Such a boundary would go through points x and y in Figure 8–2. Since the same cost-distance relation is assumed to hold for shipments in either direction, the straight-line boundary joins points which are equidistant from the two markets.

Spatial Equilibrium Models

Geographical price relationships can be analyzed in a formal way by using spatial price equilibrium models. These models make it possible to estimate (under very rigid assumptions) the net price that will prevail in each region and the quantity of a given commodity that any one region will sell or purchase from every other region. Such models enable one to determine the optimum or "least-cost" trading pattern, given supply and demand conditions within each region. From this optimum trading pattern an appropriate set of prices can be obtained, based on the principles outlined earlier: namely, that the difference in price between any two regions which trade with each other will just equal the transfer cost between these two regions, while price differences between regions not engaging in trade will be equal to or less than transfer costs.

Spatial equilibrium models are most useful in analyzing interregional price relationships and trading patterns where there are numerous consuming and producing regions. As pointed out in a previous section, if all regions except one produce surpluses and ship to a single deficit region, the structure of producer prices can be determined very simply by subtracting transfer costs from the central market price. But if each region produces as well as consumes a given commodity, one cannot always determine by inspection just which areas will have excess supplies available for sale to deficit regions and which will require imports. Nor is it always obvious which surplus regions will supply a particular deficit area.

The general principles involved in developing interregional trade models can be illustrated with the aid of diagrams showing supply and demand functions for each of two regions (Heady, et al., 1961, pp. 231–233). Such functions are shown for a potential surplus region (A) and a potential deficit region (B) in the upper part of Figure 8–3. In the absence of trade, demand and supply would be equated at a price of $30 in Region A and $50 in Region B. At a price above $30 in Region A, some product would become available for shipment to another area. Imports would be required to satisfy demands in Region B if the price were below $50.

Spatial Price Relationships

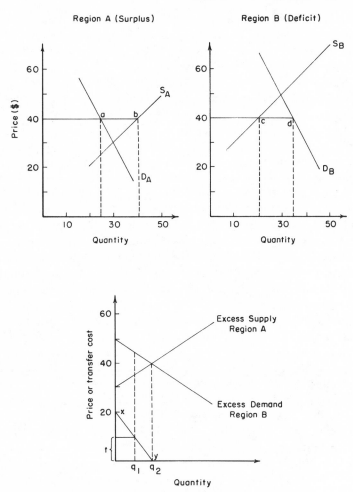

Figure 8-3. Two-region spatial equilibrium model

The information obtained from these diagrams can be used to construct excess supply and demand curves as shown in the lower half of Figure 8-3. The excess supply curve is based on the horizontal distance between the supply and demand curves in Region A at prices above the point of equilibrium (e.g., point *b* minus point *a* in the upper left-hand diagram). Excess supply is zero at the equilibrium price of $30. The excess supply curve is positively sloped like conventional supply schedules since the gap between supply and demand widens as the price increases.

Price Differences and Variability

The horizontal distance between the demand and supply curves below the point of equilibrium in Region B (e.g., point d minus point c in the upper right-hand diagram) provides the information needed to construct the excess demand curve shown in the lower half of Figure 8–3. The excess demand schedule is negatively sloped since the gap between the demand and supply curves widens as the price declines. The excess demand schedule intersects the vertical axis at the equilibrium price of $50 per unit, since there would be no unfilled demand at this price.

The excess demand and supply schedules shown in Figure 8–3 intersect at a price of $40 per unit. If no transfer costs exist between these two regions, a total of 15 units of the commodity would be shipped from Region A to Region B ($ab = cd = 15$ units). The price in both regions would then be the same, $40 per unit. The volume traded between these two regions declines with the introduction of transfer costs. No trade would occur if it cost more than $20 to transfer a unit of product from Region A to Region B. In that case, demand and supply would be equated within each region and the price difference ($20) would be less than the transfer cost.

The effect of changes in transfer costs on the amount shipped between regions can be illustrated by constructing a "volume of trade" line which is shown as the diagonal line, xy, in Figure 8–3. The vertical intercept for this line (which indicates the transfer cost at which no trade would occur) is determined by subtracting the price at which the excess supply curve intercepts the vertical axis from the price at which the excess demand curve intercepts the same axis. As shown in Figure 8–3, no trade will occur if the transfer cost equals or exceeds $20 per unit. The horizontal intercept of the "volume of trade" line (which shows the maximum trade that can occur when transfer costs are zero) is located directly under the point of intersection of the excess demand and supply schedules. In the example, this point is q_2 or 15 units.

The volume that would be exported from one region to the other at any given transfer cost can be determined by drawing a horizontal line intersecting the vertical axis at the value which represents the transfer cost per unit. The number of units which will be transferred is indicated by the point at which the line representing transfer costs (t in Figure 8–3) intersects the volume-of-trade line. For example, at a transfer cost of $10 per unit, the total amount transferred would be q_1 (about 7.5) units. Given this information, the prices that could be expected to prevail in each region can then be determined. In this case, since the slopes of the demand and supply schedules in both regions are approximately equal, the effect of introducing a transfer cost of $10 per unit would be to reduce the price from $50 to about $45 in Region B and to raise the price from $30 to about $35 in Region A.

The effect on prices in different regions of an increase in transfer costs is the same as the effect of an increase in marketing margins which was discussed in Chapter 6. An increase in transfer costs, other things remaining the same, will result in higher prices in deficit regions and lower prices in surplus regions. The larger absolute change will occur in those regions with the steeper (less elastic or more inelastic) excess demand or supply schedules.

It should be apparent from the foregoing geometric analysis that a change in the volume of trade or in price relationships between regions may occur if either (1) any regional demand or regional supply curve shifts; or (2) transfer costs change. These are the critical variables which must be considered in attempting to predict spatial price relationships.

When more than two regions are involved, it is difficult to determine the pattern of trade or the structure of prices without the aid of mathematics. In order to obtain a solution where many regions have been defined, one must know the supply and demand relationships in each region (expressed in an algebraic form) and transfer costs from every region to every other region. One can then sum the regional supply and demand schedules mathematically and solve for the price at which aggregate demand and supply will be equated (see appendix to this chapter, and Judge and Wallace, 1958). Once the equilibrium price is known, the price in each region can be estimated by adding or subtracting an appropriate differential based on average transfer costs or price differentials that have prevailed in the past between regions.

The estimated net price in each region, derived using the foregoing procedure, can then be inserted in the regional demand and supply equations to determine consumption and production. The difference between the estimated consumption and the supply available within each region determines the amount of surplus or deficit for that region. The total of excess supplies over all regions must equal the sum of all import requirements. This balance is assured since the equilibrium price was calculated so as to equate aggregate demand and supply.

Once the surplus and deficits have been estimated for each region, linear programming techniques may be used to determine the optimum or least-cost routing system (Heady and Candler, 1958, pp. 332–337). The linear programming solution insures that all the requirements of deficit areas are met and also indicates precisely how much will be shipped from each surplus region to each deficit region. The computing procedure is an iterative one, which simply means that successive solutions are obtained, each one satisfying the requirements at a lower total cost than the preceding one. In the final solution, the sum of all transfer costs is minimized and producer prices are maximized, given the supplies available and demand relationships as specified.

Information obtained from the final linear programming solution can be used to determine the geographical structure of prices that would be consistent with balancing aggregate demand and supply while meeting the deficit requirements of all regions. The price in each surplus region will be the price in the region to which it exports commodities, less the transfer cost. Price differences between regions also can be calculated directly based on the "dual" solution of the linear programming problem (Judge and Wallace, 1958).

If the regional price differentials initially assumed are inconsistent with those based on the final solution, it is necessary to recompute the equilibrium price, since the demand (or supply) in each region will change if the price differential changes. The entire process of computing an equilibrium price and then using this price together with appropriate price differentials to ascertain the amount of surplus or deficit in each region is repeated until the assumed differentials are approximately equal to those derived from the final linear programming solution.

With large computers, answers to complex problems of this kind can be obtained even when many regions are involved, provided, of course, the necessary data are available. In order to obtain solutions, one needs to derive a demand equation for each region and to know either the total supply available in each region or if supply is not fixed, the supply equations. In addition, information on transfer costs between each region and every other region must be available, which is sometimes called the matrix of transfer costs.

The final solution rests upon a number of assumptions, not all of which may be fulfilled in practice. These are as follows:

(1) All units of the product available in each region must be homogeneous with respect to quality and appearance; consumers are assumed to be indifferent as to the source of supply.

(2) Production and consumption within each region are presumed to occur at precisely the same point. Transfer costs within regions are ignored.

(3) No physical or institutional barriers exist to prevent the movement of goods between regions.

(4) Transfer costs are assumed to be uniform per unit of product, and to remain constant regardless of volume or direction of movement; however, unit costs need not be proportional to distance.

The solutions obtained from models based on these assumptions are useful mainly as a standard against which existing price differences between regions can be compared. The optimum solution is based on the concept of a perfectly competitive market. Such models do not tell us why actual prices deviate from calculated results, but the solutions obtained from the model can be used to identify situations in which marketing inefficiencies or imperfections may exist. They also have been used experimentally to determine whether regional differences in support prices for grains are consistent with those that might be expected to prevail under perfectly competitive conditions (Leath and Blakley, 1971). In theory, spatial equilibrium models could be used by administrators to calculate location differentials for support prices.

Actual prices frequently deviate quite substantially from those calculated for a given year from spatial equilibrium models. The correlation between existing prices and those obtained from least-cost solutions are frequently no higher than 0.5 and in some cases are as low as 0.2 (see King, 1963, p. 16, for a summary of the results of empirical studies). The differences between actual and calculated prices may be due to any one or a combination of the following: (1) market imperfections, including inefficiencies in marketing, institutional barriers to trade between regions, lack of knowledge, or irrational economic behavior; (2) weaknesses in the model, such as the assumption that all supplies originate or are consumed at a single point in each region; (3) inadequate or inaccurate data concerning supply and demand coefficients, estimates of population in each region, transfer costs, and so forth.

Some of the weaknesses inherent in the model may be overcome at the cost of increasing complexity. For example, the errors associated with the assumption that there are no intraregional transfer costs can be reduced simply by increasing the number of origins or destinations and hence decreasing the size of each region. One could go so far as to define each farm or each household as a region, but the problems of determining regional supply and demand relationships would increase correspondingly. Even with modern computing facilities, there are limits to how many regions can be accommodated.

One-commodity spatial equilibrium models also ignore the important interrelationships that exist among commodities (King, 1963, pp. 193–198). While theoretical models have been constructed to take account of such relationships, it is difficult to obtain realistic solutions from them because of the enormous amount of data required. Where several commodities are to be considered, one must have information on own and cross elasticities of demand and supply for each commodity in every region. Some models assume only that the supply of certain factors such as land is fixed in each region and then proceed to determine the optimum pattern of production as well as the volume and direction of trade between regions. Models also have been constructed to show how optimum plant location would affect producer and wholesale prices. These more complex models have limited usefulness in solving practical problems related to the location of production or the structure of prices, but they do serve to emphasize the importance of taking account of the interdependence that exists among commodities and regions.[4]

Once a spatial equilibrium model has been constructed, it is relatively easy to alter one or more of the variables relating to demand or supply or to change transfer costs and then trace through the effects of such a change on the pattern of trade and the structure of prices. For example, if demand increases in a particular region due to a shift in population, this influences the amount of surplus or deficit in that region. This, in turn, can affect prices in all other regions. By working through a spatial equilibrium model, both the direct and indirect effects of a change in one or a combination of variables can be anticipated. This cannot be done without the aid of a model which explicitly recognizes the high degree of interrelationship that exists among prices in different regions.

Spatial equilibrium models have been employed by a number of economists to identify optimum international trading patterns and spatial price relationships that might be expected to prevail in the absence of trade barriers. In most cases, individual countries are identified as regions. The effects of tariffs or import quotas can be appraised by incorporating these in the model. One of the important uses of such models has been to determine which countries would gain and how much producer and consumer prices would change if present trade barriers, including domestic subsidies on production, import controls, tariffs, or variable levies, were to be relaxed. Gemmill (1977), for example, employed a spatial equilibrium model to estimate the long-run structure of world sugar prices and the trading patterns that would prevail under alternative U.S. sugar policies. A somewhat similar procedure was used by Dean and Collins (1966) to measure the welfare and trade effects of changes in tariff policies applied to oranges in the European Common Market.

Conclusions

In the absence of barriers to the free movement of commodities, interregional price relationships respond to changes in supply and de-

---

[4]Day and Sparling (1977) summarize the literature relating to optimization models including spatial equilibrium models and provide an excellent list of references.

mand in different regions and to changes in transfer costs. A change in demand or supply in one region can have far-reaching effects on other regions including those not directly involved in trading with that region. Changes in transfer costs can likewise alter the relative advantage of producers in different areas. In general, a decrease in shipping costs will benefit more distant as compared with nearby producing areas. Thus, it is important to know something about the factors which influence spatial price relationships in attempting to predict changes in the competitive position of different regions.

Individuals charged with the responsibility of establishing support prices also must have an understanding of spatial price relationships. Support price differentials that are inconsistent with least-cost trading patterns and existing transfer costs can lead to uneconomic expansion of production in some regions and to higher government costs or a loss in consumer welfare.

Appendix: A Simple Spatial Equilibrium Model

This appendix illustrates a formal spatial price equilibrium model involving just two regions, assuming linear regional demands, fixed regional production, and known transfer costs. Other models might involve, for instance, regional supply relations rather than given fixed production. Of course, a "realistic" model would involve more than two regions.

Notation:

Q_1^* and Q_2^* = quantities produced in respective regions, which are indicated by subscript.
Q_1' and Q_2' = quantities demanded, including imports.
P_1 = equilibrium price in Region 1 with trade; we assume Region 1 is the area with potential excess supply.
R = transfer cost per unit.
$P_1 + R$ = equilibrium price in Region 2 with trade.
For simplicity, we assume the same linear demand relation for each region and do not include "demand shifters."

Model: with trade, the equilibrium situation is

(1) $\quad Q_1' = \alpha + \beta P_1;$
(2) $\quad Q_2' = \alpha + \beta (P_1 + R);$

and, since total production is fixed,

(3) $Q_1{}^* + Q_2{}^* = Q_1' + Q_2'.$

In these equations, α, β, R, $Q_1{}^*$, and $Q_2{}^*$ are assumed to be known. The unknowns are the equilibrium values P_1, Q_1', and Q_2'. This is a system of 3 equations with 3 unknowns.

Solution:

(a)   add equations (1) and (2)
$Q_1' + Q_2' = 2\alpha + \beta R + 2\beta P_1.$

(b)   From equation (3), we can write
$Q_1{}^* + Q_2{}^* = 2\alpha + \beta R + 2 \beta P_1.$
We are, in effect, finding the equilibrium price by equating supply and demand.

(c)   Solving for the equilibrium price,

$$P_1 = \frac{1}{2\beta}(Q_1{}^* + Q_2{}^* - 2\alpha - \beta R).$$

(d)   Having obtained P_1, equations (1) and (2) are used to solve for Q_1' and Q_2'.

References

Bressler, Raymond G., Jr., and Richard A. King. 1970. *Markets, Prices, and Interregional Trade.* New York: John Wiley and Sons.

Day, Richard H., and Edward Sparling. 1977. "Optimization Models in Agricultural and Resource Economics," in *A Survey of Agricultural Economics Literature.* Volume 2. Ed. Lee R. Martin. Minneapolis: Univ. of Minnesota Press, Pp. 93–127.

Dean, Gerald W., and Norman R. Collins. 1966. "Trade and Welfare Effects of EEC Tariff Policy: A Case Study of Oranges," *J. Farm Econ.*, 48 (Part I):826–846.

Gemmill, Gordon. 1977. "An Equilibrium Analysis of U.S. Sugar Policy," *Am. J. Ag. Econ.*, 59:609–618.

Heady, Earl O., et al., eds. 1961. *Agricultural Supply Functions—Estimating Techniques and Interpretations.* Ames, Iowa: Iowa State Univ. Press.

Heady, Earl O., and Wilfred Candler. 1958. *Linear Programming Methods.* Ames, Iowa: Iowa State Univ. Press.

Judge, George G., and T. D. Wallace. 1958. "Estimation of Spatial Price Equilibrium Models," *J. Farm Econ.*, 40:801–820.

King, Richard, ed. 1963. *Interregional Competition Research Methods.* Raleigh, N.C.: Agricultural Policy Institute, North Carolina State Univ.

Lasley, Floyd. 1977. *Geographic Structure of Milk Prices, 1975.* USDA Ag. Econ. Rep. 387.

Leath, Mack N., and Leo V. Blakely. 1971. *An Interregional Analysis of the U.S. Grain-Marketing Industry, 1966–67.* USDA Tech. Bul. 1444.

Waite, Warren C., and Harry C. Trelogan. 1951. *Agricultural Market Prices.* 2d ed. New York: John Wiley and Sons. Chapter 7.

CHAPTER 9

Price Variation
through Time

This chapter emphasizes models of price determination which seek to explain persistent patterns of price behavior through time. Such behavior includes seasonal patterns of change, year-to-year fluctuations, trends, and cycles. An objective is to provide an understanding of why temporal changes occur and to help identify regularities in price behavior.

Prices observed through time are the result of a complex mixture of changes associated with seasonal, cyclical, trend, and irregular factors. The most common regularity observed in agricultural prices is a seasonal pattern of change. Normally, prices of storable commodities are lowest at harvest time and then rise as the season progresses, reaching a peak prior to the next harvest.

Some commodities such as hogs, beef cattle, eggs, and certain vegetables exhibit cyclical behavior. Price cycles for agricultural commodities tend to vary in length and in amplitude of fluctuations, but a clear tendency does exist within agriculture for production to expand in response to favorable prices, which in turn leads to lower prices in a subsequent period.

Seasonal and cyclical price changes may be superimposed on long-term trends that persist for years. For example, the price of beef in the fall of any year reflects seasonally large supplies, whether production is currently in the rising or declining phase of a cycle and whether the general trend of price is up or down. A knowledge of all of these relationships is useful in understanding price behavior.

Economists have devoted substantial effort to an attempt to identify empirical regularities in price and quantity behavior. Mathematical techniques are available to describe the seasonal, cyclical, trend, and

168

irregular components of an economic time series. The techniques attempt to decompose the observed series into its constituent parts. Unfortunately, a variety of factors reduce the usefulness of such analyses. Reliable estimates of the future can be made only insofar as seasonal patterns, trends, or cycles persist in a uniform manner. Cycles may be lengthened or shortened by external events. Changes in government programs, a severe drought, or a new international crisis obviously can create irregular price movements which are impossible to forecast.

Short-time Price Variation

In the process of price discovery, a more or less continuous process of evaluation of factors influencing prices takes place. As negotiations and trades take place among buyers and sellers, specific prices are obtained. Hence, prices may change from week to week, from day to day, and even within the trading day.

Prices respond, in part, to current changes in economic variables. Thus, a major factor in day-to-day price changes for livestock is day-to-day changes in market receipts. The quantity of a product available on a particular day is the result of many individual decisions by sellers. Day-to-day variation in demand is usually less volatile than in supply; changes in demand can be due to strikes, health scares, previously unexpected change in exports, and so forth.

Current cash prices also may respond to expected (future) changes in factors influencing price (Working, 1958). Thus, the current price of wheat may decline in anticipation of a dock strike, which would reduce exports. Or, expected changes in government price-support or export programs may influence current price. The precise mechanism for short-time changes in prices is discussed in Chapter 12. In sum, short-term price changes arise from a process of continual evaluation of current and expected changes in factors influencing price.

Prices for some agricultural products are established within an institutional framework which tends to reduce or eliminate daily price changes. Contracts are in some cases negotiated between sellers and buyers with price fixed by a formula or by prior agreement. In addition, producers are becoming larger and more specialized, at least in the United States, which implies more stable production and marketing. Thus, one may hypothesize that the changing structure of agriculture and in marketing arrangements results in less frequent price changes today than in past years.

Seasonal Variation in Prices

Sources of Seasonality

Seasonal price behavior is a regularly repeating price pattern that is completed once every twelve months. Such a regular pattern might arise from seasonality in demand, seasonality in supply and marketing, or a combination of the two. For instance, one might visualize a continuous, constant supply over a year with regular seasonal shifts in demand resulting in a seasonal price pattern.

Most agricultural products are characterized by some seasonality in production and marketing patterns. For crops, seasonality arises from climatic factors and the biological growth process of plants. Many crops are harvested once a year and, depending on perishability, may be stored for sale through a marketing season. For livestock and livestock products, seasonality of production arises for diverse reasons including seasonal variation in climatic conditions, seasonality of feed supplies, and the biological character of the production process. However, seasonality in production is being reduced for livestock products (e.g., broilers and eggs).

Seasonality in demand also exists for agricultural products and is related to factors like climate and holidays. Thus, the demand for turkeys in the United States is greatest just prior to the Thanksgiving and Christmas holidays while the demand for ice cream rises in the summer and declines in the winter months; changes in the demand for cut flowers are closely associated with certain holidays. Seasonal differences in demand may not always be as obvious as these examples; however, some empirical research has been devoted to estimating demand relations by seasons (e.g., Stanton, 1961).

One model of seasonal price behavior is illustrated in Figure 9–1. In this model, seasonal price behavior arises from the seasonality of supply. We assume for simplicity that the year consists of three seasons and that the demand function (D) is the same for each season.

The crop is assumed to be harvested in Season 1. Sellers then have the option of selling in any of the three seasons. Since producer—inventory holders have a choice of holding inventory or of selling at harvest, the supply curves $(S_1$ and $S_2)$ for Seasons 1 and 2 have a positive slope. The slopes become progressively steeper for the successive seasonal supplies. Higher prices are required in the successive seasons to induce inventory holders to carry inventories. The seasonal price rise must cover (on the average) the costs of storage. Also, as time passes, the range of alternatives open to the inventory holder decreases.

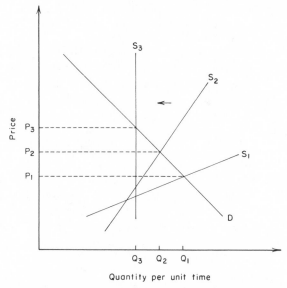

Figure 9-1. A model of seasonal supply and seasonal price change

In the model illustrated, it is assumed that the inventory carried into Season 3 must be sold in that season and cannot be carried over into the new crop year. Hence, the supply function for Season 3 is perfectly inelastic. Apples for fresh use, late summer onions, and fall potatoes are seasonal crops that cannot be carried into the next crop year. Thus, the model depicted in Figure 9-1 is a simplified version of a seasonally produced crop for which no inventories are carried from one year to the next. We turn, then, to what might be termed a "normal" seasonal price pattern.

The "Normal" Seasonal Pattern

The usual price pattern for a seasonal crop—harvested within a brief period but then sold throughout the year—is for the price to rise through the year as a function of the cost of storing the commodity. If grain merchants correctly anticipate future demands relative to supplies and hence store the "correct" quantity, the price will rise from a low point at harvest by just enough to cover storage costs from the time of harvest to subsequent points in the year (Figure 9-2). These price changes must be sufficient to induce some to sell and others to continue holding the commodity. Thus, the seasonal product is allocated through the year by the relationship of current price and expected prices to storage costs. As the next crop year approaches, price declines rather abruptly to the next seasonal low (Figure 9-2).

In essence, a merchant stores a commodity if he or she expects the benefits from storage to equal or exceed the costs of storage. If P_f is the expected future price, P_c the current cash price, and M the cost of storage between the two time periods, then in equilibrium in a perfect market $P_f - P_c = M$.

In this context, costs are broadly defined. They include the direct costs of warehouse space, fire insurance, interest on investment in facilities and inventory, and so forth. In addition, costs may be defined to include a risk premium for a possible adverse price movement while the commodity is in storage. The risk of a price decline while the merchant is holding the commodity is not a direct cost, but presumably a risk-averse warehouseman would pay, if possible, to avoid the price risk, just as he buys fire insurance. Various authors (e.g., Cootner, 1967,

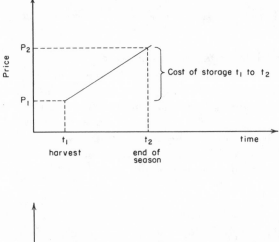

Figure 9-2. Illustrations of theoretical seasonal price behavior

p. 69) also have emphasized the "convenience yield" of holding inventories. Processors and grain merchants find some minimum inventory necessary or convenient. Thus, some inventories are held even when the expected price difference $P_f - P_c$ does not cover the direct costs of storage.[1]

For a number of reasons, the "normal" seasonal price pattern often does not prevail within any given year. Those storing the commodity may act on imperfect information—holding excess stocks, selling too much too soon, and so forth. Hence, prices may rise by more or by less than the cost of storage in a particular year. On the average, over a period of years, seasonal price rises must cover costs; otherwise in the long run there would be no storage. Intrayear price changes usually deviate from the smooth pattern depicted in Figure 9–2, but the diagram serves to emphasize the logic behind the seasonal component of prices.

The degree of storability of current inventories or the timing and size of the new crop also may influence the seasonal price pattern. End-of-season supplies of semiperishable commodities, such as apples or potatoes, are often uncertain. First, storage quality can vary from year to year. A poor quality would necessitate quick sales out of storage with a resulting small end-of-season supply. Second, storage supplies are often augmented by new crop production. Storage potatoes, for example, compete with new spring potatoes. Thus, the timing of harvest and the size of the spring potato crop influence the price of storage potatoes. If supplies toward the end of the storage season are short, prices rise dramatically; if supplies are large, seasonal prices will rise less than normal or even decline. Selected seasonal price patterns for Maine potatoes are shown in Figure 9–3. The months from October to May cover the major harvest and storage period; spring and early summer potatoes are the major source of supply in the other months.

A "nonperishable" commodity is defined as one which can be stored from one crop year to the next (e.g., wheat). The previously developed model is appropriate for this type of commodity with one modification: future expectations must explicitly consider the next crop year; the "optimal" carryover into the new crop year must be determined. Typically, new crop supplies would reduce prices sufficiently so that the carryover is small and related to the convenience of having some inventory at all times. However, a very small crop could result in an expected price

---

[1]The nature of costs and the idea of a supply-of-storage function are further explored in Chapter 12.

Price Differences and Variability

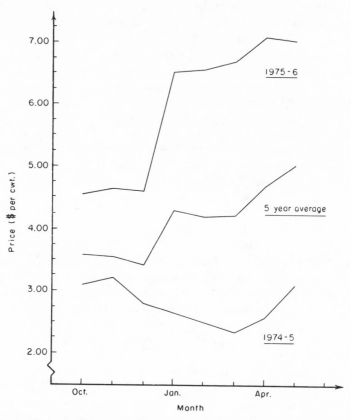

Figure 9-3. Potatoes: monthly average price received by farmers in Maine for two crop years and a five-season (1974-1975 to 1978-1979) average. Data from USDA, *Agricultural Prices,* annual summaries.

difference $(P_f - P_c)$ which would cover the direct costs of storage and hence induce a substantial carryover into the new crop year. Storage policies and seasonal price patterns clearly are influenced by price expectations for the subsequent crop year (for a formal analysis of carryover between production periods see Bressler and King, 1970).

Changing Seasonal Price Patterns

A particular price pattern, as we have seen, depends on intraseasonal supplies and demands and on storage costs over the season. Thus, price differences between months depend on these given conditions and are assumed to equal storage costs for a seasonally produced crop. It follows that changing conditions should change the seasonal pattern. In a dynamic economy, the basic factors underlying a particular seasonal pattern are likely to change. For example, a decline in the seasonality of production, as has occurred for eggs (Larson, 1967), reduces seasonal price movements. A change in storage costs, likewise, would change the seasonal price pattern.

A seasonal pattern has a fixed period of twelve months. An implication of the foregoing discussion is that the amplitude of the periodic fluctuations need not be fixed but may change systematically over the years. This potential for systematic changes plus the usual irregularities in a particular year make the use of historical seasonal price patterns for forecasting the future a very risky business.

Methods of Analysis

Various techniques, mostly descriptive, have been developed to analyze seasonality. One may begin simply by constructing a graph with, say, monthly prices on the vertical axis and time units on the horizontal axis. This helps to identify the uniformities or irregularities in the seasonal price pattern, and the observations may suggest that the seasonal pattern is changing in some systematic way. A second, common technique is to construct an index of seasonal prices. The base period is either a particular twelve months or an average of several twelve-month periods. The index for the base period is, of course, 100, and the weekly or monthly index numbers vary around the base. An index of 90 for June indicates that June prices for the period described were 10 per cent below the twelve-month average. In other words, each monthly price is expressed as a percentage of a twelve-month average. Monthly index numbers can be constructed for a period of years, and these can then be used to see if any systematic changes have occurred in the pattern. Many textbooks in statistics provide explicit details for the construction of seasonal indexes.

Regression techniques also may be used to estimate the components of a time-series variable. Regression models can specify the price (or other) variable as a function of the seasonal effect (using variables taking the values zero and one), trend, and an irregular component. Such models are discussed in numerous sources, such as Maddala (1977). Within the regression framework, the seasonal and cyclical components also can be represented by sine and cosine variables (Doran and Quilkey, 1972). The seasonal component is estimated as a smooth "cycle" with a fixed period of 12 months.

Price Differences and Variability

The multiple regression technique has the advantage of estimating the "net" values of the time-series components, such as seasonal and trend, in one equation. The equation can, in principle, be constructed to allow for changes in the amplitude of the seasonal pattern with the passage of time. Nonetheless, regression models incorporate the seasonal and other systematic components in a rather rigid, deterministic way. It is not easy to allow for the irregularities and shifts in seasonal patterns that are common in the real world.

An alternative approach is to view the sequence of observations on the time series as being drawn from some probability distribution. Again, the analyst's principal problem is to find an appropriate model, i.e., to find an appropriate description of the process generating the observations. It may involve a moving average and an autoregressive element as well as random processes. Models for seasonal time series are discussed, for example, in Nelson (1973).

By analogy with spatial price equilibrium models, it is possible to develop intertemporal price equilibrium models. The "markets" are separated by time and storage costs, rather than by space and transport costs. This approach requires that demand and supply relations be estimated for each time period (e.g., a month) within the season and that storage costs be known. With this information, optimal quantity allocations and prices for a season could be determined. It would also be possible, in principle, to analyze the effects of changing storage costs, demands, or supplies on prices and on the optimum seasonal allocation of supplies (Takayama and Judge, 1964).

Annual Price Variation

Models of price determination under pure competition (Chapter 5) can be applied directly to explain year-to-year product price variation. The demand and supply functions may be viewed as representing annual averages with annual price changes arising from shifts in these functions.

In agriculture, a principal factor in yearly price variability is changes in supply. The supply available in any one year is based mainly on current production and perhaps to some extent on imports and on carryover from the previous crop year. Annual fluctuations in the production of farm products, as we have seen, are sensitive to many economic and noneconomic factors. Demand also may change, owing to fluctuations in export demands, variations in prices of substitutes, and systematic increases (at least in the United States) in population and income.

Year-to-year variation in prices is typically greater for crops, at least for those not under price support, than for livestock products. Crops

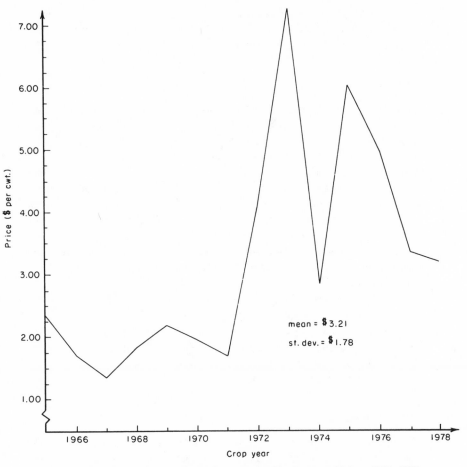

Price Variation through Time

Figure 9-4. Potatoes: season average price received by farmers, Maine, 1965–1978 crop years. Data from USDA, *Agricultural Prices,* annual summaries.

tend to have greater swings in annual production because (a) yields are sensitive to weather conditions and pests and (b) acreage planted and harvested often can be changed from year to year. Conversely, except for poultry, animal units require longer time periods to change, and yields are somewhat less sensitive to factors like weather. The demand for many crops is highly price inelastic. Hence, when substantial year-to-year shifts in supply are combined with an inelastic demand, price fluctuations are likely to be very great. This situation prevails for potatoes (Figure 9-4). Total production in the United States has varied from 296 to 365 million hundredweight in just the seven-year period

177

Price Differences and Variability

1972–1978. The average farm-level price elasticity of demand is thought to be about −0.3. The farm price in Maine averaged $3.21 in the 1965–1978 time period; the range was from $1.36 to $7.25 per hundredweight.

Trends

Trends in agricultural prices are associated with general inflation and deflation in the economy and with factors specific to agricultural products, including changes in the tastes and preferences of consumers, increases in population and income, and technological changes in production. Since World War II, technological changes have lowered costs of production and increased supplies for poultry and eggs. For example, broiler chicken production increased from about 3 billion pounds in the early 1950s to about 13 billion pounds in 1977. This increase was not completely offset by increases in demand, and farm-level prices in real terms declined about 50 per cent in the 25-year period. Thus, upward or downward trends in prices can be generated by persistent changes in either supply or demand.

Distributed lag responses also may be a factor in longer-term changes in economic variables. As previously discussed, economic responses are not instantaneous. Given a change in price, the change in quantity supplied is lagged and perhaps distributed through time. Thus, a one-time increase in price could result in observed increases in quantity supplied over two, three, or more years.

Cyclical Behavior

A cycle is a pattern that repeats itself regularly with the passage of time. A true cycle is self-energizing and not the result of chance factors. It is a matter of debate whether such cycles exist in economics. An instance of cyclelike behavior could be initiated by an external event, but such a "cycle" may dampen unless re-energized by another external event. For example, a drought reduces supply and raises price. The high price leads growers to increase production in a subsequent period, which results in a lower price. This, in turn, reduces production and so on. Such a cycle, however, could die out unless started again by another external event.

Opinions differ as to whether cycles in agriculture are of the self-generating type or are caused by external events. Indeed it is even difficult to discriminate between cyclical and random behavior. Perhaps the most common view is that agricultural cycles are initiated by such external events as drought. Presumably these "cycles" would dampen—not continue indefinitely—unless stimulated by new shocks; the combination of systematic and random behavior appears like a continuous cycle. But it is precisely because cycles appear to be continuous that some observers view them as true cycles. Conflicting views as they apply to the cattle cycle are reviewed by Breimyer (1955). Since the empirical decomposition of a time series into random and systematic components is difficult, the debate is likely to continue.

The length of a cycle is the time from one peak to the next or from one trough to the next and is usually related to the time required to produce a new generation, such as hogs or cattle, or to wear out and replace a product. The latter applies primarily to industrial goods. If a high proportion of families were to purchase automobiles in a particular year and if the average life of a car is seven years, the replacement demand for autos would be largest at the end of each seven-year period. The hog cycle is approximately four years long, though technically a new generation of hogs can be produced in 12 months. This has created some controversy about the cyclical mechanism for hogs, a topic to be discussed in a subsequent section.

If economic cycles are broadly defined to include those initiated by external events, one may conclude that cyclical behavior does exist in agriculture, especially as measured by the *number* of beef cattle, hogs, or chickens on farms. But the amplitude and length of livestock production cycles are by no means uniform. The number of cattle on farms for the period 1928–1979 is plotted in Figure 9-5. Five cycles were completed in this period, averaging about 10 years per cycle. The individual cycles range from nine to 12 years in length. Since cattle numbers have had a positive trend, each successive cycle is at a higher level. There has been more uniformity in the upward phase of the cycle than in the downward phase. The upward phase is constrained biologically by the time it takes to produce more calves and to raise female stock to breeding age. The downward or liquidation phase, in contrast, is determined by economics. It can be short or long, depending on price incentives. Obviously cattle can be slaughtered more rapidly than replacements can be produced. For this reason, it is more difficult to predict the steepness and duration of the liquidation phase of the beef cycle than the expansion phase.

Cyclical behavior in *price* variables is even more irregular than for quantity. The price of cattle, for example, may rise as the quantity of cattle increases if demand is increasing faster than supply. Eventually the larger supply may overtake demand, finally depressing prices at the

Price Differences and Variability

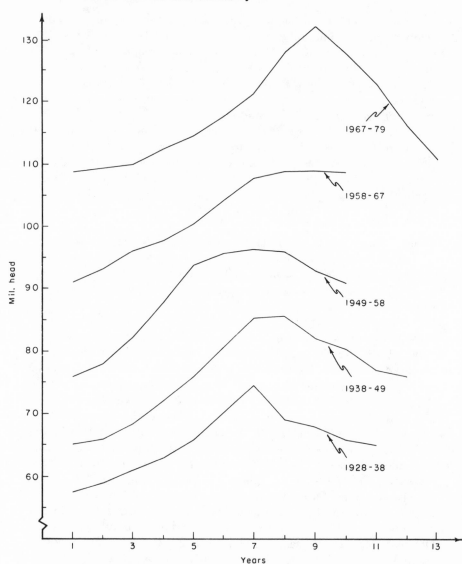

Figure 9-5. Cattle on farms, January 1, United States, 1928–1979. Data from USDA, *Agricultural Statistics,* various years.

peak level of supply. The monthly prices of barrows and gilts from July 1967 to December 1978 are plotted in Figure 9-6. These prices have been "smoothed" by a moving-average procedure to help remove the

180

Price Variation through Time

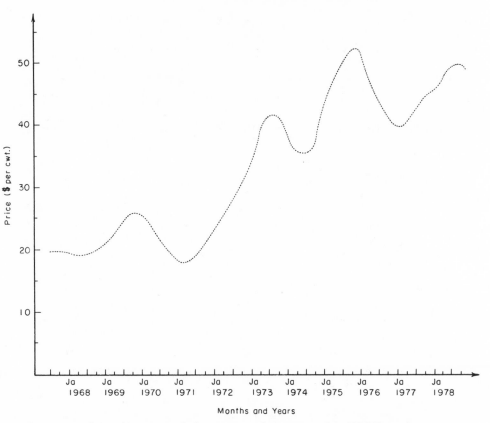

Figure 9-6. Price of barrows and gilts, seven-market average, July 1967–December 1978. Prices adjusted for seasonality. Data from *Livestock and Meat Statistics,* USDA Stat. Bul. 522 and supplements.

seasonal and irregular components of price, leaving the cyclical and trend components.[2] There is a tendency for hog prices to peak every three to five years, but prices clearly were influenced by the erratic events of the mid-1970s (e.g., the small supplies and high prices of feed grains in 1974–1975).

As indicated above, there are logical reasons why one would not expect cycles to have a constant length or amplitude; furthermore the identification of cycles is complicated by the existence of trends, sea-

[2]A danger in using moving averages is that the averaging tends to introduce autocorrelation that did not exist in the original series. Thus, cyclical behavior may be "induced" by the smoothing procedure.

181

sonal elements, and random components. Consequently, it is difficult to isolate the cyclical component and to use it for prediction; however, an understanding of what lies behind cycles is important. In economics, cycles are thought to be generated by lagged responses to changes in prices and other variables. Formal models incorporating such variables, especially lagged prices, have been developed which help explain cyclical behavior (e.g., Meadows, 1970; Gruber and Heady, 1968; Crom, 1970). The simplest of these is the cobweb model to which we now turn.

The Cobweb Model[3]

A Description

The cobweb model provides a theoretical explanation of the cyclical component of certain price-quantity paths through time. Prices and quantities are viewed as being linked recursively in a causal chain. A high price leads to large production; the large supply results in low prices, which in turn result in smaller production, and so forth. More explicitly, the cobweb model arises from three factors which, if present, would result in cyclical behavior of price and quantity. First, a time lag must exist between the decision to produce and the actual realization of production. Second, producers base production plans on current or recent past prices. Hence, realized production, because of the time lag, is a function of past prices. Third, current prices are mainly a function of current supply, which, in turn, is mainly determined by current production.[4]

Consequently, the following chain of events occurs. Current quantity supplied is a function of past prices; i.e.,

$$Q_t^{(s)} = f_1 (P_{t-1}).$$

The quantity produced in time t is sold in time t.

$$Q_t^{(s)} = Q_t^{(d)}.$$

The market clearing price for Q_t is determined by the demand relation.

$$P_t = f_2(Q_t^{(d)}).$$

[3]Ezekiel (1938) wrote one of the basic papers on the cobweb model. Waugh (1964) provides a more recent summary and bibliography. A paper by Tomek and Robinson (1977) provides additional references.

[4]The supply schedule can be adjusted for carryover, but this does not change the fundamental argument.

Thus, the basic causal chain may be written

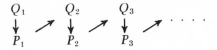

Two supply relations are implicit in the cobweb model. One is a "conventional" short-run function. However, because of the time lag in the production process, current supply is a function of lagged prices (as indicated above). More precisely, planned production is a function of current prices. Assuming plans are realized, current production is a function of past prices. An alternate statement is that production plans are based on expected prices, and expected prices are a function of current and past prices.[5]

The second supply relation is the very-short-run curve. Once production is realized, the model assumes that this quantity is sold. Current price is determined by current supply. (In other words, price is determined as illustrated in Figure 5–1, Chapter 5.) This assumption suggests that the model is most applicable to perishable or semipherishable farm products.

The name "cobweb" arises from the pattern formed by joining the successive price-quantity observations on a conventional supply-demand diagram (Figure 9–7). For convenience, we assume that poor weather resulted in a small supply and hence a relatively high price (P_0) in time t_0. The static short-run supply curve for "normal" weather, however, is shown as S. Hence, on the basis of the P_0, producers plan to produce Q_1, which will be realized in t_1 because of the time lag required for the production process. Once produced, the quantity Q_1 is sold in t_1, and the market clearing price P_1 is determined by the market demand relation D. Price P_1 is the basis for production, which is realized as Q_2, which in turn determines P_2. As the process continues, the cobweb develops.

The assumptions of the model may be summarized as follows. (1) Price is determined in a competitive market structure; producers are "price takers." (2) Price is mainly determined by shifting levels of very-short-run supply (a perfectly price inelastic relation within each time period). (3) Production *plans* are based mainly on current price. (4) An observable lag of at least one time period is required for production response. Thus, there is a clear lag between a price change and a production

---

[5] In empirical supply analysis, various alternate measures of "planned production" and "expected price" have been suggested. These are discussed in Chapter 15.

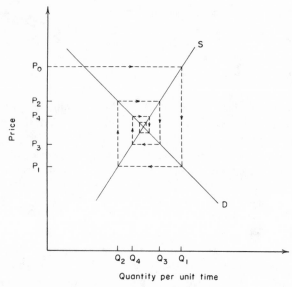

Figure 9-7. A cobweb model with a convergent cycle

change. (5) A cycle depends on actual production equaling planned production. (6) For a clear cobweb, demand and supply relations must be static.

The importance of these assumptions and the reality of the model are discussed in a subsequent section. We turn first to an exposition of the cycles that would result if the model is appropriate.

The cobweb model may lead, in principle, to divergent, convergent, or constant-amplitude (continuous) cycles in price and quantity. Typically, linear supply and demand relations are assumed. The convergent cycle is illustrated in Figure 9-7. The supply function has a steeper slope than the demand relation. The price-quantity cycles, under static conditions, would converge to equilibrium. If the demand function has a steeper slope than the supply function, then the cycle diverges. If the slopes are equal, then a continuous, constant amplitude cycle results. The appendix at the end of this chapter provides a more explicit mathematical statement.

A one-unit time lag in the production process is assumed in the foregoing discussion. The resulting cycle is two units in length. If the lag had covered two time periods, then the cycle would have been four units in length. Specifically, if monthly data were used and if twelve months elapsed between harvests, then the cycle presumably would be twenty-four months long. Thus, the model implies that the cycle will be twice the length of the production lag, where the model assumes current production is a function of the previous period's price.

Limitations

The general assumption of a lag between the planning of production and its realization, as embodied in the cobweb model, is realistic for most agricultural commodities, but the explicit assumption that current production is mechanically dictated by last season's price is weak. Expected price may not be closely tied to immediate past prices, though in some instances it is.

Current price typically is strongly influenced by current production, especially for perishable and semiperishable commodities that must be sold shortly after harvest. We also know, however, that price levels are influenced by other variables, which must be considered in a "realistic" model.

Prices of some farm products, such as livestock and livestock products, are determined in a more or less competitive market. But for commodities like the grains, cotton, and milk, prices are strongly influenced by government programs. In these cases, the simple cobweb model is not appropriate.

Realized production obviously does not always equal planned production. As we have seen, a variety of "random," noneconomic factors can influence the level of demand and supply. Thus, even if all other assumptions were met, it is unrealistic to expect a clear cycle with a constant period.

Nonetheless, the price and quantity paths of some farm products seem to have cyclical components, but two empirical "facts" about these cycles seem inconsistent with the cobweb model, at least in its simplest form. First, cycles usually do not converge or diverge; they tend to be continuous through time. On the other hand, the elementary model implies that the continuous cycle is a special case. Second, some cycles are twice the length suggested by the theory. For instance, a market-weight hog can be produced in twelve months from the time breeding decisions are made. The cobweb model would thus suggest a twenty-four-month cycle. However, the hog cycle has typically been about four years long.

At least four explanations are available for the continuity of agricultural price cycles in the context of the cobweb model. The first, most obvious, and least plausible explanation is that the elementary cobweb model is appropriate and that the slopes of the demand and supply relations are such that the special case of a continuous cycle results.

185

Price Differences and Variability

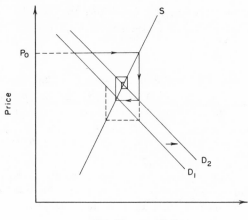

Figure 9-8. Cobweb model with changing demand

A second explanation is that the assumption that realized production equals intended production is often unrealistic. As a consequence, before a cycle can converge or diverge, a "random" shift in supply starts a new cycle. For instance, unusually favorable weather conditions could result in an unintentionally large supply and a low price. The low price would influence production plans for the next period, and consequently a new cycle would begin. The argument is plausible. However, systematic shifts in supply and demand also have the potential to speed convergence rather than prolong the cycle. The influence of a shift in demand is illustrated in Figure 9–8, and an appropriate, concurrent shift in supply (not illustrated) could result in even quicker convergence. Thus, an argument based on the invalidity of underlying assumptions would appear to be a two-edged sword.

A third explanation (Waugh, 1964, pp. 739 f.) is based on the linearity usually depicted in the cobweb model. Continuous oscillation is permitted by nonlinear functions (see Figure 9–9); that is, price could move to a stable platform and vary continuously at a constant level. However, such oscillations also may be unstable, where "stable" means that small deviations from the continuous (constant-amplitude) cycle will converge back to the original cycle.[6] Hence, one might hypothesize that the cobweb is characterized by a nonlinear, but stable, system. An alternate

---

[6]If the product of the slopes at points a, b, c, d (Figure 9–9) is less than one, i.e., if $(abcd) < 1$, then the oscillations would be stable.

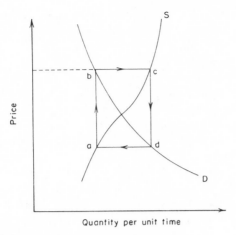

Figure 9-9. Cobweb model with curvilinear functions

hypothesis is that the cobweb is best depicted by nonlinear equations and the recognition that these functions are not static.

A fourth argument is that the cobweb is an inappropriate model for explaining agricultural cycles. Larson (1964), among others, takes this viewpoint and considers an alternate model; it permits cycles four times the length of the apparent lag, but it does not easily account for the continuity of the cycles.

Modifications and Applications

The cobweb model as depicted above is clearly too elementary for application to most real-world situations. More detailed econometric models are usually necessary for significant applied analyses; however, simplicity has the pedagogic virtue of isolating the key features of the model. The cobweb is a simple example of the recursive-type model, which views economic activity as a chain of events.

In constructing more "realistic" models, the supply and demand equations would be modified to allow for shifts in the functions. More than two equations also might be required to describe the supply-marketing-price formation-demand process. For instance, Harlow (1962), in a model of the pork sector, considered equations for (1) number of sows farrowing, (2) number of pigs raised from these farrowings, (3) marketing weights of these pigs, and (4) storage supplies of pork. Thus, four "supply" equations were used instead of a single equa-

187

tion as implied in the elementary model. In addition, the price formation–demand aspects of the commodity must be considered.

Another difficult problem in model construction is defining the prices and costs to which farmers respond (i.e., the variables in the supply equations). In some cases, as implied previously, expected prices may indeed be a function of past prices, although using only last year's price is probably an oversimplification. In other cases, discussion of a forthcoming world food shortage in the press could lead to expectations of higher prices, or anticipated prices might be based on prices of contracts for the future delivery of the commodity or on announced changes in a government price-support program.

Producers typically cannot make instantaneous adjustments from one enterprise to another in response to an expected price change (as discussed in Chapter 4). Thus, production in the current period might be viewed as modified from last year's level in response to a price change. Current quantity supplied, then, is a function of last period's quantity supplied and expected price. Nerlove (1958) has developed such a model—a distributed lag supply equation, based on a somewhat different argument. He also has developed the implications of such a supply equation for the cycles of a cobweb model.[7]

The cobweb model may be modified, as we have seen, and still contain the essential features of the cobweb. However, at some point, modifications can result in a conceptually different model. Larson (1964) has presented a "harmonic motion" model which contains many of the features of the cobweb but which modifies the static short-run supply function and hence eliminates the cobweb. Thus, the principal difference in the two models lies in the approach to production response.

While the simple cobweb model depicts supply response as a change in level along a static short-run supply curve, Larson argues that supply response is best viewed as a *rate of change* in planned production through time. Producers' decisions are constrained by such factors as resource fixity, credit rationing, and uncertainty. It takes time to alter plans, and still more time for changes in plans to affect production. Thus, current production can remain relatively large even after prices decline. A lag exists in carrying through changes in production plans, and marginal changes from an existing level of output cannot be expected to bring down total production very markedly in a short period of time. For example, farmers respond to low pork prices by reducing the

[7]For certain values of the coefficients of the equations, there will be no cycle; in other cases, a cycle is possible.

rate of breeding of sows, but both the number of pigs being fattened and the total number of sows bred (in gestation period) will remain large for some time. That is, the number of pigs in the "pipeline" of the production process, a number based on previous decisions, is large.

The time paths of price and quantity implied by the harmonic-motion model may be estimated as sine or cosine functions—hence the name of the model. Larson has applied the model to the hog cycle. He argues that the model is applicable to other commodities as well. This model does imply a cycle twice the length of the one implied by the cobweb; however, the harmonic-motion model seems most appropriate for commodities which have a more or less continuous production process or at least continuity in the decisions made by producers.

The time path solutions for price and quantity (Larson, 1964, p. 378) will be constant amplitude, cosine functions (180 degrees out of phase) only if "special" slope conditions prevail with respect to the relationships in the model. In this respect, the harmonic-motion model seems no more satisfactory than the cobweb model. Larson (pp. 380–383) discusses in detail the reasonableness of the assumptions underlying the model.

Another problem is that the period of the cycle is rigidly fixed by an assumption that planned production is realized after a fixed time interval. Producers often have some discretion in modifying production plans. Thus, the cycle may not follow a smooth and regular path, complicating the fit of a harmonic function.

Finally, any statistical model by definition will contain an error term. As emphasized above, prices are a function of systematic and random components. Thus, cycles that might dampen and have a regular period in a theoretical, deterministic framework may very well be continuous and irregular in practice.

Some Final Comments on Temporal Price Variability

Temporal price variability for agricultural commodities can be broadly attributed to three factors. One is the biological nature of the production process which makes output partly dependent on uncertain events, including weather and pest damage, and creates seasonal peaks in production. A second, closely related, factor is the prevalence of lagged response relationships in agriculture. The lag between a decision to produce and the realization of output is a function of the biological production process, and since farmers seem to use prices prevailing at the time of the production decision, current output is influenced by past prices.

Hence, cyclical changes in output occur. A third factor is the price inelasticity in both supply and demand, which means that small changes in supply or demand can lead to large changes in prices.

Price variability generally is greater for agricultural commodities than for industrial products. This creates uncertainty, both for producers and consumers. Farmers are handicapped in making future plans when prices are highly variable. Price uncertainty can lead to an unwillingness on the part of producers to make investments (internal capital rationing) or to lenders refusing to make loans (external capital rationing) because of the risks involved. Consumers, processors, and retailers also would prefer to have more stable supplies and prices of farm commodities. Thus, pressures exist to moderate price instability. This can be done, but at a cost. Storage stocks can be increased to moderate price changes within a marketing year and between years, but someone will have to bear the higher costs of maintaining larger stocks. Government intervention through price-support loans and guaranteed prices to producers also may serve to dampen price instability or to provide better guides for planning future production, but again this may involve substantial public costs. Contracting in advance with buyers is another way for farmers to shift price risks.

But stability can be overdone. Prices must be permitted to fluctuate over a considerable range if they are to serve as guides to production, marketing, or consumption decisions. For example, as we have noted, seasonal price changes help ration a fixed supply over the marketing year, or if consumers are to benefit from technological improvements, prices must be free to reflect changes in the costs of production. Thus, it is important to preserve sufficient flexibility for prices to perform their economic function, which is to ration consumption and guide production. Ideally, one would like to protect producers, marketers, and consumers from random or irregular fluctuations while permitting systematic changes in prices to occur in response to underlying economic forces.

Appendix: An Elementary Cobweb Model

The simplest cobweb model can be written as three equations.

$$Q_t^{(s)} = \delta + \gamma P_{t-1} \text{ (supply)}$$
$$Q_t^{(s)} = Q_t^{(d)} \text{ (market clearing).}$$
$$P_t = \alpha - \beta Q_t^{(d)} \text{ (demand).}$$

With price on the vertical axis, the slopes are

$$\frac{dP}{dQ} = -\beta \text{ for the demand relation, and}$$

$$\frac{dP}{dQ} = \frac{1}{\gamma} = \gamma^{-1} \text{ for the supply relation.}$$

Thus, the slope conditions for the three types of cycles are

$$|-\beta| > |\gamma^{-1}| \quad \text{a divergent cycle,}$$
$$|-\beta| < |\gamma^{-1}| \quad \text{a convergent cycle, and}$$
$$|-\beta| = |\gamma^{-1}| \quad \text{a continuous cycle.}$$

One method of computing the *paths* of Q and P through time is by the "brute strength" technique of substitution. While not recommended for actual computations, it may help the reader to understand the conditions leading to various types of cycles.

Since $\quad P_t \quad = \alpha - \beta\ Q_t$ and

$\quad\quad\quad Q_{t+1} = \delta + \gamma\ P_t$, it follows that

$\quad\quad\quad Q_{t+1} = \delta + \gamma\ (\alpha - \beta Q_t)$

$\quad\quad\quad\quad\quad = (\delta + \gamma\alpha) - \gamma\beta\ Q_t$.

Also, $\quad Q_{t+2} = (\delta + \gamma\alpha) - \gamma\beta\ Q_{t+1}$ and

$\quad\quad\quad\quad\quad = (\delta + \gamma\alpha) + \gamma\ \beta\ [(\delta + \gamma\alpha) - \gamma\beta\ Q_t]$

$\quad\quad\quad\quad\quad = (\delta + \gamma\alpha)(1 - \gamma\beta) + (\gamma\beta)^2\ Q_t$.

Let $t = 0, 1, 2, 3, \ldots$ and the equations for computing Q in each period may be summarized as follows:

$$Q_1 = (\delta + \gamma\alpha) - \gamma\beta\ Q_0.$$
$$Q_2 = (\delta + \gamma\alpha)(1 - \gamma\beta) + (\gamma\beta)^2\ Q_0.$$
$$Q_3 = (\delta + \gamma\alpha)(1 - \gamma\beta) + (\gamma\beta)^2 - (\gamma\beta)^3\ Q_0.$$
$$.$$
$$.$$
$$.$$

Of course, to compute the sequence of Q's we must have estimates of α, β, γ, and δ and know the initial value of Q_0.

Since β is negative, the levels of Q are oscillating from period to period. The conditions for the three types of cycles also may be stated as

Price Differences and Variability

$(\gamma\beta)^2 > 1$ for a divergent cycle,
$(\gamma\beta)^2 < 1$ for a convergent cycle, and
$(\gamma\beta)^2 = 1$ for a continuous cycle.

For instance, if $(\gamma\beta)^2 = 1$, i.e., $|-\beta| = |\gamma^{-1}|$, then our sequence of Q's becomes

$$Q_1 = (\delta + \gamma\alpha) - (1)\, Q_0;$$
$$Q_2 = (\delta + \gamma\alpha)\, (0) + Q_0 = Q_0;$$
$$Q_3 = Q_1;$$
$$Q_4 = Q_0.$$

In other words, the Q's oscillate between

$$[(\delta + \gamma\alpha) - Q_0] = Q_1 = Q_3 = Q_5 = \text{etc.}$$
and $\quad Q_0 = Q_2 = Q_4 = \text{etc.}$

Readers with some mathematical background may have observed that

$$Q_{t+1} = \gamma\beta\, Q_t \text{ and}$$
$$P_{t+1} = \gamma\beta\, P_t \text{ are first-order difference equations.}$$

General solutions are available for such equations at various points t through time, but a development of this topic is beyond the scope of this chapter.

References

Breimyer, Harold F. 1955. "Observations on the Cattle Cycle," *Ag. Econ. Res.*, 7:1–11.

Bressler, Raymond G., Jr., and Richard A. King. 1970. *Markets, Prices, and Interregional Trade*. New York: John Wiley & Sons, Inc. Chapter 11.

Cootner, Paul H. 1967. "Speculation and Hedging," *Food Res. Inst. Studies*, 7:65–106 (Supplement).

Crom, Richard. 1970. *A Dynamic Price-Output Model of the Beef and Pork Sectors*. USDA Tech. Bul. 1426.

Doran, H. E., and J. J. Quilkey. 1972. "Harmonic Analysis of Seasonal Data: Some Important Properties," *Am. J. Ag. Econ.*, 54:646–651.

Ezekiel, Mordecai. 1938. "The Cobweb Theorem," *Quart. J. Econ.*, 53:255–280.

Gruber, Josef, and Earl O. Heady. 1968. *Econometric Analysis of the Cattle Cycle in the United States*. Iowa State Univ. Res. Bul. 564.

Harlow, Arthur A. 1962. *Factors Affecting the Price and Supply of Hogs*. USDA Tech. Bul. 1274.

Larson, Arnold B. 1964. "The Hog Cycle as Harmonic Motion," *J. Farm Econ.*, 46:375–386.

———. 1967. "Price Prediction on the Egg Futures Market," *Food Res. Inst. Studies*, 7:49–64 (Supplement).

Maddala, G. S. 1977. *Econometrics*. New York: McGraw-Hill Book Co. Sections 9–2 and 15–3.

Meadows, Dennis L. 1970. *Dynamics of Commodity Production Cycles*. Cambridge, Mass.: Wright-Allen Press.

Nelson, Charles R. 1973. *Applied Time Series Analysis for Managerial Forecasting*. San Francisco: Holden-Day Inc. Chapter 7.

Nerlove, Marc. 1958. "Adaptive Expectations and Cobweb Phenomena," *Quart. J. Econ.*, 73:227–240.

Stanton, B. F. 1961. "Seasonal Demand for Beef, Pork, and Broilers," *Ag. Econ. Res.*, 13:1–14.

Takayama, T., and G. G. Judge. 1964. "An Intertemporal Price Equilibrium Model," *J. Farm Econ.*, 46:477–484.

Tomek, William G., and Kenneth L. Robinson. 1977. "Agricultural Price Analysis and Outlook," in *A Survey of Agricultural Economics Literature*. Volume 1. Ed. Lee R. Martin. Minneapolis: Univ. of Minnesota Press. Pp. 328–409.

Waugh, Frederick V. 1964. "Cobweb Models," *J. Farm Econ.*, 46:732–750.

Working, Holbrook. 1958. "A Theory of Anticipatory Prices," *Am. Econ. Rev.*, 48:188–199.

CHAPTER 10

Changes in the
General Level of Farm Prices

Thus far, the discussion has focused mainly on the factors that determine the prices of individual commodities. In this chapter, we examine the causes and economic consequences of changes in the general level of farm prices and, more particularly, the relationship between average farm and nonfarm prices. Changes in the general level of farm prices affect the ability of farmers to repay debts, the profitability of investments in land, buildings, and equipment, and the competitive position of one country relative to another in selling farm products on world markets. Changes in relative prices are of even greater importance from a social and political point of view, since they affect the welfare of farm families and the level and distribution of income between the farm and nonfarm sectors of the economy.

Farm prices, like those of other goods and services, are strongly influenced by overall trends in the economy. The prices of farm products have generally risen in the United States during periods of inflation, and have declined as much or more than the prices of nonfarm goods and services in periods of deflation. Since the Civil War, the United States has experienced two major periods of deflation. The first began in 1866 and ended in 1895; the second began with the collapse of prices following World War I and ended in 1933. During the 1920s and 1930s, deflation was a major issue in the United States; since World War II, inflation has replaced deflation as one of the foremost economic issues and has persisted despite widespread efforts to control it.[1] While inflation has been pervasive, the rate at which prices have risen since the

---

[1] A discussion of the causes of inflation lies beyond the scope of this book (for a review of the literature on the causes of inflation see Frisch, 1977).

194

1940s has varied widely among countries and from year to year. In the 1970s, for example, the average annual rate of inflation ranged from over 50 per cent in Argentina to around 6 per cent in Germany and Switzerland. In the United States, the annual rate of inflation accelerated during the 1970s from just under 4 per cent in the early part of the decade to over 10 per cent in 1979.

All prices, of course, do not move up or down precisely at the same time or at the same rate. This is particularly true of farm prices which at times have moved counter to the general trend. In the 1950s and 1960s, for example, the average level of farm prices remained relatively stable in the United States while nonfarm prices continued to rise. Livestock and grain prices sometimes move in opposite directions. Whenever such divergent trends exist, it is somewhat misleading, or at least not very helpful, to make statements about the general level of farm prices.

Measuring Changes in the Average Level of Prices

Index numbers are used to measure changes in the general level of prices. An index number, like any average, is influenced by what is included in the index and the weights attached to each of the component items.[2] Thus, in interpreting index numbers, it is important to find out what items are included or excluded and how they are weighted.

Measures of the rate of inflation can be biased upward or downward depending on the nature of the weights given to the prices of the items in the index. Generally, an index which uses fixed, base-year weights has a slight upward bias, while one which uses current weights has a slight downward bias. This occurs because consumers change their expenditure patterns in response to changes in relative prices. Base-year weights tend to give too much weight to those items whose prices have gone up relative to the average and too little weight to those items whose prices have lagged behind. Index numbers based on current expenditure patterns have the opposite tendency, that is, they give greater weight to items that have risen less than the average since the base year. In principle, this bias problem in index numbers could be minimized by using a combination of base and current year weights, but in practice such indexes would be very costly to compute.

Changes in the quality of items included in an index also create a problem. The latest model tractor or a new combine with an air-

---

[2]See the appendix at the end of this chapter for a more complete discussion of index numbers and the manner in which they are constructed.

conditioned cab will cost more than earlier models, but the new equipment probably will handle a larger acreage in a given amount of time with more comfort to the operator. Thus, a part of the price increase is related to a change in quality, and it is not appropriate to use the price of the new item in constructing an index without adjusting for the change in quality. An analogous problem arises when a new product, such as a more effective herbicide, enters the marketplace.

Index numbers measure changes in prices relative to a particular year (say, 1967) or period of years (say, 1910–1914). If fixed weights are used (which is the common practice), percentage changes in prices between years will be the same whether one calculates them using an index based, say, on prices in 1937 or in 1967, but the absolute level of the index will be much larger when the earlier base period is used (assuming, of course, that prices have been rising over this time period).

The principal index numbers used to measure changes in the general level of prices in the United States are the Consumer Price Index (CPI), the Producer Price Index (formerly the wholesale price index, but now referred to as the PPI), and the GNP deflator. Because each of these index numbers includes different items with different weights, it is not surprising that the rate of inflation calculated using each of these indexes frequently differs. In the late 1970s, the GNP deflator generally increased less rapidly than the CPI, in part because the former uses what amounts to current year weights while the latter uses fixed weights, and in part because the prices of products such as food which rose more rapidly than the average during this period are weighted more heavily in the CPI than in the GNP deflator.

Raw material prices are important in the PPI, and these prices tend to be more volatile than the prices of finished products and services. Thus, the PPI often fluctuates more from month to month than does the CPI.

The Index of Prices Received by Farmers is the most frequently quoted measure of changes in the average level of U.S. farm prices. This index uses fixed weights based on the relative value of different commodities included in the index. Unlike the CPI, the quality of products included in the index is not held constant. Thus, changes in a particular component of the index, such as the average price of wheat, can reflect changes in the average quality of the product that can occur in a particular year and not just the price of a standard or uniform commodity.

The Impact of Inflation on Agriculture

Traditionally, farmers have been among those who have gained from inflation. This was especially true during the two world wars. In each of these periods, the prices of farm products rose relative to the prices of production items. The value of farm land also rose, thereby adding to the potential capital gains of those who had bought land earlier. In contrast, farmers did not gain from inflation in the 1950s and 1960s. During this period, the prices of farm products lagged behind changes in the price of industrial products, labor, and most services. Thus, it is not always true that inflation benefits farmers. Deflation, however, has almost invariably brought hardship to those in agriculture simply because farm prices tend to fall faster and further than nonfarm prices.

The effects of moderate or creeping inflation, say 1 or 2 per cent per year, are clearly different from rapid or hyperinflation during which prices may increase by as much as 50 or 100 per cent per year. The latter type of inflation leads to a "flight from cash." When money depreciates rapidly, every individual seeks to convert cash into goods as quickly as possible. This can lead to even more rapid increases in the prices of tangible assets, such as land, gold, and silver. If everyone seeks to beat inflation by purchasing such items, the prices of these items will eventually be bid up to the point where they can no longer serve as a hedge against inflation.

The obvious beneficiaries of inflation are those who purchased land earlier, since land usually appreciates relative to other assets, and debtors, since they are able to pay off their obligations with depreciated currency. Beyond these widely recognized effects, one can draw few conclusions about who benefits and who loses from inflation, because relative price changes do not necessarily follow a uniform pattern from one period of inflation to another. Even factor costs do not rise uniformly. In the 1960s, for example, the cost of labor rose relative to the prices of machinery and fertilizer; in contrast, during the 1970s the prices of land, machinery, and fertilizer rose more than the cost of labor. Thus, gains or losses from inflation will depend partly on the mix of inputs employed by farmers as well as the combination of products which they offer for sale.

Leads and lags in price adjustments during periods of inflation can result in a substantial redistribution of income, even within agriculture. In the mid-1970s, for example, grain prices rose relative to the prices of livestock products, thus transferring income from areas in which livestock feeding was important to regions specializing in cash grain production. The flow of funds within agriculture was reversed in 1978 and 1979 when livestock prices rose relative to the price of grain.

Rapid inflation is often accompanied by an increase in speculative activity which, in turn, contributes to increased instability in commodity prices. Under such circumstances, returns to farmers will be strongly

197

influenced by the time at which they sell commodities or purchase inputs such as feed and fertilizer. Gains or losses from speculative buying or selling can exceed returns from increasing efficiency. This includes inventory gains from appreciation in land and other assets. Inflation, according to Solow (1975), distorts incentives away from lowering costs of production toward speculation, rewarding those who are either exceptionally astute or fortunate in their timing of sales or purchases rather than those who are simply efficient managers.

One of the serious consequences of inflation is that it may result in the loss of export markets if domestic costs rise relative to those in competing exporting nations. The adverse effects of inflation on exports can be averted if the country with the more rapid rate of inflation devalues its currency by enough to compensate for the increase in its prices. If this is not done, the incomes of those producing export crops will decline. Eventually, this may lead to a drop in the output of export crops as producers shift the use of their land and other resources to alternative enterprises or seek employment outside of agriculture.

Argentina provides an excellent case study of the adverse effects of high rates of internal inflation, not fully compensated for by devaluation, on the returns to those producing export crops. During the 1940s and 1950s, the government devalued the currency periodically, but in some cases not frequently enough or by an amount sufficient to prevent the incomes of farmers producing export crops from being squeezed. The long-run effect of this was to reduce incentives to produce export commodities and thus potential export earnings.

The Effects of Currency Revaluation

Currency revaluation, that is, a change in the foreign exchange rate, can serve either to offset the effects of changes in relative prices between countries or to give the country which devalues its currency a competitive advantage in export markets. The ultimate consequences of devaluation can be extremely complex, but the first-round effects are quite straightforward. Assume the dollar is devalued 10 per cent relative to the German mark. For simplicity, assume also that the exchange rate before devaluation is two marks to the dollar and that the price of U.S. hard wheat delivered to Hamburg, Germany, is $4.00 per bushel. With a 10 per cent devaluation of the dollar a German importer can now obtain $4.40 for the eight marks formerly required to purchase a bushel of wheat. Eight marks will buy 10 per cent more wheat than formerly, provided the U.S. price of wheat remains at $4.00 per bushel. In terms of German marks, the U.S. price of wheat has become 10 per cent cheaper. Under these circumstances, there will be an increase in demand for U.S. wheat which ultimately can lead to an increase in the U.S. price of wheat, assuming the supply is inelastic.

Devaluation of the U.S. dollar in the 1970s contributed to inflation by making imports more expensive, but, at the same time, benefited export commodities. Part of the increase in grain prices in the early 1970s can be attributed to the fact that, after devaluation, buyers were able to obtain more dollars per unit of their currency than they did previously. This resulted in bidding up the price of U.S. grain. Overvaluation of the dollar prior to 1971 according to some analysts depressed U.S. farm prices (Schuh, 1976).

If prices in the country devaluing its currency rise by the same percentage that the currency is devalued, the initial competitive advantage will be lost. Other countries, fearing a loss of markets, also may decide to devalue their currency. Thus, a country's decision to devalue its currency will not always succeed in increasing the volume of exports or in raising internal prices.

The Terms of Trade of Farm Products

The welfare of farmers is influenced as much or more by relative price movements as by the absolute level of farm prices. Relative price movements are frequently referred to as the "terms of trade" of farm products.[3] An improvement in the terms of trade of farm products, that is, an increase in the average level of farm prices relative to the prices of other goods and services, leads to a gain in the welfare of farmers, while the reverse, unless accompanied by offsetting improvements in productivity, leads to a loss of real income.

Agriculture has experienced widely fluctuating terms of trade during the twentieth century. The prices of farm products increased relative to the prices of nonfarm products during each of the two world wars, but the terms of trade moved against agriculture very dramatically in 1920–1921 and again between 1929 and 1932. Farm prices tend to be more volatile than the prices of nonfarm goods and services. Hanau (1960)

[3]This term as commonly used in economic literature refers to the ratio of the prices of goods and services exported to the prices of items imported. When one reads of an improvement in the terms of trade, this usually means that export prices have risen relative to import prices; however, the concept can be applied equally well to the ratio of farm to nonfarm prices.

Price Differences and Variability

attributes the greater instability of farm as compared to nonfarm prices to a combination of the following factors:

(1) the nature of the aggregate demand and supply curves which tend to be more price-inelastic for agricultural commodities than for many industrial products;

(2) greater year-to-year fluctuations in the production of agricultural commodities combined with unequal rates of growth in demand and supply, the latter due mainly to improvements in technology;

(3) instability in international market prices, which are more important for a number of agricultural products than for many nonfarm goods and services;

(4) differences in market organization and structure which make it possible for many nonfarm firms to exercise some degree of control over prices and to adjust production in response to a change in demand rather than to accept lower prices.

The aggregate demand for farm products in most countries is highly inelastic unless producers have access to export markets that can absorb varying quantities with little effect on prices.[4] Empirical studies indicate that the aggregate farm-level price elasticity of demand for all food in the United States is less than -0.25 (Cochrane, 1958, pp. 37–41; and Mann and St. George, 1978). This means that a 1 per cent increase in the per capita availability of food will depress average farm prices by 4 per cent or more. The demand for exports and nonfood crops such as fibers probably is less inelastic (Tweeten, 1967; and Johnson, 1977), and for this reason the aggregate price elasticity of demand for all farm products in the United States may be closer to -0.3 or -0.4, but all evidence points to the fact that it is substantially less than -1.0.

The aggregate short-run supply of farm products also is extremely inelastic. Tweeten and Quance (1969) estimate that the short-run price elasticity of aggregate supply of farm products in the United States falls somewhere between 0 and 0.2. Their analysis suggests that the elasticity of supply is slightly lower in response to falling prices than to rising prices, although the differences are not very great. Long-run elasticity, as one might expect, tends to be somewhat higher.

For reasons that were discussed in Chapter 4, farmers usually find it unprofitable to reduce the use of inputs such as land, family labor, and

---

[4]The demand schedule facing a minor exporting country may be elastic even though the aggregate demand for all farm products on world markets is highly inelastic. This is analogous to the situation in which the demand schedule facing an individual farmer is infinitely elastic (horizontal demand schedule) despite the fact that total demand is inelastic.

machinery in the short run in response to lower farm prices. They can sometimes switch from the production of one commodity to another; however, aggregate production tends to remain the same, given normal weather. In contrast, manufacturing firms are more likely to reduce the length of the work week and to cut production if orders drop. Thus, the short-run effect of a general recession or depression is to bring about a sharp decline in agricultural prices but a reduction in output and employment in the industrial sector, often with little or no change in published prices.

Because of the biological nature of agricultural production, its widespread geographical dispersion, and the unpredictable rates of development of new production technologies, it is difficult to maintain equality between the rates of growth in aggregate supply and demand. During the 1940s, demand shifted to the right abruptly because of wartime needs. The adjustment in supply lagged behind changes in demand, with the result that prices rose very sharply. In contrast, during the 1950s, the aggregate supply curve moved to the right as a result of improvements in agricultural technology (Cochrane, 1958). This occurred at a time when export demands for U.S. farm products were declining. Given the severe inelasticity of both the demand and supply functions, this combination of events led to a substantial drop in the equilibrium level of average farm prices. Actual market prices did not decline to the equilibrium level, however, because of government intervention. Surplus commodities were acquired by the government at support prices, and programs were introduced in an attempt to curb production. In the absence of such programs, farm prices would have fluctuated over a much wider range in the 1950s and 1960s.

Fluctuating export demands have been one of the major contributors to instability in grain prices in the 1970s. The United States, as the principal residual supplier of grain, has been especially vulnerable to changes in export demands. Modest shifts in production in a few key countries like Canada, Australia, the Soviet Union, or China can lead to large changes in the demand for U.S. grain. National support policies, which have encouraged self-sufficiency and prevented grain use from responding to changes in world prices, also have contributed to price instability in the principal residual markets. Sugar, beef, butter, and cheese are among the other commodities that have suffered from instability in export prices because of national support policies designed to protect domestic producers.

Changes in policies are an obvious source of instability. The decision of the Soviet Union to expand livestock output and to rely on imports of grain to meet deficits resulting from unstable internal production had an enormous impact on world markets in the 1970s. The imposition of export embargoes by the United States has had an equally dramatic impact on grain and soybean prices during the past decade.

Agriculture's terms of trade may deteriorate as a result of a rise in the prices of industrial products as well as a fall in the prices of commodities sold by farmers. Raul Prebisch (1964), an economist from Argentina with a special interest in the export problems of the less developed countries, attributes at least a part of the decline in the terms of trade of agricultural exporting nations in the 1950s and 1960s to the failure of the industrial countries to share the fruits of technical progress with those purchasing industrial goods. A large fraction of the gains from technical improvements in manufacturing, according to Prebisch and others, have been captured by workers in the form of higher wages rather than passed on to consumers in the form of lower prices. Strong unions demand wage increases that frequently exceed productivity gains. Firms operating in oligopolistic industries then pass on the higher costs to their customers, but agricultural producers, operating as they do under more competitive conditions, have no opportunity to do likewise and in fact may suffer from lower prices as a result of increasing supplies associated with changes in technology. Thus, a concentrated market structure combined with the actions of strong trade unions can lead to higher industrial prices at a time when agricultural commodity prices are falling.

Historical evidence regarding price movements of agricultural and industrial products is not entirely consistent with the Prebisch hypothesis. The prices of several major agricultural export crops such as coffee, cocoa, and rice rose relative to the prices of industrial products in the 1970s, thereby improving the terms of trade for a number of agricultural exporting nations. Furthermore, neither labor unions nor multinational firms have succeeded in capturing all the gains from improvements in technology. Despite general inflation, the average prices paid by farmers for fertilizer and for agricultural chemicals were no higher in 1970 than they had been a decade earlier. The evidence clearly supports the conclusion that the terms of trade of farm products have been highly unstable, but the historical record does not indicate that the terms of trade have moved consistently against agricultural exporting nations (Hanau, 1960, pp. 135–137; McCrone, 1962, pp. 111–117; Morgan, 1963; and Hallett, 1968, pp. 40–44).

Ratios of index numbers are used to measure changes in the terms of trade; that is, an index of farm prices is divided by an index of nonfarm prices to obtain a ratio. If both farm and nonfarm prices increase or decrease by the same percentage relative to the base period, the ratio remains equal to 1.0 (or 100 if converted to an index number by multiplying the ratio by 100). The ratio obviously is influenced by the index used in the denominator. Two types of index numbers are commonly used for this purpose. One is an index of wholesale industrial prices; the other is the index of prices paid by farmers, which includes farm-produced items such as feed, seed, and livestock as well as the prices of land, farm labor, machinery, fertilizer, and other industrial inputs used by farmers. When the latter index is used in the denominator, the result is commonly referred to as the "parity ratio."

Since the 1930s, the parity ratio has played an important role in farm policy in the United States. This ratio was first defined in legislation adopted in 1933 as the Index of Prices Received by Farmers divided by the Index of Prices Paid by Farmers for items used in production and family living, both on a 1910–1914 base. Later, farm wage rates were added to the index of prices paid by farmers. The family living component is now based on the CPI. Average farm prices are said to be at "parity" when the ratio is equal to 1.0, that is, when prices received by farmers have risen by exactly the same percentage as the index of prices paid by farmers since 1910–1914.

Great care must be exercised in drawing inferences from this ratio. Merely changing the base year or period of years can make the terms of trade look more or less favorable for farmers. For example, the parity ratio on the original 1910–1914 base was 71 in 1979, while on a 1967 base it was 97. Since not all farmers buy the same "mix" of items which make up the index of prices paid by farmers, the parity ratio may be misleading as an indicator of the well-being of a particular group of farmers like corn producers or dairymen. Furthermore, the ratio takes no account of changes in productivity. Gains in efficiency can offset all or part of a decline in the terms of trade. For this reason, the parity ratio which reflects only changes in relative prices and ignores changes in output per unit of input is not a reliable indicator of changes in the welfare or real income of farmers.

Conclusions

In summary, two features of general price movements are of concern: persistent trends (inflation or deflation) and instability. For both political and economic reasons, there is likely to be a continuing bias toward inflation in the years ahead. When inflation is correctly anticipated, most producers and consumers can adapt to it. We can expect farmers, like everyone else, to attempt to beat inflation by buying assets now and going into debt with the expectation of paying off the debt with depreciated dollars. Attempts to "stay even" with inflation will lead to greater use of the principle of indexing, that is, by using a general price index such as the CPI or the Index of Prices Paid by Farmers to adjust support prices or those negotiated under private contracts.

Instability in the terms of trade of agricultural products also is likely to persist. Export crops are especially vulnerable to changes in demand. This, combined with weather-induced variations in output, will continue to produce highly unstable terms of trade for farm products in the absence of national or international intervention. Relative price changes often serve a useful function, as pointed out earlier, but they also can lead to a misallocation of resources and to capricious changes in income, especially if they occur as a result of natural disasters, abuse of economic power, or political decisions. We can expect continued efforts to reduce the amplitude of price fluctuations, especially for storable commodities, through the use of such devices as storage or reserve policies and international commodity agreements.

Appendix: Price Indexes

Price-level movements are measured by index numbers, including indexes of retail, wholesale, and farm prices. That is, index numbers are used to measure average changes in prices (or other variables) at some point in time relative to a base year or period of years. A specific index number series, such as the Consumer Price Index, provides an empirical measure of a general concept, such as the level of retail prices. Clearly, there is likely to be a problem in obtaining observations that represent the concept being measured. This appendix briefly reviews selected methods of constructing index numbers, some problems encountered in computing such numbers, and the interpretation and use of index numbers. This appendix, however, does not contain a complete discussion, and the reader should consult other references for greater detail (such as Yamane, 1967).

Constructing an Index

In its simplest form, an index number may be thought of as a ratio. The denominator of the ratio contains the "base period" observations and the numerator the "current" observations. The resulting ratio measures current observations as a percentage of the base period. The ratio of the current price of a particular product (or service) to a base period price is defined as the "price relative."

$$R = \frac{P_{1i}}{P_{0i}},$$

where P_{1i} = current price of the ith commodity and
P_{0i} = base period price of the commodity.

As time passes, current price changes, and we obtain a series of price relatives for a given base period.

An index number can be constructed as an average of price relatives. For example, the arithmetic mean for n commodities and services would be

$$I = \frac{\sum_{i=1}^{n} \frac{P_{1i}}{P_{0i}}}{n}.$$

In 1967, the average price received by farmers for beef cattle was \$22.30 per 100 pounds, for hogs \$18.90, and for sheep \$6.35. Selecting 1967 as the base year, the price relatives would be 1.0 in that year. In 1977, the prices of meat animals had risen; the respective prices for beef cattle, hogs, and sheep were \$34.40, \$39.40, and \$13.40. An index of meat animal prices for 1977 may be constructed as an average of the three price relatives.

$$I_{77} = \frac{\dfrac{34.40}{22.30} + \dfrac{39.40}{18.90} + \dfrac{13.40}{6.35}}{3} = 1.912.$$

It is common practice to multiply the index by 100 and write 191.2.

Other averages such as the geometric or harmonic mean could be used. These generally give different numerical results. Perhaps a more important problem, however, is that simple averages give each item in the index equal weight. In the meat animal illustration, sheep received equal weight with beef cattle, but sheep marketings are clearly much smaller than beef cattle marketings in the United States. One weighting method is to use percentage weights based on the value of marketings of each commodity in the index relative to the total value of marketings.

Price Differences and Variability

Weights may be formulated as follows. For one commodity,

$$W_{0i} = \frac{V_{0i}}{\Sigma V_{0i}} \,,$$

where $V_{0i} = P_{0i}Q_{0i}$ = value of marketings of commodity i in base period 0,

and $\sum\limits_{i=1}^{n} V_{0i}$ = total value of n items in index.

By definition, $\sum\limits_{i=1}^{n} W_{0i} = 1$.

A weighted arithmetic mean gives the following index number definition:

$$I = \frac{\Sigma W_{0i} \dfrac{P_{1i}}{P_{0i}}}{\Sigma W_{0i}} = \Sigma W_{0i} \frac{P_{1i}}{P_{0i}} \,, \text{ since } \Sigma W_{0i} = 1.$$

This formula is one way of defining the *Laspeyres* index, which uses quantities (Q_{0i}) in a base period as weights. To see this, recall

$$W_{0i} = \frac{V_{0i}}{\Sigma V_{0i}} = \frac{P_{0i} Q_{0i}}{\Sigma P_{0i} Q_{0i}} \,.$$

Then substitute for W_{0i} in the definition of I.

$$I = \sum_{i=1}^{n} \frac{P_{0i} Q_{0i}}{\Sigma P_{0i} Q_{0i}} \frac{P_{1i}}{P_{0i}} = \frac{\Sigma Q_{0i} P_{1i}}{\Sigma Q_{0i} P_{0i}} \,.$$

In this equation, only P_{1i} changes with the passage of time. The preceding equation is also defined as a *weighted aggregative price index*.

There are a number of alternative weighting systems for index numbers. The *Paasche* index replaces the base period weights (Q_{0i}) in the Laspeyres formula with current year weights (Q_{1i}). It is difficult, however, to obtain and maintain current quantity weights. *Fisher's ideal index* is the square root of the product of the Laspeyres and Paasche formulations. Most price indexes in the United States use a Laspeyres or a modified Laspeyres formula.

Problems in Constructing Indexes

The difficulties of index number construction can be classified under three headings: (1) selecting components of the index, (2) choosing the base period, and (3) choosing the weights.

As mentioned previously, an index is constructed to represent a particular concept, but the cost of collecting data generally prohibits exhaustive coverage. The Consumer Price Index uses the prices of almost 400 items, and these prices are collected in 85 urban areas. The price index is based on a sample of all possible retail prices. Thus, the analyst has the problem of selecting items to include in the index. The sampling problem is complicated by the numerous outlets selling the various items, by the possibility that posted or listed prices are not the actual sale prices, by price specials not coinciding with the day or days price information is collected, and so forth.

In the Consumer Price Index, prices are obtained for items that are precisely defined (in terms of quality specifications) and for which observations are readily available. Thus, this index attempts to preserve uniformity of quality through time. As new products become available or items change in quality and others become obsolete, the index must be modified to reflect these changes.

To compute the Index of Prices Received by Farmers, the U.S. Department of Agriculture obtains the average price received for each commodity by farmers each month. No quality specifications are contained in the instructions. Hence, the index can change simply because the average quality of the product sold changes. This again emphasizes that indexes, by the selection of data, can measure quite different concepts (either intentionally or unintentionally). The intent in the prices received index is to use prices that, when multiplied by quantities sold, give the total revenue received by farmers.

Since index numbers are constructed for the purpose of making comparisons, the base period is often thought of as a time of "normal" prices. A common practice is to use an average of prices for several years as the "base price." The denominator P_{0i} then is not a single price but is an average of prices over, say, three years. Because of the changing product mix and changing quality, the base period should not be too far removed from the current period.

The quantity weights need not come from the same time period as the price base, and indeed they often do not. The weight for each commodity in the Index of Prices Received by Farmers is a ratio, which is the commodity's proportion of total income for the years 1971–1973. While the current price base is 1967, the index also is available on a 1910–1914 base. Index numbers calculated by the Department of Agriculture, including both the Index of Prices Received by Farmers and the Index of Prices Paid by Farmers for items used in production and family living are modified from time to time to reflect changes in the relative importance of different commodities and services. When changes are made in weights and/or base periods, the new index can be chained or spliced to the old index (Yamane, 1967, pp. 281–294).

In computing a farm-prices-received index, the weights could be based on quantities produced or quantities marketed. Quantities marketed are typically used. In the United States, the quantity produced and the quantity marketed are nearly identical. In a developing country, a high proportion of the food produced is often consumed on farms and not sold. In this situation, quite different weights would be obtained from quantity produced as contrasted with quantity marketed.

The quality or accuracy of an index depends, in part, on the quality of the data going into the index and hence on the amount of resources devoted to obtaining accurate price and quantity information. Personal judgments inevitably enter into the decision-making process of index number construction, but this does not necessarily mean that index numbers are biased. Government agencies, including the U.S. Department of Agriculture, take great care in trying to make the index numbers as representative of the price or production series they are trying to measure as financial resources will permit.

Uses of Price Indexes

The major use of a price index is simply to describe the average price movement of a combination of goods and services with the passage of time relative to the base period (when I = 100). A current index number of 180.7 means that prices on the average are 80.7 per cent higher than in the base period. For a Laspeyres-type index, it also is valid to compare adjacent years, such as the values 180.7 and 185.0. The period-to-period change in this case is 4.3 points or 2.4 per cent. The user should understand the concept being measured (and conversely what is not measured) by the index. For example, the Consumer Price Index for all urban consumers uses prices paid by urban residents; it excludes farm families, military personnel, and persons in institutions.

The principal problem encountered in using index numbers is to interpret them correctly. If carefully constructed, they provide a reasonably accurate measure of changes in relative prices over a period of years, but they are not a good indicator of well being or of relative income changes. The selection of alternative base periods for purposes of comparison can lead to widely different conclusions about relative price movements and the welfare of different groups. Between 1940 and 1950, average farm prices rose relative to the Consumer Price Index, but between 1950 and 1960, the situation was reversed. Thus, one would be tempted to conclude that farmers were relatively well off in the late 1960s if the comparison between farm and all retail prices was based on 1940 = 100; he would conclude just the opposite if he were making the comparison based on index numbers of farm and retail prices using 1950 as a base.

Sometimes monthly price indexes are seasonally adjusted. Prices are assumed to have a "normal" seasonal pattern within the year; for this reason alone, a monthly index would move up and down. The seasonal adjustment attempts to remove the effect of the "normal" seasonal pattern. The appropriate comparison in a seasonally adjusted index is between different years for the same month. Comparisons between adjacent months within a year can be confusing. The *unadjusted* index, for example, may rise from one month to the next, but if the price rise is less than the normal seasonal rise, then the seasonally *adjusted* index would decline.

In addition to their descriptive functions, price indexes are used to "deflate" various price and income series. The deflated series is obtained simply by dividing a price or income series by an appropriate index. The resulting price series indicates how the individual price has changed relative to the denominator which usually is selected to reflect general price movements. For instance, if the price of pork remains constant while the retail price index rises, the "real" or "deflated" price of pork falls. The same principles are involved in calculating prices or incomes in "constant dollars." For example, the per capita income of farmers in "1972 dollars" is the actual income in current dollars for each year divided by an appropriate index of prices for the same year with 1972 equal to 100. The resultant series shows changes in "real" or "deflated" income. Some of the advantages as well as problems associated with using deflated rather than actual data in empirical work are discussed in Chapter 15.

References

Cochrane, Willard W. 1958. *Farm Prices: Myth and Reality.* Minneapolis: Univ. of Minnesota Press.

Price Differences and Variability

Frisch, Helmut. 1977. "Inflation Theory 1963–1975: A 'Second Generation' Survey," *J. Econ. Lit.*, 15:1289–1317.

Hallett, Graham. 1968. *The Economics of Agricultural Policy.* Oxford: Basil Blackwell.

Hanau, A. F. 1960. "The Disparate Stability of Farm and Nonfarm Prices," in *Proceedings of the Tenth International Conference of Agricultural Economists, 1958.* London: Oxford Univ. Press. Pp. 124–156.

Johnson, Paul R. 1977. "The Elasticity of Foreign Demand for U.S. Agricultural Products," *Am. J. Ag. Econ.* 59:735–736.

Mann, Jitendar S., and George E. St. George. 1978. *Estimates of Elasticities of Food Demand in the United States.* USDA Tech. Bul. 1580.

McCrone, Gavin. 1962. *The Economics of Subsidising Agriculture.* London: George Allen and Unwin, Ltd.

Morgan, Theodore. 1963. "Trends in Terms of Trade and Their Repercussions on Primary Producers," in *International Trade Theory in a Developing World.* Ed. R. Harrod. London: Macmillan, Pp. 52–72.

Prebisch, Raul. 1964. "The Economic Development of Latin America and Its Principal Problems," as reprinted in *Leading Issues in Development Economics.* Ed. Gerald M. Meier. New York: Oxford Univ. Press. Pp. 339–343.

Schuh, G. Edward. 1976. "The New Macroeconomics of Agriculture," *Am. J. Ag. Econ.*, 58:802–811.

Solow, Robert M. 1975. "The Intelligent Citizen's Guide to Inflation," *The Public Interest*, No. 38 (Winter 1975):30–66.

Tweeten, Luther G. 1967. "The Demand for United States Farm Output," *Food Res. Inst. Studies*, 7:343–369.

_____, and C. Leroy Quance. 1969. "Positivistic Measures of Aggregate Supply Elasticities: Some New Approaches," *Am. J. Ag. Econ.*, 51:342–352.

Yamane, Taro. 1967. *Statistics: An Introductory Analysis.* 2d ed. New York: Harper & Row. Chapter 11.

III

PRICING
INSTITUTIONS

Institutional arrangements related to agricultural product prices are considered in this section. In Chapter 11, alternate methods for discovering or establishing farm prices are described and appraised. The mechanics and performance of commodity futures markets—institutions that are somewhat unique—are discussed in greater detail in Chapters 12 and 13. Topics related to agricultural price policies are considered in Chapter 14, including the objectives of support programs and the economic consequences of alternative methods employed to support or stabilize farm prices.

CHAPTER 11

Mechanisms for
Discovering Farm Prices

This chapter deals with alternative mechanisms for discovering or establishing farm prices.[1] Price discovery is distinct from price determination. Price determination deals with the theory of pricing and the manner in which economic forces influence prices under various market structures and lengths of run (Chapter 5). The term "price discovery" is used to describe the process by which buyers and sellers arrive at specific prices and other terms of trade. But not all agricultural commodity prices are "discovered" through the process of higgling between buyers and sellers or on the basis of bidding at auctions or on organized markets. Some prices are negotiated by producer organizations, calculated using some type of formula, or established by a public agency. We prefer to use the terms "pricing arrangements" or "pricing mechanisms" to denote the complex set of institutions and methods used to discover farm prices.

In this chapter, the first section describes the mechanisms used to arrive at specific prices and the alternative ways of classifying these pricing methods. Next, the factors influencing the evolution and change of pricing mechanisms are discussed. Finally, problems associated with these changes are considered, including criticisms of pricing mechanisms, criteria for appraising pricing mechanisms, and possible ways of improving pricing arrangements.

---

[1]The discussion is limited to methods employed in pricing farm products, mainly at the farmer-first handler level. Sometimes, however, the principal price-making institution is located at the wholesale and retail level. Where appropriate, these arrangements are considered (for information on the pricing of industrial products and at retail see Caves, 1977; Kaplan *et al.*, 1958; and Padberg, 1968). A monograph edited by Marion (1976) contains descriptions of pricing specific farm commodities.

Pricing Institutions

Alternative Pricing Mechanisms

Pricing arrangements for farm products have been classified in several ways. One method is to base categories on what is commonly called "market structure" (Rogers, 1970). Market structure can be viewed as a continuum from pure competition to absolute monopoly (Chapter 5). A simple division is possible, however, between "competitive" and "noncompetitive" or "supply and demand" and "administered" pricing. Implicit in this approach is the use of market structure characteristics, such as the number of buyers and sellers or the share of sales controlled by, say, the four largest firms; however, the characteristics used to classify pricing mechanisms usually are not made explicit.

A second approach is to categorize pricing arrangements by the institutions or mechanics used to establish prices. The following categories cover most of the pricing systems now employed in agriculture:

(1) informal negotiation between individuals,
(2) trading on organized exchanges or auctions, including both specific market places and electronic exchanges or auctions,
(3) pricing via formulas,
(4) bargaining conducted by producer associations or cooperatives, and
(5) administrative decisions, both in the private and public sectors.

The foregoing categories are largely self-explanatory. Many transactions involve a private treaty between a buyer and a seller; the trade may be negotiated in person or by telephone. Organized exchanges often involve third parties, such as auctioneers, commission firms, or those running the computerized system; the seller may not be present when the transaction occurs. In some instances, farmers have organized to negotiate with buyers; the actual negotiation may be conducted by a negotiating team, leading to a formal contract. In formula pricing, the specific transaction price is, in effect, computed from an equation; the formula may be quite simple, specifying that price will be a fixed differential from some previously agreed upon base price; or the formula may be more complex, as in the case of milk-marketing orders (Manchester, 1971). Administered prices are those set by a government agency or a firm that has substantial market power. Government price supports are an example of a legislatively or administratively determined price.

More than one mechanism, of course, may be used to price a particular commodity. Some milk prices are negotiated, while others are fixed by formulas. Feeder cattle, for example, may be priced at an auction or alternatively may be sold directly by a rancher to a cattle feeder with price negotiated individually or tied to a futures market quotation. Both the diversity and relative importance of different methods used in pricing livestock products are illustrated by the data shown in Table 11-1. At least three different methods are used in pricing most livestock products. Formula pricing has been the principal method used to price carcass beef, cheese, and eggs, but negotiation remains important for fresh pork and processed turkeys.

A purely descriptive system of categorizing pricing arrangements for farm products, such as the foregoing, has limited usefulness in judging performance. Prices established under each of the systems referred to in the preceding paragraphs may or may not approximate those that would prevail under pure competition, although futures markets often come close to the competitive ideal. Even the distinction between administered and competitive pricing becomes blurred in practice. For example, an elevator operator, buying grain from farmers, customarily posts buying prices, and in this sense the prices can be said to be administratively determined, but the posted prices are usually based on a central market quotation which may have been discovered under relatively competitive conditions. Formulas, likewise, may be negotiated or tied

Table 11-1. Pricing systems for selected commodities, 1978

			Commodity, by per cent of total transactions				
			Cheese		Turkeys		
Pricing system	Carcass beef	Fresh pork	First handler	Packaged and processed	Live	Processed	Nest run eggs
Intrafirm transfer*			20		65		35
Formula	70	40	65-70	25-35	29	16	60
Negotiation	30	50	10-15	1-2	6	29	10†
Administered (price list)		10		60-70		55	

Source: Hayenga, Marvin L., and Lee F. Schrader. 1980. "Formula Pricing in Five Commodity Markets," *Am. J. Ag. Econ.,* 62: forthcoming. Copyright by the American Agricultural Economics Association.

*Vertically integrated production facilities, producer-owned cooperatives, and contracts.

†Includes direct sale of eggs to processors (breakers) and resales among egg handlers; there is some double-counting in the estimates.

to a central market quotation. Some formulas, like those used to price milk under marketing orders, are modified infrequently and only after a lengthy process, but others may be changed from week to week based on individual negotiations between buyers and sellers. In some instances, the base price in the formula may be competitively determined, but not in other cases. Thus, it is difficult to generalize about the behavior of prices established under different mechanisms. Nevertheless, one does need to have an understanding of the institutions which help establish prices before attempting to judge the relative performance of the different pricing arrangements.

Individual Negotiations

Millions of pricing decisions are made each year on the basis of individual negotiations between buyers and farmers without benefit of a formal market. Prices established under such a decentralized system will approximate the equilibrium prices implicit in a competitive market only if reasonably accurate economic information is readily available to both buyers and sellers. Even with such information available, prices will vary with each transaction. A range of prices rather than a single equilibrium price is likely to prevail. This range may reflect "true" differences among the lots of the product based on quality and location, but it also probably reflects imperfections in the pricing method, including the relative bargaining power and trading skills of the participants. Price reporting where so much variability exists is time-consuming, expensive, and sometimes inaccurate.

A decentralized pricing system provides scope for individuals who like to capitalize on their trading skills or who enjoy participating in the bargaining process. However, it is a relatively expensive method of determining prices if a high value is placed on the time of those involved in the negotiations. In less developed countries, where alternative uses for family labor are limited, there may be little or no real cost to society and certainly no sacrifice in income to the individual if he or she spends half a day in a market or bazaar selling a few pounds of produce. But this system of pricing becomes progressively less satisfactory as the volume of production per farm increases and the opportunity cost of time spent in bargaining rises. For this reason, as agriculture becomes more commercialized, the price a farmer receives is less likely to be determined by individual negotiation.

Organized Exchanges or Auctions

Two types of trading occur on organized markets. One is the "spot" or cash market which involves trading in actual commodities, normally on the basis of samples. The other is in futures contracts which specify the minimum grade or particular grades of a commodity which must be delivered in fulfillment of the contract at some future date. In markets where both types of trading take place, the near futures price serves as the base for discovering the cash prices paid for specific lots of commodities; buyers and sellers negotiate cash prices as discounts or premiums from the near futures with differences based on the grade, moisture content, etc. of a particular lot of grain. Even when cash transactions do not take place on a central market, the futures market is often used as a reference for pricing (Heifner, *et al.*, 1977). The mechanics of trading futures contracts and their function in pricing farm commodities are discussed in much greater detail in the two succeeding chapters.

Auction markets provide facilities for arriving at prices for those commodities which are more difficult to standardize, such as feeder cattle and tobacco. Physical inspection of these items is important since quality varies greatly. Under the auction system, buyers are able to observe each animal or each lot of produce. Prices are then determined on the basis of competitive bids for each lot. Conventional auction markets make it possible to establish prices efficiently for a wide range of commodities, but they have the disadvantage of requiring the physical assembly of the commodities to be sold at a particular location. This can be time-consuming and more costly than direct buying and selling.

In order to avoid the costs of assembling products in one place, electronic auctions have been instituted for some commodities. Buyers must rely on accurate descriptions of the specific lots rather than actual observation. Through the use of computers, the auction concept might be extended over a much broader area, enabling individuals in various parts of the country to bid on specific lots of commodities designated by grade (e.g., eggs) and to match bids and offers without requiring the presence of buyers and sellers in one place.

The major advantage of organized commodity markets is that they provide an impersonal method of pricing which typically is not subject to control by either buyers or sellers. They perform the important function of discovering prices that will equate short-run demand and supply. The prices established in such markets approximate equilibrium prices when the following conditions are met: (1) the volume of transactions is large; (2) the quality of the produce sold on the exchange is broadly representative of total production; (3) a sufficiently large number of buyers and sellers participate in trading so that manipulation of prices is difficult or impossible; (4) unbiased and complete information with respect to supplies of the commodity and factors affecting demand are available to traders; and (5) prices are above government support levels.

Pricing Institutions

The major criticism directed against commodity markets (assuming the preceding conditions are met) is that prices tend to fluctuate "excessively," and at times, perhaps, irrationally, in response to rumors or mass psychology. Unfavorable weather, for example, can lead to buying in anticipation of a price increase. This may attract other buyers who want to capitalize on a rising market. The reverse may occur in a falling market. Such changes in speculative demand, as discussed in Chapter 2, can serve a useful purpose to the extent that the expectations are correct. Problems arise, however, when expectations are wrong or exaggerated. They unnecessarily reinforce or magnify price changes, thereby leading to greater amplitude of fluctuations than required simply to clear the market or to allocate inventories. With the passage of time, markets tend to correct excessive changes in prices. Moreover, it is difficult to demonstrate empirically that prices on terminal markets have unwarranted "runs" (Chapter 12).

The trend toward direct marketing of livestock, eggs, fruits, and vegetables has complicated the process of price discovery and price reporting. Buyers and sellers are no longer brought together in one or a few places. Meat packers, for example, have abandoned plants in central cities and erected new ones in areas closer to sources of supply. It obviously is more difficult to obtain a representative price quotation from a large number of decentralized markets than from a few central ones.

As the volume sold through central markets becomes smaller, the prices established on such markets are likely to fluctuate more and may reflect different qualities than the average of the entire output. For example, terminal markets for fresh fruits and vegetables tend to become residual markets, i.e., markets where shippers send products that could not be sold directly to buyers. If the residual supplies happen to be large on a particular day and the number of buyers seeking to augment normal supplies is small, prices will be depressed; on the other hand, prices will be high if chain stores find their usual sources of supply inadequate and seek to make up the deficits through purchases on terminal markets. Of course, if the average quality of produce sold on a terminal market differs from that of produce sold direct, the price quotation for that market would be lower. If the terminal market price is used as a basis for pricing commodities bought directly, differentials should be established to reflect such quality differences. Terminal quotations can be used as a basis for shipping point pricing as long as the average quality of products sold on such markets is approximately equal to that of products sold directly, or if quality differs in a consistent and recognized manner.

Mechanisms for Discovering Farm Prices

As mentioned above, some of the functions formerly performed by terminal markets can be replaced by electronic trading, and since the pricing process is divorced from physical assembly, there is potential for lowering marketing costs relative to those of central markets (though not necessarily relative to those of direct marketing). If a large number of buyers and sellers participate, the cost per transaction of electronic trading would be small, and it may be possible to broaden the information base for negotiation. Cotton, eggs, and hogs are being priced in this manner, although at present on a limited scale. Obviously, the system can operate successfully only if the product's description can be accurately communicated and has the confidence of both buyers and sellers.

Formula Pricing

The use of formulas in pricing agricultural commodities has increased in the United States during the past two decades. Among the commodities now priced in this way are eggs, wholesale meat, and milk. Pricing formulas are usually based on some reported price, such as a quotation derived from a central market or the price paid to producers in a particular region or location. More complex pricing formulas for milk have been developed incorporating price movers, such as the percentage of deliveries sold as fluid milk, and index numbers reflecting changes in the general level of prices, costs, or demand.

A well-designed formula offers the advantages of providing an impersonal, prompt, and low-cost method of adjusting prices. Once adopted, a pricing formula makes it possible to change prices more or less automatically in response to changes in the designated base price or whatever movers are incorporated in the formula. For government administrators, this is a desirable feature, particularly if it becomes necessary to reduce prices. A formula can perform this function impersonally, thereby taking pressure off the administrator. Formulas also provide a relatively prompt method of adjusting prices. Prior to the introduction of formulas for pricing milk, fluid prices were changed only after a hearing and referendum conducted among producers. This procedure made it possible for all interested parties to express their views before a change was made, but it often required several months to complete the process. Prices are now adjusted automatically in response to changes in the movers incorporated in the formula; no hearings are required as long as the formula remains the same.

From the viewpoint of private firms, formula pricing frees people from the task of negotiating prices. Formula pricing also is attractive in the context of long-term contracts; the parties to the contract, by using a formula tied to a market quotation, are assured of a transaction price

219

similar to competitor's prices at the time of delivery (Hayenga and Schrader, 1980). The Urner-Barry quotations of egg prices and the *National Provisioner* (often called the "Yellow Sheet") reports of carcass beef prices have been popular sources of base prices used in formulas.

A potential weakness of formulas based on such published prices is that the base price itself may be biased or unrepresentative. As the volume of sales priced on the basis of a formula increases, the number of negotiated transactions which can serve as a foundation for the formula diminishes. Furthermore, there have been questions about whether reporters (say, for the *National Provisioner*) obtain an adequate sample of the negotiated prices, whether the prices they publish accurately reflect the sample information, and whether traders deliberately give false information to the reporters. Despite these criticisms, the Yellow Sheet has survived and has been widely used in pricing carcass beef and as a basis for establishing buying prices for live cattle (Ward, 1979). The extensive use of the Yellow Sheet suggests that such price quotations provide a useful service and that formula pricing is likely to persist until a clearly preferable alternative is identified by sellers and buyers.

Group Bargaining

Dissatisfaction with price levels and other terms of trade has led farmers, in some cases, to form bargaining associations (or cooperatives) in an attempt to negotiate with buyers. Farmers hope to achieve results similar to those obtained by the more successful labor unions. Under the National Labor Relations Act in the United States, an employer is compelled to enter into negotiation with representatives of a union provided it has been certified as the appropriate bargaining agent, but thus far this law has not been extended to include farmer bargaining. Farmers in the United States have sought this legal authority for many years, and the Congress continues to consider such bills. If passed, this legislation would force processors and handlers to bargain in good faith over prices and other contract terms with an organization of producers certified as a qualified bargaining agent.

The concept of organizing farmers in an attempt to influence prices is by no means new. During the latter part of the nineteenth century and again in the 1920s, numerous attempts were made to organize large-scale cooperatives or associations of farmers with the objective of obtaining higher prices from meat packers, milk distributors, and other buyers of farm products (Galbraith, 1952, pp. 163–167). The most famous attempt to organize farmers into national selling organizations occurred immediately following World War I. At that time, Aaron Sapiro, a dynamic and convincing speaker, encouraged farmers to combine and sell collectively through their own organizations rather than individually. As a result of his efforts, several national cooperatives were formed, including one for grain and another for livestock. But within a few years, these organizations had collapsed. They failed because they could not prevent their members from selling outside the organization despite "iron-clad" contracts "compelling" members to market through the association. This occurred because producers who were not members continued to sell and benefit from the action of the cooperative in holding farm products off the market, while members received little or nothing since their produce was not being sold.

The experience of the 1920s demonstrates the fundamental weakness of voluntary associations formed in an attempt to raise prices on a national scale. It is difficult to get everyone to join, especially when the potential benefits of remaining outside of the association are so great. Even if an organization is successful in signing up a large number of producers initially, it is difficult to hold them if they find others gaining at their expense.

The ability of bargaining associations of producers to negotiate more favorable prices depends first and foremost on their ability to control a substantial proportion of the total supply. If large numbers of producers who grow the same or competing crops refuse to join, a bargaining association can do very little to raise prices. Voluntary efforts to control supply generally have been unsuccessful for the reasons mentioned above. To overcome this weakness, cooperatives or bargaining associations interested in raising prices have frequently made use of federal or state marketing orders to restrict marketings or to divert part of the supply to secondary markets. A marketing order cannot be put into effect, however, unless it is first approved by a two-thirds vote of producers and conforms to specifications set forth in the federal or state enabling legislation. Orders have been successful in enhancing prices, at least in the short run, for cling peaches in California, raisins, and several other specialty crops. Over the longer run, producers have been less successful in maintaining above-equilibrium prices through the use of marketing orders because it has not been possible to prevent growers from increasing production, either within the area covered by a marketing order or in competing areas.

The success of a bargaining organization depends not only on the degree of control they are able to exercise over supply but also on the characteristics of the firms to which they sell and the price elasticity of demand for their products. Labor unions have learned from experience that it is easier to obtain substantial wage increases from employers in industries in which a few firms are dominant, such as the rubber tire, automobile, or aluminum industries, than from those composed of many small firms scattered over a wide geographical area, like the textile industry. The profit position of firms also has a bearing on the success of wage negotiations, and presumably the same would be true of producer efforts to raise prices.

In general, the more inelastic the retail-level demand schedule for a commodity, the easier it will be for producers to negotiate a higher price, since middlemen can readily pass the increase on to consumers without any substantial loss of sales. On the other hand, if those to whom farmers sell must compete against lower priced imports from other countries or regions or substitute products, it is more difficult to raise prices. An implication of an elastic demand, of course, is that higher prices reduce total revenue.

There is a lack of empirical evidence about the price effects, if any, of farmer bargaining. Numerous studies have dealt with the potential returns to monopoly pricing schemes (e.g., Piggott, 1976), but little analysis of actual bargaining exists. Some of the alternative views and such evidence as does exist on cooperative bargaining is contained in a publication edited by Marion (1978).

The market power of farmer cooperatives and their ability to enhance prices received by farmers have come under attack by the U.S. Department of Justice and by consumer groups. One of their targets has been the classified pricing system for milk which, in effect, provides the legal authority to raise fluid milk prices and hence extract more money from consumers. This results in a loss of consumer welfare (Eisenstat and Masson, 1978). However, the prices established under market orders also have helped to stabilize returns to milk producers, thus leading to greater production.

Farmers are unlikely to be granted additional power to enhance prices in the United States, but they may still seek to stabilize prices through collective bargaining efforts. Bargaining associations can play a useful role in moderating price fluctuations for commodities like red tart cherries. Such associations also can help to improve pricing efficiency by supplying additional information, scheduling deliveries, and by negotiating appropriate premiums and discounts for quality and for time of delivery.

Administrative Decisions

Few agricultural commodity prices are administratively determined in the United States except for price-support loan rates or the buying prices announced by the government for supported commodities such as wheat, corn, cotton, and manufactured dairy products. In this respect, agriculture differs substantially from the industrial sector of the economy. Administered pricing in agriculture is almost exclusively a government function, whereas in the nonfarm sector such decisions are often made by private firms. In addition, of course, the prices of electricity and other public services are regulated by public agencies.

Individual farmers, unlike many firms producing nonfarm goods, have little opportunity to control or administer prices. The opportunity to do so is limited to those firms which produce a unique or differentiated product or otherwise have some monopoly power (i.e., the firm must face a demand curve that is less than perfectly elastic). Firms producing a differentiated product do have some discretion in deciding at what price to sell, but in most cases the zone of discretion in pricing is quite narrow. The upper limit is determined by the prices offered by competitors for similar products. A firm which attempts to raise prices unduly will find its market position undermined by competition from existing products, by the development of substitute products, and by the entry of new firms.

The competitive nature of agriculture makes it difficult for farmers or even those marketing farm products to administer prices and especially to maintain them substantially above competitive equilibrium levels without government assistance.[2] If prices are to be raised, farmers and processors must accept some degree of control over supply (i.e., to limit sales or ration the right to produce). The only alternatives to limiting production are to develop secondary outlets for surplus commodities or to request the government to purchase whatever quantities cannot be sold at the higher price.

The objective of government-administered pricing in agriculture in some cases is simply to provide a floor under prices in years of large crops so as to limit price fluctuations, while in others it is to provide incentives to increase production, as during World War II, or to assure farmers of a "fair" or equitable price. The resource allocative function of prices is often sacrificed in order to achieve some welfare objective. There is no reason why society should not elect to do so, but if prices are to be used as an instrument to raise or maintain incomes, other methods must be employed to guide production or maintain consumption.

---

[2]Food processors and food retailers, of course, administer prices in the sense that administrative decisions are involved in announcing or quoting wholesale or retail prices.

Pricing Institutions

Changes in Pricing Mechanisms

Pricing mechanisms change and respond to economic forces and market structure, although existing institutions tend to persist partly because of inertia. The evolution of pricing mechanisms is influenced, among other things, by the relative prices and costs of the mechanisms themselves. When the cost of labor and management rises relative to the price of capital, there is less incentive for individuals to spend the time necessary to negotiate prices, and consequently they turn to alternative pricing arrangements. As transportation and other assembly costs increase, central markets decline and electronic pricing becomes a viable alternative.

Market structure also influences pricing mechanisms, especially the growing concentration among buyers of farm commodities. Large buyers prefer not to purchase small lots of produce which are frequently all that is available in local market places. It is more convenient and economical for them to contract with large producers for specific quantities and qualities and to arrange for delivery at specified times. As firms grow larger, they tend to take over functions previously performed by markets. For example, food processors often seek to integrate back to the production level either through direct ownership or through contracts in order to obtain raw products in the desired amounts at the desired time and with the preferred characteristics.[3]

The costs and benefits of various coordination arrangements are also influenced by the nature of the product—its bulkiness, perishability, homogeneity, and form in which it is sold. Changes in technology alter relative costs of storage, processing, and transporting commodities and thus indirectly influence pricing mechanisms. For example, a commodity may become less perishable if storage technology is improved, which then makes forward contracting or delayed pricing more feasible.

As a result of the economic and technical changes which have occurred in the United States since World War II, central or terminal markets have declined as pricing institutions. They have been replaced by direct marketing. In 1975, 66 per cent of all cattle and over 70 per cent of hogs were sold directly to processors (Holder and Hepp, 1978). In addition, the use of futures markets has increased enormously. Electronic pricing methods are likely to play an ever more important role in establishing farm product prices in the future.

---

[3]These topics have been discussed in the economics literature for many years—see Coase (1937); Gray (1964); and Alchian and Demsetz (1972).

Assessing Performance

The persistence of numerous mechanisms suggests that no one system of pricing is inherently superior for all commodities or situations. The diversity of pricing mechanisms is mainly a function of the diversity and complexity of the agricultural sector, but also may reflect differing perceptions of what a pricing system should do. Numerous criteria for evaluating pricing mechanisms exist in the literature, and no single criterion has been universally accepted as the basis for appraising pricing arrangements. The criteria that have been suggested can be conveniently grouped under three headings: private and public costs, pricing and productive efficiency, and various welfare measures.

The most obvious costs of price discovery are those associated directly with negotiating prices. These include the time spent by participants in searching for the most advantageous trade and in conducting negotiations; the physical costs of exchange including the capital invested in marketing facilities and communication equipment, the direct cost of labor, and the cost of grading and transporting commodities; and finally, costs associated with settling disputes or guaranteeing performance on contracts.

There are hidden costs that should be considered as well. Pricing information constitutes one element of such costs. A shift to direct marketing reduces the amount of information available and probably results in more uncertainty about how much supply is available or the current strength of demand. Price reporting under such circumstances becomes more costly and perhaps less accurate. Individuals may make errors in marketing decisions because of poor information. Decision makers administering public programs also require accurate information about prices, for example, to compute deficiency payments or tariffs.

In economics, efficient prices are usually defined as those generated under perfect competition. Thus, one of the obvious criteria for judging performance of a pricing mechanism is the competitive norm. Pricing mechanisms create inefficiencies, i.e., deviations from the competitive ideal, to the extent they permit or encourage price manipulation or detract from the information base of traders.

Pricing aberrations may appear in the level of prices (bias), in the variability of prices, and in the nature of price adjustments. That is, price levels may differ from the level justified by economic conditions, and prices may vary too much or too little relative to the competitive norm. Moreover, after a change in economic conditions, price may initially overadjust or underadjust, necessitating still further adjustments to reach the level warranted by current information.

A pricing and coordination system also may influence productive efficiency (French, 1977). For example, as discussed above, contracting and direct marketing may lower assembly costs relative to marketing through a central market place. On the other hand, direct marketing may permit more concentration of economic power in the hands of buyers.

A welfare norm is particularly difficult to apply to pricing mechanisms, partly because concepts of welfare differ. The economist's technical definition of welfare is not the same as the layman's. It can be shown mathematically that combined consumer and producer surplus (and hence total welfare) is maximized when prices are competitively determined. But prices which equate demand and supply may yield returns which are deemed "unfair" to farmers because such prices will not provide the majority of producers with a reasonable return for their labor.

Several problems are encountered when trying to use the foregoing concepts in an attempt to appraise pricing mechanisms. One difficulty is the lack of evidence about the relationship of alternative mechanisms to the criteria. In particular cases, it is often difficult to ascertain whether "unsatisfactory" prices are due to deficiencies in the pricing mechanism itself or to fundamental economic forces. In addition, empirical analyses of whether prices are biased or too variable are fraught with such difficulties as a lack of a standard for measuring bias (for examples of such studies see Garoyan and Thor, 1978, or USDA, 1978).

A second problem is a lack of agreement about the relative importance of the various criteria. Not everyone agrees that a price-discovery mechanism that simply "clears the market" is best under all circumstances. But a pricing mechanism that is designed to achieve welfare objectives, like stable prices or a given level of farm income, may lead to surplus production and the loss of markets as consumers substitute lower-priced alternatives for the price-supported product.

A third problem is the lack of information regarding trade-offs among the various performance criteria for the alternative mechanisms. For example, what are the consequences of shifting from negotiated to formula prices for private transactions costs, for public information, and for price behavior?

Issues related to pricing mechanisms, such as the influence of futures trading on the behavior of cash prices or the dangers associated with basing farm prices on thin markets, will continue to attract widespread interest and concern among farmers. Disenchantment with existing pricing mechanisms has led some to suggest that formula pricing be restricted or that futures markets for particular commodities be eliminated. Others have suggested that buyers and sellers be compelled to report transaction prices so as to provide a broader basis for pricing formulas. Advocates of reform frequently urge greater use of electronic auctions.

The dearth of empirical information makes it difficult to assess the impact of shifting to a different pricing mechanism. Each of the proposed changes would involve trade-offs in performance relative to the existing situation. Pricing efficiency, for example, might be improved, but with higher transaction costs if electronic auctions were to be more widely employed. Each proposed modification must be subjected to careful analysis of gains and losses if informed decisions are to be made.

References

Alchian, Armen A., and Harold Demsetz. 1972. "Production, Information Costs, and Economic Organization," *Am. Econ. Rev.*, 62:777–795.

Caves, Richard. 1977. *American Industry: Structure, Conduct, Performance.* 4th ed. Englewood Cliffs, N.J.: Prentice-Hall.

Coase, R. H. 1937. "The Nature of the Firm," *Economica*, 4:386–405.

Eisenstat, Philip, and Robert T. Masson. 1978. "Cooperative Horizontal Market Power and Vertical Relationships: An Overall Assessment," in *Agricultural Cooperatives and the Public Interest*. Ed. Bruce W. Marion. North Central Project 117, Mono. 4. Pp. 281–292.

French, Ben C. 1977. "The Analysis of Productive Efficiency in Agricultural Marketing: Models, Methods, and Progress," in *A Survey of Agricultural Economics Literature*. Volume I. Ed. Lee R. Martin. Minneapolis: Univ. of Minnesota Press. Pp. 91–206.

Galbraith, J. K. 1952. *American Capitalism: The Concept of Countervailing Power*. Boston: Houghton Mifflin.

Garoyan, Leon, and Eric Thor. 1978. "Observations on the Impact of Agricultural Bargaining Cooperatives," in *Agricultural Cooperatives and the Public Interest*. Ed. Bruce W. Marion. North Central Project 117, Mono. 4. Pp. 135–148.

Gray, Roger W. 1964. "Some Thoughts on the Changing Role of Price," *J. Farm Econ.*, 46:117–127.

Hayenga, Marvin L., and Lee F. Schrader. 1980. "Formula Pricing in Five Commodity Markets," *Am. J. Ag. Econ.* 62:No. 4 (forthcoming).

Heifner, Richard G., et al. 1977. *The U.S. Cash Grain Trade in 1974: Participants, Transactions, and Information Sources.* USDA Ag. Econ. Rep. 386.

Pricing Institutions

Holder, David L., and Ralph E. Hepp. 1978. *Cooperative Strategies for the Pork Industry*. USDA Mkting. Res. Rep. 1097.

Kaplan, A. D. H., J. B. Dirlam, and R. F. Lanzillotti. 1958. *Pricing in Big Business*. Washington: The Brookings Institution.

Manchester, Alden C. 1971. *Pricing Milk and Dairy Products: Principles, Practices and Problems*. USDA Ag. Econ. Rep. 207.

Marion, Bruce W., ed. 1976. *Coordination and Exchange in Agricultural Subsectors*. North Central Project 117, Mono. 2.

———. 1978. *Agricultural Cooperation and the Public Interest*. North Central Project 117, Mono. 4.

Padberg, Daniel I. 1968. *Economics of Food Retailing*. Ithaca, N.Y.: Cornell Univ. Food Distribution Program.

Piggott, R. R. 1976. "Potential Gains from Controlling Distribution of the United States Apple Crop," *Search*, Cornell Ag. Exp. Sta., 6:2.

Rogers, George B. 1970. "Pricing Systems and Agricultural Marketing Research," *Ag. Econ. Res.*, 22:1–11.

USDA. 1978. *Beef Pricing Report*. Ag. Mkting. Ser. (December).

Ward, Clement E. 1979. *Slaughter-Cattle Pricing and Procurement Practices of Meatpackers*. USDA Ag. Info. Bul. 432.

CHAPTER **12**

Commodity Futures Markets: Their Mechanics and Price Relationships

This and the next chapter are devoted to a more detailed discussion of one pricing mechanism, namely, commodity futures markets. The discussion begins with a review of the mechanics of futures market operations but also provides additional depth with respect to the theory of price determination in such markets. The objectives of these two chapters are to enable the student to obtain greater insight into one method of price discovery and to understand more clearly why certain commodity prices behave as they do.

Futures markets are important pricing institutions for many of the major farm commodities in the United States, such as live cattle, hogs, soybeans, wheat, and corn. Moreover, the importance of futures markets, as measured by the volume of trading, has been growing. The number of contracts traded increased from less than four million in 1960 to about 34 million in 1978. These volumes pertain only to farm products. In addition, futures markets for industrial raw materials, precious metals, financial instruments, and foreign currencies have grown, but the discussion in this book is limited to futures markets for agricultural products.

A Description of Futures Trading[1]

Organized Market Places

A distinction must be made between cash sales and trading in futures contracts. Cash sales involve the actual delivery of the commodity, and

---

[1]This section is intended as a review to facilitate subsequent discussion; for more detail see Gold (1975).

most cash sales are not made in central market places. Trading on futures markets involves buying and selling standardized *contracts* for the future delivery of the commodity. Trading in futures contracts takes place only on formally organized central market places. Typically, buyers and sellers do not intend to take or make delivery on the contract. Trading in futures contracts started in Chicago in the 1860s (for additional discussion of the historical evolution see Irwin, 1954).

An organized market provides a trading place, aids in disseminating market information, facilitates the mechanics of trading, and helps regulate the business dealings of members—hence, helps settle disputes. In futures markets, trading must take place at a designated place and time by open outcry. The level of price and price changes are public knowledge. A market reporter continuously provides this information. A communications network swiftly distributes price information. The right to buy and sell in the specific market goes only to members of the exchange. (The Chicago Board of Trade is the largest futures market.) Nonmember traders place orders through a professional broker, who is a member, at established commission charges.

A futures contract is a legal contract, enforceable by the rules of the exchange on which it is traded, to deliver or accept delivery of a definite amount of a commodity during a specified month at a specified price. For example, on October 1, trader A buys 5,000 bushels of May wheat at $4.75 per bushel from trader B. A contract has been made in October for the delivery of wheat in May.

The contract calls for the delivery of a specific grade of the commodity at a specific location or locations. All contracts for a particular commodity on a given exchange are identical, but contract specifications may differ from market to market (e.g., wheat contracts at Chicago, Kansas City, and Minneapolis). In most cases, substitute grades may be delivered at discounts or premiums which are specified in the contract. Traders also understand that the definitions of a grade represent the minimal standards for the grade and that it is this minimal quality which usually is being priced.

Trading on futures markets is facilitated by the device of a clearing house whose purpose is to keep records and record each member's market position at the end of each day. The clearing house operation removes the individual responsibility of one member to another. In effect, the clearing house substitutes for the other party to the contract. Trader A, for example, may make both purchases and sales of contracts for the May delivery month for wheat during the course of the day. But trader A is responsible to the clearing house for his or her net position—not to separate individuals involved in the original trades. Trader A may sell contracts to B, who in turn subsequently sells to C, D, and E, but with the clearing house mechanism, trader A is not obligated to follow the movement of specific contracts which he has sold to other traders. The traders may make numerous transactions through time. As any particular delivery month approaches, however, the trader is responsible only for the net position with the clearing house. This responsibility is usually discharged by taking an offsetting position. A purchase "cancels" a previous sale.

The contracts are seller's options. The seller has the option of making delivery at any time during the delivery month. Notice of delivery must be given. "First notice day" usually is several days before the beginning of the delivery month. When traders who have net positions representing sales give notice of delivery, the clearing house in turn notifies a trader or traders with net positions representing purchases. In some cases, the notice goes to the trader with the oldest net purchases; in others, the notices are apportioned by the size of position. The trader receiving notice of delivery may be able to sell and pass on the notice, or he may choose to accept delivery. A very small percentage of the volume of transactions result in actual delivery. (Actual delivery is usually in terms of a warehouse receipt indicating that the commodity is at a designated location. The warehouse receipt is also the instrument of title transfer used in cash transactions. The person taking delivery can, of course, sell the commodity on the cash market.)

In principle, a seller's contractual obligation could be covered by a financial settlement with a buyer rather than by physical delivery of a product. If this option were exercised, the major issue would be to establish a settlement price that did not disadvantage either the buyer or seller. This concept has been used in broiler contracts (Paul, 1976) and is being considered for other contracts. Thus, financial settlements may become an increasingly important substitute for delivery of a product in futures trading.

Types of Traders and Trading

Actual traders on the floor of the exchange include (1) floor traders buying and selling for their own accounts and (2) brokers trading for others. The floor traders and those placing orders through brokers are classified as "hedgers" and "speculators." However, an unambiguous definition of these terms is difficult because positions in a futures market often have elements of both speculation and hedging.

A perhaps oversimplified view of hedging is establishing a position in futures opposite from the one held in the spot (cash) market. A futures market transaction may be made as a hedge, however, even though the trader has no explicit position in a cash market. For example, a Maine potato grower may sell November futures contracts in the spring, while planting the crop. While no offsetting purchase of cash potatoes has been made, the sale of contracts is principally a hedge. The grower anticipates producing and selling potatoes. Holbrook Working (1953) defines a hedge as the use of a futures contract as a temporary substitute for a later transaction in the cash market. A selling hedge starts with the sale of futures contracts, and a buying hedge starts with the purchase of contracts.

In the "classical" example of a selling hedge, a grain warehouseman sells futures contracts as he buys grain for storage. Later, as the grain is sold out of storage, the warehouseman covers or offsets the original futures position by buying futures contracts. The main economic justification for futures markets rests with hedging. We elaborate on this topic subsequently.

Speculators take market positions with the expectation of making a profit. They do not take offsetting positions (explicitly or implicitly) in the cash market. For purposes of exposition, speculators may be divided into three groups. (1) "Scalpers" and "day traders" are professional speculators who trade frequently on small price changes. Their profits and losses are based on minute-to-minute and day-to-day transactions, rather than longer-time price trends. (2) "Position traders" take positions based on expectations about longer-term price movements. If the trader thinks a price is going to rise, he or she buys contracts hoping to sell at a higher price. Avocational speculators are typically position traders. There are also professional position traders. In practice, a continuum of speculators may exist based on the length of time positions are held, ranging from those offsetting positions every few seconds or minutes to those holding positions for weeks. (3) A "spreader" purchases one futures contract and at the same time sells another. This typically is done when the trader believes the difference in price between contracts will change.[2] For example, if a trader thinks the current price difference between the December and May contracts for corn is too large, then he would buy one and sell the other. *If* the appraisal is correct and the spread subsequently narrows, then the speculator makes a profit by offsetting his initial transactions.[3]

---

[2]Other reasons exist for taking offsetting positions in different contracts; these are discussed in Chapter 13.

[3]Assuming the May contract price is above the December, the initial transactions are to

The spread between two delivery months for a given commodity is an interdelivery spread. Intermarket spreads involve contracts in different markets (e.g., Kansas City and Chicago wheat), and intercommodity spreads involve contracts for different commodities (e.g., oats and corn). Spreading tends to keep prices among contracts in "normal" (to be defined) alignment. Also, as we shall see, trading by speculators—especially the professional scalpers—provides market liquidity.

Market Positions and Volume of Trading

A trader may establish a market position by either buying or selling. It is *not* necessary to buy futures before selling. To be "short," a trader has sold contracts not covered by purchases. The seller simply has assumed a contractual obligation to deliver the specified commodity at a specified price and to receive the agreed-upon price. This is not unlike a tailor who agrees to make a suit of clothing for later delivery to a customer. A difference arises in that normally the seller of a futures contract offsets the short position by buying an equivalent amount of the same contract at a later date. This removes the obligation to make delivery. To be "long," a trader has purchased contracts not covered by an equivalent amount of sales. The buyer is obligated to accept delivery and pay for the contracted amount unless he or she subsequently offsets the long position with appropriate sales.

Assuming the trader does not make or take delivery, the cost of the futures trading includes commission charges to a broker and the possible adverse price movement while holding the contract.[4] Because of the possibility of adverse price movements, traders are required to make a margin deposit. Margins vary from commodity to commodity and by type of trader (speculators pay higher margins). Margins are typically a small percentage (perhaps 5 per cent) of the total value of the contracts. This could amount to 10 cents per bushel ($500 for a 5,000 bushel contract) in absolute terms. The objective is to provide protection against default by the trader. Thus, a margin is not a down payment but is more like "earnest money." Margin calls occur with adverse price movements (a price decline for the purchaser and a price increase for the seller).

The ideas associated with margins and margin calls are perhaps best clarified with an illustration. Suppose that the *initial margin* on a 5,000

---

buy December contracts and sell May. Subsequently, the trader makes the offsetting transactions; if the December price has risen relative to the May, the trader makes a profit.

[4]A member of the exchange has purchased a "seat" on the exchange and pays a smaller fee.

bushel contract is 15 cents per bushel ($750) and that the *maintenance margin* is 10 cents per bushel. As prices fluctuate, the speculator's margin deposit fluctuates—the equity in the contract changes. If the trader holds a long position, a price increase is favorable and the margin is increased; a price decrease is unfavorable and the margin is decreased. Given an unfavorable price change, the trader is asked (margin call) to provide additional funds when the margin goes below the maintenance level. In our example (with the trader long), if price declines more than 5 cents per bushel, the trader is asked to deposit (within a certain time limit) sufficient funds to bring the margin back to the initial level of 15 cents per bushel. If the trader fails to meet the margin call, the broker will sell out the position.

"Open interest" is the number of contracts remaining to be settled for a particular contract. For example, if a trader with a net zero position buys a December contract from another trader with a net zero position, the open interest in this contract increases by one. If this trader subsequently sells a December contract, the open interest is reduced by one. The open interest is equal to the net number of long or short positions. The number of contracts long and short must be equal.

The "volume of trading" is the total number of transactions in a given time period, say a day. It may be quoted as the number of contracts or the physical volume of contracts traded. A numerical example of volume of trading and open interest is given in Table 12-1.

Establishing Price

A well-developed futures market comes close to exemplifying the economist's concept of a perfectly competitive market. There are many buyers and sellers dealing in a standardized commodity (the futures contract). Traders do not have perfect knowledge, but in principle, they have equal access to available information. For example, USDA crop-

Table 12-1. Illustration of open interest and volume of trading in a futures market for three "days"

Day	Transaction	Volume during day (number of contracts)	Open interest end of day (number of contracts)
1	A sells 5 to B	5	5
2	C sells 10 to D		
	E sells 5 to F	15	20
3	F sells 5 to A	5	15

size estimates which may influence price are released at the end of the trading day. Traders have until the next day to "digest" this information. Prior to release, the USDA maintains strict secrecy so that traders have equal access to the available information. Exchanges facilitate the collection of information on factors influencing price.

The price at any point in time represents the *collective* judgments of buyers and sellers as indicated by their decisions to buy and sell. Potential buyers and sellers enter the market with numerous objectives (e.g., to speculate or to hedge various cash positions). However, the ultimate goal, one may assume, is to enhance profits. Traders, including hedgers, hope to make money on their transactions. Thus, potential traders know current prices, including the relationships among prices of different contracts, and they have some expectations, either implicit or explicit, about the future movements of prices. On the basis of this knowledge, purchases and sales are made, and price is the outcome.

Price Relationships: Seasonally Produced, Continuous Inventory Commodities

The relationships among the constellation of futures and cash prices for such commodities as wheat and corn are explored in this section. The relationships include the differences between prices at a point in time, and the movement of prices (and the differences) through time. The theory developed in this section is particularly relevant to those commodities produced once a year but stored and consumed throughout the year. Futures markets were first developed and are better understood for storable commodities. Price relationships for certain other commodities are considered in a subsequent section.

The Constellation of Monthly Prices

The annual (or seasonal) average cash price for a commodity is determined by the annual demand and supply conditions. A set of monthly prices is associated with the annual average. As explained in Chapter 9, the lowest price for seasonally produced crops occurs at harvest, and prices must rise through the year, on the average, by an amount to cover storage costs. Thus, a particular monthly price reflects (1) the average economic conditions for the crop year and (2) the specific conditions necessary for allocating inventories through time.

A hypothetical pattern of cash prices over a crop year is shown in upper Figure 12-1. If traders in futures contracts had perfect knowledge about forthcoming cash prices, then prices of the contracts would be

Pricing Institutions

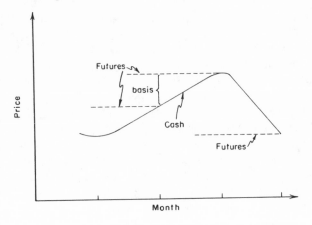

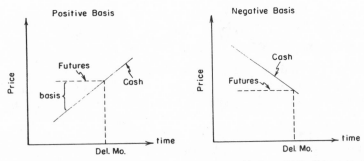

Figure 12-1. A seasonal pattern of cash prices with hypothetical futures prices superimposed

stable reflections of the known future prices. Several such futures price patterns are also illustrated in Figure 12-1.

Prices of futures contracts for certain delivery months may be above the current cash price at a point in time. This is sometimes called the *premium* relationship (illustrated in lower Figure 12-1). A difference between a futures price and a cash price at a point in time is called a *basis*. A premium market has a positive basis. The basis narrows as the delivery month approaches. For a commodity with identical quality and location to that specified in the futures contract, the difference between the current cash price and the futures price is due to temporal differences. The narrowing basis is a reflection of the decreasing cost of storage as the delivery month approaches.

The current cash price also may be above the futures price; this is sometimes called a *discount* relationship (illustrated in lower Figure 12-1). This occurs when current inventories are small relative to expected supplies. For instance, at the end of the old crop year, the price of the futures representing the harvest month for the new crop may be below the current cash price.

In defining a basis, we will usually assume that the cash price pertains to the particular quality, location, and delivery conditions specified in the futures contract. Of course, the cash price for any particular lot of the commodity may vary from the futures price because of quality and location considerations. For instance, the farm price of wheat in a Kansas or Nebraska town differs from the Kansas City price by a transportation and handling differential. Hence, to understand a particular empirical basis, the definition of the cash price used must be carefully compared with the price defined by the futures contract. These alternative definitions of the basis are of interest to the potential hedger for reasons which are explained in the next chapter.

The Supply of Storage

An economically rational merchant will hold inventories only if benefits are expected to equal or exceed the costs of storage between two points in time. The difference between the price for a future delivery month and the current cash price (or between the prices for two delivery months) defines the expected revenue from storage. This difference (the basis) may be defined as the price of storage.[5] It may be positive or negative.[6]

In its simplest form, the supply-of-storage concept states that the price of storage (i.e., the basis) is mainly a function of the size of current inventories.[7]

$$P_f - P_c = f(I),$$

where P_f = current price of a futures contract or, more generally, expected future price;

P_c = current cash price;

I = current level of inventory.

[5]Holbrook Working wrote the fundamental paper on the supply of storage (1949). His empirical research used the difference between the prices of the last old crop and the first new crop futures as the price of storage. Brennan (1958), Cootner (1967), and Weymar (1966) have provided elaborations and extensions of the concept of the supply of storage.

[6]Other terminology includes "carrying charges" and "inverse carrying charges."

[7]The concept refers to the supply of the commodity as inventory, *not* to space available for storage.

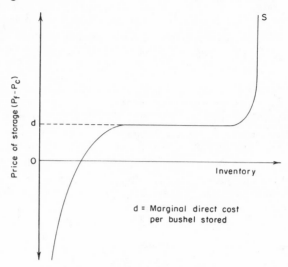

Figure 12-2. Hypothetical supply-of-storage relationship

The relation is analogous to the usual supply function; it may be viewed as derived from the marginal cost of storage. The form of the function (see Figure 12-2) is justified by a broad concept of costs. The direct costs of storage (e.g., the price of warehouse space) are thought to be constant over a fairly wide range of inventories, i.e., the added cost per bushel of additional inventory is approximately constant. However, in principle, inventories could approach the limit of available warehouse space, and at this point the marginal direct cost of storage would increase sharply. For instance, grain stored in inadequate facilities would deteriorate in quality. The supply-of-storage function becomes highly price inelastic as the limit of available space is approached.

Inventories have a convenience yield (Chapter 9), which is treated as a negative cost. The convenience yield is thought to be largest when inventories are smallest and to decline rapidly as inventories increase. At some point, merchants will carry added inventory only if the price difference is expected to cover direct costs; the marginal convenience yield becomes zero. Thus, some inventories are carried even with a negative price of storage, but the function rises rapidly as inventories increase (for additional elaboration see Cootner, 1967, pp. 68–73).[8]

---

[8]The carrying of inventories also involves risks, and the marginal risk factor rises as *unhedged* inventories increase. Thus, the function may not be perfectly horizontal for

Futures Markets: Mechanics and Price Relationships

Weymar (1966) hypothesizes that the price of storage is a function of the expected behavior of inventories over the time interval, say, from now to the delivery month. In other words, if expectations about the size and change in size of inventory over the time interval change, then the price of storage changes (pp. 1228f.).

$$P_f - P_c = f(I^*),$$

where $I^* = $ inventory level expected at a future time.

The level of current inventory is apparently a good proxy variable for expected inventory for seasonally produced commodities harvested over a short time period. Weymar argues that it is not such a good approximation for commodities where harvest is spread substantially through time; he uses the example of cocoa. By implication, the level of *current* inventories may not satisfactorily explain the basis of continuously produced commodities with inventories (e.g., pork bellies).

To this point, the concept of the supply of storage has been emphasized. Theoretically, the equilibrium level of the basis and the size of inventory at a point in time is jointly determined by the supply of and demand for storage. The demand for storage is related to consumption demand. Thus, the demand for storage for a crop year is related to consumption demand for the season and demand for inventory at the end of the season. With the passage of time, the demand-for-storage function shifts. The function shifts especially with changes in production in successive years. Specifically, the demand for storage from period t to period $t + 1$ would increase with an increase in production in period t or with a decrease in production in period $t + 1$. A decrease in production in t or an increase in production in $t + 1$ would reduce the demand for storage (Brennan, 1958, p. 52).

---

moderate and large inventories; Brennan (1958, pp. 54–55) writes the net marginal cost (m) of storage as a function of three components, each a function of the size of inventory. Namely,

$$m = d + r - c,$$

where

$d = $ marginal direct outlay (costs)
$r = $ marginal risk aversion
$c = $ marginal convenience yield.

However, the risk of adverse price movements does not increase on inventories hedged in futures contracts. This raises the question of whether speculators require a "risk premium" to take a position opposite the one held by hedgers. This is a question considered in the next chapter.

Pricing Institutions

Empirical evidence suggests that the supply-of-storage function is stable relative to the demand for storage. Shifts in demand are largely the outcome of exogenous changes in production for the seasonal crop. Thus, a scatter diagram of inventory level and price differences gives an estimate of the supply function,[9] and it is appropriate, at least for a commodity like wheat, to view the price of storage as a function of current inventory (see Brennan, 1958, pp. 63–67).

This theory, in effect, sets an upper limit to the positive price difference—namely, the positive marginal cost of storage. A basis larger than the cost of storage would provide a large incentive to store, and it is just this incentive and consequent competition to acquire stocks which prevents the cash price from dropping below the futures price by more than the cost of storage. (How a grain merchant may use hedging to assure himself of the price difference is illustrated in the next chapter.)

However, there is no theoretical limit to the size of the negative basis. A current shortage of inventory may imply a very high cash price relative to the price of a distant futures contract; consequently, the basis will be a large (absolute value) negative number. Price-support programs can place a practical limit on increases in cash prices (as well as a floor under prices) for some commodities. As prices increase, sales can be made from government-owned stocks accumulated under support programs, and farmers can be encouraged to sell from government-subsidized, farmer-held reserves at certain specified prices. Expectations of release of stocks or of a change in government policy also can affect the relationship between current cash and futures prices.

The theory outlined to this point implies a constellation of prices, including the current cash price and the prices of progressively more distant futures. The *level* of the constellation of prices may change with the passage of time, and the differences (prices of storage) also may change. It is of interest to explore more fully the nature of these changes.

Price Levels and Price Differences

Short-term changes. The constellation of prices at a point in time represents the market's judgment of economic forces influencing prices. With the passage of time, judgments change. New information on current and expected economic conditions becomes available, and market

---

[9]For a fuller discussion of the interpretation of scatter diagrams involving prices and quantities, the reader is referred to the section on "the identification problem" in Chapter 15.

participants are continually evaluating information. Thus, prices of futures contracts change from moment to moment based on revised expectations.

Since new information influencing price tends to occur randomly, price *changes* appear to be nearly random. Indeed, in a perfect market, price changes would be random (Working, 1958; Samuelson, 1965). But markets are not perfect. Market participants do not receive perfect information; they may not have equal access to existing information; different individuals react in different ways to new information. Thus, new information is not likely to cause a single once-and-for-all change in the price of a particular commodity; rather, the effect is likely to be distributed through time as a series of price adjustments. That is, one may hypothesize that a price series will have some correlation with itself through time; this is called autocorrelation.[10]

Nonetheless, actual markets may adjust rapidly to new information, so that day-to-day changes in prices could be random. On the other hand, a dramatic change in information may cause a large change in the price, and this impact may be spread over several days. This could be the consequence of market rules that limit the size of a price change from one day to the next. For example, if trading must be suspended after a price change of 10 cents per bushel, then several days may be required to work out a large change in expectations. Or, autocorrelation may occur as the "natural" process of adjustment in an imperfect market.

A common hypothesis is that futures prices tend to overreact to new information. For instance, "bullish" news is thought to cause price rises not warranted by the information; hence, prices subsequently decline to the warranted level. This type of behavior is sometimes called "price reaction." It implies negative autocorrelations in a futures price series: price increases followed by decreases, or decreases followed by increases. An initial under-reaction to new information with gradual adjustment to the warranted level is sometimes called "price continuity." Price continuity implies positive autocorrelations in a price series.

Empirical analyses of futures prices have produced mixed results (e.g., Cargill and Rausser, 1972; Mann and Heifner, 1976; Working, 1967; Labys and Granger, 1970; and references therein). Unfortunately the results seem to depend, in part, on the particular statistical method used, but a few generalizations are possible. If one uses changes in daily closing prices, there often is evidence of significant, though small, au-

---

[10]This simply means that price in time t is correlated with price in time $t + j$, where $j = 1, 2$, etc.

tocorrelations. Both positive and negative autocorrelations have been found, and there does not appear to be a pervasive tendency toward price reaction (Brinegar, 1970).

Large transactions cause temporary dips and bulges in prices on futures markets. For instance, a large selling hedge tends to depress price. The size of the price effect depends on the size of the transaction relative to the liquidity of the market, which illustrates the economic importance of speculation. A scalper makes his profit from small price changes. For example, a scalper may take the opposite side of a large selling hedge for one-fourth cent less than the previous price. He hopes to resell the contracts gradually at the original or higher prices. The scalper, while making a profit on dips and bulges in price, is providing the service of temporally distributing the impact of a large transaction. It is this type of liquidity which minimizes the transactions cost (the price effect) of a large hedge (Gray, 1967; Working, 1967).

The level of the constellation of prices is more variable through time than the price differences (Working, 1942 and 1949). The prices for different delivery months tend to move up and down together; minor changes in the differences occur with changes in the cost of storage or in expectations about future inventories. New information which affects cash and near futures tends to influence more distant futures by an equivalent amount. The parallel movement of prices in different delivery months is demonstrated in Figure 12-3. If traders, for example, anticipate a dock strike which is likely to reduce the demand for grain, this will tend to depress both distant and nearby futures since the different delivery months are linked by inventories.

There is a close, but not a perfect, relationship among the constellation of prices. New information about the level of inventories, rates of use out of inventory, possible quality deterioration of inventory, and so forth, may influence the price differences. Working (1942, p. 44) writes: "Variations from week to week in the relations between prices . . . appear mainly attributable to changes in the market estimate of the marginal cost of carrying." Further, as the price for the July future in the current year expires and the price for the next July future is established, the new price relationship may involve a substantial change in the price of storage (from one year to the next). This is a topic for the next subsection.

In sum, we started with a model of seasonal price variability and of "fixed" futures prices associated with perfect knowledge (Figure 12-1). However, knowledge is not perfect, and the level of this constellation of

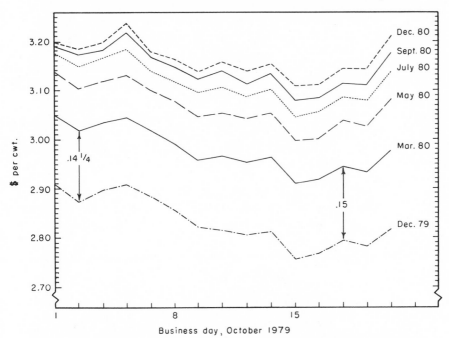

Figure 12-3. Closing prices of corn futures contracts, Chicago Board of Trade, October 1-19, 1979

prices moves up and down through time with changing information.[11] Since changes in factors influencing price occur somewhat randomly through time, a time-series sequence of futures prices has the superficial appearance of a "random walk."[12] Nonetheless, such time-series data have systematic components. The differences between prices of successive delivery months (the prices of storage) are a function of the size of inventories. These differences tend to be stable relative to price level changes.

Year-to-year changes. The foregoing discussion emphasizes the

[11]Whether or not futures prices are unbiased estimates of cash prices in the subsequent delivery month is a controversial question and is considered in the next chapter. Loosely speaking, the question is whether or not the average of past futures prices for a contract equals the average cash price for that delivery month.

[12]If price changes are serially independent and have no trend, the price series form a random walk. Actual price series sometimes produce patterns that resemble a random walk, though chart traders believe that graphs have predictive significance. As suggested in the text, some evidence of autocorrelation in price series does exist.

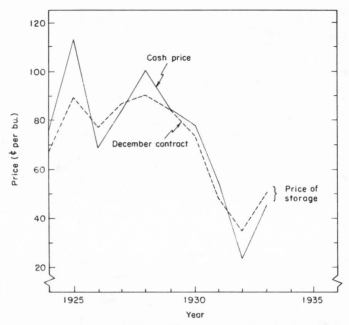

Figure 12-4. Closing prices of May and December corn futures, Chicago Board of Trade, May 15, 1924-1933. Cash price is price of current May future on May 15; price of a contract near its expiration is essentially a cash price. Data from Annual Reports of the Chicago Board of Trade.

character of short-term price behavior. One must be cautious in extending these results to longer time periods, especially the relationship between current price and the price of futures for delivery in the next crop year. Prices of all delivery months do tend to move in a parallel fashion from year to year in response to changes in demand and supply (Chapter 9), but the basis also may change from year to year. It can be positive in some years and negative in others. A small current inventory relative to the prospective crop usually is associated with a negative basis, whereas a relatively large current inventory will generally lead to a positive basis. The contrast between years in which there is a positive and a negative basis is shown in Figure 12-4. This shows the price on May 15 for the May and December corn futures for the years 1924 through 1933.[13] The price of the May futures is essentially a cash price since it falls near the

[13]The years 1924-1933 are used to avoid the large influence of recent price-support programs of the federal government on prices and inventories.

expiration date of the contract. The difference between the two prices is positive in some years and negative in others. The price of May futures in 1925, for example, was well above the price of December futures (a large negative basis or price of storage), whereas in 1932, the price of May futures was below the price of December futures due to the relatively large inventories existing in May 1932.

An empirical consequence of the annually changing carrying charges is that futures prices apparently are somewhat less variable from year to year than cash prices. For instance, observations of the cash price on May 15 and the price of the December futures on May 15 over a period of years reveal that the cash price has a slightly larger variance (Tomek and Gray, 1970). Also, the price of the December future in May tends to be less variable than the cash price in December from year to year. A futures price is not going to be higher than a cash price at any point in time by more than the cost of storage, and in practice, the lowest cash price through time implies the lowest futures price. On the other hand, a small inventory can mean a current cash price very much higher than a futures price in a particular year. In sum, a futures price can never be above a cash price by more than the cost of storage, but no such principle limits the cash price from being above a futures price.

Price Relationships: Other Commodities

Since World War II, futures markets have developed for commodities which are not in the "traditional mold." These commodities don't fall into nice, clear-cut categories, but some classification is useful to illustrate different models of price behavior. Three groups can be distinguished as follows: (1) semiperishable commodities that are produced seasonally, stored within the season but not from one season to the next, such as potatoes; (2) perishable commodities more or less continuously produced, but with some seasonality of production and modest inventories, such as pork bellies; and (3) perishable commodities more or less continuously produced, but with very small stocks, such as fresh eggs. Futures prices for these commodities behave differently in some respects than the prices of commodities that can be stored for longer periods. These distinctions are discussed below.

Intertemporal Price Relationships

One of the principal differences between the behavior of futures prices for the different categories of commodities is the linkage or degree of association between the prices of near and distant delivery

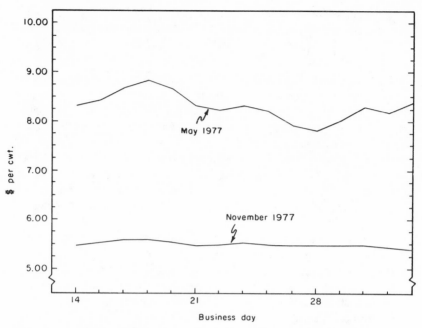

Figure 12-5. Maine potato futures, daily closing prices for May and November contracts, three weeks in March 1977

months. For commodities with continuous inventories, like corn, changes in daily prices for both near and distant contracts tend to move together (Figure 12-3), but this is less true for commodities where nearby and distant futures are not closely linked by inventories. Potatoes provide a special case of a commodity without an inventory linkage between crop years, and hence changes in daily prices for contracts maturing in different crop years have little or no correlation (Figure 12-5). Note in this figure that the November futures price in March 1977 was much more stable than the May futures price. The November futures price presumably reflected conditions expected to prevail at the time of harvest for the next crop, while the May futures was strongly influenced by the size of stocks remaining from the preceding harvest.[14]

[14]Within a crop year, the prices of the various potato contracts are linked by inventories, and price differences can be viewed as prices of storage. However, the cost of storage is more difficult to estimate for potatoes than for the grains. An important cost is the spoilage and shrinkage while potatoes are in storage; hence, cost depends on the amount of loss and the value of the loss. With a small crop and a high price, the cost of a given quantity loss is larger than with a low price. Thus, the price of storage for potatoes varies inversely with the size of crop.

Futures Markets: Mechanics and Price Relationships

Price linkages between futures prices for most nonstorables, such as live cattle, represent an intermediate position between the corn and potato examples. Daily prices for different cattle contracts tend to move in the same direction; however price differences, even between nearby contracts, are less stable for cattle than for corn, and the correlation between the near futures contract and the subsequent contracts decreases as the time interval between contracts lengthens. Some of these characteristics are illustrated in Figure 12-6, which shows the daily closing prices in March 1979 for the nearby (April) and a more distant (June) futures for live cattle. The difference between the two prices widened during March although day-to-day changes were highly correlated. Expectations were changing about the supplies of cattle available

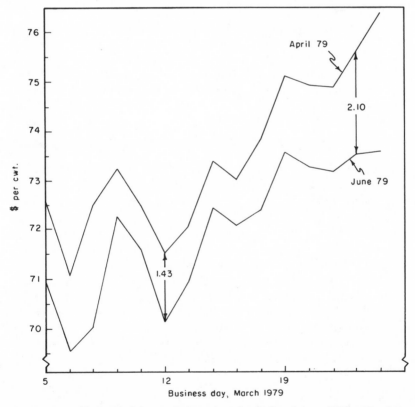

Figure 12-6. Live cattle futures, closing prices for April and June 1979 contracts in March 1979. Data from the Chicago Mercantile Exchange, *1978-1979 Yearbook.*

247

for immediate delivery relative to supplies available by June, thus depressing the price of the June contract relative to the April contract.

Producers of nonstorables, almost by definition, have limited flexibility in their production and marketing decisions. In the very short run, cattle feeders may be able to defer marketings a few days or weeks; in the intermediate run, feeding programs can be altered, for example, by using more roughage and less grain; for the longer run, female animals may be withheld from feedlots for breeding purposes. It is for these reasons that the prices of live cattle futures (which require the delivery of grain-fed steers) are interrelated. All futures prices for cattle are influenced by factors like changes in the price of corn, soybeans, and feeder calves, but prices for distant contracts respond more to anticipated changes in future supplies, while prices for near contracts reflect current economic conditions. Thus, there is more scope for the independent movement of nearby and distant futures for nonstorables like cattle than for storable commodities like corn.

Empirical analysis of prices for live cattle futures by Leuthold (1979) is consistent with the foregoing observations. His analysis indicates that, given the current cash price, the prices of forthcoming futures are a function mainly of the expected supply of fed cattle in the particular delivery month being analyzed.

Distant cattle futures prices also are related to the current cash price of feeder cattle placed in feedlots. The difference between these two prices is analogous to the price of storage, but in this case the difference is determined by the cost of feeding cattle. The relationship is somewhat more complex for cattle than for grain, because steers are being transformed into finished full-fed steers. The cost involved is that of feeding cattle instead of carrying an inventory. Paul and Wesson (1967) and Ehrich (1969) analyze price differences, such as $P_f - P_d$, where $P_f =$ current price of a contract for the future delivery of fed cattle and $P_d =$ current price of feeder cattle placements in feedlots.

In a well-functioning market, cash prices and the price of the near futures contract will move in sympathy and converge toward the maturity date of the contract. In theory, the cash and futures prices will be identical in the delivery month (except for any quality and transportation differentials related to defining the cash price). It is, however, relatively difficult to write provisions for the delivery of a nonstorable commodity, and the delivery process for any futures contracts, including the grains, may have imperfections. Moreover, even in a market that is functioning well, there will be some costs in making and taking delivery. Thus, in practice, futures prices at contract maturity have typically been slightly below cash prices for farm commodities. But, with major imperfections in delivery, futures prices can have large premiums or discounts relative to cash prices near the end of the life of a futures contract. For example, if sellers of futures find it very costly to make delivery, they may prefer to buy back the contracts even though futures are at a substantial premium over the cash price. When such imperfections exist, a futures market's effectiveness as a hedging medium is reduced.

Short-Term Price Changes

Daily price changes for any single futures contract tend to have similar characteristics for all commodities; namely, price changes reflect changing information about the forces determining prices. Thus, the "random walk" hypothesis of a perfect market is a benchmark for the analysis of short-term price changes whether one is considering the June contract for live cattle, the December contract for corn, or any other futures contract.

Short-term price changes for different delivery months are likely to be less closely related for perishables than for storables, as we have noted, but also may show a growing variance. Samuelson (1965) hypothesized, using a theoretical model, that the variance of price changes for any (individual) futures contract should increase as the maturity date of the contract approaches. Observed price changes for the grains are not consistent with this hypothesis. The variance of distant futures is about the same as that of nearby futures (Figure 12-3), and there does not appear to be a significant increase in the variance of grain futures over the life of such contracts.

The behavior of daily prices for potato futures, however, is consistent with the Samuelson hypothesis. There is little information about the expected size of the potato crop (or other factors determining price), say, 10 months prior to harvest, and since inventories are not carried from one crop year to the next, prices of the November contract 10 months prior to harvest will not be linked to the current cash prices. Few reasons exist for the prices of the November futures to change in the months prior to the planting of the potato crop, but as the crop is planted, develops, and matures, additional information about the forces determining November prices becomes available. Moreover, this information is likely to change more and more frequently as harvest-time approaches. Hence, daily prices of November futures for potatoes, for example, do tend to show a growing variance as the maturity date approaches if plotted in a manner similar to those shown in Figure 12-5.

For most commodities, one cannot infer from a simple inspection of the data whether or not the variance of prices increases with the life of the contract. Miller (1979) tested this hypothesis for live cattle futures and concluded that the variance of price changes for this commodity did, in fact, increase as the maturity date approached. It seems reasonable to assume that the prices for other perishable products behave in a similar fashion.

Summary

Prices for the different contract maturities for storable commodities are closely linked. Both cash and futures prices are influenced by changes in expected economic conditions. For futures that specify the delivery of nonstorables, the linkage of cash, near futures, and distant futures is less close, but changes in expectations may have some influence on cash prices and clearly influence futures prices.

In any futures market that functions well, the futures price converges to the cash price in the delivery month, and the daily changes in futures prices are essentially a random walk. But markets are not perfect, and at least some minor deviations from the random walk model may be found. Also, futures and cash prices will not be identical at delivery because there are costs in making or taking delivery on a contract.

References

Brennan, Michael J. 1958. "The Supply of Storage," *Am. Econ. Rev.*, 48:50–72.

Brinegar, Claude S. 1970. "A Statistical Analysis of Speculative Price Behavior," *Food Res. Inst. Studies*, 9:1–58 (Supplement).

Cargill, Thomas F., and Gordon C. Rausser. 1972. "Time and Frequency Domain Representations of Futures Prices as a Stochastic Process," *J. Am. Stat. Assoc.*, 67:23–30.

Cootner, Paul H. 1967. "Speculation and Hedging," *Food Res. Inst. Studies*, 7:65–105 (Supplement).

Ehrich, R. L. 1969. "Cash-Futures Price Relationships for Live Beef Cattle," *Am. J. Ag. Econ.*, 51:26–40.

Gold, Gerald. 1975. *Modern Commodity Futures Trading.* 7th ed. New York: Commodity Research Bureau.

Gray, Roger W. 1967. "Price Effects of a Lack of Speculation," *Food Res. Inst. Studies*, 7:177–194 (Supplement).

Irwin, Harold S. 1954. *Evolution of Futures Trading.* Madison, Wis.: Mimir Publishers.

Labys, Walter C., and C. W. J. Granger. 1970. *Speculation, Hedging and Commodity Price Forecasts.* Lexington, Mass.: D. C. Heath and Co.

Leuthold, Raymond M. 1979. "An Analysis of the Futures-Cash Price Basis for Live Beef Cattle," *North Central J. Ag. Econ.*, 1:47–52.

Mann, Jitendar S., and Richard G. Heifner. 1976. *The Distribution of Shortrun Commodity Price Movements.* USDA Tech. Bul. 1536.

Miller, Katherine Dusak. 1979. "The Relation Between Volatility and Maturity in Futures Contracts," in *Commodity Markets and Futures Prices.* Ed. Raymond M. Leuthold. Chicago: Chicago Mercantile Exchange. Pp. 25–36.

Paul, Allen B. 1976. *Treatment of Hedging in Commodity Market Regulation.* USDA Tech. Bul. 1538.

_____, and William T. Wesson. 1967. "Pricing Feedlot Services Through Cattle Futures," *Ag. Econ. Res.*, 19:33–45.

Samuelson, Paul A. 1965. "Proof That Properly Anticipated Prices Fluctuate Randomly," *Ind. Mgt. Rev.*, 6:41–49.

Tomek, William G., and Roger W. Gray. 1970. "Temporal Relationships among Prices on Commodity Futures Markets: Their Allocative and Stabilizing Roles," *Am. J. Ag. Econ.*, 52:372–380.

Weymar, F. Helmut. 1966. "The Supply of Storage Revisited," *Am. Econ. Rev.*, 56:1226–1234.

Working, Holbrook. 1942. "Quotations on Commodity Futures as Price Forecasts," *Econometrica*, 10:39–52.

_____. 1949. "The Theory of the Price of Storage," *Am. Econ. Rev.*, 39:1254–1262.

_____. 1953. "Hedging Reconsidered," *J. Farm Econ.*, 35:544–561.

_____. 1958. "A Theory of Anticipatory Prices," *Am. Econ. Rev.*, 48:188–199.

_____. 1967. "Tests of a Theory Concerning Floor Trading on Commodity Exchanges," *Food Res. Inst. Studies*, 7:5–48 (Supplement).

CHAPTER **13**

Commodity Futures Markets:

Their Functions and Controversies

With the background of Chapter 12, we turn to a discussion of the functions of a futures market. The general function is to facilitate various types of resource allocation through hedging and through the provision of forward prices. Within this context, speculators play a role in facilitating hedging.

Trading in futures contracts has resulted in controversies about, among other things, the influence of futures markets on cash prices received by producers and paid by consumers. We review some of these controversies and such evidence as is available in answering these questions. The chapter closes with brief discussions of price manipulation, regulation, and biases which make some markets unsuccessful.

Functions of Futures Markets

In an uncertain world, economic activity (production, distribution, processing, etc.) has speculative elements. For example, a farmer who commits seed, land, and other resources to wheat production is subject to yield and price risks; there may be a crop failure, and/or price at harvest may be below the costs of the resources committed to the production process. Sometimes economic institutions exist to help shift risk. The farmer, for example, could negotiate a forward contract at planting time to sell the crop at a particular price at harvest time; this shifts the price risk from the farmer to the buyer.

Futures markets are simply a particular kind of forward contracting institution. As we have seen, standardized contracts are traded under well-known rules. If it is functioning well, a futures market is the least-cost way for many firms to enter into and liquidate contracts, and competitive prices are openly established for all to see. Typically futures markets have more integrity than individual forward contracts in cash markets. Gains and losses are taken as they occur in futures markets, while there is more potential for defaults on forward contracts in cash markets in the face of large price changes (Gray, 1976).

Thus, in principle, futures markets provide a low-cost method of hedging decisions taken in cash markets. The objectives of hedging probably include both enhancing profits and shifting risk. In discussing the potential benefits of futures markets, various authors have stressed different functions. Telser and Higinbotham (1977) emphasize the low cost of transactions on organized futures markets, arguing that other benefits could be obtained through forward contracts in cash markets. Historically, many authors have stressed the risk-shifting role of hedging in futures, while Working (1953) has placed greater emphasis on profit enhancement. More recently, using ideas of portfolio theory, analysts have discussed optimal hedges for a firm in terms of the best attainable combination of average profit and risk (Heifner, 1973). In the foregoing context, we examine some specific hedging and speculative uses of futures markets.

Temporal Allocation of Seasonally Produced Commodities

The carrying of inventories of seasonally produced commodities is facilitated by the existence of a futures market and is perhaps the role most emphasized by economists. The accumulation and decumulation of inventories is often accompanied by hedging. In addition, forward cash sales made without inventories on hand are frequently offset by buying hedges (as are forward requirements of processors).

Decisions by grain merchants with respect to inventory carrying and hedging are related to the constellation of prices observed by them. The price of storage is a minimum return which is essentially assured through hedging; it is an incentive or disincentive to store. To illustrate, using a hypothetical example, the merchant might observe on September 1 the following price relationship:

Cash wheat at $3.80 per bushel and

May wheat futures at $4.00 per bushel.

The positive price of storage is 20 cents per bushel, and the merchant may view this price as sufficient for profitable storage. If so, he or she buys wheat and sells an equivalent quantity of May futures contracts.

The initial positive price of storage and the narrowing of the basis through time can provide a 20-cent-per-bushel return for storage. The merchant is, in a sense, "guaranteed" a minimum return of 20 cents per bushel. If, for instance, price is $4.00 per bushel in May (the cash and futures price are identical in the delivery month for identical quality,

253

location, and delivery conditions), then the merchant is able to sell the wheat at a 20-cent increase in the cash price and is able to buy back the futures contracts at no gain or loss. However, this return is not contingent on cash prices rising to $4.00. For example, if price declined to $3.76 in May, then the hedger still gains at least 20 cents per bushel. The final set of transactions is

a cash sale of wheat at $3.76 and

purchase of futures contracts at $3.76.

The 4-cent loss on the cash transaction is offset by a 24-cent gain on the futures market transaction. The direct costs of storage, of course, are constant whether prices move up or down.

In addition, the merchant hopes to sell and, in fact, typically does sell the inventory through private transactions to buyers at cash prices which reflect gains beyond those guaranteed by the hedging transaction. The typical merchant has no intention of holding the inventory, say, through to May to sell on the central market or to make delivery on the futures contracts at the then prevailing price. (However, it is the *potential* to deliver on the contracts which results in the observed price relationships.) Rather, the trader will be alert to various merchandising opportunities to sell wheat at a gain above that implied by the initial basis. This possibility exists because the merchant often has grain of a quality or in a location of special advantage to a particular buyer and the seller.

If the grain merchant is faced with inverse carrying charges, then the incentive is not to store (although, as previously noted, there may be a convenience yield in carrying some inventories). However, the merchant may have an opportunity to make a contract for delivering grain in some future month without having grain in inventory. This forward cash sale can be covered by the purchase of futures contracts—a buying hedge.

For example, a merchant might contract in March to deliver corn in November at $2.70 per bushel, and at the same time offset this forward contract by the purchase of December corn futures at $2.48. If on October 10 the merchant buys corn at $2.50 (to deliver on the forward contract) and sells December futures at $2.40 (to cover the hedge), he has gained 20 cents in the cash transaction and lost 8 cents on the futures market transaction for a gain of 12 cents on the net transaction. These particular figures are hypothetical, but they illustrate the principle that an inverse carrying charge combined with a narrowing basis is an incentive for this type of merchandising transaction (i.e., a buying hedge covering a forward cash sale).

In sum, both positive and negative carrying charges provide incentives for particular types of transactions by grain merchants. The positive carrying charge reflects ample current inventories and an incentive to carry stocks. Negative carrying charges reflect current shortages of stocks relative to forthcoming supplies and a disincentive to carrying stocks, and in addition, there is an incentive for merchants to make forward contracts covered by a buying hedge. Since the trader can take advantage of these price relations through hedging, a futures market is an institutional mechanism which facilitates temporal allocations of seasonally produced commodities.

Risk Aversion

The oversimplified textbook example of pure risk aversion (perhaps more accurately risk shifting) frequently assumes a constant basis. Thus a selling hedge is placed as follows:

Buy cash wheat at $3.80 per bushel and

sell futures contracts at $4.00 per bushel.

Later, the hedge is lifted.

Sell wheat at $3.70 (loss of 10 cents) and

buy futures at $3.90 (gain of 10 cents).

With the constant basis, the loss in the cash market is just offset by the gain in the futures market.

Holbrook Working (1953) has emphasized that most hedging does *not* have the objective of pure risk aversion or pure price insurance. Rather, hedging is a tool which the user hopes to employ in making a profit. The intelligent hedger knows that the basis tends to narrow as the delivery month approaches. This changing basis, which may be positive or negative, may work in favor of or against various hedges. The hedger is unlikely to employ a hedge which has the potential of being unprofitable.

Given the same initial transaction with a positive carrying charge of 20 cents, however, the hedger is protected against a price decline, and a narrowing basis works in favor of the inventory holder. The selling hedge also would assure a gain if prices had increased and the basis had narrowed. For instance, the final offsetting transactions might have been

sell cash wheat at $4.10 (gain of 30 over 3.80) and

buy futures at $4.20 (loss of 20 from 4.00).

Notice that, if the hedge had not been placed, the gain in the cash transaction would have been 30 cents per bushel. Thus, while a selling hedge assures a minimum return from holding inventories with a positive basis, it also precludes larger returns when prices rise. The potential hedger has an incentive to make a judgment about the direction of price changes. The case of rising prices with a selling hedge is an illustration of a "speculative element" of hedging.

Pricing Institutions

The selling hedge, as implied by previous discussion, is less effective with inverse carrying charges. In contrast, the buying hedge works best with inverse carrying charges and provides protection against price increases. A buying hedge precludes potential profits if price declines, and it is not an effective hedge with positive carrying charges. The student should develop examples of these various alternatives to more fully understand the applicability of the buying hedge under alternate situations.

The basis often remains fairly constant over short time periods, and a hedge can be placed purely as insurance against an adverse price movement over a short time span, even if the basis is adverse. Working's argument is that the *typical* motive for hedging is not pure price insurance. The placement of a hedge depends on (1) the purpose of the hedge in relation to (2) the size of the basis and (3), to some extent, the expected movement of the constellation of all prices. An inverse carrying charge implies that the cash price will eventually decline relative to the distant future and a positive basis implies the opposite.

The ability of a hedge to achieve its purpose depends, in part, on the degree of association between the cash and futures prices involved in the transactions. Assuming the same quality, location, and delivery conditions for the cash commodity as specified in the futures contract, the two price series move up and down together in a closely related fashion with the basis narrowing as the delivery month approaches. However, the hedger may have grain of a different quality or in a different location such that the cash and future prices are less closely related. This implies a less perfect hedge which may work in favor of or against the hedger. He or she may, as previously implied, be able to take advantage of the imperfections by completing the hedge on more favorable terms than suggested by the initial basis.

A hedge may be less than perfect also because futures contracts specify the delivery of fixed quantities (say, 5,000 bushels per contract) which may differ somewhat from the quantities involved in the cash transactions. In addition, the typical hedging example assumes that the hedge can be placed and lifted at two points in time. In practice, the purchase of grain and the sale of futures contracts and the subsequent offsetting transactions may not precisely coincide. Thus, the usual textbook examples oversimplify the real situation.

Operational and Margin Hedging

Processors and other purchasers of farm commodities may use futures markets as a part of their business operations. For example, a flour miller may buy wheat without having offsetting forward flour sales. Thus, the firm may temporarily sell wheat futures contracts; eventually, the miller hopes to cover the wheat inventory with forward flour sales and then lift the hedge on the wheat inventory. Or, the miller may make a forward flour sale without having a wheat inventory. This forward sale can be covered by the purchase of wheat contracts. Covering forward flour sales with purchases of wheat contracts assumes flour and wheat prices are closely related, which they are.

Soybean processors can, in principle, hedge their processing margins directly because futures contracts exist for whole soybeans, soybean oil, and soybean meal. A 60-pound bushel of beans is processed into about 48 pounds of meal, about 11 pounds of oil, and approximately one pound of waste (these numbers are rounded to simplify computations). If a processor bought beans at $6.50 per bushel and sold meal at $180 per ton (9 cents per pound) and oil at 25 cents per pound, then the gross margin would be 57 cents per bushel.[1] Clearly, the possibility exists for a soybean processor to hedge stocks of beans in bean contracts or, by the sale of oil and meal contracts, to buy bean contracts and sell oil and meal contracts in anticipation of subsequent purchase and processing of beans, and so forth. In other words, the processor has a chance, through hedging, to "fix" the gross processing margin.[2]

These potential uses of the futures market further illustrate Working's definition of a hedge in futures as a temporary substitute for a later transaction in the cash market.

Price Discovery and Forward Pricing

A principal justification for futures trading for the seasonally produced, continuously held commodity has been, and is, the hedging of stock carrying, exporting, and processing activities. Price discovery can be viewed as essentially a by-product of the main function of inventory-hedging markets. The views of many buyers and sellers are focused on a single market. They have diverse objectives in terms of hedging and

[1] 48 lb. × 9 cents = $4.32 for meal
11 lb. × 25 cents = 2.75 for oil
total value = 7.07 per bushel
cost of beans = 6.50 per bushel
gross margin = 0.57.

[2] Meal and oil prices sometimes are not high enough relative to bean prices to cover processing costs. Apparently, losses in processing have been more than covered by gains from holding stocks of beans—the inventory has been an asset which has typically increased in value (for more detail see Paul, 1966). Henry Arthur (1971) provides further discussion of business uses of futures.

speculation, but the process leads to a continual appraisal of price-making forces. This might be viewed as a complementary function of inventory-hedging markets.

Price discovery and forward pricing are especially important in such markets as those dealing with fresh eggs, live cattle, and iced broilers. The carrying of inventories is of little or no importance; hence, these markets might be termed forward-pricing markets.

The forward-pricing function of futures markets is potentially useful both to sellers and buyers. Farmers might use futures prices as a guide to production decisions. Current prices for futures contracts may be treated as predictors of delivery-month prices and might be useful measures of expected prices in supply analysis (Gardner, 1976). Thus, farmers and others may use futures prices as guides to delivery-time prices even if they do not hedge (Helmuth, 1977).

But, if a firm wants to assure itself of a particular (existing) price, a hedge is required. A farmer can "lock in" a particular price during the growing season by selling futures. Subsequently, when the crop is harvested and sold, the futures position is offset. Likewise, a processor can hedge ingredient requirements by buying futures now in anticipation of raw commodity needs. When the commodity is actually purchased, the futures position is offset by a sale. This is sometimes called an anticipatory hedge.

Hedges, however, do not assure an exact price, and profits may be foregone by hedging. The sale (or purchase) price assured by the hedge equals the futures price minus the firm's basis (the difference between the futures and cash prices based on the actual cash price received by the firm), but at the time the hedge is placed the basis is not known with certainty. To illustrate, a corn grower might sell December futures in June at $3.00 per bushel assuming the harvest-time basis will be $0.20. This implies an expected return to the grower of $2.80 per bushel.[3] If, however, the actual basis at harvest is $0.25, then the actual return is $2.75. Since basis variability is usually much smaller than price-level variability, hedging does assure an approximate return, but it is extremely important for the person hedging to know the behavior of the basis relevant for the hedging decision (Tomek, 1978).

There also is a speculative element in hedging in the sense that profits

[3]The hedge is initiated by selling futures at $3.00. If the price level subsequently declined to $2.60, then futures would be purchased at harvest for a $0.40 gain in the futures transaction. But, given a $0.20 basis, the farmer would be selling corn in the cash market at $2.40 per bushel, and the return to the grower is $2.80 (the cash sale at $2.40 plus the $0.40 return on the futures transactions).

may be foregone (as well as losses prevented). If a farmer has placed a selling hedge and if prices rise subsequently, then the hedge has prevented the farmer from benefiting from the higher price. Or, if a processor has locked in a procurement price via a buying hedge, this negates the possibility of benefiting from a subsequent decline in price.

Thus, a critical question is whether or not to enter into a selling (or buying) hedge. A futures market provides great flexibility in the timing of forward sales or purchases. One need not wait until the end of the production period to sell; sales can be made at any time, and these sales can be spread over time. But this does not tell the potential trader when to buy and sell.

Most firms hedge selectively, not routinely. An obvious rule is that a firm does not want to lock in a loss by hedging. Hedges will normally be placed only at futures prices that, when the relevant basis is subtracted, will cover costs. Thus, the costs of production and marketing are a benchmark in selective hedging.

Government price-support programs are another consideration in selective hedges for some farm commodities. If prices are at or near the support level, then no down-side price risk exists—prices will either stay the same or go higher—and hence there is little incentive for a farmer to place a selling hedge. On the other hand, a processor realizes that prices cannot go much lower and may want to assure this low procurement price via a buying hedge.

Still another factor in making decisions about hedging is expectations about price changes over the period the hedge will be held. If prices are trending upward, a farmer considering a selling hedge would not want to lock in a price until the higher price level is reached. But this clearly involves speculative judgments. If a farmer does not hedge now in the hope of selling at a still higher price later, the danger exists that prices will collapse and the opportunity of assuring a profitable price will be missed.

The timing of the placement and lifting of hedges is a difficult problem. Large firms often have research departments which assist with these decisions. They may develop quantitative models (such as those discussed in Chapters 15 and 16) which help predict, say, the seasonal low price. If and when this price is reached in the futures market, the firm can assure it via a hedge. But many small firms—particularly farmers—do not have access to such information.

Some analysts recommend the use of relatively simple trend-following methods to aid in hedging decisions (e.g., Franzmann and Lehenbauer, 1979). These methods, conservatively used, may help identify short-term trends in prices and thereby aid the decision maker in placing and lifting hedges. A danger exists, however, that the methods will be misused. A moving-average technique, for example, may suggest the initiation of a selling hedge on one day and then provide a buy signal just a few days later. "In-and-out" trading is speculation on price changes, and speculative profits, if any, can be offset by the commissions involved in frequent trades. Indeed, while trend-following methods are widely used, they are controversial. A futures market, in the aggregate, provides zero returns to traders; total losses must equal total gains.

Systematic Components in Hedging Positions

If the main justification for futures trading rests with hedging use (i.e., if futures trading is not just a game with random trades), then hedging open interest should be related to the pattern of economic activity in the cash market. For example, grain exports from the United States trended upward in the 1960s and 1970s, and this implies that long hedging should have increased. And indeed it did. Based on the reports of large traders, the open interest of long hedgers in wheat on the Chicago Board of Trade averaged 16.1 million bushels per month in 1965–1966, 22.1 in 1970–1971, and 74.5 in 1977–1978.

With seasonally produced crops with large inventories immediately after harvest, short hedging tends to be large, and as inventories decline seasonally, short hedge positions also decline (e.g., Paul *et al.*, 1979). Of course, firms hedge for many reasons. Hedge positions in the wheat market are held by a combination of growers, storage operators, millers, exporters, and others. This can lead to complex patterns of hedging use. Little empirical analysis has been done on the demand for hedging. An exception is a study of short and long hedging of soybeans by Rutledge (1972).

The Role of Speculators—Some Further Comments

Speculators, in a sense, provide two types of liquidity. As we have just observed, particular types of hedging are related to patterns of behavior in the cash market, and hence it is unrealistic to expect short hedging to be completely offset by long hedging. When short hedging is seasonally large, this must necessarily be offset in large part by long speculation. Further, it is unrealistic to expect a potential long hedger to enter the market at precisely the same moment as a potential short hedger, nor are their hedges likely to be of the same size. Hence, traders who take the opposite side of such hedges are needed. In a well-developed market, these traders are primarily professional speculators.

Futures Markets: Functions and Controversies

The objective of the speculator is, of course, to make a profit. The decision to buy or to sell is based on expectations about the forthcoming movements of price—in a rather general sense, a forecast. However, some evidence suggests that a significant proportion of speculation is not based on formal forecasts of longer-term price level changes (Working, 1967). Rather, speculation tends to respond directly to the (small) price changes implied by the placement of hedges. The position taken by scalpers is essentially that the current market-determined price is correct, that a large transaction (usually a hedge) can cause a deviation from this price, but that price will return to its previous level. Thus, for example, a scalper may buy on a ¼-cent price decline, hoping to resell the contracts, perhaps a few at a time, at higher prices over the next few minutes. This speculator is providing liquidity and is temporally spreading the effects of a large transaction.

Clearly, the market price can show "trends" of a few minutes, days, or weeks. A speculator trading on a minute-to-minute basis must be proficient in recognizing the longer trends to cut losses quickly when necessary. Hopefully, gains and losses from longer trends will balance for the scalper. In a well-developed market, professional speculators tend to specialize in particular types of activities. Working (1967, pp. 17f.) classifies scalpers as (1) those who devote attention primarily to the smallest dips and bulges, (2) day traders who give most of their attention to dips and bulges of more than unit size, yet occurring fairly often within a day, and (3) day-to-day scalpers who give attention to price changes of such size and duration that positions are carried through several days. Working concludes, "it must be largely, if not almost wholly, scalping that contributes to the fluidity of the market" (p. 19).

Some speculators, of course, are trading on expectations of price changes over a longer time period. These traders contribute less to market liquidity, but they help in the continual appraisal of factors influencing price. These traders take positions based on new information or the re-evaluation of old information.

Some people seem to believe that speculators are free to drive prices up (to the detriment of consumers) or to drive prices down (to the detriment of farmers), getting rich in the process. A large speculator may on occasion attempt to "corner the market" (see subsequent section) and influence price; this is illegal and a relatively infrequent occurrence. Futures prices are typically the outcome of numerous transactions by many buyers and sellers and hence represent a collective evaluation of market forces. Since futures markets have zero sum returns (gains equal losses), not all traders are getting rich on futures markets. The evidence (Hieronymus, n.d.; Stewart, 1949; Wise, 1962) suggests that small, nonprofessional speculators are, on balance, losers. A study of 462 speculator customers of a large commission firm for one year found that 164 made profits totaling $462,123, while 298 lost a total of $1,127,355. However, regular traders, as defined in the study, did better than the occasional traders (Hieronymus, pp. 7–8). It seems likely that professional speculators and perhaps hedgers are gainers. This is their vocation. They are likely to be better informed and can place more "timely" trades than the nonprofessional.[4]

One other class of speculator deserves comment, namely, the "spreader." These are often professional speculators who place offsetting transactions in different futures contracts. These positions are based on the supposition that the price difference between the two contracts will change. These differences, as previously discussed, tend to be more stable, at least in inventory-hedging markets, than price-level changes. The interdelivery spread (the price of storage) is related to the size of inventories. The intermarket spread, say, between wheat contracts in Minneapolis and in Chicago is related to space (transfer costs) and quality differences. The intergrain spread, say, between oats and corn contracts is a function of the substitutability between the two grains. If the price spreads are viewed as functions of certain economic variables, then the spreader by trying to recognize potential profit opportunities from changes in price differences plays the role of keeping the price differences consistent with prevailing economic conditions—that is, in "normal" alignment.

In addition, spread positions are held by scalpers in the course of their trading, and a position trader may spread to another contract to "hold" a profit. For instance, if a trader is long March contracts and if he has a profit from a price rise but does not wish to take it by selling, perhaps because of tax considerations, then he or she may sell May futures. The prices of March and May futures, of course, tend to move together; hence, with a spread position, the gains in one contract tend to be offset by losses in the other. It is in this sense that a spread may hold a profit.

In sum, speculators enter a futures market to make a profit, although many do not. One consequence is an increase in market liquidity, which assists hedgers. In addition, speculators contribute to the process of price discovery.

---

[4]If the small speculator faces a high probability of loss, why does such speculation continue? This question is considered in a subsequent section of this chapter.

Some Theoretical and Empirical Issues

To this point, we have presented a majority viewpoint, among professional economists, of the "facts" of futures trading; we now turn to a few of the controversies.

Risk Premiums and the Supply of Speculative Services

Until the 1950s, economists tended to view hedgers as purchasers of price insurance from speculators (in contrast to the emphasis in this book). Grain merchants were thought to hedge inventories solely as protection against price declines. Speculators were presumably induced into taking long positions (against the short hedges) by some clear indication of a positive return. If hedgers are typically short and speculators are typically long, then positive return to speculators must come from an increase in price through time to the maturity date of the contract. In other words, hedgers "pay" speculators to absorb a price risk (on the average), and it is this risk premium that attracts a supply of speculative services to the market. If this view is correct, then futures prices are *not* unbiased estimates of forthcoming cash prices but are biased downward to induce speculators to take long positions (as shown in Figure 13-1).

Keynes (1923) and Hardy (1923) apparently were the first to discuss the issue. Keynes believed that speculators received positive returns;

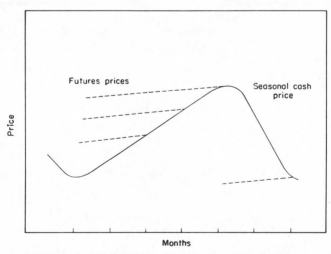

Figure 13-1. Hypothetical biased relationship of futures prices to cash prices under the assumption of a risk premium

Hardy (p. 225) states, "it [that hedgers pay speculators] does not seem probable." Considerable empirical research has been devoted to the question of the existence of a risk premium. The majority view is that a risk premium is nonexistent (Dusak, 1973; Gray, 1961; Rockwell, 1967; Telser, 1967), but several researchers (Cootner, 1967; Houthakker, 1957) believe that a small positive risk premium does exist.

If a risk premium is not transferred, if the majority of speculators are losers, and if hedgers are not hedging purely against price declines, then what induces speculation? Successful speculators are, by definition, persons who make a profit on speculation. However, they are a minority of the total number of speculators, and their profits do not necessarily come from a risk premium. As previously discussed, profits are a return for providing liquidity (Working, 1967). But some professional speculators presumably are successful in forecasting price-level or price-difference changes, and this implies that some professional speculators have developed special skills in making certain types of forecasts.[5]

While the avocational amateur speculator typically is a loser, there is a possibility of making a large gain, and the amateur speculator may gain pleasure from the process of speculation. "To these amateurs speculation represents a 'good' for which they are willing to pay and not a 'bad' for which they must be paid to undertake. The losses of speculation, if any, are made up by other sources of income. Amateurs who cannot sustain the losses and who leave the market are replaced by others; a rapid turnover of amateurs is compatible with the maintenance of a large stock of them. Thus to the amateurs speculation in commodities is comparable to the purchase of a lottery ticket which has a small probability of a large gain" (Telser, 1967, p. 132).

Influence of Futures Trading on Cash Prices

The public, as represented by the Congress of the United States, seem to believe that trading futures contracts "adversely" influences cash prices.[6] This belief has taken many forms. Futures trading is thought to influence the *level* of cash prices. Thus, high wheat prices in 1947 were blamed on futures trading (Wise, 1962), but, on the other

[5]The issue under discussion has in fact been stated in terms of a forecasting problem (see Houthakker, 1957; Rockwell, 1967). In reviewing the literature, the reader should be reminded that Keynes' term "normal backwardation" is analogous to the concept of an inverse carrying charge; however, he viewed this carrying charge as including a risk premium.

[6]For example, trading in onion futures was declared illegal by an act of the Congress in 1958. Of course, such laws tend to reflect the views of certain special-interest groups (e.g.,

hand, relatively low potato prices in Maine also were thought to be due to futures trading (Bagnell, 1963). Further, futures trading, some argue, increases the *frequency* and *magnitude* of the variation of cash prices.

Before discussing specific allegations, it is useful to try to put them in a general perspective. First, cash and futures prices in inventory-hedging markets are highly correlated. Also, cash prices and futures prices for nearby delivery months in forward-pricing markets are related. However, current cash prices and prices for distant futures in forward-pricing markets are not closely related. We have discussed theoretical reasons for these various levels of correlation. In other words, logical reasons exist for the correlations in futures and cash prices, and this does not somehow imply that these prices are inconsistent with existing economic conditions.

Second, where high correlations exist, the allegations imply that cash prices would behave differently without the institution of a futures market and that this behavior would in some sense be "better" without futures trading. The source of adverse price behavior is alleged to be excess speculation in futures. Clearly there are difficult problems involved in judging performance. What is "adverse" price behavior? If it can be identified, is its source in the futures market? If so, would the different behavior be "better" or "worse" than the alternative behavior? What is "excess speculation"?

Third, in analyzing the effects of speculation on price behavior, a distinction should be made between ordinary speculative activity and deliberate manipulation. This suggests two questions: to what extent is the manipulation of prices on futures markets a problem, and if no manipulation exists, does the existence of a futures market inject artificial influences into price behavior? With respect to the latter question, one may argue that ill-informed traders contribute to unwarranted price changes and that futures markets contribute to the supply of poorly informed traders, or one may hypothesize that the existence of futures markets increases the availability and distribution of information and on balance improves the evaluation of the information. Stated another way, speculation in futures may help anticipate needed price adjustments in the light of new information, or it may result in unneeded price changes. Whether or not price responses in futures markets are appropriate should be answerable by empirical analysis, but in practice, such analyses are difficult. We turn now to some specific questions.

---

onion growers) rather than those of the general public. The public image of futures markets is in contrast to the views of most professional economists, who typically argue that such markets serve useful purposes.

Pricing Institutions

Does trading in futures contracts influence the level of annual average prices? In other words, would these commodity prices be significantly higher (or lower) without futures trading? Logically, the answer is no. A futures market is a price-discovery mechanism interpreting economic forces; it is these forces which determine the level of price. But like any other pricing mechanism, a futures market's "unbiasedness" depends on a lack of market imperfections. High-quality information about price-making forces should minimize bias, and even if unwarranted prices occur over short periods of time, they may balance out on average so that the annual average price is appropriate. However, a few futures markets have had persistent price biases (see below).

Does trading in futures contracts increase the magnitude of the variance of annual cash prices? The variability of prices from year to year, as we have seen, depends on the magnitude of shifts in supply and demand and on the slopes of these functions. Thus, for instance, the large variability of onion prices (for which no futures trading now exists) is mainly a function of a highly price inelastic demand and variable supplies. Futures markets may, in some instances, help stabilize production by providing relatively stable forward prices that can be assured by hedging. In addition, available evidence (see previous chapter) suggests futures prices tend to have smaller annual variances than cash prices. The influence of futures markets on annual variability of cash prices, if any, would seem to be in the direction of reducing them.

Does trading in futures contracts influence the variance of seasonal price patterns? There is some logic and evidence which implies that futures trading reduces the variability of seasonal price fluctuations. Futures trading, through its inventory-hedging function, should contribute to an "optimal" distribution of a seasonally produced commodity through the marketing year. Hedging by reducing the price risk of carrying inventories in a sense reduces the costs of storage. One may hypothesize that without futures trading "too little" of the commodity would be stored with consequent lower prices at harvest and higher prices at the end of the storage period.

Does futures trading influence the short-run behavior of cash prices? This is perhaps the most important question of the ones posed. Diverse answers have been obtained, depending on the markets and time periods studied and on the statistical techniques applied. Several analyses of weekly cash prices have found that the variability of the random component decreased after futures trading was instituted (Powers, 1970; Cox, 1976). We were not able to reproduce Cox's results for cattle and hog prices, however, using a longer time period after the start of futures trading.

Nathan Associates (1967) studied daily price changes for soybeans in conjunction with information about the types of traders in the market. Liquidity and a good balance between the demand for short and long positions appear to contribute to stable daily prices. Day-to-day price changes were relatively small when the percentage of total volume attributed to scalpers was relatively large (p. 88). On the other hand, a lack of market balance and of the liquidity provided by scalpers helps explain day-to-day price changes (for more detail see pp. 84–89).[7] The type of speculator in the market influences the level of price stability.

Speculators are more likely to be active in markets in which prices are moving sharply up or down than in stable markets. Thus, the volume of trading is usually correlated with the magnitude of price changes, but the effect of increased trading activity could result in damping down price fluctuations rather than accentuating them. In a study of potato futures, Paul *et al.* (1979) found that, while the volume of trading in the May contract increased relative to the other delivery months, the variability of price changes for the May contract increased less than for the other months. Working's theory of floor trading (1967) implies that hedging typically attracts the volume of speculation required to provide adequate liquidity.

Regulation and Price Manipulation

The Commodity Futures Trading Commission (CFTC) is the federal regulatory agency for futures markets in the United States. It is concerned with fraud and manipulation and requires that markets protect the public with adequate rules; it also registers firms that buy and sell contracts on behalf of others and requires that such firms meet certain financial requirements. In addition, each exchange has a set of by-laws or regulations which cover the operations of members of the exchange.

While there is relatively little fraud, some inevitably does exist. Manipulation of prices can be conveniently categorized into two parts: man-

---

[7]The study cited defines day-to-day price change as the difference between the closing and opening prices. The empirical analysis is for the prices of the May 1961 soybean contract in Chicago in February and March 1961. This was a period in which the Commodity Exchange Authority (now the Commodity Futures Trading Commission) collected daily reports on the classification of reporting traders and other daily data. The concept of "market balance" can be approached in several ways. One is the approximate equality of the ratios long hedging/short hedging and short speculation/long speculation. These ratios typically are below one because short hedging and long speculation tend to dominate futures markets. Values between zero and 2.5 have been observed. The concept of a "thin market" may be defined by the ratio volume traded/open interest. The market is thin when the ratio is small.

ipulation during the life of the contract and manipulation at the expiration of a contract. It is relatively difficult and costly to manipulate prices in an active market during most of its life. When a market has a large volume, then by definition large financial resources are required to undertake sufficient trades to influence prices. Moreover, if a trader is successful in moving price in one direction, the price is likely to move back to the original position as the trader attempts to take "profits" via offsetting transactions. The trader also will have incurred some costs in placing the transactions. It is alleged, however, that three or four very large traders were successful in running up the price of silver contracts in 1979 (Maidenberg, 1979).

Manipulation near the expiration of a contract is relatively easier because of the potential costs of making or taking delivery. The classic attempt to "corner" a market involves one or more traders taking large long positions in futures contracts for a particular month while simultaneously having control of the physical supplies which could be delivered to fulfill these contracts. Thus, the manipulator is in a position to force prices up as sellers of futures attempt to cover their positions by buying or as they attempt to obtain the commodity to deliver on the contracts.

A more subtle squeeze or corner can occur when traders observe that it will be costly for sellers of futures to make delivery on a particular contract. In this case, the holders of long positions do not formally control the deliverable supplies, but they can force sellers to buy back their contracts at prices that are high relative to those in the cash market. The reverse also can occur. Sellers of futures may have ample deliverable supplies well positioned for delivery and at the same time buyers of futures may find it costly to take delivery. As a consequence, some large price movements can occur in futures in the last day or two of the life of the contract, and the price difference between the futures and cash markets may be unusually large. The difference, in effect, reflects the costs of making and taking delivery, and in some instances large imperfections may exist in the delivery mechanism. From a legal viewpoint, these pricing aberrations may not be fraud, but hedgers and amateur speculators should avoid holding positions in futures near the close of the contract.

A "bear raid" involves manipulative selling to force down a futures price. In this case, the manipulator presumably has identified a situation in which his or her selling can precipitate a price decline. For instance, traders holding long positions may have stop-loss orders under their contracts, and a small price decrease may set off a wave of sales that lowers prices still further. If this occurs, then the manipulator is able to cover his or her initial sales with purchases at lower prices.

What Makes a Futures Market Successful?

A successful market is one that meets an economic need, an attribute which often is measured indirectly by volume of trading. Many years ago economists argued that the commodity should be seasonally produced and storable for it to be traded on futures markets. Presumably the major economic justification in this case was considered to be the hedging of inventories. It is now clear, however, that many other types of hedging are feasible and useful.

There appear to be at least two conditions necessary, though not necessarily sufficient, for a futures market to be successful: technical feasibility and economic need. Technical feasibility involves writing contract terms (remember contracts for a particular market are homogeneous) that do not give special advantages either to buyers or sellers. As implied in the previous section, it is important to minimize the imperfections in the delivery process. Trading in seasonally produced, storable commodities is technically feasible because of the relative ease of writing delivery provisions for such commodities. Writing contracts for other commodities has proved to be more difficult, but gradually the problems have been solved. The original contracts written for livestock products, for example, were not very successful (Powers, 1967); over a period of years they have been modified and now attract a large volume of trading.

Economic feasibility is related to the potential demand for short and long hedging. This, in turn, is related to such factors as the quantity of product that in principle could be hedged, the potential to shift price risk or enhance profits through hedging, the possible substitutes for hedging (e.g., cash forward contracts and diversification), the relative costs of the alternatives, and so on. An interrelated factor is the number of buyers and sellers, including speculators. If the market is liquid, then the price effect of a single transaction is small, and hence the cost of using the market is small. Thus, the "many-buyers-and-sellers" condition implies that the market is not highly concentrated and that the market is able to attract sufficient speculative volume for liquidity.

Even if a futures market seems justified from an economic perspective, it may not attract traders. Among the reasons for lack of use of futures markets are the following. First, the delivery terms may favor either buyers or sellers. Consequently, only buyers or only sellers will

269

want to use the market, leading to a lack of balance and a possible bias in prices.[8] Second, inertia or lack of experience may preclude potential traders from participating. Farmers typically have not used futures markets, although this situation appears to be changing. The demise of the "bran and shorts" (wheat milling by-products) market has been attributed, in part, to the fact that feed manufacturers (potential buyers) were less inclined to use the market than flour millers (potential sellers). Third, government intervention in pricing may reduce price risks to the point where there is little scope for speculative gains, and it becomes unnecessary to hedge inventories. Trading in cotton, for example, declined greatly in the 1960s as a result of government support and resale policies which kept cotton prices within a narrow band.

Markets have declined in use and disappeared as their main economic justification has declined. The storage-egg contract is an example. The seasonality of egg production has been reduced. Hence, the need to store eggs and to hedge these inventories decreased. A contract for eggs now calls for the delivery of the fresh product. The delivery of potatoes on the Maine futures contract became more costly in the mid-1970s, and this reduced the effectiveness of the market for hedging. As a consequence, the volume of trading in potato futures declined.

Increased price variability and improved contract provisions have been among the factors contributing to a large increase in the volume in the 1970s. The incentives to hedge or to speculate in grain contracts became much greater once prices rose above support levels and governmental stocks had been exhausted. Futures trading in livestock contracts also has grown as prices have become more variable and contract provisions improved. The futures market for grain sorghum, however, has not grown despite the growth in production and despite its similarity to corn. This may be due to the option of cross-hedging positions in grain sorghum in the corn market, since the prices of corn and sorghum are closely related. A futures market for hams has attracted little interest; in contrast, the market for frozen pork bellies (the raw material for bacon) has a large volume. Apparently the success of a futures market is influenced by intangibles beyond those which have been discussed.

[8]The existence of a persistent bias through time in price leads one to ask why it continues. Traders aware of the bias could be expected to exploit that knowledge, which would tend to eliminate the bias. For instance, coffee futures were once thought to be biased downward. This implies that a trader could make a profit by consistently buying a futures contract, holding it, and then selling it close to the delivery month. Of course, if enough traders did this, the bias would be eliminated. But potential buyers failed to enter the coffee market apparently because of uncertainty regarding possible currency devaluation which would have lowered prices. Hence, the bias persisted (Gray, 1960).

Clearly all the factors contributing to success have not yet been identified.

References

Arthur, Henry B. 1971. *Commodity Futures as a Business Management Tool.* Boston: Harvard Univ. Graduate School of Business Administration.

Bagnell, Douglas B. 1963. "Irish Potato Futures Trading," *Hearing before a Subcommittee of the Committee on Agriculture and Forestry, United States Senate,* 88th Congress, 1st Session on S. 332 (Sept. 30). Pp. 43–54.

Cootner, Paul H. 1967. "Speculation and Hedging," *Food Res. Inst. Studies,* 7:65–105 (Supplement).

Cox, Charles C. 1976. "Futures Trading and Market Information," *J. Pol. Econ.,* 84:1215–1237.

Dusak, Katherine. 1973. "Futures Trading and Investor Returns: An Investigation of Commodity Market Risk Premiums," *J. Pol. Econ.,* 81:1387–1406.

Franzmann, John R., and Jerry D. Lehenbauer. 1979. *Hedging Feeder Cattle with the Aid of Moving Averages.* Oklahoma St. Univ. Ag. Exp. Sta. Bul. 746.

Gardner, Bruce L. 1976. "Futures Prices in Supply Analysis," *Am. J. Ag. Econ.,* 58:81–84.

Gray, Roger W. 1960. "The Characteristic Bias on Some Thin Futures Markets," *Food Res. Inst. Studies,* 1:296–312.

———. 1961. "The Search for a Risk Premium," *J. Pol. Econ.,* 69:250–260.

———. 1976. "Risk Management in Commodity and Financial Markets," *Am. J. Ag. Econ.,* 58:280–285.

Hardy, C. O. 1923. *Risk and Risk-Bearing.* Chicago: Univ. of Chicago Press.

Heifner, Richard G. 1973. *Hedging Potential in Grain Storage and Livestock Feeding.* USDA Ag. Econ. Rep. 238.

Helmuth, John W. 1977. *Grain Pricing.* Com. Futures Trading Com. Econ. Bul. 1.

Hieronymus, Thomas A. N.d. *Commodity Speculation as an Investment Medium.* New York Coffee and Sugar Exchange, Inc., pamphlet.

Houthakker, H. S. 1957. "Can Speculators Forecast Prices?" *Rev. of Econ. and Stat.,* 39:143–151.

Keynes, J. M. 1923. "Some Aspects of Commodity Markets," *Manchester Guardian Commercial,* section 13 (March 29).

Maidenberg, H. J. 1979. "Squeezing the Market in Silver," *The New York Times,* p. D2, (October 29).

Nathan Associates. 1967. *Margins, Speculation and Prices in Grains Futures Markets,* Econ. Res. Ser., USDA.

Paul, Allen B. 1966. "Pricing below Cost in the Soybean Processing Industry," *J. Farm Econ.,* 48 (Part II):2–22 (Aug.).

———, et al. 1979. *Potato Futures Study.* Committee Print, U.S. Senate Committee on Agriculture, Nutrition, and Forestry, 96th Congress, 1st Session (Nov. 5).

271

Pricing Institutions

Powers, Mark J. 1967. "Effects of Contract Provisions on the Success of a Futures Contract," *J. Farm Econ.*, 49:833–843.

———.1970. "Does Futures Trading Reduce Price Fluctuations in Cash Markets?" *Am. Econ. Rev.*, 60:460–464.

Rockwell, Charles S. 1967. "Normal Backwardation, Forecasting, and the Returns to Commodity Futures Traders," *Food Res. Inst. Studies*, 7:107–130 (Supplement).

Rutledge, David J. S. 1972. "Hedgers' Demand for Futures Contracts: A Theoretical Framework with Applications to the United States Soybean Complex," *Food Res. Inst. Studies*, 11:239–256.

Stewart, Blair. 1949. *An Analysis of Speculative Trading in Grain Futures.* USDA Tech. Bul. 1001.

Telser, Lester G. 1967. "The Supply of Speculative Services in Wheat, Corn, and Soybeans," *Food Res. Inst. Studies*, 7:131–175 (Supplement).

———, and Harlow N. Higinbotham. 1977. "Organized Futures Markets: Costs and Benefits," *J. Pol. Econ.*, 85:960–1000.

Tomek, William G. 1978. *Hedging in Commodity Futures: A Guide for Farmers in the Northeast.* Cornell Univ. Ag. Exp. Sta. Inform. Bul. 147.

Wise, T. A. 1962. "Do You Have a Future in Commodity Futures?" *Fortune* (April), pp. 120–121, 200–206.

Working, Holbrook. 1953. "Hedging Reconsidered," *J. Farm Econ.*, 35:544–561.

———. 1967. "Tests of a Theory Concerning Floor Trading on Commodity Exchanges," *Food Res. Inst. Studies*, 7:5–48 (Supplement).

CHAPTER **14**

Government Intervention
in Pricing Farm Products

Governments now attempt to influence the prices of at least some farm products in nearly every country of the world. Political considerations obviously play a dominant role in the decision to support or not to support the price of a particular commodity. Although government price-support programs remain controversial in the United States, a majority of those in Congress have voted in favor of continuing such programs. Price supports in some form have been maintained since 1933 for most cereals, cotton, tobacco, oilseed crops, wool, sugar, and milk. These commodities account for about half the cash receipts of farmers in the United States. Prices of commodities which account for the remaining half of gross farm receipts, including poultry and eggs, beef, pork, fruits, and vegetables, have not been supported directly, although the prices of these commodities have been influenced by support programs on grains, and to a modest degree by government purchase programs and marketing orders for selected fruits and vegetables.

The objective of this chapter is to provide a framework that will enable the student to appraise the economic consequences of alternative forms or degrees of government intervention in pricing. While policy decisions are inevitably influenced by political pressures and social considerations, economists can play a useful role by pointing out which groups are likely to gain or lose if a particular policy is adopted. In this chapter, we illustrate how economic principles and a knowledge of demand and supply relationships (or elasticities) can be used to predict the consequences of alternative policies on such variables as the level and stability of farm prices and incomes, consumer prices, the magnitude of surpluses or deficits, the volume of imports, and government costs.

273

Pricing Institutions

Objectives of Government Intervention

Governments generally intervene in pricing farm products to achieve one or a combination of the following objectives:

(1) to reduce price and income instability,
(2) to improve the allocation of resources,
(3) to increase self-sufficiency in food and fiber,
(4) to raise the average level of prices and incomes.

As we have observed, farm prices tend to fluctuate more than the prices of many nonfarm goods and services. This can lead to cycles in production with excess resources being devoted to certain commodities during some periods and can lead to underutilization of processing and marketing facilities during others. Consumers gain relatively little from price instability, especially if it leads to fluctuating supplies. Under reasonable assumptions regarding the nature of utility functions, it can be demonstrated that consumers generally are better off with relatively stable rather than fluctuating supplies of farm products (Johnson, 1947, pp. 151–153). Waugh (1944), on the other hand, argues that consumers are made worse off if the price of a commodity is stabilized at the arithmetic mean of the fluctuating prices. This argument is based on the concept of consumer surplus which is defined (approximately) as the area under the demand curve and above the market price. With a downward sloping demand curve, gains in consumer surplus at prices below the mean will exceed the loss in consumer surplus from prices above the mean. Producers may or may not gain from price stabilization. The effects on producer returns depend on a complex set of circumstances including the shapes of the demand and supply curves, the source of instability, and how producers respond to stabilization programs.[1]

Unstable prices also may have an adverse effect on the demand for agricultural raw materials. For example, in periods of high prices for fibers, textile manufacturers are likely to switch to synthetic materials. Once processors and consumers have become accustomed to the substitute materials, it may be difficult to regain markets even when prices subsequently decline. A compelling case can be made for collective action on the part of producers or for the introduction of public policies

---

[1] The theoretical effects of price stabilization, especially in terms of the welfare (consumer and producer surplus) effects, have been explored by many authors (e.g., Helmberger and Weaver, 1977; Just, 1977; Just, et al., 1977; and Turnovsky, 1978). The articles by Just and by Turnovsky provide useful surveys of the literature on the welfare effects of price stabilization.

designed to reduce price fluctuations under such circumstances. Alternative methods of stabilizing supplies are discussed in a subsequent section.

Government intervention in pricing also has been advocated by some economists to provide producers with better guides for planning. Current or past prices, as pointed out in Chapter 4, do not always provide reliable guides for the future. Such prices may be depressed or abnormally high as a result of temporary shifts in demand or supply. This may lead producers to make what turn out to be unwise production decisions. Where local market prices are depressed, perhaps as a result of an overvalued exchange rate or export taxes, incentives to maintain or increase production are reduced. Under such circumstances it may be desirable to adopt what Krishna (1967) refers to as a "positive price policy," that is, a support level that will encourage farmers to make use of additional inputs. Myrdal (1968) likewise believes that government intervention in pricing can serve a constructive role if it provides producers with appropriate guides for planning.

Efficiency in the use of capital may be enhanced through measures to stabilize prices. Price uncertainty leads to what Johnson (1947) calls "capital rationing." This means that creditors refuse to lend as much money to farmers as they could profitably use, or alternatively that farmers decide to borrow and hence invest less than optimum amounts of capital because of discounting for uncertainty. With more stable prices, Johnson argues that more capital would be employed, leading to greater output and efficiency.

In food-deficit countries, support programs have been introduced and maintained in an attempt to reduce dependence on imports, conserve foreign exchange, and insulate domestic producers from international price instability. These arguments were used to justify supporting farm prices in the United Kingdom following World War II (McCrone, 1962, pp. 14–20; and Hallett, 1968, pp. 206–208) and have been advanced in defense of the Common Agricultural Policy of the European Community. Prices of grains and livestock products within the European Community have been maintained well above those prevailing in the principal exporting countries, including the United States, during the past three decades. By doing so, these countries have succeeded in achieving a high degree of self-sufficiency in food production and in stabilizing internal prices but at the expense of residual suppliers.

In the United States, the major purpose of government intervention in pricing farm products has been to improve the welfare of farmers. Programs were adopted in the 1930s with the primary objective of raising the average level of farm prices so as to avoid further foreclosures and to give farmers a "fair" return for their labor. Even with such programs, the average income of the farm population in the United States has generally lagged behind that of the nonfarm population except during periods of war or exceptionally strong export demand, such as occurred in the mid-1970s. Supporting farm prices also has been justified as a means of preserving small farms. In the absence of such programs, proponents argue, the drift to the cities would accelerate, and larger farms would displace family farms, thus contributing to the demise of rural communities.

Methods of Reducing Price Instability

Fluctuations in prices received by producers can be reduced by a storage or reserve program, that is, by storing a portion of the crop in years of low prices and releasing stocks in years of high prices. Obviously, prices can be held down only if reserve stocks have previously been acquired. The range over which prices are permitted to fluctuate depends on decisions made with respect to acquisition and resale prices. The narrower the price band, the larger the stocks required to keep prices within that range. Subsidies will be necessary to compensate those storing commodities if the price is to be held within a range that is not sufficient to cover the costs of storage.

The size of storage stocks required to achieve a given degree of price stability depends on the variability of production and demand as well as the slopes of the demand and supply schedules. With highly unstable yields and/or large fluctuations in demand, substantial reserves will be needed to keep prices within a prescribed range.

An attempt on the part of one country to achieve internal stability, by importing in short-crop years and exporting in large-crop years, clearly can add to instability in export markets. Thus, the size of reserve stocks needed to keep export prices relatively stable will depend in part on policies pursued in the major importing countries. Larger stocks will be needed by the principal residual suppliers if importing countries do not permit prices to rise so as to ration consumption in short-crop years (Johnson, 1975).

World attention was focused on reserve policies for grains in the mid-1970s following the sharp increase in prices that resulted from the entry of the Soviet Union into the world market on a large scale and the elimination of government-held surplus stocks in the United States. Economists responded by initiating a large number of both theoretical and empirical studies of alternative reserve strategies.[2] The general conclusion of these studies is that privately held stocks of grain are not likely to be sufficient to hold prices within an acceptable range, but that the size of publicly held stocks need not be large unless the objective is to hold prices within a very narrow range, for example, a range of 5 per cent above or below the anticipated long-run equilibrium price.

A reserve program that succeeds in reducing the amplitude of price fluctuations does not necessarily lead to stable returns to producers. When prices are free to fluctuate in response to changing output, high prices are normally associated with small crops and vice versa. If the price elasticity of demand is equal to -1.0 (i.e., unitary elasticity), price changes are just sufficient to compensate for variations in output, and hence total revenue remains the same regardless of the level of production. Income instability will increase as demand becomes more or less inelastic (i.e., deviates from -1.0). Price stabilization will reduce income instability compared with what would happen in the absence of a stabilization program only under certain conditions. If the price elasticity of demand is less than -0.5 (in absolute value), a stable price will reduce income instability as compared to fluctuating prices, although income will still be unstable. If the elasticity exceeds -0.5, income will be more unstable with a constant price than with prices that are allowed to respond freely to changes in supply or demand.

Average returns to producers may or may not be enhanced by reducing price fluctuations through a storage program. The effect on average returns of acquiring stocks and then reselling them later depends on demand conditions at the time of acquisition relative to the time of sale, the cost of holding commodities, and the length of time they are held. In general, farmers gain over a period of years from storing commodities only if demand shifts during the period by enough to cover storage costs and if the price elasticity of demand at the time reserves are sold is greater (or less inelastic) than when stocks are acquired (Gislason, 1959, pp. 593–597). With a linear demand curve, the latter condition is met since the elasticity of demand increases as one moves upward along the demand curve.

The effects of withholding stocks in years of high production and selling them in years of short crops when the demand function is linear are illustrated in Figure 14-1. Assume that a monopoly selling organiza-

---

[2]A single reference cannot do justice to the wealth of information available on this topic. Cochrane and Danin (1976), Reutlinger (1976), and Walker, Sharples and Holland (1976) provide a good introduction to the empirical literature dealing with the size of reserve stocks and include references to many other useful studies.

Pricing Institutions

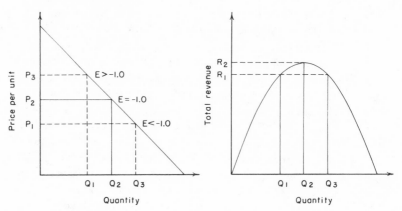

Figure 14-1. Effect of a buffer-stock scheme on average prices and total revenue with a linear demand function

tion knows the shape of the demand curve and that high-production years are normally followed by low-production years so that it is possible to acquire stocks in the first period for sale in the second. If production in t_1 (represented by Q_3 in Figure 14-1) were sold in that year, price would be equal to P_1 and total revenue as shown in the right-hand diagram would be R_1. But by withholding $Q_3 - Q_2$ of the product in t_1, price would be raised to P_2 and total returns to R_2. In the following period, with production equal to Q_1, the accumulated stocks could be sold. This would drive down the price from P_3 to P_2, but total revenue would rise to R_2 (since demand over this range is price elastic, total revenue rises with an increase in sales). At the price P_2 and volume Q_2, total revenue is maximized. Thus, producers would benefit by acquiring stocks any time the price fell below P_2 and releasing them whenever the price exceeded P_2. In this case, they benefit from both the acquisition and the release of stocks, a special situation which is attributable to the fact that demand is inelastic over the low range and elastic over the upper range of prices.

Producer returns are reduced by a storage program designed to equalize supplies when demand is inelastic at high prices and elastic at low prices; producer returns are increased by a stabilization program when the opposite elasticity conditions prevail. Whether it pays producers to stabilize supplies and prices, once the demand curve is known, can be determined simply and directly by noting the shape of the total revenue function (price multiplied by quantity) (Eckstein and Syrquin, 1971). It will not pay producers to store part of the crop in years of high

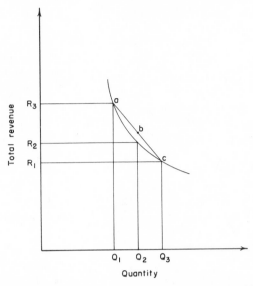

Figure 14-2. Difference in average revenue between two periods with fluctuating and stable supplies and prices

production and resell in years of low production if the total revenue function is concave from above, that is, if it falls below a straight line joining points on the total revenue function which show how returns would vary with fluctuating supplies in the absence of a storage program. This relationship prevails if the price elasticity of demand is constant and less than unity.[3] The relationship between the average revenue obtained with fluctuating supplies and that earned from selling a constant amount each year is illustrated in Figure 14-2. The average revenue over a two-year period with production at Q_1 and Q_3 is represented by point b, the midpoint of the line ac joining R_1 and R_3. If sufficient supplies were withheld in the high-production year and sold in the low-production year so as to maintain supplies at Q_2, the average revenue in the two years would be R_2. This clearly falls below point b. The opposite would be true if the total revenue function is curved upward, as shown in the right-hand side of Figure 14-1.

Storage programs are expensive. Interest costs alone may amount to

[3]Eckstein and Syrquin (1971, p. 332) point out that with constant elasticity functions (admittedly a special case), "farmers' revenue will rise as a result of supply fluctuations when price elasticity is *smaller* than unity and fall when it is greater."

10 to 15 per cent per year, and annual storage costs for grains, the least expensive products to store, generally average somewhere between 5 and 10 per cent of the market value of such commodities. Storage charges for semiperishables such as butter and cheese are even higher. Thus, access to substantial amounts of capital is required if large reserve stocks are to be maintained.

Without accurate forecasts, it is difficult to decide when to acquire stocks, how much to store, and under what circumstances they should be sold. If demand and supply conditions turn out to be less favorable for producers than anticipated, stocks may accumulate to the point where they become a major financial burden. Furthermore, the presence of large stocks has a depressing effect on prices even though they are not sold. A stabilization program is most likely to be successful if prices fluctuate around a stable or reasonably predictable upward trend in equilibrium prices.

Past experience with stabilization schemes has been mixed. Consumers in the United States as well as some in other countries benefited in the 1940s when the government-financed Commodity Credit Corporation sold excess stocks of grains and cotton which had been acquired in the 1930s. In this case, producers also gained since the government absorbed storage costs and any losses on the commodities held off the market. If excess stocks must be held for long periods before being sold, the cost of storage may more than offset any gains realized from shifts in demand. Gislason (1959) concluded that Canadian wheat producers did not gain from storage operations of the Wheat Board in the 1930s and 1940s despite the fact that the average price of wheat when sold was considerably greater than when it was acquired. Storage costs (which were not subsidized by the government) exceeded the gains from higher prices.

The United Nations Conference on Trade, Aid and Development (UNCTAD) has proposed making greater use of reserve schemes to help stabilize the prices of internationally traded commodities such as coffee, cocoa, rubber, and jute. The proposed plan includes provisions for the creation of a common fund to finance the acquisition of stocks. Since the prices of different commodities tend to move somewhat independently, proponents of the plan argue that less money would be required to support a group of commodities than for each commodity separately. Furthermore, through pooled funding, risks to lenders would be reduced. One of the limitations of previous stabilization efforts has been the lack of adequate capital or borrowing capacity to finance the acquisition of stocks during periods of low prices. In 1958, for example, administrators of the International Tin Agreement were unable to keep prices from falling below the floor specified in the agreement because they had exhausted the funds provided for this purpose. Later, when demand conditions improved, they were unable to prevent prices from rising above the ceiling because of insufficient stocks (Hallett, 1968, p. 197).

Net producer returns, but not market prices, can be stabilized by creating a stabilization fund. In this case, money is set aside in years of high prices by withholding payments from producers. The proceeds can then be used to augment returns to producers in years of low prices. Such a scheme is feasible only if the entire output is marketed through a monopoly selling organization like a marketing board. Deductions can be made relatively easily from the average or "pooled" price paid to producers in years of high market prices. Australia and New Zealand are among the countries that have used such schemes to reduce fluctuations in returns paid to producers from the sale of export commodities.

The major advantage of a stabilization fund over a reserve scheme is that it is less expensive, since funds are not tied up in acquiring and storing commodities. But a stabilization fund offers no protection for consumers, since market prices cannot be held down unless physical stocks have been set aside for this purpose. Furthermore, serious equity problems may arise whenever a substantial interval exists between the time funds are accumulated and dispersed. Farmers from whom deductions were made in the early years of the program will have no opportunity to recover any benefits if, in the interim, they have left farming or now produce other commodities. Finally, such a scheme may become a burden to the government if the stabilization fund is exhausted and prices remain low. In the case of the wheat stabilization scheme in Australia, Campbell (1964) points out that the government was compelled to step in and underwrite losses in the 1950s and 1960s when export prices fell and remained below the guaranteed price. Thus, a stabilization scheme adopted initially for the purpose of stabilizing returns may end up as a disguised price-support program.

Price-Support Programs in the United States

An extremely complicated array of support programs has evolved in the United States since such programs were first introduced during the depression years of the 1930s. Government intervention in pricing continues to be selective and the degree of influence which the government exercises over commodity prices varies greatly from commodity to commodity. Support programs have been implemented mainly for storable commodities. Congress has been reluctant to extend supports to perishables for a number of reasons, including the unwillingness of producers to accept controls on production or sales, especially for livestock products, and the potential high cost to the government of extending support to these commodities. Part of the reluctance to extend supports to perishable farm products is traceable to the unfortunate experience with the attempt to maintain the prices of eggs and potatoes above equilibrium levels during and immediately after World War II. Costs proved to be so high that support programs for these commodities were abandoned in the late 1940s.

During the 1940s and 1950s, support prices for most commodities were closely linked to parity prices. Parity prices, as defined in legislation adopted in the 1930s, are those prices which give farm products the same purchasing power with respect to articles farmers buy as they had in 1910–1914 (USDA, 1970, p. 22). To calculate the parity price for any commodity, the adjusted base price (defined below) is simply multiplied by the current Index of Prices Paid by Farmers and divided by 100. This is equivalent to "indexing" prices, that is, multiplying all base-period prices by a common mover which presumably reflects the overall rate of inflation. If prices were supported at a uniform percentage of parity, the relationship prevailing among current support prices would be the same as that which existed during the base period. Originally, the prices used in computing current parity prices were those actually received by farmers in the 5-year period, 1910–1914.

The limitations of the original parity formula as a method of establishing support prices for farm products are now widely recognized. The indexing procedure takes no account of changes in efficiency or in the relative costs of producing different commodities that have occurred since the base period. In general, gains in efficiency have been greater over the past 60 years for grains than for beef cattle, hogs, and milk. Thus, if current support prices were based on the original parity formula, cereal crops would be overpriced relative to most livestock products. The parity formula also fails to take account of shifts in demand or potential competition from new products.

In an attempt to overcome some of the limitations of the original parity formula, Congress modified the formula in 1948. Under the modernized version, parity prices are calculated using "adjusted base prices" rather than those actually prevailing in 1910–1914. The adjusted base prices reflect price relationships prevailing among commodities in the most recent ten-year period.[4] The modernized parity formula is an

[4]Adjusted base prices are calculated by computing an average of actual market prices for the most recent ten-year period, and then adjusting these back to the 1910–1914 base by

improvement over the original formula; however, parity prices still do not take full account of changes in efficiency or relative demands that may have occurred in recent years. Current parity prices reflect recent changes in demand and supply only insofar as actual prices in the most recent ten-year period have responded to these forces.

Support prices for most commodities except milk are no longer closely linked to parity prices. The move away from basing support prices on a fixed percentage of parity prices began during the 1950s. More recent legislation has given the Secretary of Agriculture even greater discretionary authority in establishing loan rates for storable commodities. This has been done to encourage use and avoid the need for export subsidies that might be required to make U.S. farm products competitive in world markets if support levels were tied to parity prices.

Alternative Methods of Supporting Prices

The economic effects of programs designed to support farm prices depend on the level of support in relation to equilibrium prices and the method used to make supports effective. If a country produces less of any commodity than it consumes, internal prices can be maintained above import prices simply by imposing tariffs or by restricting imports. This is the method of support most commonly used in food-deficit nations. In countries where actual or potential production at the support or guaranteed price exceeds consumption, the government has the choice of purchasing the excess production (presumably for disposal abroad or in some market that does not compete with normal commercial sales), subsidizing consumption so as to shift the demand curve to the right, restricting production to what can be sold at the support price, or making deficiency payments to producers. The costs to the government of maintaining a given level of support will differ depending on the support method used and the elasticities of demand and supply. In practice governments frequently use a combination of devices to maintain or raise prices.

---

dividing each ten-year average price by the Index of Prices Received by Farmers for the same ten-year period (USDA, 1970, pp. 26–28). The effect of this is to raise the base price of any commodity that goes up faster than the average of all farm products and to lower the base price of commodities that go up more slowly. The adjusted base price for wheat, for example, in January 1980 was $0.69 per bushel, which was based on the average price for the 120-month period ending December 1979 divided by 4.39. The parity price for wheat in January 1980 was $6.27 per bushel, which was the base price ($0.69) multiplied by the Index of Prices Paid by Farmers and divided by 100 (909/100).

Pricing Institutions

Tariffs, Variable Levies, and Import Restrictions

The United States makes use of tariffs on such commodities as meat and wool to maintain domestic prices above import prices. In addition, quotas are employed to restrict imports of frozen beef and dairy products. The European Economic Community makes use of similar devices, including variable levies, to maintain internal farm prices well above import prices. For most temperate-zone products there is no longer a single world market but rather a series of national markets with widely varying levels of protection.[5]

The effect of most protectionist policies is to raise internal prices, thereby encouraging domestic production and reducing the market for potential exporting nations. The degree to which internal production and consumption are affected by the imposition of a tariff depends on the slopes or elasticities of the demand and supply curves in the importing nation: the more elastic these relationships are, the greater will be the impact on residual exporters for a given tariff or import duty. This assumes that import supply is perfectly elastic at the import price. If it is not, the imposition of a tariff will affect the import price as well as the internal market price.

The potential effect of an import duty on domestic production, consumption, and imports is illustrated in Figure 14-3. The supply of an imported commodity such as feed grains is assumed to be perfectly elastic at the price P_1. In the absence of any tariff or other protectionist measures, domestic production will be equal to Q_1 and consumption will be equal to Q_4, with imports making up the difference between total consumption and domestic production ($Q_4 - Q_1$). If a tariff is imposed on imports such that the domestic price rises to P_2, producers will eventually increase output to Q_2 and consumers will reduce purchases to Q_3. These changes are usually referred to as the production and consumption effects of a tariff policy. If the import price remains the same, costs to consumers will rise by the full amount of the tariff and imports will decline from $Q_4 - Q_1$ to $Q_3 - Q_2$. Obviously, the flatter the slopes of the supply and demand curves, the more production will be increased and consumption reduced if a tariff is imposed. Even a modest increase in the

[5]Johnson (1964, pp. 922–923) has estimated the average degree of protection afforded agricultural producers in a number of countries in the early 1960s using a method devised by McCrone (1962, pp. 50–57). The level of protection is computed by valuing output at national or internal prices and then dividing this total by the same output valued at import prices. According to Johnson's estimates, the degree of protection (i.e., the percentage that the internal value of agricultural production exceeded the import value) ranged from over 50 per cent in Norway and Sweden to between 10 and 20 per cent in Belgium, Netherlands, France, and the United States.

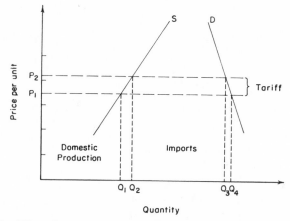

Figure 14-3. Effect of a tariff on domestic production, consumption, and imports

degree of protection can lead to a substantial decline in the volume of imports. The percentage effect will depend on the elasticities of the demand and supply schedules in the importing country and the proportion of the total amount consumed which is imported.[6]

As long as some quantity is imported, tariffs have the additional advantage of creating a source of government revenue. Consumers clearly pay the full cost of supporting agriculture if this is done through the use of tariffs or import restrictions. The same effect on prices as shown in Figure 14-3 could be obtained simply by restricting imports by means of

[6]The elasticity of demand for imports is often used to indicate the percentage effect on the quantity imported of a 1 per cent change in the import price (or the equivalent percentage effect on the internal price of a change in the tariff or an import quota). The elasticity of import demand can be high even though the price elasticities of demand and supply within the importing country are quite low. This is attributable to the fact that the elasticity of import demand is a multiple of the combined elasticities of domestic demand and supply in the importing country. The weights or multiples used to derive the import elasticity of demand are equal to the ratio of total consumption to imports for the domestic demand elasticity and the ratio of domestic production to imports for the internal supply elasticity. Assume imports make up one-fifth of the total supply and domestic production four-fifths and that the elasticity of domestic demand (E_d) is equal to -0.2 and domestic supply (E_s) is equal to 0.15. The elasticity of import demand (E_i) is then equal to -1.6. Specifically,

$$E_i = \frac{consumption}{imports} (E_d) - \frac{production}{imports} (E_s) = \frac{5}{1} (-0.2) - \frac{4}{1} (0.15) = -1.6.$$

If only one-tenth of the total supply had been imported with the same internal elasticities, the import elasticity of demand would be still higher (-3.35).

a quota to the amount $Q_3 - Q_2$. In this case, however, the government would obtain no revenue. The benefits of higher prices would accrue to exporting countries which were offered quotas. By restricting imports in this way, benefits can be distributed selectively to preferred suppliers. The allocation of such rights is likely to become a sensitive political issue since it leads to discrimination among suppliers. The United States used a quota system to restrict sugar imports in the 1960s. Since the domestic price of sugar was well above the prevailing world price during most of this decade, privileged suppliers earned several hundred million dollars more for their sugar than they would have received if they had sold it elsewhere (Horton, 1970).

With a fixed or *ad valorem* tariff rate on imports of agricultural commodities, exporting countries can maintain the existing volume of sales simply by reducing their own export prices. If this occurs, the internal price may not increase or will rise less than the amount of the tariff. But if the importing country makes use of variable levies which are adjusted up or down to compensate for any change in import prices, there is no way (short of negotiating for a guaranteed share of the market) that exporters can increase sales. This type of protection has been adopted by the European Community for grains and livestock products.

Government Purchases

Protectionist policies are not sufficient to maintain producer prices above equilibrium if potential supply exceeds demand at the support or guaranteed price. A country which produces surpluses above domestic needs, such as the United States, must then rely on some other method to maintain prices above equilibrium. Support prices have been made effective in the United States by offering farmers price-support loans or the opportunity to sell surplus commodities to the government (acting through the Commodity Credit Corporation). The price-support loan rate is, in effect, a buying price if the market price falls to the loan level. Farmers who comply with acreage restrictions or other supply-control measures are eligible to obtain price-support loans on storable commodities such as grains and cotton. Such loans need not be repaid. If a farmer does not repay his loan, the government simply takes title to the commodities pledged as security for the loan. The government also may acquire surplus commodities by direct purchase, as with dairy products. Any surplus stocks which the government acquires can be resold only if they are in danger of spoiling or if the price rises above the loan rate or purchase price by a specified percentage. This percentage has ranged from as low as 5 per cent to as high as 50 per cent over the past two decades.

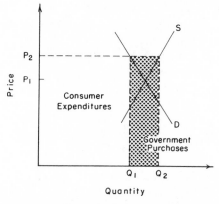

Figure 14-4. Consumer expenditures and government costs of supporting prices above equilibrium through a government purchase program

The economic effects of a government purchase or acquisition program are illustrated in Figure 14-4. Assume the support price is maintained at P_2, which is above the equilibrium price P_1. In the absence of effective supply controls, an amount Q_2 will be produced in response to the favorable support price. In order to maintain the price at P_2, the government will have to acquire an amount represented by the shaded area, which is the difference between Q_2 and Q_1. Total consumer expenditures are represented by the unshaded rectangle ($P_2 \times Q_1$). Producers will receive the sum of what consumers spend plus the value of government purchases.

Initial government costs will depend on the price elasticity of demand, the level of support in relation to the equilibrium price, and the price elasticity of supply if production is uncontrolled or the effectiveness of control measures when an attempt is made to hold down production. The more elastic the demand and supply curves, the higher will be the cost to the government of maintaining a given level of support. Losses incurred by the government will depend on how long the commodities are held before being resold (or given away) and the recovery value of commodities which are sold. The government may even gain if demand shifts by more than enough to cover storage costs or a series of unfavorable crop years reduces production.[7] Storage and associated

[7]This occurred in the mid-1930s in the United States, for example, when two years of severe drought made it possible for the government to unload accumulated stocks. Surpluses acquired in the late 1930s were used to meet emergency needs during and immediately after World War II. Proponents of such programs argue that in an uncertain world in which drought or insect and disease damage may cut production or food-aid demands may suddenly increase, it is desirable for the government to maintain emergency reserves.

handling costs are relatively high, however, especially for semiperishable commodities like dairy products. They are lower for grains, but annual costs may still amount to 15 per cent or more of the value of commodities placed in storage. For this reason, the government is likely to incur losses on stored commodities if they must be held for several years before they can be sold.

Consumption or Export Subsidies

Surpluses of farm products can be avoided, even if prices are maintained above free-market levels, provided the government is willing to subsidize domestic consumption or exports. This is equivalent to shifting the demand curve to the right. Producers generally prefer programs that make use of farm products rather than those that compel them to limit output. The welfare of certain nonfarm groups also may be enhanced by programs designed to increase consumption, such as the school lunch program and the food stamp plan.

The economic effects on producers of a domestic food-subsidy program depend on the amount of the subsidy and how it is spent, that is, whether it is used to buy additional food or more services. If the subsidy simply enables consumers to substitute public for private expenditures on food, their welfare is increased, but farmers do not gain. At least a part of the additional purchasing power made available under a domestic food-subsidy program is normally used to pay for packaging and marketing services rather than for more farm products. Any benefits accruing to agriculture also are likely to be distributed very unevenly among producers of different commodities. Only those producing commodities with relatively high income elasticities of demand such as meat, cheese, snack foods, and certain fruits and vegetables can expect to gain. Such programs offer little to those producing wheat, rice, dry beans, or cotton. Domestic food-subsidy programs can be used to improve nutrition and the welfare of certain consumer groups, but the benefits to agriculture as a whole are likely to be modest except in countries where the income elasticity of demand for additional calories or physical quantities of food is quite high.

Export subsidies have been employed, most often by relatively high-income countries, to reduce or eliminate surpluses of farm products. The European Community and the United States have been among the principal offenders. Both have used export subsidies or extremely generous credit terms to dispose of such commodities as wheat and dairy products. Export subsidies are regarded by other exporting nations as an unfair form of competition, especially by those nations lacking the financial resources to compete with the U.S. Treasury in subsidizing exports.

Limiting Production or Sales

The government can hold prices above equilibrium levels in the short run simply by accumulating surpluses in storage, but unless additional outlets can be found, this becomes very expensive. In the long run, it is cheaper for the government to limit production, or even to pay farmers not to produce, rather than to purchase commodities and then attempt to dispose of them.

Supply-adjustment programs have been a major feature of agricultural support programs in the United States since the 1930s. In theory, the supply of any agricultural commodity can be limited simply by assigning each producer a sales or marketing quota with sufficiently high penalties to discourage anyone from exceeding the quota, but, in practice, it has proven difficult to gain political support for sales quotas except for tobacco. Instead, the government has relied mainly on acreage-control or land-retirement programs in an attempt to curb production. It is much easier to administer an acreage-allotment or land-retirement program than to enforce sales quotas or to check on the use of other inputs. Land restrictions are relatively easy to police using maps and aerial photographs. But it is generally conceded that limiting the area of land that can be planted to certain crops is a relatively inefficient method of attempting to restrict production. Large areas of land must be held out of production to compensate for the fact that farmers will remove the poorest land first and use additional fertilizer plus other inputs to increase yields on the remaining acreage. An acreage-allotment or land-retirement program can effectively reduce production, but only if the acreage planted is cut back substantially.

Farmers benefit from reducing the output of a commodity only if the demand for that product is price inelastic. In the short run, the demand for most of the major crops produced in the United States is sufficiently inelastic so that returns can be increased by cutting back on production, or at least by limiting expansion. But, over a period of years, the demand for a controlled commodity may become more elastic as alternative sources of supply or substitute products are developed. Thus, an effective supply-control program ultimately may lead to a serious loss of markets, especially for commodities which are exported. Cotton is a good example of a commodity that lost markets during the 1950s owing to persistent overpricing made possible by an effective supply-control program.

Any additional revenue obtained by farmers under a supply-control program comes directly from consumers, not from the government. If production or marketing controls are sufficiently comprehensive and enforced, the government need not purchase any commodities. No government purchases will be required if production can be limited to what consumers will purchase at the support price (Q_1 in Figure 14-4). The total revenue obtained by producers will be less under an effective supply-control program than under a government purchase or subsidized consumption program since a smaller quantity will be produced and sold. But farmers may be as well or better off since they will not have incurred the additional costs that would be required to produce the larger output. Agribusiness firms supplying inputs to farmers or marketing services obviously will be adversely affected if output is reduced. Thus, it is not surprising to find such firms generally opposed to programs which limit production.

A selective supply-control program that limits the area planted to only one or a small number of commodities can adversely affect producers of noncontrolled commodities if land is diverted from controlled to uncontrolled crops. This is precisely what happened in the 1950s when acreage restrictions were reimposed on wheat and cotton. The area planted to substitute crops, including barley, sorghum, and soybeans increased, thereby adding to the surpluses of these commodities. A similar problem could arise under a sales quota program. For example, if quotas were imposed on milk production, forage supplies and grain no longer needed to produce milk probably would be diverted to the production of beef and pork.

The secondary effects on other producers of selective acreage-control programs can be minimized by imposing comprehensive restrictions on all commodities or by adopting programs to keep cropland idle. Successive administrations have opted for the latter approach in the United States since the late 1950s. Opposition to limiting production has been minimized by making participation in supply-management programs voluntary and by paying farmers to keep part of their cropland idle. This gives farmers who want to plant additional land the option to do so, although they forego substantial cash benefits if they do not sign up to participate in the various programs that are offered. Experience during the 1960s demonstrated that this is a relatively expensive method of holding down production since farmers are willing to keep acreage idle only if the payments offered by the government are equivalent to what they would have earned above cash or output-of-pocket costs had the additional acreage been planted. The added costs of planting the last 10 or 20 per cent of a farmer's total acreage tend to be low, and consequently the marginal gains are relatively high unless the weather is unfavorable for planting or the farmer has alternative uses for his equipment and labor. The government must compete against these relatively high marginal returns if a voluntary set-aside or land retirement program is to be effective.

The benefits accruing to producers under a successful supply-control program tend to be capitalized into the value of the rights to produce or to sell the controlled commodity. Where acreage allotments or the right to receive payments go with the farm, the original owners of land with such rights reap most of the gains. The market price of the factor of production which is restricted rises because producers are willing to bid for the privilege of obtaining higher returns. This applies equally well to allotments, bases, or marketing quotas. The capitalization problem, of course, is a feature of all programs in which the rights to obtain higher returns are restricted and negotiable.

Deficiency Payments

By making use of compensatory or deficiency payments, it is possible to maintain above-equilibrium prices to producers while permitting market prices to fall to whatever level is necessary to equate production and consumption. The government is responsible for making up the difference between market-clearing prices and those guaranteed to farmers. Storage, handling, and disposal problems are eliminated. Consumers benefit from increased supplies of commodities and lower market prices; however, some families will pay more in taxes. In contrast to supply-control programs, deficiency payments make the cost of supporting agriculture a visible item in the government's budget. If the money to finance deficiency payments is raised through a progressive income tax, low-income groups benefit at the expense of upper-income families.

One of the obvious advantages of using deficiency payments to support farm prices is to avoid the loss of markets. This is particularly important for those products faced with close substitutes as well as those which must compete with imports or exports from other suppliers.

The economic effects of an unlimited deficiency-payment program (i.e., one with no restrictions imposed either on production or on the total amount of money that can be paid to an individual producer) are illustrated in Figure 14-5. Assume the price guaranteed to producers (P_3) is above the equilibrium price (P_2). Total supply is determined by the point at which the guaranteed price intersects the supply schedule. The total amount produced (Q_2) is then placed on the market and will be consumed at a price P_1, which is below the equilibrium price since output exceeds what would be produced under free-market conditions. Government payments will be equal to the dif-

291

Pricing Institutions

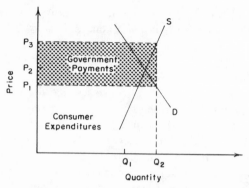

Figure 14-5. Consumer prices and expenditures and government costs of supporting farm prices above equilibrium by making deficiency payments

ference between the guaranteed price to producers (P_3) and the market-clearing price (P_1) multiplied by the total volume of production. This is represented by the shaded area in Figure 14-5. Consumers benefit from below-equilibrium prices, while producers receive above-equilibrium returns. Thus, both production and consumption are subsidized. Consumers and agribusiness firms also gain because the total volume produced and marketed is larger than it would have been if the same level of support to producers had been made effective by a supply-control program.

The slopes of the demand and supply schedules are critical in determining the cost to the government of supporting prices above equilibrium by making deficiency payments to producers. If the supply curve is relatively flat so that producers respond to the guaranteed price by adding substantially to total output, and if the demand curve is relatively steep so that a large reduction in price is required to induce consumers to buy the additional output, the gap between the guaranteed and market price will be large and hence costs to the government will be high. Government costs will be modest if supply is inelastic and demand is relatively elastic.

The price elasticity of demand also is critical in determining the cost of supporting agriculture using deficiency payments *relative* to the cost of a direct-purchase program. A deficiency-payment program will be less costly to the treasury, at least initially, than a government-purchase program (assuming the same level of support is maintained in both cases) if the price elasticity of demand is greater than unity (i.e., elastic); a deficiency payment scheme will be more expensive than a government purchase program if demand is inelastic (Schickele, 1954, pp. 217–221). The relative costs of a deficiency payment and a purchase program can be ascertained visually by comparing the area cross-hatched in Figure 14-5 with the area $Q_2 - Q_1$ bounded by the guaranteed price (comparable to the cross-hatched area in Figure 14-4).

The government's liability under a deficiency-payment program can be limited in a number of ways. For example, payments can be restricted to something less than 100 per cent of the total output of all farms combined, or a payment limitation may be imposed on the total amount of money that will be paid to an individual producer. Individual farm bases or quotas also could be assigned, with no payments made for production in excess of the quota. If such a program were in effect, over-quota production could be sold but only at the market price which presumably would be less than the guaranteed price. This would reduce the incentive to maintain or increase output. Thus the level of production is likely to be less if payments are tied to individual farm bases than it would be under an unrestricted payment program.

Few governments have been willing to offer unlimited deficiency payments to producers. In the United States, price-support payments have been made in recent years only to producers who agree to participate in voluntary supply-management or acreage-diversion programs. Thus, payments have been used as an inducement to limit output. Congress also has imposed ceilings on the total amount of money that can be paid to an individual producer, partly to hold down costs, but also to avoid pyramiding benefits on large farms.

For food-deficit countries that want to protect home agriculture or increase their degree of self-sufficiency, a deficiency-payment scheme has a number of advantages over tariffs or import quotas. Domestic production can be encouraged by making payments to producers above the prices of imported commodities, while consumers continue to benefit from the relatively low import prices. Exporters are less adversely affected by a deficiency-payment scheme than by tariffs or import quotas, since consumption is not reduced; they will, however, lose markets insofar as domestic production expands in response to the guaranteed prices.

Conclusions

Government intervention in agriculture now takes many forms. In most instances, governments have attempted to maintain prices above equilibrium levels, either to encourage production or to improve the incomes of farmers. In the United States, support programs have been used successfully to transfer income from the nonfarm sector of the economy to agriculture. Such programs also have contributed to the growth of output, and, by providing farmers with additional income, have enabled them to make productive investments leading to increases in efficiency. This has provided some long-run benefits to consumers, although such programs clearly have held prices above where they otherwise might have been in the short run.

While income unquestionably can be transferred to agriculture by supporting prices, most economists would argue that this is not the most efficient or socially desirable means of improving the welfare of the farm population. The benefits of support programs usually are distributed among farmers roughly in proportion to sales, which means that a high proportion of the gains go to the larger farms. Few low-income farmers are likely to be liberated from poverty by programs which result in raising the average level of farm prices. Furthermore, the benefits of farm programs tend to be capitalized into the value of farms. Thus, subsequent landowners may be no better off with higher product prices than they would be with lower prices.

The effects on welfare and government costs of maintaining farm prices above equilibrium depend on: (1) the level of support; (2) the mechanism used to make supports effective; (3) the price elasticity of supply, unless production is controlled; and (4) the price elasticity of demand. The social costs of overpricing farm products are likely to be less serious if the supply and demand curves are relatively inelastic than if they are elastic. The allocation of resources is not seriously distorted and welfare losses to society are modest if neither consumption nor production is materially altered by raising prices.[8] Under such conditions, prices can be maintained above equilibrium by either a supply-control program or a government purchase and diversion program at a cost to the treasury which is low in relation to the amount of money transferred to agriculture.

Countries that are residual suppliers of farm products on world markets are among those who have been most seriously affected by the widespread adoption of national support policies. They have been subjected to greater price instability and have lost markets as a result of

---

[8]At least some of the welfare costs of overpricing farm products can be neutralized or offset by using nonprice allocative mechanisms to limit supply and by subsidizing consumption. For an excellent discussion of the concept of welfare costs applied to agricultural support programs and the relative social costs of alternative support methods, see Wallace (1962).

measures adopted to increase self-sufficiency and insulate internal prices from changes in world demand or supply. By relying on imports to compensate for variations in internal production, much of the instability in grain production caused by variable weather in importing countries has been shifted to the principal exporters including the United States.

References

Campbell, Keith O. 1964. "National Commodity Stabilization Schemes: Some Reflections Based on Australian Experience," in *International Explorations of Agricultural Economics*. Ed. Roger N. Dixey. Ames, Iowa: Iowa State Univ. Press. Pp. 55–63.

Cochrane, Willard W., and Yigal Danin. 1976. *Reserve Stock Grain Models, The World and the United States, 1975–1985.* Univ. Minn. Ag. Exp. Sta. Tech. Bul. 305.

Eckstein, S., and M. Syrquin. 1971. "A Note on Fluctuations in Supply and Farmers' Income," *Am. J. Ag. Econ.*, 53:331–334.

Gislason, Conrad. 1959. "How Much Has the Canadian Wheat Board Cost the Canadian Farmers?" *J. Farm Econ.*, 41:584–599.

Hallett, Graham. 1968. *The Economics of Agricultural Policy.* Oxford: Basil Blackwell.

Helmberger, Peter, and Rob Weaver. 1977. "Welfare Implications of Commodity Storage under Uncertainty," *Am. J. Ag. Econ.*, 59:639–651.

Horton, Donald C. 1970. "Policy Directions for the United States Sugar Program," *Am. J. Ag. Econ.*, 52:185–196.

Johnson, D. Gale. 1947. *Forward Prices for Agriculture.* Chicago: Univ. of Chicago Press.

———. 1964. "Agriculture and Foreign Economic Policy," *J. Farm Econ.*, 46:915–929. Reprinted in *Agricultural Policy in an Affluent Society.* Ed. Vernon W. Ruttan *et al.* New York: W. W. Norton and Co. (1969). Pp. 264–281.

———. 1975. "World Agriculture, Commodity Policy, and Price Variability," *Am. J. Ag. Econ.*, 57:823–828.

Just, Richard E. 1977. "Theoretical and Empirical Possibilities for Determining the Distribution of Welfare Gains from Stabilization," *Am. J. Ag. Econ.*, 59:912–917.

———, et al. 1977. "The Distribution of Welfare Gains from International Price Stabilization under Distortions," *Am. J. Ag. Econ.*, 59:652–661.

Krishna, Raj. 1967. "Agricultural Price Policy and Economic Development," in *Agricultural Development and Economic Growth.* Ed. H. M. Southworth and B. F. Johnston. Ithaca, N.Y.: Cornell Univ. Press. Pp. 497–540.

McCrone, Gavin. 1962. *The Economics of Subsidising Agriculture.* London: George Allen and Unwin Ltd.

Myrdal, Gunnar. 1968. *Asian Drama.* Volume 3. New York: Pantheon. Appendix 5, pp. 2031–2039.

Pricing Institutions

Reutlinger, Shlomo. 1976. "A Simulation Model for Evaluating Worldwide Buffer Stocks of Wheat," *Am. J. Ag. Econ.*, 58:1–12.

Schickele, Rainer. 1954. *Agricultural Policy: Farm Programs and National Welfare.* New York: McGraw-Hill.

Turnovsky, Stephen J. 1978. "The Distribution of Welfare Gains from Price Stabilization: A Survey of Some Theoretical Issues," in *Stabilizing World Commodity Markets.* Ed. F. Gerard Adams and Sonia A. Klein. Lexington, Mass.: Lexington Books. Pp. 119–148.

USDA. 1970. *Major Statistical Series of the U.S. Department of Agriculture,* Volume 1: *Agricultural Prices and Parity.* Ag. Hb. 365.

Walker, Rodney L., Jerry A. Sharples, and Forrest Holland. 1976. "Grain Reserves for Feed Grains and Wheat in the World Grain Market," *Analysis of Grain Reserves, A Proceedings.* USDA ERS-634. Pp. 114–135.

Wallace, T. D. 1962. "Measures of Social Costs of Agricultural Programs," *J. Farm Econ.*, 44:580–594.

Waugh, Frederick V. 1944. "Does the Consumer Benefit from Price Instability?" *Quart. J. Econ.*, 48:602–614.

IV

INTRODUCTION TO
EMPIRICAL PRICE ANALYSIS

Two subjects are stressed in this section: (1) the formulation of models to explain the behavior of agricultural product prices or related variables and (2) the use and appraisal of the results of quantitative price analyses. Our intent is to provide sufficient discussion of model building to show how the economic principles presented in the earlier part of the book can be combined with statistical methods to produce useful empirical results. An additional objective is to enable the student to understand and interpret empirical studies. We do not present a formal discussion of statistical inference although some prior background in statistics, particularly in regression analysis, would be helpful. Excellent references in econometrics are available.

CHAPTER **15**

Background for

Price Analysis

The term "price analysis" usually refers to the quantitative study of demand-supply-price relationships. Much of price analysis is simply applied econometrics.[1] However, quantitative analyses may range from the construction of tables and graphs to the use of a variety of rather advanced mathematical tools. No attempt is made here to survey all available quantitative methods.

Two reasons for engaging in price analysis are (1) to estimate specific economic coefficients (parameters) such as price and income elasticities of demand and (2) to provide forecasts of prices or the variables affecting prices. As mentioned in previous chapters, estimates of elasticities are necessary to determine the effects of alternative policies such as a supply-control program. Forecasting is the objective of an important part of the price analysis work done by the U.S. Department of Agriculture, by extension economists in land-grant universities, and by economic research departments in private industry. In addition, price analysis is sometimes used simply to describe the behavior of prices and related variables. For example, one may want to determine whether or not there are persistent trends, cycles, or other regularities in the price series.

---

[1]Econometric techniques found rather early and wide use in agricultural economics, particularly in the estimation of demand and price relationships. Henry L. Moore (1914; 1917) is considered to be the founder of statistical estimation of economic relationships. Over the past 50 years, a large literature has developed with much of today's research firmly based on the pioneering research of the 1920s and 1930s (e.g., Schultz, 1938; Warren and Pearson, 1928; H. Working, 1922). Modern econometric methods are discussed in such books as Johnston (1972) and Maddala (1977). Judge (1977), Tomek (1977), and Tomek and Robinson (1977) provide reviews of various aspects of this rather large literature.

Empirical Price Analysis

This chapter is devoted to a discussion of alternative techniques of analysis, procedures in formulating models, sources of data, and the identification problem. More detail concerning the interpretation and use of results will be presented in the next chapter. This should enable the student to see the relationship between certain economic principles outlined earlier and empirical work. We hope that this will also help the student to gain an appreciation of the complexities of price analysis as well as some of the uses and limitations of statistical studies based on time-series data.

Alternate Techniques

Some individuals appear to have the ability to judge events qualitatively without the aid of formal methods of analysis, but it usually helps to have at hand the results of quantitative studies. Quantitative approaches to price analysis are emphasized in this book, but of course judgment is important in all types of analysis. Among other advantages, quantitative studies serve the purpose of making relationships among variables explicit.

A common type of quantitative analysis is based on persistent patterns of behavior in time-series data. Thus, price forecasts might be based on observed trends, seasonals, or cycles. One of the simplest approaches in forecasting is to assume that the recent past trend will continue in the immediate future. Other models could be based on the assumption of a changing rate of change, such as a diminishing rate of increase in production. Graphic methods provide a simple means of identifying trends or other persistent patterns of behavior. The most common procedure is to graph the variable of interest (such as price) on the vertical axis with time on the horizontal axis. In this way, the behavior of the variable through time can be observed (Figure 15-1). Of course, linear trend lines, harmonic functions, and so forth may be fitted, or moving averages computed. These relatively simple procedures often yield surprisingly accurate forecasts for the short run. But, forecasts based on trends miss all of the turning points (changes of direction) for the variable. Such changes can be extremely important in economics. The simpler techniques of analyzing patterns of behavior in time-series observations (trends, seasonal indexes, and moving averages) are developed in numerous introductory textbooks in statistics.

The "balance-sheet approach" is sometimes used by private business firms to summarize information which will help to indicate whether surpluses or deficits in supplies are likely to exist in the forthcoming year

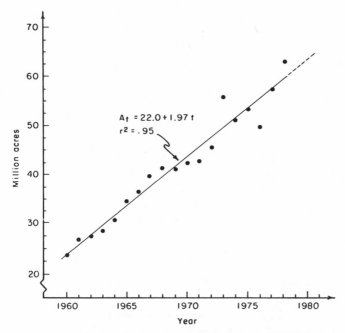

Figure 15-1. Acreage harvested, soybeans, United States, 1960-1978. *A* = million acres and *t* = time (1960 = 1, 1961 = 2, etc.). Data from USDA, *Agricultural Statistics 1977* and *Agricultural Statistics 1978.*

if current prices prevailed (see Ashby, 1964). Thus, an informed judgment can be made about whether or not prices in the future are going to rise or fall from current levels. The technique is essentially a method of organizing large quantities of data, especially for important farm commodities in international trade. The accuracy of the method depends mainly on the judgment and experience of the user.

A third quantitative approach to price analysis is to consider the relationships among variables.[2] Demand and supply functions are examples of particular economic relationships. Relationships among variables might be examined graphically, or they may be explicitly estimated by statistical methods. Scatter diagrams, which show relationships visually, are often a useful preliminary step in the analysis.

[2]Other quantitative techniques available to economists include operations research methods like linear programming. We concentrate on the formulation and use of simple econometric models, but this does not imply that other approaches are poorer methods of analysis. Each has its place, depending on the problem to be analyzed.

301

Empirical Price Analysis

Regression analysis provides a method of estimating relationships among variables. A multiple linear regression equation considers the net relationship between each explanatory variable (X) and a dependent variable (Y). Specifically,

$$Y_t = \beta_0 + \beta_1 X_{t1} + \beta_2 X_{t2} + \ldots + \beta_K X_{tK} + e_t,$$

where Y_t = observable dependent variable,
           X_{tk} = observable independent variables, K in number,
           e_t = unobservable error or disturbance term,
           β_k = unknown population parameters to be estimated,
and $t = 1, 2, \ldots, T$ observations on the variables.

The equation states that Y_t depends linearly on the observed X_{tk} and on the unobserved disturbances e_t. One statistical problem is to estimate the parameters $(\beta\text{'s})$ given the observations on the variables in the equations. Naturally, an estimation technique which provides "good" estimates is desired, and ordinary least squares is a commonly used method. The appropriate technique, however, depends on how the observations on Y_t and X_{tk} are generated (see Johnston, 1972, chapters 3 and 5; Maddala, 1977, chapters 7 and 8).

Varying assumptions may be made about what constitutes an appropriate model. The researcher must determine which observable variables will appear in the equation, whether the relationship is linear, what assumptions may reasonably be made about the nature of the error term, and so on. Moreover, more than one equation may be required to describe and analyze a particular problem. Then, an estimation method must be selected to obtain the coefficients and the results appraised and used. The appraisal of results will often suggest modifications of the initial model followed by re-estimation of the modified model.

Getting Started

Some General Comments

The first step in model specification is problem definition. For example, the growers of a particular commodity may want to know whether or not a supply-control program might raise their income. Hence, the analyst would need to test the hypothesis that the demand for the commodity is price inelastic in the relevant range of prices—one of the requirements for the proposed program to raise total revenue.

The second step in the analysis is to formulate a model that is oriented toward solving the stated problem. The model should be consistent with the logic and theory underlying the commodity sector being analyzed. The term "model" implies some abstraction from the real world. A model of a particular economic sector may be thought of as one or more equations that describe the important relationships among the variables.

Model building may be viewed as having two parts. One involves the specification of the economic model, that is, the general economic relationships. Economic theory can be thought of in terms of functions and certain variables within these functions. The second part of model building involves the explicit definition of equations which are to be estimated. For example, what variables appear in a particular equation, and how are these variables explicitly defined? Is the relationship linear or nonlinear? Based on the anwers to these and other similar questions, explicit equations are defined.

Given the equations to be estimated, the next step is to obtain observations on the variables and to estimate the coefficients which relate the variables. In practice, the specification of the equations to be estimated is likely to be influenced by the data available. The final step in analysis is to evaluate and use the results. The evaluation includes appropriate statistical and logical "tests." The use of results may include computation of elasticities, preparation of forecasts and simulation of alternative policy decisions.

There are perhaps three requirements for doing a good job of price analysis. First, a good knowledge of economic theory aids the researcher in model formulation. Second, the analyst needs to have a thorough knowledge of the economic sector being analyzed. This helps to provide specific details for the model, prevent errors, and correctly interpret the results. A third requirement is a good knowledge of statistical principles and methods, which is essential for correct estimation and hypothesis testing.

Economic Models—Some Elementary Examples

Economic theory suggests the general types of functions that may be appropriate for a particular research problem and also the economic variables that should appear in each equation. For example, in a demand relation, quantity is assumed to be a function of the commodity's own price, the prices of substitutes, income, and perhaps other variables. Theory also often suggests how these variables are related. The commodity's quantity and price are expected to be inversely related (negative sign); income and quantity would be positively related for most products. Theory typically does not tell us the precise functional relationship among variables, nor does it specify the magnitude of the coefficients which relate one variable to another. Thus, while price and quantity demanded are inversely related, we do not know whether a straight line or a curvilinear relationship is most appropriate.

To illustrate the use of models, we begin with a simple model of competitive price determination using linear demand and supply functions. The static equilibrium situation, which simultaneously determines price and quantity, can be defined by two equations with the third equation specifying that quantity demanded must equal quantity supplied in equilibrium.

$$Q_t^d = \alpha - \beta P_t \text{ (demand equation)}.$$
$$Q_t^s = \delta + \gamma P_t \text{ (supply equation)}.$$
$$Q_t^d = Q_t^s.$$

The subscript t indicates that P and Q are observed within some specific time period.

The first modification to make the model more realistic would be to permit changes in supply and demand, that is, shifts in these functions. For instance, assume R is a variable, say rainfall, which influences the level of supply but which is not in turn influenced by supply. Given these assumptions, the supply equation can be rewritten as

$$Q_t^s = \delta + \gamma P_t + \pi R_t.$$

As R increases, the level of Q increases, and vice versa (Figure 15-2). Other supply shifters may include variables like factor prices and technology.

Other elements of realism may come from the analyst's personal knowledge. Theory does not exhaust the factors that explain the level of supply in a particular time period, but theory does provide clues as to which variables are likely to be most important. There also may be "random" or "special" factors (e.g., a disease affecting yields) which have an impact on supply. If e_t is set equal to these disturbances or equation errors, then the supply equation can be rewritten as

(1) $\qquad Q_t^s = \delta + \gamma P_t + \pi R_t + e_t.$

In addition, total supply may equal production in the current period, stocks carried over from the previous period, and net imports. That is,

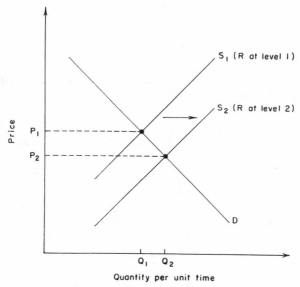

Figure 15-2. Changes in price and quantity as the result of changes in the variable R

$$(2) \qquad S_t = Q_t{}^s + C_t + I_t,$$

where S = total supply
        Q = current production
        C = carryover stocks
        I = imports.

It may be appropriate to have separate equations to explain Q, C, and I, rather than one equation to explain S. Again, this comes from the analyst's special knowledge of the economic sector rather than from economic theory.

In the terminology of econometrics, equation (1) is an example of a behavioral equation. Demand, consumption, and investment functions are other examples of behavioral equations. They contain parameters to be estimated, and since they are not exact functions, a disturbance term (designated e_t) is added. Equation (2) is a definitional equation. It is an exact relationship. Just as one plus one equals two, we are saying in equation (2) that by definition total supply equals the sum of current production, carryover stocks, and net imports.

Returning to the model depicted in Figure 15-2, the equations are (ignoring the disturbances for the moment):

(3) $\qquad Q_t{}^d = \alpha - \beta P_t$

(4) $\qquad Q_t{}^s = \delta + \gamma P_t + \pi R_t$

(5) $\qquad Q_t{}^d = Q_t{}^s.$

If the model is a correct approximation of the real world, then price does not determine quantity nor does quantity determine price; rather the two are simultaneously determined within time period t. When R changes, both P and Q change, and, over a discrete time interval, P and Q interact to determine the new equilibrium. Price influences quantity and quantity is influencing price. If this takes place within time t, then P and Q are, in effect, simultaneously or jointly determined. In this over-simplified model, the different levels of P and Q are generated by the shifts in supply resulting from changes in R. The variable R is assumed to be determined by outside conditions. If R is rainfall, then its level is determined by hydrological factors and certainly not by P and Q.

Equations (3), (4), and (5) form a simple simultaneous equations model. The variables that are simultaneously determined are called jointly determined or endogenous variables. Their values are determined simultaneously within the sector being studied. Variables that influence the endogenous variables but whose own level is determined by factors entirely outside the economic sector under consideration are called exogenous variables. In our illustration, R is exogenous, and P and Q are endogenous.

The cobweb model exemplifies a recursive system of equations such as those presented in the appendix to Chapter 9. In a recursive system, the endogenous variables are determined sequentially as a chain through time rather than simultaneously. In the cobweb model, quantity supplied in t is hypothesized to be a function of lagged price (not current price). The level of price in the previous period is determined by events at that time; it is a lagged endogenous variable. Exogenous and lagged endogenous variables are grouped under the general heading of predetermined variables.

The parameters of equations in a recursive system often can be appropriately estimated by a simpler method than the analogous parameters in a simultaneous model. Fortunately, a recursive model is appropriate for numerous agricultural commodities. A supply equation which is part of a recursive system, for example, can be treated as a single equation without specifying the other equations in the model.[3] Thus, in general,

---

[3] The analyst must decide whether or not single equation procedures are appropriate for the particular problem. If price and quantity are simultaneously determined within the

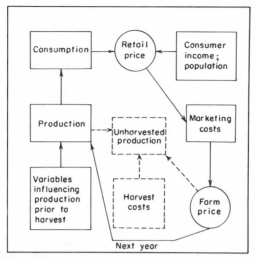

Figure 15-3. Simplified demand-supply structure for perishable commodity

when an equation can be considered part of a recursive system, some useful simplifications in specification and estimation are often possible.

Diagrams

The economic structure of agricultural commodities is more complex than the elementary models discussed so far. But the important economic relationships can be clarified through the use of a diagram. Rectangles represent variables; sometimes circles are used to represent price. Arrows show the direction of influence among variables (one-way or two-way), with heavy lines indicating the major paths of influence and dashed lines indicating the negligible or occasional paths.

A diagram for a simple recursive model is illustrated in Figure 15-3. In this illustration, production is determined by lagged endogenous and exogenous variables (the one-way arrows). The commodity is perishable; no stocks exist; consumption depends solely on the level of production. Usually, the quantity produced is consumed, but occasionally prices may be so low relative to harvesting costs that a part of the crop is abandoned (the dashed lines). Retail price is depicted as a function of the

time period covered by each observation, then the demand equation cannot be ignored, though the main interest is in the supply equation. The simultaneity in the determination of price and quantity should be taken into account in estimating the supply relation. A discussion of methods for estimating equations which are part of a simultaneous system are discussed in standard econometrics textbooks (e.g., Johnston, 1972, chapter 12).

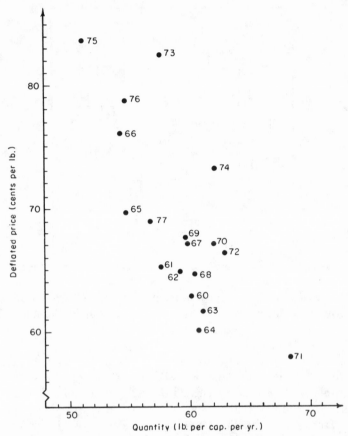

Figure 15-4. Relationship between retail price of pork (deflated by Consumer Price Index, 1967 = 1.0) and consumption of pork, United States, 1960-1977

quantity available for consumption and certain demand variables. The one-way arrow from income to price is technically not correct. The level of national income depends on prices and quantities of sales. Assuming that the product in question is a small proportion of the national economy, income is often treated as a predetermined variable.[4]

A diagram such as Figure 15-3 summarizes the analyst's knowledge, and of course the diagram is no better than the information going into it. The model would be more complicated if the product could be used in alternative ways. Producers may have a choice in selling their crop for fresh use or for processing. Under these circumstances, quantities sold

[4]Klein (1962, p. 69) points out that the absolute size of the error made by using this assumption may be small but that the relative bias can be large.

308

for different uses and the corresponding prices would be simultaneously determined although total output would still be predetermined by past events.

The scatter diagram (Figure 15-4) is a particularly useful tool in price analysis. It is relatively easy to construct and read, and it can help answer questions such as the following: Are changes in prices associated mainly with one variable such as changes in volume? Does the relationship appear to be linear or curvilinear? Is there evidence of systematic shifts in demand? When time-series data are used, it is useful to label each dot so as to see any systematic changes associated with the passage of time.

The scatter diagram depicts the simple relationship between two variables, but as we shall see, the "net" relationship between two variables, after taking account of the influence of other variables, differs from the simple two-variable relationship. Thus, while the two-dimensional diagram is a very useful tool, it is also subject to misuse.

Data Sources

In economics, the observations on variables typically are *not* generated by a formal experiment.[5] Rather, economic behavior is reflected in various nonexperimental data sources. Such data are the outcome of the many complex interactions of the real world.

Two major types of data are used in economic analyses: time series and cross section. Time-series data are sums or averages collected with the passage of time, e.g., monthly or annual average prices. The use of time-series data is emphasized here because such data are the cheapest and most readily available observations for most economic analyses. Cross-section observations are obtained from some population at a point in time. For instance, a sample of households in New York State might be interviewed over a short period of time with the objective of obtaining observations on household income, other household characteristics, and expenditures on various items.

Regardless of the source, the analyst should become thoroughly acquainted with the data, including the sources and methods used to construct the series. For example, how is beef "consumption" computed?[6] It is also important to make sure that the series being used accurately reflects the desired concept. If the objective is to develop a

---

[5] In an experiment, if $Y = f(X)$, then the experimenter can control X and observe the outcome Y. Occasionally, an economist can rely on an experiment to generate data for a specific problem.

[6] The USDA does not conduct a survey to measure consumption directly. Rather, data on beginning inventories, domestic production, exports and imports, and ending inven-

price-forecasting equation for apples used in processing, one should not use the average prices based on combined fresh and processing sales.

Agencies compiling data sometimes change the definition of a variable or the method of obtaining and computing it. For instance, the states included in a particular region might be changed, and consequently the production reported for a commodity in this region would change. Obviously, the reason for the change in production is a change in definition of the region and has nothing to do with the economics of supply. Therefore, an analysis of production in this region could be very misleading unless the analyst were familiar with the change in definition.

In another example, the "marketings" of cattle and calves in the United States have exceeded "production" by about 18 billion pounds in recent years (USDA, 1979, p. 26). The casual user who did not examine the definitions of these variables might assume that production (by his intuitive usage of the term) exceeds marketings. The careful user would study the definitions of both variables to determine the one appropriate for the analysis.

If more than two sources exist for the observations on a particular variable, the most recent source should be used. It presumably contains any recent revisions. Thus, in obtaining data, the analyst should start with the most recent source and work back as necessary, checking, where possible, for consistency in the different sources. Observations issued by a particular agency, say the Bureau of Census, may be reprinted in a variety of other sources. It is usually a good policy to go to the original source to obtain the observations.

The Identification Problem

Assume the problem is to estimate a market demand function based on annual observations. The data are nonexperimental time-series observations. Thus, price is an annual average and quantity is an annual total for each year. The price may be viewed as an average equilibrium price and quantity as the equilibrium quantity exchanged. In this example, the identification problem is whether or not a demand equation can be estimated from the observed prices and quantities. It is possible to compute coefficients that relate price and quantity, but the question is whether the coefficients obtained really are estimates of the true demand coefficients. This is not a easy question to answer. The discussion which follows assumes that a competitive market structure is appropriate.

---

tories are used to compute "domestic disappearance" during a given time period. This quantity is assumed to be "consumed."

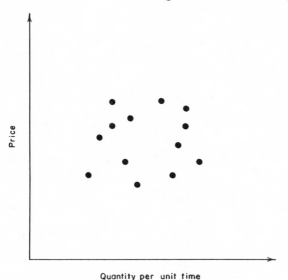

Figure 15-5. Scatter diagram with no identifiable relationship

If the economy were perfectly static, then the observed outcome would be a single price and quantity—the point of equilibrium. In this case, it would be impossible to estimate either a demand or a supply function since an infinite number of curves could be constructed to go through the equilibrium point.

With the passage of time, supply and demand functions are expected to change (shift), and these changes may help identify one or the other or both of the relations. However, this is not guaranteed because these average equilibrium points may form a "shot-gun pattern" (Figure 15-5), and without specific information on how the pattern was generated, neither relationship can be inferred from the data. In other words, the scatter of observations may have been the result of many combinations of changes in demand and supply. These changes "do not carry any labels accommodating to analysts which explain whether they were due to demand forces or supply forces" (Breimyer, 1961, p. 56). This means that additional information must be obtained (or assumed) about how the observations were generated.

If the demand curve shifted through time and the supply curve remained stable, then the observations trace out a supply curve (Figure 15-6). If the supply curve shifts (either for systematic or random reasons) and the demand curve remains stable, then the observations would trace out a demand curve (similar to Figure 15-2). The additional information necessary to achieve identification in these cases is the knowledge that

311

Empirical Price Analysis

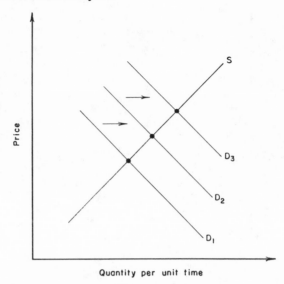

Figure 15-6. A supply relation identified

one function is stable while the other is changing (E. Working, 1927).

However, even if the observations form a definite pattern on a scatter diagram, it is still possible that neither function can be identified. This occurs if the shifts in the functions are highly or perfectly correlated, as they might be if both were shifting to the right through time with changes in population and technology. In Figure 15-7, the shifts in the functions are negatively correlated; the observations form a negative slope; but the function connecting the dots clearly is not a demand function.

Thus, (1) if the demand function is relatively stable and the supply function shifts and (2) if the shifts in the two functions are not highly correlated, then the demand function is identified. An analogous argument can be made for the identifiability of the supply equation.

The preceding discussion is based on the simplest possible simultaneous equations model. With more complex models, the question of whether or not the equations in the model are identified is handled in an explicit mathematical fashion (see Johnston, 1972, chapter 12; Maddala, 1977, pp. 220-231).[7]

[7]Identification is achieved through knowledge about the explicit predetermined variables which are "shifters" in the various functions. We argued that identification might be achieved if one function changed relative to the other and if these changes were uncorrelated. This is typically achieved when the functions have different predetermined variables. For instance, in Figure 15-2, R is assumed to be a systematic predetermined variable in the supply equation, and these shifts in supply trace out a demand function.

The identification problem is a general one in the estimation of economic relationships, but it is in simultaneous-equations models that the identification problem is explicitly considered. The question of identification also arises for equations in a recursive system. Fortunately, equations in a "true" recursive system are identifiable, and the question of identification typically is not explicitly considered (however, see Klein, 1962, pp. 75–81). Thus, assuming current supply is solely dependent on lagged price and other predetermined variables, estimates of the coefficients relating these variables (using an appropriate technique) are estimates of the true supply coefficients. This means that as long as the equations considered subsequently can be viewed as part of a recursive system, they are identified.

Equations in a Recursive System

The price structure for some agricultural commodities is best represented by a recursive model. As previously discussed, current production is a function of lagged prices as well as exogenous factors, and this quantity, once produced, is a principal factor determining current price. Annually produced crops often fall within this framework. Fox's research (1953) suggests that the supply of certain types of livestock also is largely predetermined for any given year. For example, on January 1, the

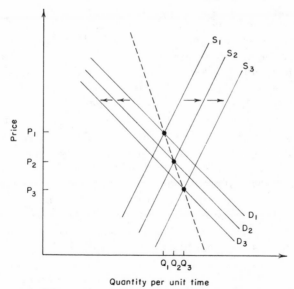

Figure 15-7. Correlated changes in supply and demand and neither a supply nor a demand curve identified

number of pigs in various age categories is known and fixed. The size of the coming spring pig crop also can be estimated and essentially is fixed by the number of sows already bred. Thus, the quantity of hogs marketed in one year is largely predetermined by the events of the previous year.

Recursive models, if applicable to a problem, are appealing. The parameters of the model are identifiable, and generally the relatively simple method of least squares can be used to estimate the parameters. Thus, we turn to some details of specifying equations. Numerous decisions must be made by the analyst in building a model. We can only convey information about the types of decisions to be made, but no precise guides exist to determine "the" appropriate model. Model building is partly an art which must be refined by experience, and the correctness of a particular model depends, in part, on the objectives of the analysis.

Market-Supply Equations

The complex, chainlike process of production in agriculture permits substantial latitude in building supply equations. Careful definition of terms is essential. Total supply in a specific time period may depend not only on current production but also on carryover stocks and imports and exports. The analyst may wish to develop separate equations to explain storage stocks and net imports. In this section, we concentrate on equations relating to current production.

Production in a given time period equals yield per unit multiplied by the number of units. Units may be in area or animal number terms. For instance, total milk production equals the number of producing cows multiplied by average pounds of milk per cow. Thus, while the analyst may consider making total production dependent in one equation, it may be more appropriate to consider yields and units separately in two or more equations. Using total production as the dependent variable is simpler since only one equation is involved, but some detail is lost in the process. There are often several measures of production, including total production, harvested production, and sales to particular markets (e.g., for fresh or for processing uses). Total production presumably is not related to current price because of the lag in the production process. However, current price may influence quantities harvested or allocated to various uses; such quantities and price would be simultaneously determined.

The producer usually has more control over the number of units planted than over yields. Thus, acres planted (sows farrowing, etc.) is often used as the dependent variable in analyzing producers' supply response to various factors. Yields, on the other hand, may be largely influenced by factors over which the producer has little or no control (moisture, temperatures, pests). Some factors, like level of fertility, can be controlled, but yield equations typically are difficult to specify, and they frequently exhibit strong underlying trends.

We especially consider, then, equations which explain units like acres or cow numbers. The general nature of the independent variables is suggested, in part, by theory. The product's price, the prices of other products competing for the same production resources, and input prices are logical explanatory variables, but with the substantial lag between the decision to produce and the actual realization of production, a problem exists in specifically defining the price variables to which producers respond. One hypothesis is that production responds to expected prices and costs and that expectations are based on current or recent experience. Thus, assuming the dependent variable is acres planted in the current time period, then the independent variables for prices and costs typically are those for the previous year. Other hypotheses about the appropriate definition of variables, of course, are possible. Prices lagged two or more periods also might be considered; other alternatives include some weighted average of past prices or perhaps prices of contracts for future delivery of the product.

Two considerations in specifying the time lag between prices and quantity are the units of time (month, year, etc.) in which the variables are observed and the actual biological lag in the production process. There are clearly differences in the speed of response possible in egg production on the one hand and milk on the other. Producers in both cases can control the rate of culling from existing herds or flocks rather quickly, but new additions to producing units can be made much faster for chickens than for cows.

Equation specification must emphasize the major factors thought to influence supply. It is not possible to include an exhaustive set of variables. For instance, the price of a single major input or an index of input prices is commonly used to represent costs. The price of corn in a pork supply equation represents the major input in pork production. Similarly, prices of one or two major substitutes (on the production side) might be included, e.g., the price of corn in a soybean supply equation.

Supply schedules for many agricultural commodities have shifted because of technological change. In fact, changes in technology often seem to be the dominant factor in explaining supply changes, but unfortunately there is no direct measure of "changes in technology." We must resort to the rather unsatisfactory device of a proxy variable. The most common proxy is a trend variable, e.g., the numbers 1, 2, . . . , T. This specification assumes a smooth change in technology of equal amounts each time period. Sometimes general measures of changes in productivity are used, such as an index of changes in productivity (changes in output per unit of input).

Using trend as a proxy for the concept "technology" illustrates a rather common practice in empirical price analyses. In cases where the variable itself is not directly observable, the analyst is compelled either to use a substitute or to omit the concept from the model. One can ask whether it is better in a statistical sense to include the proxy variable. No simple answer exists for this question, though the usual practice is to include proxy variables rather than omit the concept from the model. Maddala (1977, pp. 158–162) provides a useful discussion of the problem.

Current production is usually highly correlated with production in the previous time period. We noted in Chapter 4 that the production of various farm commodities in particular regions is influenced by physical and climatic considerations. For example, many acres devoted to wheat simply have no viable alternatives over a wide range of prices. Further, large changes in production tend to be restricted by factors like resource fixity, managerial ability of farmers, and habitual production patterns. As a result of such considerations, some researchers have specified the dependent variable lagged one time period as an independent variable (if Q_t is dependent, then Q_{t-1} is independent).[8] This simply says that current production is influenced by the level of production in the previous period, and current production may be viewed as changing from the previous level in response to various price and cost factors. Unfortunately, the lagged dependent variable often tends to be highly correlated with the influence of technology and other trending explanatory factors; in such cases the lagged variable becomes, in part, a proxy for other variables. As a consequence, the effect of the lagged variable may be overstated. Models with lagged dependent variables are popular, but they create statistical problems and are subject to misuse, especially by the inexperienced analyst.

When specifying yield or total production equations, independent variables may include noneconomic factors influencing the dependent

---

[8]The inclusion of the lagged dependent variable as an independent variable may also be justified by means of distributed lag concepts. The distributed lag view implies that if Q_{t-1} is an appropriate variable, then expected price (to which producers respond) is a geometric average of all past prices (Nerlove, 1956).

variable. Such factors might include rainfall at critical growth periods, soil moisture reserves, or a weather index. An illustration of a supply relation is given in Chapter 16.

Market Demand and Price Equations

If prices and quantities are indeed determined recursively, then price is the logical dependent variable in the demand equation while the quantity of the commodity as well as the quantities of the major substitutes are specified as the independent variables. However, the quantity variables for some agricultural commodities are not predetermined. Production of an annual crop is predetermined, but the quantity harvested may be influenced by price. Imports and exports also may be influenced by current prices. Furthermore, a commodity like broilers has a sufficiently short production period so that supply and price may be jointly determined within a twelve-month period. Nonetheless, the quantity available for domestic consumption of a number of agricultural products appears to be largely predetermined for periods of twelve months or less. The analyst, of course, must make the ultimate decision as to whether or not the quantity variable is predetermined for the commodity being considered.[9]

Income is thought to be one of the important demand "shifters," and is often included as an independent variable. Again, the regression model assumes that income influences the dependent variable but not vice versa. This is technically not correct because the level of income in an economy is influenced by the quantities and prices of all (final) goods and services which are sold. Hence, income is jointly determined with prices and quantities. However, any one commodity typically is a very small part of the economy, i.e., makes a small contribution to income. For example, a change in the marketings and price of beef changes the level of national income, but the change is small relative to the total. Therefore, income is typically treated as if it were a predetermined variable in demand equations for agricultural commodities.[10]

The most commonly used measure of income is consumer-disposable income—income after taxes. The consumer can allocate this income among an almost infinite array of goods and services. However, most

---

[9]Waugh (1964), a greatly respected price analyst, takes the position that the objective of most studies should be forecasting, and hence that the variable to be forecast naturally determines the variable to be treated as dependent.

[10]In some economies, national income can depend largely on one commodity so that this would be an incorrect assumption. (Also, see comment and citation in footnote 4, this chapter.)

consumers have fixed commitments like utility bills and rents to pay. Therefore, some economists have suggested that a measure of discretionary income—that part of income over which the consumer has discretion—is most appropriate in demand analysis. Other variables like tastes and preferences can change systematically with the passage of time. It is sometimes difficult to separate statistically the effects of the upward trend in income from other factors which systematically influence demand. If income alone is treated as the major demand shifter, then the influence of income on demand may be understated or overstated depending on the correlation of income with the other variables which are omitted. If other variables that change systematically are included, they are often so highly correlated with income that it is impossible to estimate accurately the separate effects of each variable. This is the problem of multicollinearity (high intercorrelation) among the independent variables of regression analysis.

Changes in population have a direct influence on market demand relations. The population variable is commonly taken into account by putting the quantity and income variables on a per capita basis (dividing total quantity and income by population). Sometimes a question of the relevant population arises. Typically, this is the population of the entire country, but for a commodity like beer the relevant population might include those 18 years and older. Changes in the distribution of the population by age, occupation, or region may have an impact on demand. For example, the aging of the U.S. population probably has a negative effect on the demand for fluid milk. Hence, in a study of the demand for milk, a variable representing the age distribution of the population might be considered.

Substitutes and complements probably have important impacts on demand, but these effects are often difficult to measure. There are two reasons for this. The first is that individual substitutes or complements may have only a small influence on demand, and the second is that the variables measuring the influence of substitutes are often highly correlated. The common practice is to include one or two variables representing major substitutes. If price is the dependent variable, then a quantity variable for the substitute is usually used. The assumption is that this variable is predetermined. For example, the price of pork could be made a function of the quantity of beef. Sometimes an aggregate measure of substitutes is used. This might be the sum of several variables. For example, substitutes in a pork demand equation might be measured by the aggregate consumption of all other meats. Index numbers of prices or quantities of substitute commodities are occasionally constructed. This approach attempts to take account of a number of substitutes in one variable, but it does not permit the measurement of the separate influences of individual commodities.

In a price equation for an individual state, the analyst must not forget that the most important substitute for the product grown in the state is the same product grown in other states. The farm price of apples in New York State depends on New York production and production in other states. Similarly, the most important substitute for a particular grade of a commodity is other grades of the same commodity.

Changes in tastes and preferences may influence demand, and such changes are perhaps the most difficult to handle in statistical demand analyses. There is no direct measure of tastes. Hence, the researcher must either assume that there was no change in tastes and preferences during the period analyzed or use a proxy variable. The most common proxy variable is simply a linear trend. This approach assumes that tastes have changed in a continuous and regular fashion over the period analyzed. An analyst may believe in some cases that the change in tastes is associated with such factors as urbanization or shifts to more sedentary work. This suggests the possibility of using a proxy variable like the percentage of the labor force in blue-collar jobs.

Depending on the objective of the study and on the commodity sector being studied, other variables might be considered. If the equation is a derived demand (say, farm-level) equation, then it is appropriate to consider the effects of a change in the marketing margin. Or, the analyst may wish to consider the influence of advertising by using a measure of the amount of money spent advertising a particular commodity or the space devoted to advertising (e.g., see Thompson and Eiler, 1977).

Deflating

One of the issues that arises in model specification is whether or not to deflate and by what variables. In price analyses, deflating often involves dividing nominal prices and incomes by a price index to obtain real prices and incomes. For example, personal disposable income (Y_t) may be divided by the Consumer Price Index (I_t) to obtain real disposable income (X_t). That is, $X_t = Y_t/I_t$, where $t = 1, 2, \ldots, T$ time periods. More broadly, deflating includes placing variables in ratio form rather than incorporating them as separate explanatory variables in the equation.

The reasons for deflating can be categorized under two general headings: one is related to economic theory and the other to statistical problems. For example, demand theory suggests that it is appropriate to deflate if, when all prices and income increase or decrease by the same percentage, demand remains unchanged. As pointed out in Chapter 3, this follows from the homogeneity assumption. Thus, if this assumption is correct, it is appropriate to deflate the individual price and income variables in a linear demand equation by a general index of prices.

If, however, changes in the general price level have an "illusion effect" on the demand for the product under study, then deflating is not appropriate. An illusion effect simply means that the demand for the product changes in response to nominal prices even though real prices have not changed. An alternative to deflating in this case is to include the product's price and the general index of prices as separate variables.

Deflating a price series may be inconvenient or even unnecessary when the objective of the analysis is to forecast prices. The researcher usually wants to forecast the nominal price, not a deflated price. The simplest model in such cases is to make the nominal price the dependent variable. On the other hand, as suggested above, the economic hypothesis to be tested may best be stated in real terms, and, in this case, deflating is appropriate.

Another practical consideration in deciding whether or not to use a deflated series is the amount of information conveyed. Clearly a ratio combines two variables into one with a single coefficient. The hog-corn price ratio is typical of such variables. In using such a ratio, one cannot distinguish between the effects of the price of corn and the price of hogs on the supply of hogs. With the passage of time, the relative importance of the two variables may change. For example, in the 1950s and 1960s, the ratio changed mainly because the price of hogs changed, while in the 1970s both corn and hog prices were highly variable. Under the latter conditions, it may be useful to have estimates of the separate effects of each variable. Meilke's research (1977) does suggest that forecasts of hog supply may be improved by using separate variables.

At least two statistical reasons have been used to justify deflating. One is to help reduce the high correlations among explanatory variables. Prices and price indexes often have strong underlying trends and thus tend to be highly correlated. Population and income often follow the same pattern through time. Thus, including such variables separately in an equation may make it difficult to disentangle statistically the separate effects of the variables. This is the problem of multicollinearity or high intercorrelations. Sometimes analysts attempt to reduce the problem by converting quantity and income variables to per capita figures and by deflating prices and income by a general price index. In other words,

320

some variables are combined in ratio form rather than appearing separately in the equation. (Maddala, 1977, pp. 192–193 discusses some of the issues which arise when using ratios as a solution to the multicollinearity problem.)

A second statistical problem has to do with the nature of the variance of the error term of the equation being estimated (the variance of e_t). This variance is often assumed to be a constant over the range of the data (the assumption of homoscedasticity), but if this assumption is not true, then the classical least-squares method of estimating the coefficients of the equation cannot be justified statistically. However, if the variance of e_t is assumed equal to $\sigma^2 X_t^2$ where σ is a constant and X_t is one of the explanatory variables, then the analyst is justified in dividing (deflating) all of the variables in the equation by X_t. Least squares is then applied to the transformed equation (Maddala, 1977, pp. 265–268). For example,

$$Y_t = \alpha + \beta W_t + \gamma X_t + e_t, \text{ var } (e_t) = \sigma^2 X_t^2 \text{ and}$$
$$Y_t/X_t = \alpha/X_t + \beta (W_t/X_t) + \gamma + u_t, \text{ var.}(u_t) = \sigma^2.$$

In the foregoing example, the deflator was selected on statistical grounds. The deflator is probably selected more often on economic grounds. A common practice in demand analysis for a single food product is to divide the nominal prices by the Consumer Price Index (CPI) for all items. The CPI also may be the appropriate deflator for farm-level or wholesale-level demand equations provided the equations contain a measure of the marketing margin (Foote, 1958, p. 28). A common practice in estimating aggregate consumption functions or systems of demand equations is to use an implicit price deflator based on the Gross National Product (GNP). The GNP deflator for a particular year contains all of the goods and services produced in the economy that year. In contrast, the CPI measures the cost of a fixed bundle of goods that does not vary over time except for periodic revisions.

By deflating, one seeks to obtain the best possible measure of real prices (or whatever concept is under consideration), where by "best measure" we mean the variable that comes closest to measuring the relative prices to which consumers respond. That is, assuming relative prices are important, the practical problem is to find a precise, relevant measure of relative prices.

As explained in Chapter 10, an index based on fixed weights, like the CPI, can exaggerate the price-level changes faced by consumers. The GNP deflator is not subject to this problem (Dornbusch and Fischer, 1978), but since it implicitly contains all goods and services in the economy, its relevance for studying the demand for a particular product is not clear. Government services, for example, are an important component of the GNP deflator, and whether this is necessary in defining, say, the real price of beef is not especially clear. Unfortunately, there is no simple rule or guide for selecting the appropriate deflator. The final decision must be made problem by problem, and the analyst's experience is an important base for decision-making.

If the index used in the deflation procedure contains the price series being deflated, then the coefficients relating the deflated variable to other variables are likely to be biased. The amount of bias depends on the relative weight which the price series being deflated has in the index. If it is a large component of the index (e.g., the price of beef in an index of meat prices), then the bias is large. A regression equation with price as a function of quantity illustrates the point. A small quantity produced implies a high product price, and this also means a higher price index. The larger index, however, means that the ratio is reduced. In other words, since the index changes because of the change in this particular commodity's price, deflating by that index tends to "cancel" the influence of the price change. Consequently, the regression coefficient relating quantity to deflated price is biased.

Some analysts also have felt that deflating two variables, say Y and X, by a common deflator may result in spurious inferences about the relation of Y to X, and if the empirical problem is in terms of Y and X, these are the variables to use in the analysis. On the other hand, if logic suggests deflating, then one should deflate. Whether or not to deflate is basically a question of correct model specification. Moreover, the deflated variables do not necessarily have a larger correlation than the undeflated variables; this is an empirical question which must be answered for the particular pair of variables (Maddala, 1977, p. 267).

Alternative Functional Forms

The researcher also must decide which specific functional form is appropriate for the behavioral equation being estimated. The criteria used in selecting functional forms can be conveniently placed in three groups. One is the mathematical properties of the function relative to the logic underlying the relation, but theory and logic often are not very helpful in suggesting specific functional forms.

A consumption function for an individual product illustrates the thought that may go into selecting a functional form. A household's consumption of a particular product may very well be zero at and below some level of income. As income increases, consumption normally rises. But consumption growth may level off and approach a maximum at high levels of income. For some products, consumption may even reach a maximum within the range of observable data and turn down. Thus, in specifying a consumption-income relation, the functional form should be flexible enough to intersect the income axis (consumption equals zero) at a positive level of income and then curve upward (a changing positive slope) approaching a maximum. Since a number of functions have this general shape, logic still does not dictate the specific form to select. The form might vary from product to product.[11]

The reasonableness of the elasticities implied by the functional form over the range of the data is another aspect of selecting the form on the basis of logic. Different functional forms also will give similar forecasts of the dependent variable when the explanatory variables are near their means, but give very different predictions at the extreme values. Since economic variables often exhibit strong trends, forecasts are likely to be based on values far from the means of the variables. Thus, the behavior of the equation at the data extremes may be more important than the behavior near the means of the variables.

A second type of criterion involves statistical tests and the fit of the equation to the sample of data. The intuitive idea is to find the functional form that "best" fits the data, where best is defined in terms of statistical measures. A few goodness-of-fit measures, like the coefficient of determination, are discussed in Chapter 16. Unfortunately, a goodness-of-fit measure may have similar magnitudes for different functional forms (even though the functions may behave differently at the data extremes). Also, if the dependent variable is measured in different units for different functions (Y and the logarithm of Y), then the coefficients of determination are not directly comparable. Moreover, a rule based on goodness-of-fit can lead to selection of the wrong model; it is not an infallible rule (Theil, 1971, p. 544). It is true, however, that formal statistical tools are available for comparing functional forms; interested readers may consult Maddala (1977, pp. 314–317).

A third criterion in selecting functional forms is simplicity. Other

---

[11]A logical reason exists, however, for using the same functional form for all goods and services. In consumption function analysis, consumption is sometimes measured by the expenditure on each product, and total expenditures is used as a proxy for income. If n equations are fitted for all goods and services, then the sum of the dependent variables for the n equations should equal the explanatory variable, total expenditure, which appears in each of the n equations. This is the so-called adding-up criterion. In this situation, the analyst may select a single functional form for all n equations that meets this criterion.

things being equal, the simplest possible equation is preferred. "Simple" is usually defined as the equation with the fewest parameters.

In principle, the decision on a functional form should be made prior to the empirical analysis, based on the logic of the problem. In practice, however, theory and logic alone are not powerful enough to suggest a unique form for a particular behavioral equation, and consequently the functional form is usually based on the analyst's judgment, which in turn is implicitly or explicitly based on the criteria outlined above.

Some common functional forms used in empirical price analyses are summarized in Table 15-1. The slope coefficients shown in the table are the first derivative of Y with respect to X, and when the function contains logarithms of the variables, the derivatives assume natural (base e), not common, logarithms. The slope coefficient is one mathematical property that can be used to compare a particular form with the logic of the problem under analysis. The selection of a specific function automatically implies a restriction on the nature of the slope, and the analyst can ask whether this restriction is sensible.

The simplest, and most common, specification is the linear equation, i.e., a straight-line relationship. In this case, the slope is a constant over the entire range of the data. For each one unit change in X, Y is specified as changing by the fixed amount, beta (β). This simple specification has proved applicable to a rather large number of problems. The general applicability of the linear relation is perhaps the result of the modest range over which data are observed; a linear approximation may be reasonable even if the "larger" relation is curvilinear.

Table 15-1. Some alternative functional forms used in price analysis

Name	Equation	Slope (dY/dX)
Linear	$Y = \alpha + \beta X$	β
Quadratic	$Y = \alpha + \beta X + \gamma X^2$	$\beta + 2\gamma X$
Hyperbola	$Y = \alpha - \beta/X$	β/X^2
Semi-log	$Y = \alpha + \beta \ln X$	β/X
Double log	$\ln Y = \alpha + \beta \ln X$	$\beta(Y/X)$
Log-inverse	$\ln Y = \alpha - \beta/X$	$\beta(Y/X^2)$
Transcendental	$\ln Y = \alpha + \beta \ln X + \gamma X$	$Y(\beta/X + \gamma)$
Log-log-inverse	$\ln Y = \alpha + \beta \ln X - \gamma/X$	$Y/X^2(\beta X + \gamma)$

Comment: Derivatives, dY/dX, assume natural logarithms (base e).

The second most common functional form is the double logarithm specification. This model is curvilinear in the original observations.

$$Y_t = \gamma X_t{}^\beta.$$

By taking logarithms, the model is made linear in the parameters.

$$lnY_t = ln\gamma + \beta lnX_t = \alpha + \beta lnX_t, \text{ where } \alpha = ln\gamma.$$

In this case, the coefficients $ln\gamma$ and β are constants that may be estimated after the equation has been transformed to logarithms.[12] The slope is not a constant (Table 15-1), but the parameter β is a constant. Hence, the percentage relationship between a change in X and a change in Y is a constant. That is, as

$$dY/dX = \beta(Y/X), \quad \beta = (dY/dX)(X/Y).$$

Since the percentage relationship is equivalent to the elasticity concept, the double logarithm specification, in effect, forces the elasticity to be a constant over the range of the data (see also Chapter 3, footnote 2).

To summarize, the assumption of a constant slope or of a constant elasticity is not necessarily good or bad. Rather, the point is that the analyst must recognize the implications of the mathematical properties of the function used relative to the logic of the behavioral, economic relationship.

First Differences

The first-difference transformation has been proposed as a pragmatic solution to a variety of problems encountered in price analysis. The transformation can best be understood by starting with a model in terms of the original data.

$$(6) \qquad Y_t = \alpha + \beta X_t + \gamma t + e_t.$$

The dependent variable, Y, depends linearly on the variable X and on the time trend t as well as an error term e. This model is, of course,

[12]For convenience the Greek letters alpha, beta, and gamma are used in each of the equations presented in Table 15-1. Of course, if each of the equations were fitted to the same data, the coefficients would differ from equation to equation.

assumed to hold for the entire sample period $t = 1, 2, \ldots, T$. Thus, one is justified in writing the equation lagged one time period.

(7) $\qquad Y_{t-1} = \alpha + \beta X_{t-1} + \gamma(t-1) + e_{t-1}.$

The first-difference transformation simply involves taking the differences between the adjacent observations in a time series. In effect, equation (7) is subtracted from equation (6) to give

(8) $\qquad Y_t - Y_{t-1} = \alpha - \alpha + \beta(X_t - X_{t-1}) + \gamma(t - (t-1)) + e_t - e_{t-1},$

or $\qquad\qquad \Delta Y_t = \beta(\Delta X_t) + \gamma + v_t, \ v_t = e_t - e_{t-1}.$

In practice, the data are transformed to first differences, and equation (8) is estimated directly, say, by least squares. The estimated slope coefficient receives the same interpretation in equation (8) as in (6). However, the intercept coefficient, gamma, in first differences is a measure of the trend, if any, in Y. Equation (8) states that, even if the change in X is zero, Y is changing by gamma amount each time period (for a discussion of first differences of logarithms see Foote, 1958, pp. 29, 43).

First differences have been suggested as a solution for two statistical problems. One is the possible autocorrelation of the error term e_t. The classic least-squares estimation method assumes that the successive values of e_t in equation (6) have zero correlations; that is, the covariance between e_t and e_{t-1} is assumed to be zero. Likewise, applying least squares to equation (8) assumes that the v_t have zero autocorrelations. Thus, the first-difference transformation has been used when the analyst has thought that the assumption of zero autocorrelations was more nearly applicable to equation (8) than to (6). Note, $v_t = e_t - e_{t-1}$ or $e_t = e_{t-1} + v_t$. If r in $e_t = re_{t-1} + v_t$ is near one, and if v_t has the classic regression properites, then least squares should be applied to the first-difference equation, but if r is near zero, then least squares should be applied directly to the original equation (Maddala, 1977, pp. 274–291).

A second potential problem is a very high correlation between X and t: the problem of multicollinearity mentioned above. If the right-hand-side variables are in differences, they may be less correlated than the original data. Hence, the first-difference transformation may permit more precise estimates of the separate effects of the explanatory variables. The difficulty with this solution, however, is that the error term of the transformed equation (the v_t) may not meet the classical assumptions.

Some analysts just prefer to work with first differences. If they are making forecasts of Y, they may prefer viewing the problem as one of forecasting the change in Y from its previous level. A scatter diagram of the first differences of Y and X gives a picture of the slope relation between Y and X as well as a measure of the trend, if any, in Y. In the 1950s, the use of first differences was quite popular in agricultural price analysis (Foote, 1958; Fox, 1953). Then, as newer approaches to the problem of autocorrelated error terms were devised, the use of the first-difference transformation declined. First differences still have a role to play in empirical price analyses, but like other procedures, the judgment of the analyst is important in determining appropriate applications.

Time-Series Data

We have previously noted that the selection of variables, how accurately the series are measured, and whether or not they are deflated and by what index, has a bearing on the results. Among the additional decisions that have to made in using time-series observations are the following:

(1) What specific years should be covered (included) by the analysis? Dropping some years and adding others may alter the results.

(2) Should one make use of annual, quarterly, monthly, weekly, or daily observations?

Two conflicting factors enter into the decision as to what historical time period to use. One consideration is the number of observations. Other things being equal, we prefer a long time series simply to increase the number of degrees of freedom—that is, we prefer a large number of observations relative to the number of variables in the equation. A second factor, however, is the desire to have the analysis cover a relatively homogenous time period, which would yield results relevant to the immediate future. This usually implies a recent, relatively short, series. "Abnormal" years, including war years or periods with special government programs, may sometimes be excluded. If this is done, it should be based on logic prior to the analysis and should not involve dropping observations simply to improve the fit.

A second question is the choice of time unit for analysis. The researcher may have access to daily, monthly, or quarterly, as well as annual, observations. Which should be used? The objectives of the study usually dictate the choice. Obviously, annual observations would not be appropriate if the objective is to estimate seasonal demand relations. Observations for short time units do require more complex models; seasonal and other short-time variations must be explained. Conversely, annual observations which are essentially averages of short-time variations may make it possible to use somewhat simpler models.

Many price-analysis studies have been based on annual observations. This is a natural period for summarizing data, and hence annual data are readily available. If the objective is to make specific short-term forecasts, then it is essential to have monthly or quarterly data. Recent studies have included more complex models using shorter units of time. Of course, such data increase the number of observations (as compared with annual observations).

A third problem with time-series data is that of consistency. There are calendar, crop, and fiscal years. The researcher must guard against obtaining quantity observations on a crop-year basis and prices on a calendar-year basis. Also, the data should be obtained at the same market level: farm, wholesale, or retail. And, as previously mentioned, the researcher should be sure that the definition or method of construction of the variable has not changed over the time period being considered.

A Final Comment

Some of the foregoing comments can be illustrated by the following price-dependent demand equation for pork. Mnemonic notation, rather than conventional Y's and X's, is used.

$$\left(\frac{P}{I} \right)_t = \beta_0 + \beta_1 \left(\frac{Q}{L} \right)_t + \beta_2 \left(\frac{Q_b}{L} \right)_t + \beta_3 \left(\frac{Y}{LI} \right)_t + e_t,$$

where
P = retail price of pork, cents per pound,
Q = consumption of pork, pounds,
Q_b = consumption of beef, pounds,
Y = disposable personal income, dollars,
I = Consumer Price Index,
L = July 1 U.S. population,
t = 1, 2, . . . , T observations,
e = unobserved disturbance or error term.

This specification states that the deflated price of pork is a linear function of the per capita quantity of pork, the per capita quantity of beef, real per capita disposable income, and a disturbance term. The simple scatter diagram for deflated price and per capita quantity of pork on an annual basis is given in Figure 15-4.

Assuming the specification is correct, the analyst obtains the necessary data (observations on the variables) and estimates the values of the unknown β's. If the explanatory variables are predetermined, then the most commonly used estimation method is ordinary least squares (for a discussion of the method see Johnston, 1972, Chapters 2 and 3).

The equation represents one possible specification. Numerous other alternatives are available. The analyst, for instance, might wish to consider other substitutes, such as broilers, or to consider alternate functional forms.

A major problem in building econometric models is that many alternative specifications are more or less consistent with the theory undergirding the model. Either a linear or a curvilinear relationship may be appropriate for a demand equation. More than one measure of the income variable exists; income may or may not be deflated; and so on almost *ad infinitum*. Thus, in selecting a model, the analyst is faced with numerous choices, and sometimes no clear guides exist for making choices.

The problem of choice is compounded by the "requirements" of statistical inference that the model be specified, the sample data collected, the estimates made, and the hypotheses tested. It is (from the viewpoint of statistical inference) inappropriate to experiment with alternate models, using one set of data, until good results are obtained. Clearly, if a sufficiently large number of alternate specifications are tried, then some specification is likely to be found that gives "good" (but perhaps spurious) results.

Since specification of the best model prior to estimation is nearly impossible for many problems in economics, some experimentation is generally necessary. The judgment of the analyst is critical in model selection, although different models sometimes give similar results. The problem of choice is further considered in the next chapter.

References

Ashby, Andrew. 1964. "Forecasting Commodity Prices by the Balance Sheet Approach," *J. Farm Econ.*, 46:633–643.

Empirical Price Analysis

Breimyer, Harold F. 1961. *Demand and Prices for Meat—Factors Influencing Their Historical Development.* USDA Tech. Bul. 1253.

Dornbusch, Rudiger, and Stanley Fischer. 1978. *Macroeconomics.* New York: McGraw-Hill. Pp. 38–42.

Foote, Richard J. 1958. *Analytical Tools for Studying Demand and Price Structures.* USDA Ag. Hb. 146.

Fox, Karl A. 1953. *The Analysis of Demand for Farm Products.* USDA Tech. Bul. 1081.

Johnston, J. 1972. *Econometric Methods.* 2d ed. New York: McGraw-Hill.

Judge, George G. 1977. "Estimation and Statistical Inference in Economics," in *A Survey of Agricultural Economics Literature.* Volume 2. Ed. Lee R. Martin. Minneapolis: Univ. of Minnesota Press. Pp. 1–49.

Klein, Lawrence R. 1962. *An Introduction to Econometrics.* Englewood Cliffs, N.J.: Prentice-Hall.

Maddala, G. S. 1977. *Econometrics.* New York: McGraw-Hill.

Meilke, Karl D. 1977. "Another Look at the Hog-Corn Ratio," *Am. J. Ag. Econ.,* 59:216–219.

Moore, Henry L. 1914. *Economic Cycles: Their Laws and Causes.* New York: Macmillan.

———. 1917. *Forecasting the Yield and Price of Cotton.* New York: Macmillan.

Nerlove, Marc. 1956. "Estimates of the Elasticities of Supply of Selected Agricultural Commodities." *J. Farm Econ.,* 38:496–509.

Schultz, Henry. 1938. *The Theory and Measurement of Demand.* Chicago: Univ. of Chicago Press.

Theil, Henri. 1971. *Principles of Econometrics.* New York: John Wiley.

Thompson, Stanley R., and Doyle A. Eiler. 1977. "Determinants of Milk Advertising Effectiveness," *Am. J. Ag. Econ.,* 59:330–335.

Tomek, William G. 1977. "Empirical Analyses of the Demand for Food," in *Food Demand and Consumption Behavior.* Ed. Robert Raunikar. Univ. of Georgia, Athens. S-119 Southern Regional Research Committee. Pp. 1–30.

———, and Kenneth L. Robinson. 1977. "Agricultural Price Analysis and Outlook," in *A Survey of Agricultural Economics Literature,* Volume 1. Ed. Lee R. Martin. Minneapolis: Univ. of Minnesota Press. Pp. 327–409.

USDA. 1979. *Livestock and Meat Statistics.* Supplement for 1978 to Stat. Bul. 522. ESCS.

Warren, G. F., and F. A. Pearson. 1928. *Interrelationships of Supply and Price.* Cornell Univ. Ag. Exp. Sta. Bul. 466.

Waugh, Frederick V. 1964. *Demand and Price Analysis: Some Examples from Agriculture.* USDA Tech. Bul. 1316.

Working, Elmer. 1927. "What Do Statistical 'Demand Curves' Show?" *Quart. J. Econ.,* 41:212–235.

Working, Holbrook. 1922. *Factors Determining the Price of Potatoes in St. Paul and Minneapolis.* Univ. Minn. Ag. Exp. Sta. Bul. 10.

CHAPTER **16**

Using Results
of Price Analysis

This chapter provides a basis for interpreting and using results of price analyses based on regression techniques. An appraisal of results of an empirical study depends, in part, on the basic objectives and how well it fulfills these objectives. The usefulness of a particular result is likely to vary with the intended application. The discussion in this chapter must necessarily be rather general; it cannot cover applications of specific pieces of research. But this chapter does suggest tools for using and appraising specific studies.[1] The first section discusses the interpretation of regression results, and a second section covers the appraisal of results. The topic "errors in model specification" is selected for special attention, as it is the single most important problem in empirical price analyses. The computation and interpretation of empirical elasticities also is considered. The final section is devoted to forecasting from regression equations.

Interpreting Estimated Parameters

Net Regression Coefficients

Using the notation of the previous chapter, the unknown relationship among variables is represented by the following equation:

$$Y_t = \beta_0 + \beta_1 X_{t1} + \beta_2 X_{t2} + \ldots + \beta_K X_{tK} + e_t.$$

[1]The intent, as in the previous chapter, is not to give a rigorous statistical treatment, but to provide an intuitive review and some insights into uses and appraisal of quantitative economic analyses.

Empirical Price Analysis

The equation estimated by least squares may be written

$$Y_t = b_0 + b_1 X_{t1} + \ldots + b_K X_{tK} + u_t.$$

Also, $\quad \hat{Y}_t = b_0 + b_1 X_{t1} + \ldots + b_K X_{tK},$

where the computed residuals, which are estimates of the disturbances, are

$$u_t = Y_t - \hat{Y}_t.$$

The $b_1, \ldots, b_K$ are estimates of the net relationship between the respective X_{tK} and Y_t. Each is an estimate of the change in the dependent variable in response to a one-unit change in the particular X_{tK}, the other independent variables held constant. This interpretation holds regardless of how Y_t and X_{tk} are measured. However, the magnitudes of the estimated coefficients do vary with the units (e.g., pounds or tons) used to measure the variables. For this reason, the absolute magnitudes of the estimated coefficients are not measures of the "importance" of the independent variables.[2]

Interpretation is easier if the variables are in comparable units, e.g., quantities in bushels and prices in dollars per bushel. However, variables should be of roughly similar orders of magnitude to help insure computational accuracy. Adjusting variables by powers of 10 only influences the placement of the decimal in the coefficient (Friedman and Foote, 1957, p. 6).

Multiple regression equations are quite flexible in incorporating different functional forms, but this can lead to incorrect interpretations. For the quadratic form, the independent variable and the square of the independent variable both appear as regressors. The effect of a change in this variable must be evaluated by using the coefficients of both regressors (X_t and X_t^2). Another specification sometimes uses the level of a variable and its change from last period (e.g., the current level of income and the change in income are separate regressors).

$$Y_t = b_0 + b_1 X_t + b_2 (X_t - X_{t-1}) + \ldots$$

In this case, the net effect of X_t must be computed from $b_1 X_t + b_2 X_t = (b_1 + b_2) X_t$, that is, $b_1 + b_2$.

[2]Three measures of the relative importance of independent variables in the regression are the level of significance of the coefficients of the variables (to be discussed), partial r^2 coefficients, and beta coefficients (Maddala, 1977, pp. 108–124).

The estimate of the intercept coefficient b_0 places the level of the equation. Technically, it estimates the level of the dependent variable when all of the independent variables are zero. Often the intercept has little meaning because the range of observations of the X_{tk} usually does not extend back to zero. Hence, it is not reasonable to assume a linear relation between Y_t and X_{tk} from zero to the beginning of the observations on the variables. For example, annual per capita beef consumption has ranged upward from 80 pounds in recent years. Thus, while a linear relation may hold between price and quantity within the range of the data, it probably does not hold all of the way back to zero consumption. In this context, the intercept coefficient has little economic meaning. However, if the variables are in first differences, then, as noted in Chapter 15, the intercept is interpreted as the coefficient of a trend variable.

Standard Errors

Courses in introductory statistics emphasize the concept of the variance and standard deviation of a single variable. These statistics are based on the variability of the individual observations about their mean. For the variance, the individual deviations from the mean are computed, squared, summed, and divided by "degrees of freedom."

The variance of regression is simply an extension of the single variable concept. The variance of regression measures the variability of the observed Y_t about the computed regression "line" (the $\hat{Y}_t$). For T observations and $K + 1$ parameters, the regression equation has $T - K - 1$ degrees of freedom. Thus, the variance of regression is

$$s_u^2 = \frac{\displaystyle\sum_{t=1}^{T} u_t^2}{T - K - 1} = \frac{\Sigma\,(Y_t - \hat{Y}_t)^2}{T - K - 1}\ .$$

In the classical regression model, the error terms, e_t, are assumed to have a constant variance, σ_e^2, and s_u^2 is an estimate of this unknown variance.

The standard error of estimate is the square root of the variance of regression. This provides a measure of variability in the same units of measure as the dependent variable. Naturally, the analyst would like to have a relatively small standard of error of estimate.[3] This is consistent

---

[3]The standard error of estimate is not the appropriate statistic for computing a confidence interval of the forecast of Y_t. This is discussed in a subsequent section.

with a high degree of "explanation" of the dependent variable by the independent variables. However, it is possible for a particular economic sector to have large random variations which are not susceptible to systematic explanation.

The standard errors of the regression coefficients (s_b) also may be interpreted by analogy with the standard deviation of a variable. Each b is an estimate of an unknown β. The conceptual possibility of repeated samples means that many possible estimates of β exist, and these alternate estimates are likely to be distributed about the true value. In practice, one sample is available, but nonetheless the standard error of the distribution of each b_k can be estimated. This arises from assumptions made about the model. The e_t are usually assumed, for example, to have a normal distribution. Thus, the b_k are usually assumed to be normally distributed about the true, but unknown, β_k. It is important to note that the estimates of the variances and standard errors of the coefficients (as well as the associated statistical tests) are based on the underlying assumptions of the statistical model. If the assumptions are not met, then the estimated standard errors and the associated statistical tests may not be appropriate.

The analyst would like to have a small standard error of each regression coefficient relative to the size of the respective coefficients. Loosely speaking, this means that the analyst can have considerable confidence that the true, but unknown, parameter is within a relatively small range of the estimate. The importance of small standard errors relative to the regression coefficients is also emphasized in a following section on statistical tests.

Residuals

The residuals, u_t, are estimates of the true, but unobservable, errors, e_t ($t = 1, 2, \ldots, T$). The residuals estimated by least squares have certain properties. First, the sum of the squared residuals, Σu_t^2 is the minimum for any estimator; no other method of estimating the β's can have a smaller sum.

Second, the sum of the residuals is zero. $\Sigma u_t = 0$. This implies that the least-squares regression equation passes through the point of means of the variables in the equation $(\overline{Y}, \overline{X}_1, \ldots, \overline{X}_K)$.

Third, the correlation between any one of the explanatory variables, X_{tk}, and the residuals, u_t, is zero. In this sense, the explanatory variables are independent of the residuals. Hence, the term "independent variable" means that the right-hand-side (explanatory) variables are assumed to have a zero covariance with the error term. The least-squares estimation method forces this condition to be true, although in practice the assumption could be wrong. If so, then least-squares estimation is inappropriate.

Coefficients of Determination

The coefficient of multiple determination, R^2, is a measure of the degree of linear association between the dependent variable and the collective independent variables. Strictly speaking, the coefficient is applicable only for the least-squares estimator, since it forces the covariancès between the explanatory variables and the error term to be zero. Thus, the total variability of Y_t can be divided unambiguously between the variability of the X_{tk}'s and of e_t.

$$R^2 = \frac{\text{variability in } Y \text{ associated with } X\text{'s}}{\text{total variability of } Y} \ .$$

R^2 is a ratio with a range from zero to one. For example, if $R^2 = 0.75$, then 75 per cent of the variability in Y_t is estimated as being associated with the variability of the X_{tk}.

Adding independent variables tends to increase R^2 at least slightly even if there is no "true" relationship between the added independent variable and the dependent variable. Also, as the number of independent variables increases, the degrees of freedom of the equation decrease. Thus, for instance, two observations exactly determine the regression line for a simple two-variable equation; there are no degrees of freedom, and $r^2 = 1$. In general, $R^2 = 1$ in a multiple regression when degrees of freedom is zero. Intuitively, a R^2 near one with very few degrees of freedom suggests a misleading overestimate of the actual degree of association. This idea has led to the use of a corrected coefficient of determination,

$$\bar{R}^2 = 1 - (1 - R^2) \frac{T - 1}{T - K - 1} \ , \text{ where}$$

T = number of observations and
K = number of independent variables.

The interpretation of $\bar{R}^2$ is the same as the interpretation of R^2, i.e., the proportion of the variation in Y_t associated with the variation in the X_{tk}'s. It is mathematically possible, however, for $\bar{R}^2$ to be negative. A negative coefficient should be treated as a zero level of association.

$\bar{R}^2$ is also useful in comparing alternate equation specifications. One of the considerations in selecting among alternate specifications of a model is R^2. The user typically would like to have a high R^2 with a large number of observations relative to the number of independent variables. The corrected coefficient of determination takes this idea into account by penalizing the equation with the larger number of independent variables in relation to the number of observations. Thus, adding a new independent variable increases $\bar{R}^2$ only if R^2 increases sufficiently to offset the "penalty" of the adjustment factor for the larger K. Therefore, in comparing the results of alternate model specifications, $\bar{R}^2$ is a more appropriate statistic than R^2.[4]

As defined above s_u^2, like $\bar{R}^2$, has been used to select among alternative model specifications. The criterion is to select the model with the smallest s_u^2. This is analogous to selecting the model with the largest $\bar{R}^2$. To see this, let s_y^2 be the variance of Y_t ($s_y^2 = \Sigma(Y_t - \bar{Y})^2/(T-1)$), then $\bar{R}^2$ may be specifically defined as

$$\bar{R}^2 = 1 - s_u^2/s_y^2.$$

Since s_y^2 is a constant for a given sample of size T, $\bar{R}^2$ will become larger as s_u^2 gets smaller.

If the dependent variable is transformed in the process of equation specification, the coefficients of determination are no longer comparable between the transformed and the untransformed versions. In particular, R^2 for an equation transformed to logarithms cannot be directly compared with the R^2 for the untransformed equation. In the logarithmic equation, R^2 estimates the proportion of the variation of the logarithm of Y_t which is associated with the variation of the logarithms of the X_{tk}. This is clearly not the same as measuring the proportion of the variance of the observed Y_t associated with the variation of the observed X_{tk}. The antilogs of the calculated values of log Y_t must be obtained and these values used with the observed Y_t to compute the R^2 value for a direct comparison with the untransformed equations. To re-emphasize the point, a larger R^2 for an equation transformed to logarithms does not necessarily mean that transformation is the preferred alternative. It is not clear without additional computations whether the transformation increases the degree of explanation of the observed Y_t.

---

[4]Explicit statistical tests are availalbe to determine if the added independent variable contributes a "statistically significant" explanation of the dependent variable. If the t ratio (defined in the next section) for the coefficient of a particular variable has an absolute value greater than one, $\bar{R}^2$ will decrease if this variable is dropped from the equation.

Appraising the Results

Tests of Logic

In constructing an econometric model, the researcher typically, but not always, has an idea about the expected signs of the coefficients of the equation. In a demand equation, price and quantity of the commodity are logically inversely related. Thus, the price coefficient is expected to have a negative sign. The income coefficient would usually have a positive sign, but there are inferior commodities which would have negative income coefficients. Sometimes the researcher may be uncertain whether a particular commodity is superior or inferior in a particular economy. For example, pork might be considered a superior commodity in some households and an inferior good in others.

If the sign of an estimated coefficient is not consistent with the logic of the model, then the estimated equation is suspect. Perhaps there is specification error in the equation, or there may be high intercorrelation between several independent variables.

The analyst usually has some idea of the expected magnitudes of the coefficients being estimated. This knowledge may be based on logic or on related research results. This does not mean that the researcher must know the precise magnitudes of coefficients, but he or she should have sufficient knowledge to raise questions about coefficients which appear to be excessively large or small. For example, the price-quantity coefficient in a demand equation for onions would be expected to yield a price elasticity less than -1.0 (in absolute value) and probably less than -0.5.

Statistical Tests

In evaluating estimated parameters, the most common statistical procedure is the t test. Consider the model

$$Y_t = \beta_0 + \beta_1 X_{t1} + \beta_2 X_{t2} + \ldots + e_t.$$

The hypothesis usually tested is the null hypothesis of no relationship between an independent variable and the dependent variable. For example, $\beta_1 = 0$. There are two possible alternative hypotheses. The broadest is simply that there is a relationship. Namely, $\beta_1 \neq 0$. This requires a two-tail test. However, if the researcher has strong logical reasons for believing that the true parameter must be negative (or positive), then a one-tail test is appropriate. The alternate hypothesis is $\beta_1 < 0$ when the true parameter must logically be negative. This is the appropriate alternate hypothesis for the price-quantity coefficient in a demand relation.

The test statistic is

$$t = \frac{b_1 - \beta_1}{s_{b_1}} \ .$$

Given the hypothesis $\beta_1 = 0$, the computed statistic simply becomes $t = b_1/s_{b_1}$.

The statistical test is, of course, based on principles of probability. The t-statistic has a probability distribution—the t distribution. Conceptually, we can ask what is the probability of obtaining the computed t for a sample with the given degrees of freedom from a population in which the true parameter is indeed zero? Tables of the t distribution can be constructed; modified versions of such tables are available for testing hypotheses.

In practice, the mechanics of the test are as follows. The t statistic is computed from b_k and s_{b_k}, where the null hypothesis is $\beta_k = 0$. This statistic is compared with the table value of t, which depends on the degrees of freedom of the regression ($T - K - 1$ in our notation) and on the "level of significance." The selection of the level of significance sets the level of type I error (i.e., the probability of rejecting a true null hypothesis), which the analyst is willing to accept. The researcher has discretion in selecting the level of significance, typically designated as α. Commonly used levels of α are 0.01, 0.05, and 0.10.

If the computed t statistic is larger than the critical value of t (from table), then the null hypothesis is rejected. A sample with $T - K - 1$ degrees of freedom from a population with $\beta = 0$ *might* give the computed t, but the probability is sufficiently small (α or less) that the alternate hypothesis is accepted. If the computed t is less than the table value, then the null hypothesis cannot be rejected. In empirical research, a common statement is that the coefficient is not statistically significant, say, at the 5 per cent level. This means that the researcher has not rejected the null hypothesis when $\alpha = .05$.

The analyst may be interested in a small probability of type I error. This gives a high confidence that the true parameter is not zero. However, selecting type I (α) error smaller does increase the probability of making type II error, that is, accepting the null hypothesis when the alternate is true. There are numerous occasions when type II error is more important than type I error to the researcher's decision making. However, the typical researcher selects an arbitrary level of type I error for hypothesis testing, which sometimes is inappropriate (Manderscheid, 1965). Indeed, analysts include variables in an equation precisely because these variables are thought to influence Y (i.e., to have nonzero parameters). Hence, if a variable is logically important in the model, it should not be lightly discarded.

The following equation is based on 18 observations. Hence, there are 14 degrees of freedom. The standard errors of each coefficient appear in parentheses below the coefficient. A one-tail test is assumed to be appropriate for each parameter, and the coefficients do have the expected signs.

$$\hat{Y}_t = 184.3 - 1.057\ X_{t1} - .384\ X_{t2} + .013\ X_{t3}.$$
$$\phantom{\hat{Y}_t = 184.3\ -\ }(.232)\phantom{X_{t1}\ -\ }(.164)\phantom{X_{t2}\ +\ }(.010)$$

For a one-tail test with $\alpha = 0.05$ and 14 degrees of freedom, the table value of $t = |1.761|$. The computed t_1 in the example for the hypothesis $\beta_1 = 0$ is

$$t_1 = \frac{-1.057}{.232} = -4.556.$$

In this example, the null hypothesis is rejected in favor of the alternate hypothesis. There is a high probability that the true parameter is not zero, but rather is negative. This, however, is not a surprising conclusion as X_{t1} was a logically important variable in the model.

A criterion for adding or dropping variables from models may be based on the size of t ratios under the null hypothesis $\beta_k = 0$. (Technically, this practice is called pretest or sequential estimation, and a t-test criterion is implicit in stepwise computer programs.) One practice was to drop variables that had coefficients less than twice the size of their standard errors (a t ratio less than two in absolute value). This rule of thumb arose from the observation that the critical value of t (from table) is approximately two for $\alpha = 0.05$ and about 20 degrees of freedom. A common rule today is to retain variables with t values of one or larger. This is based on the notion that variables, which are a logical part of a model, should not be dropped on stringent statistical grounds. In any case, the analyst's judgment is important.

Price analysts have sometimes used inappropriate procedures in sequential estimation and hypothesis testing. One problem has been to use levels of significance for t tests in the final equation as if no prior experimentation had been done with the data used to fit the final equa-

339

tion. A t test for a regression parameter assumes, among other things, that the researcher has built the appropriate model, estimated it from a given sample of data with no model revisions, and then tested a hypothesis. With model revisions based on prior t tests, the level of significance is rapidly eroded, and since such sequential estimation is almost universal in applied econometrics, the practice of reporting regression coefficients as being significant at the one (or similar) per cent level is misleading (Wallace, 1977). The true levels of significance are without doubt much larger, i.e., poorer. In general, the routine reporting of coefficients as being statistically significant at some specific level should be avoided. If the standard errors of the coefficients as well as the research procedures are reported, readers can draw their own conclusions.

A second problem, which is often associated with the first, is the routine testing of the hypotheses $\beta_k = 0$ ($k = 1, 2, \ldots , K$) *seriatim*. The t test and the corresponding level of significance was designed for a single, simple hypothesis, not for a sequence of tests. For example, if 10 tests were done for 10 different parameters at the 10 per cent level of significance, then one hypothesis is likely to be rejected even if all ten are true (Freund and Debertin, 1975).

Moreover, as suggested above, the hypothesis $\beta_k = 0$ may not be meaningful. The researcher should test just those hypotheses that flow naturally from the research. It may be, for example, that $\beta_k = 1$ is a more appropriate hypothesis for a particular research problem. In this case, the test statistic is $t_k = (b_k - 1)/s_b$.

Of course, a researcher wants regression coefficients that are large relative to their standard errors, i.e., have large t ratios. But, given the model experimentation that lies behind most final results, t ratios usually should be interpreted qualitatively rather than in terms of formal probability statements.

Analysis of Residuals

An important part of appraising results is a study of the residuals of the equation (Maddala, 1977, pp. 83–89). This involves computing $u_t = Y_t - \hat{Y}_t$ ($t = 1, 2, \ldots , T$) and analyzing them. The analysis, of course, covers the sample period. In addition, forecasts might be made beyond the sample period, and then when the actual values are ultimately observed, the forecasts can be appraised. A variant of this procedure is to "save" some data from the original sample (not use it for estimation), and, after estimation, study immediately how well the equation fits the omitted data. The evaluation of forecasts is explored in more detail in a subsequent section. This subsection reviews briefly the analysis of residuals for the sample period.

Residuals can be analyzed by goodness-of-fit measures such as R^2, by formal statistical tests, and by visual inspection of graphs. In essence, one is interested in how well the equation fits the data and whether the residuals have systematic patterns of behavior.

A researcher is naturally interested in having an equation with a large $\bar{R}^2$, other things being constant. With modern computers, it is easy to estimate a large number of alternative equations, and often one can find a particular specification that fits the sample of data very well. The $\bar{R}^2$, however, may be large for just this sample and not represent the true population relation. Measures of goodness-of-fit taken alone can be rather poor measures of the quality of results.

The least-squares estimation procedure makes explicit assumptions about the nature of the error term; specifically, the errors are assumed to have a mean of zero, to have a constant variance over the range of the data, and to have no serial correlation among any of the time periods. Serial correlation (also called autocorrelation) is simply the lagged correlation of a series with itself; for instance, first-order autocorrelation involves e_t and e_{t-1}. Such behavior usually is a sign of specification error in the model, such as the omission of a variable or the use of an incorrect functional form.

Another reason for systematic behavior in the residuals is a structural change within the sample period. For example, if the residuals in recent years are generally positive while those in earlier years are negative, a structural change may have occurred. If a change in structure has occurred, then the coefficients of the equation will not accurately represent the relationships which prevailed in either of the subperiods.

Statistical tests exist for specific hypotheses about the structure of the error term. For example, the Durbin-Watson test is commonly used for the hypothesis of first-order autocorrelation in the errors (for details of the test see Maddala, 1977, pp. 284–291). Visual inspection of a plot of the residuals against time is a useful supplement to formal statistical tests. Systematic patterns of behavior may show up on a graph. For instance, the variability of the residuals may increase with the passage of time, or, if the serial correlation is associated with seasonality in quarterly data, then the residuals four quarters apart would be related (fourth-order autocorrelation). A visual inspection also can indicate the existence of one or two exceptionally large residuals (outliers). The analyst should be concerned if the model cannot explain a large change in a particular time period. Whenever an outlier is observed, one should try to find out whether the observation is the result of an error in the data, the omission of an important variable, or a random event such as a natural disaster. A single outlying observation can have a great influence on the values of the regression coefficients. If a large residual is observed for a particular time period, the analyst has to decide whether the observation should be retained or deleted, and, if retained, whether the model should be altered.

The foregoing comments all serve to emphasize an important point, namely that the behavior of the residuals must be examined. Any non-random behavior is a sign of danger, and every effort should be made to uncover the source of the systematic element which has been observed. It is possible for an estimated equation to have a large $\bar{R}^2$ but also have significant serial correlation in the residuals. In this case, the researcher should be skeptical about the estimated coefficients and the forecasting ability of the equation (Granger and Newbold, 1977). A respecification of the model that reduces the serial correlation also is likely to result in large changes in the estimated coefficients.

Specification Error and Multicollinearity

Specification error in its broadest sense is any error in model specification. In practice, the term "specification error" usually refers to the omission of relevant explanatory variables or to the inclusion of irrelevant variables.

A relevant variable may be omitted from an equation because the analyst is unaware of the importance of the variable or is unable to obtain observations on the variable. The omission of a relevant variable also can be interwoven with the problem of multicollinearity. Multicollinearity, as mentioned in Chapter 15, is the problem of large correlations among explanatory variables; the correlations are so large that regression procedures cannot disentangle the separate effects of the variables. One way of dealing with this problem is to drop one of the intercorrelated variables, but this may result in omitting a relevant variable from the model. In this case, the analyst is confronted with a trade-off between two problems.

If a relevant variable is omitted and if it is correlated with the explanatory variables in the equation, which is the usual case, the estimates of the parameters of the included variables are biased. The sign and magnitude of the bias depend on the sign and magnitude of the (unknown) parameter of the excluded variable and on the relationship of the excluded variable to the included variables (Maddala, 1977, pp. 155–157).

The consequences of omitting relevant variables can be illustrated by alternative specifications of equations to represent the demand for pork. Using the arguments outlined in Chapter 15, deflated price is the dependent variable in each equation (Table 16-1). Equation (1) contains just two explanatory variables: the per capita consumption of pork and per capita real income. The coefficients of both variables have relatively small standard errors, but the Durbin-Watson statistic (d) is relatively small. This implies positive first-order serial correlation in the residuals (Maddala, 1977, p. 285); and a plot of the residuals against time also implies a systematic pattern of behavior (Figure 16-1). As indicated above, ill-behaved residuals can be a sign of specification error.

The consumption of beef is added in equation (2), and both the consumption of beef and of chicken are added in equation (3). As the variables are added, the Durbin-Watson statistic becomes larger. A statistic "near" two implies that there is no autocorrelation. Thus, the addition of variables appears to be reducing the autocorrelation in the residuals of the pork equations.

The coefficient of income increases almost sixfold as variables are added, while the coefficient of the consumption of pork changes little. The income, beef, and chicken variables were positively correlated in

Table 16-1. Estimated retail price relationships for pork, United States, 1955–1977

| Equation number | Intercept | Independent variables* | | | | $\bar{R}^2$ | d |
		X_1	X_2	X_3	X_4		
(1)	127.9	−1.264	—	—	0.006	.68	0.88
	(14.5)†	(0.218)			(0.002)		
(2)	138.2	−1.279	−0.662	—	0.021	.74	1.03
	(13.7)	(0.197)	(0.277)		(0.007)		
(3)	130.0	−1.233	−0.620	−0.881	0.034	.78	1.58
	(13.2)	(0.182)	(0.255)	(0.413)	(0.008)		

*X_1 = consumption of pork, lb. per cap. per year ($\bar{X}_1$ = 59.3); X_2 = consumption of beef, lb. per cap. ($\bar{X}_2$ = 76.1); X_3 = consumption of chicken, lb. per cap. ($\bar{X}_3$ = 34.4); all consumption variables retail weight; X_4 = disposable personal income, $ per capita deflated by Consumer Price Index, 1967 = 100 ($\bar{X}_4$ = 2635). Dependent variable is retail price of pork deflated by the Consumer Price Index, cents per lb. (mean = 68.6). Scatter diagram of price-quantity observations for 1960–1977 is shown in Figure 15-4.

†Standard errors of respective coefficients shown in parentheses.

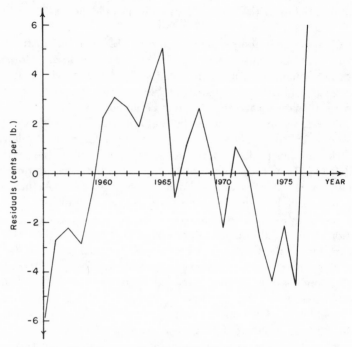

Figure 16-1. Residuals for equation (1), Table 16-1

the 1955–1977 sample period; all three were trending upward. The quantity of beef and of chicken each should have negative effects on the price of pork; that is, a larger supply of beef would, other things constant, depress the price of beef which in turn would reduce the price of pork. Thus, when beef and chicken were omitted from the pork equation, as in equation (1), the effect of income on the demand for pork was underestimated; i.e., the coefficient is biased downward since income is picking up part of the negative effects of the omitted variables. On the other hand, the quantities of beef and chicken have little correlation with the quantity of pork,[5] and hence the omission of the two variables had little influence on the coefficient associated with the quantity of pork.

The last pork equation, even with quantities of beef and poultry included as explanatory variables, still might be improved. The autocorre-

---

[5]The quantity variables are based on supplies available to be consumed, and prices adjust to the changes in supplies. Thus, the quantity variables need not be correlated.

lation has been reduced, but an examination of the residuals for equation (3) (not shown) indicates that the residual for 1977 is still very large. It would be important to understand the reason for the unusual behavior of pork prices in that year.

The inclusion of an irrelevant variable in an equation does not cause bias. This is true since an irrelevant variable, by definition, has a true parameter of zero. Since there is no bias, the inclusion of an irrelevant variable may appear to be less serious than the exclusion of a relevant variable. But this is not necessarily true. If the included irrelevant variable is correlated with one or more of the other explanatory variables, then the variances of the regression coefficients are unnecessarily increased.

The analyst would like to have a model that includes all relevant variables, but excludes irrelevant variables. As suggested above, one can examine the signs of coefficients, the size of t ratios of coefficients, and the residuals of the equations to obtain guides to model specification. But, ultimately, the experience and judgment of the analyst are extremely important in selecting the "final" model.

An especially difficult situation arises when coefficients have relatively large standard errors because of multicollinearity and when compelling reasons exist for including all of the intercorrelated variables in the equation. "Solutions" that retain the variables in the model require additional information either in the form of more observations or in the form of restrictions on the parameters of the equation being estimated.[6] The time series might be extended in the hope that the variables will be less correlated over the longer sample period. It may be possible to pool cross-section and time-series data for some problems, although this usually requires more complex statistical models (Maddala, 1977, Chapter 14).

Additional data, however, may be costly to obtain or simply not available. A common approach to multicollinearity involves imposing an implicit or explicit constraint on parameters of the model. Examples of implicit constraints include using ratios of variables, first differences of variables, simple or weighted sums or averages of variables, or perhaps dropping a variable from the model. Adding two variables, for instance, implies that each variable has the same parameter, i.e., $\beta(X_1 + X_2)$ is the appropriate relationship rather than $\beta_1 X_1 + \beta_2 X_2$. A ratio implies an

---

[6]Some alternative estimation methods, such as ridge regression, have been developed for the problem of multicollinearity. These methods also require a particular kind of additional information. The topic, however, is beyond the scope of this book.

345

analogous restriction, and, as mentioned in Chapter 15, the first-difference transformation implies special restrictions on the nature of the error term of the transformed equation.

Analysts sometimes drop a variable from the model when multicollinearity exists even though the omitted variable is logically relevant in the model. The omission, of course, restricts the parameter of that variable to zero and results in bias in the estimates of the other coefficients. In this situation the analyst is making the judgment that the gain from reducing the variances of the coefficients of retained variables exceeds the loss resulting from an increase in bias. Bias and variance can be combined in a concept called the "mean square error," and in principle this concept could be used to decide whether or not a variable is retained in the model. Unfortunately, the true mean square error is unknown for specific problems, and moreover the topic is beyond the scope of this book. In essence, the analyst is making the very difficult judgment of whether the specification error of omitting the variable or the multicollinearity associated with retaining the variable is a more serious problem. Such judgments must be made on a case-by-case basis.

Errors in Variables and Proxy Variables

The variables in a model may be measured with error. Mistakes may be made in compiling, publishing, and using data, and the measured variable may not correctly represent the economic concept relevant to the model. For example, in specifying a consumption function, the analyst may use the annual income reported by households, but the households may be making consumption decisions based on what they perceive to be their permanent income. Or, in supply analysis, a geometric weighted average of past prices has been used as a measure of the concept "expected price," but this measure may not capture the true expectations of suppliers. If the explanatory variables are measured with error, then the least-squares estimates of the parameters of the equation are biased (Johnston, 1972, pp. 281–291). Nonetheless, the errors-in-variables problem is usually assumed to be relatively unimportant, although, of course, variables are likely to have some measurement error.

Proxy variables are often used when observations on a variable are not available or when the variable cannot be measured (e.g., changes in tastes and preferences of consumers). Trend, code, and zero-one variables are examples of proxies used to substitute for nonmeasurable concepts. These artificial variables are included to "improve" the estimates of the parameters of the other variables in the equation. For example, the analyst may be mainly interested in the coefficient relating price to quantity, but thinks consumer preferences are changing. Thus, to avoid the specification error of omitting a preference variable from the model, a trend variable is included. This assumes that the bias related to an error in variable (trend as a proxy for preferences) is smaller than the bias from omitting the concept from the equation. The price-quantity coefficient is assumed less biased with the trend variable in the equation than without it.

Proxy variables, however, can be misused, and alternative specifications of proxy variables can have a profound effect on the coefficients of other variables in the equation. Tomek (1972) shows how alternative methods of allowing for shifts in a supply function for cotton influenced the price coefficient. It is rather common to use time trends to allow for unmeasurable, systematic shifts in supply functions. Thus, one plausible model is

$$\hat{A}_t = 6.319 + .566\ P_{t-1} + .565\ A_{t-1} + .271\ t,$$
$$(5.396)\ (.154)\qquad (.150)\qquad\quad (.104)$$
$$\bar{R}^2 = .71, d = 1.60,$$

where A_t = cotton acreage planted, million acres (A_{t-1} same variable lagged one year),

P_{t-1} = season average price of cotton, deflated by the Index of Prices Paid by Farmers, cents per pound,

t = trend (= 1, 2, ...).

The coefficients are large relative to their standard errors, and the results seem reasonable. The coefficient of the trend variable suggests a positive trend of 271,000 acres per year, net of the effects of the other variables. This implies a positive shift in supply each year of a fixed amount for given levels of past price and past acreage.

An inspection of a scatter diagram, however, suggests a large shift in supply from the 1910–1924 to the 1925–1933 period (Figure 16-2). This type of shift can be accommodated by using a zero-one variable (Johnston, 1972, p. 177). The variable D is defined as zero in the years 1910–1924 and as one in the years 1925–1933, and D is substituted for t in the equation.

$$\hat{A}_t = 22.417 + .749\ P_{t-1} + .068\ A_{t-1} + 9.352\ D.$$
$$(4.312)\ (.100)\qquad (.127)\qquad\quad (1.321)$$
$$\bar{R}^2 = .89,\ d = 1.19.$$

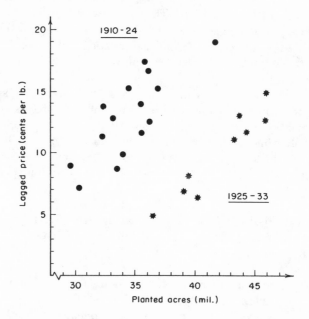

Figure 16-2. Relationship between cotton acreage and lagged deflated price, United States, 1910-1933. Data from USDA, *Agricultural Statistics 1937,* pp. 88-89 and p. 399.

The coefficient of lagged price is more than 30 per cent higher in the second specification, while the coefficient of lagged acreage declines from 0.565 to 0.068.

The zero-one variable is interpreted as simply shifting the intercept (level) of the equation. In 1910–1924, $D = 0$ and the intercept is 22.417. In 1925–1933, $D = 1$ and the intercept is $22.417 + 9.352 = 31.769$. The D variable, like the t variable, does not tell why supply changed, but in this example the D variable appears to provide a better method of taking account of the one-time shift. In this sense, the net effect of P_{t-1} on A_t is probably better measured in the second specification.

The decline in the Durbin-Watson statistic from 1.60 in the first specification to 1.19 in the second is of some concern. Since both equations contain the lagged dependent variable, A_{t-1}, the d statistic is biased toward the acceptance of the hypothesis of no autocorrelation, and in this context, a small d certainly is suggestive of the existence of autocorrelation. Thus, both equations apparently have problems, the first because the specification of the trend variable appears inconsistent with the nature of the actual shift in supply and the second because of the small d value. The point to be made here, however, is that substituting the proxy variable D for the proxy variable t had a large effect on the magnitude of the other coefficients in the equation. Proxy variables should not be inserted into equations in a casual manner.

Imprecise data also have implications for model revisions and for reporting results. When an initial model specification gives unsatisfactory results, the usual practice, as discussed above, is to revise the model, that is to drop or add variables, to change the functional form, etc. But the model may be correct, and the source of the poor results may be poor data. It is rather uncommon for analysts to investigate whether their data are appropriate or accurate relative to the research problem.

In addition, a few analysts, using results just as they come from the computer, report a large number of digits for each coefficient. This implies a false sense of accuracy. The number of digits reported for the regression coefficients should not exceed the number of significant digits in the original data, and at best this will be two or three.

Computing and Appraising Elasticities and Flexibilities

Since elasticities play an important role in economics, they are frequently computed from the coefficients of regression equations. Elasticities (or flexibilities) are given directly by the coefficients of equations which are linear in the logarithms of the variables, but for most other functional forms, they must be calculated. A linear demand equation illustrates how elasticities are obtained. Assume we have estimated

$$\hat{Q} = b_0 - b_1 P + \dots .$$

The coefficient b_1 is an estimate of the net slope relating price (P) and quantity (Q), holding the other independent variables constant. The price elasticity of demand is defined as

$$E = \frac{\Delta Q}{\Delta P} \ \frac{P}{Q} \ , \text{ holding other factors constant.}$$

Since b_1 can be viewed as a measure of the change in Q given a one-unit change in P, the ratio $\Delta Q / \Delta P$ equals b_1, where b_1 is negative. Thus, the elasticity is computed from

$$E = b_1 \ \frac{P}{Q} \ .$$

The ratio P/Q must represent a point on the estimated demand function; actual observations (from the original sample) cannot be used because such observations typically are not on the regression line. The usual practice is to use the arithmetic means of P and Q, since (1) the least-squares fit is known to go through this point and (2) it is a point in the "middle" of the data.

With a demand function that is linear in the original observations, the elasticity varies as the ratio P/Q changes. To compute an elasticity at any point on a linear function, the relevant values of the independent variables are inserted into the equation and the corresponding value of Q on the regression line is computed. The selected level of P and the resulting computed value of Q are then used in the ratio P/Q to obtain the elasticity.

As previously noted, price-dependent equations are frequently estimated for recursive models in agricultural economics.

$$\hat{P} = a_0 - a_1 Q + \ldots .$$

In this case, it is natural to estimate flexibility coefficients. The own-price flexibility is

$$F = \frac{\Delta P}{\Delta Q} \ \frac{Q}{P} \ , \text{ holding other variables constant.}$$

Thus, the estimated flexibility at the point of means is

$$F = a_1 \left(\frac{\bar{Q}}{\bar{P}} \right).$$

The price elasticity of demand is frequently approximated by using the reciprocal of the flexibility coefficient. As mentioned in Chapter 3, with price-dependent equations, the same variables are not held constant as with quantity-dependent equations; for this and other reasons, the reciprocal of a_1 above does not equal b_1. The reciprocal of the flexibility sets the lower limit of the elasticity. Sometimes a system of price-dependent equations has been developed for a set of substitutes. These equations can be transformed to quantity-dependent equations with prices as the explanatory variables. In this special case, the elasticity can be computed from the transformed equations (computational details are given in Foote, 1958, pp. 87ff.).

Estimates of price elasticities of supply, income elasticities of demand, and flexibility coefficients can be computed from linear equations using analogous procedures. For instance, an acreage response equation for cotton was presented above. The price elasticity of supply is estimated at the point of means as

$$E_s = \frac{\Delta Q}{\Delta P} \frac{P}{Q} = 0.749 \frac{11.87}{37.32} = 0.24,$$

where 0.749 is the slope coefficient, $\bar{P} = 11.87$, and $\bar{A} = 37.32$. In this case, the elasticity measures the responsiveness of acreage, rather than total quantity, to price.

Elasticity estimates should not be accepted uncritically, and in appraising elasticity estimates, the procedures used in obtaining the elasticities must be considered. Since some type of statistical analysis usually is the basis for the computed elasticity, the economist must specify and estimate an appropriate relationship. Hence, one question is whether or not the mathematical relationship can be called a "demand curve." As discussed in Chapter 15, simply obtaining observations on prices and quantities does not necessarily specify the slope of the demand curve. It also is obvious that *all* other factors cannot be held constant in a statistical analysis. The economist, at best, will be able to hold some major variables constant. Thus, for this reason alone, the estimated coefficient is an approximation of the theoretical concept. However, these approximations often are useful.

The numerous choices with respect to the data used in demand analysis will affect the magnitude of the elasticity coefficients which are obtained. Elasticities will, of course, vary depending on whether the price-quantity relationship is estimated using farm, wholesale, or retail data. The market area covered and the time period used for the analysis also influence results. This influence on the magnitude of measured elasticities arises, in part, because different demand relationships are involved. One should not be surprised to discover, for example, that the price elasticity of demand for center-cut pork chops at retail in New York City differs from the elasticity of demand for hogs in Iowa.

Elasticity estimates also are influenced by the degree of product aggregation. The more products are combined, the fewer the number of substitutes and therefore the less elastic (or more inelastic) demand is likely to be. For example, there are fewer substitutes for all livestock products combined than for beef alone; hence, one would expect to obtain a lower elasticity estimate for all meat than for beef.

In addition, as the reader may recall, two different samples from the same popuation are not likely to provide exactly the same estimates of the unknown parameters. Differences arise due to sampling error, and for a particular data set there is no guarantee that the estimated coefficients equal the "true" parameters. For reasons given in previous sections, the estimated coefficients may be biased. For example, the slope coefficient, 0.749, used to compute the price elasticity of supply for cotton may be seriously in error.

Notwithstanding the above qualifications, empirical elasticities have often displayed some internal consistency. For example, different studies have obtained similar elasticities for retail-level demand equations for meats, such as beef and pork. Farm-level demand relations are typically found to be more price-inelastic than retail-level functions. The important conclusion is that the potential user must select the elasticity which is relevant for his particular problem.

Forecasting from Regression Equations

Mechanics

The actual computations for making a point forecast of the dependent variable in a regression equation are simple. The analyst has presumably estimated an appropriate equation. For example,

$$\hat{Y}_* = b_0 + b_1 X_{*1} + b_2 X_{*2}.$$

The procedure is to obtain the relevant values of the independent variables for the forecast period (the X_{*k}), insert them in the equation, and compute the dependent variable.

Once the appropriate equation has been estimated, the major problem remaining is to obtain the relevant values of the independent variables for the forecast period.[7] If the independent variables are pre-

---

[7]This is sometimes called the problem of making "ancillary forecasts."

determined, then their levels are determined by outside or prior events. Nonetheless, obtaining observations to make the forecast may be difficult. For example, in forecasting price, production is predetermined, but it is difficult to know even at harvest the precise level of production.

There are various methods and sources for obtaining estimates of the independent variables for the forecast period. Government agencies sometimes publish relevant estimates. The Crop Reporting Service of the USDA makes monthly preharvest estimates of the size of many crops. Data are also available on planted acres, weather conditions, and other factors, which enable the analyst to make estimates of production. Regular reports are also made on size of inventories and on expected levels of inventories. Some variables, like population and income, have rather smooth growth rates over short periods of time so that reasonable short-term projections can be made.

Sometimes there is a sufficient time lag between the specified independent variables and the dependent variable that the analyst can wait until the independent variables are observed before making the forecast. When an equation is part of a recursive model, its sequential nature is helpful in obtaining estimates of independent variables in successive equations. For example, supply next year may depend on current or recent past prices and costs. These observations can be used to forecast supply. The forecast level of supply, then, can be used to help forecast price in the next period.

Short-run forecasts of supply can take advantage of known fixed biological relationships in the production process, particularly those for animals (see, for example, Walters, 1965). Units produced are limited by the size of the breeding herd or flock; gestation and hatching periods are known; live chicks hatched per 100 eggs, for instance, is a well-established rate. Thus, a forecast of current broiler production can be related to the hatch of broiler-type chicks two or three months earlier. The number of chicks hatched, in turn, depends on the number of eggs placed in incubators and their hatchability rate.

Interpreting Forecasts

The point estimate of the dependent variable ($\hat{Y}_*$ in the equation above) is said to be a conditional forecast. It is conditional on the values selected for the independent variables (the X_{*k}, $k = 1, \ldots, K$). If the values of the independent variables are changed, then $\hat{Y}_*$ changes.

A point of some confusion is that $\hat{Y}_*$ can be given two interpretations: as an estimate of a conditional mean or as an estimate of an individual Y_t (where t now refers to some forthcoming time period). Conceptually, there is a conditional distribution of individual Y_t's for a given set of X_{tk}'s, and the distribution has a true, but unknown, mean. The distribution of Y_t's arises from the assumptions made about the error term of the equation. Thus, if many replications of Y_t were obtained for fixed values of the explanatory variables, the individual Y_t's will be distributed about a mean and will have a variance based on the variance of the error term. If new levels of the explanatory variables were used, the individual Y_t's would be distributed about a new mean. Consequently, the particular values X_{*k} imply a particular conditional distribution with a fixed mean, and the computed Y_* may be interpreted as an estimate of this mean. In this case, the error term is assumed to be zero, which is correct on the average.

The usual forecast, however, is for a specific, individual time period, not for the conceptual average obtained from repeated samples for fixed values of the explanatory variables. That is, a particular Y_t in the distribution is being forecast, and $\hat{Y}_*$ may be interpreted as an estimate of this individual Y_t. In this case, of course, the error term will not be zero. The single, observed Y_t is not likely to be the same as the average.

The forecast of an individual Y_t is always subject to two errors. First, the equation is an estimate of the true population relation. Even if the equation is correctly specified and has no sources of bias, the equation is still an estimate. The estimated coefficients will not exactly equal the true parameters, and the forecast is, therefore, subject to sampling error. Second, since the forecast is for an individual Y_t, the error term for the tth (forecast) period will not be zero. Random factors will influence the actual level of Y_t, while in computing Y_* from the equation, the random factors are treated as being zero. These two sources of error are taken into account in the derivation of the variance of forecast, and the standard error of forecast (the square root of the variance) can be used to estimate confidence intervals for a forecast.[8]

Unfortunately, individual forecasts are often subject to additional sources of error. Values of the explanatory variables used in making the forecasts may themselves be wrong. Frequently, they are estimates derived from other equations. For instance, as discussed above, the level of supply forecast from one equation may be used to forecast price from a second equation. Thus, the conditions supporting the forecast may turn out to have been erroneous. The variance of forecast can be

[8]Formulas for computing the standard error of forecast and confidence intervals are given in many textbooks (e.g., Maddala, 1977, p. 82 and pp. 119–120). A distinction must be made between the variances pertaining to estimating the conditional mean and those pertaining to individual forecasts.

modified to take account of this additional source of error (Feldstein, 1971), but the resulting confidence intervals may be very large and hence not very useful.

There are at least two other potential types of errors. The equation may have been incorrectly specified or estimated, and hence the regression coefficients may have serious biases. Finally, the structure of the model may change with the passage of time. Thus, while the forecast equation may have been applicable to the sample period, it may not be applicable to the forecast period.

As has already been discussed, an equation should be appraised for possible errors, such as the omission of a relevant variable, but problems may not become obvious until actual forecasts are attempted. If the analyst recognizes that a structural change has occurred, it may be possible to make adjustments in the old coefficients to help the equation reflect the change in structure. In all cases, the forecast generated by an equation is simply a starting point in making a forecast. The analyst will typically modify the estimate derived from the regression equation on the basis of informed judgment. If the apple crop is known to be of poor quality, for example, a larger proportion than average may go into processing uses, thereby lowering the prices paid farmers for processing apples. An analyst would take such information into account in making a forecast of the price received by farmers for processing apples.

Evaluating Forecasts

This subsection introduces some methods for appraising forecasts (for more information see Dhrymes *et al.*, 1975; Granger and Newbold, 1977; and Theil, 1965 and 1966). Emphasis is placed on forecasting beyond the sample period, although many of the techniques could be used to evaluate an equation's performance within the sample period. Forecasts beyond the sample period can take two forms. As mentioned before, one is to save some data to generate "forecasts" of the dependent variable. This approach to evaluation is not a full test because the explanatory variables used to make the forecasts have already been observed. In an actual forecasting situation, precise estimates of the right-hand-side variables may not be available.

The second approach is to evaluate actual forecasts. Obviously, time must pass before an evaluation can be made. In appraising forecasts, it is helpful to identify possible sources of errors. Is the basic model wrong? Has there been a structural change? Were the values used for the explanatory variables erroneous? Did the analyst make poor judgmental modifications of the values computed from the equation?

355

Empirical Price Analysis

Criteria for evaluating forecasts can be categorized as goodness-of-fit and tracking measures. Tracking measures are designed to test the ability of an equation to identify turning points (changes in direction) at the time they occur. The analyst naturally would prefer an equation that correctly predicts turning points (a large proportion of the time relative to the alternatives) and that does not predict turning points which do not occur.[9] It is especially important to be able to forecast major changes in direction, but appraisal of this characteristic of a model usually involves qualitative judgment.

Numerous measures of goodness-of-fit of forecasts exist. An obvious statistic is the simple coefficient of determination, r^2, between the predicted (P_t) and the actual (A_t) values of Y_t, but a more informative basis for evaluation is the simple linear regression equation

$$A_t = \alpha + \beta P_t + e_t.$$

For a perfect forecast, $r^2 = 1$, $\alpha = 0$, and $\beta = 1$. Errors in forecasts can be evaluated in terms of the differences of the estimates of α from zero, β from one, and r^2 from one.

A commonly used measure of goodness-of-fit is the mean-square error (MSE) of the predictions or its square root, RMSE.

$$\text{MSE} = \frac{1}{I} \Sigma (P_t - A_t)^2,$$

where $t = 1, 2, \ldots, I$, the number of comparisons. The RMSE would be in the units of measure of the variable A. Thus, the percentage obtained from the ratio $\text{RMSE}/\bar{A}$, where $\bar{A}$ = mean of A, is often used to compare the forecasts of different variables or of different models. The MSE can be decomposed into components analogous to those of the regression equation above, and in this sense the two measures are related (Theil, 1965, Chapter 2). Theil also proposes a decomposition of the MSE into bias (unequal means of P and A), unequal variability (different standard deviations), and unequal covariation.

[9]Theil (1965, Chapter 2) provides a rigorous discussion of the evaluation of turning-point errors. He points out that there are two kinds of correct forecasts and two kinds of errors. A correct forecast occurs when the dependent variable changes direction and this is predicted, and also when the dependent variable does not change direction and this is predicted. Incorrect forecasts occur when the dependent variable changes direction, but this is not forecast (type I error), and when the variable does not change direction, but a change is predicted (type II error). One could compute the proportions of an equation's forecasts that fall in the four categories.

An evaluation of the forecasting performance of a particular equation is not very informative unless one has a standard of comparison. An equation could have a mediocre forecasting ability in an absolute sense, but still be relatively good compared with the alternative forecasts. Thus, the forecasting performance of one model should be compared with alternatives, which might be other models or even judgmental forecasts. Sometimes price forecasts from a quantitative model have been compared with prices for the future delivery of a commodity that are observable in futures markets.

Another basis for comparison is the so-called "naive forecast." The simplest naive forecast is $P_t = A_{t-1}$. This standard is implicit in coefficients of inequality (u) proposed by Theil (see Leuthold, 1975 for a discussion of alternative u's). One version of the coefficient of inequality is

$$u = \frac{\sqrt{\frac{1}{I} \Sigma (P_i - A_i)^2}}{\sqrt{\frac{1}{I} \Sigma A_i^2}} \quad .$$

In effect, the root mean-square error (RMSE) is standardized by a component using the actual values. Theil apparently intended that A_i and P_i be defined as differences: $P_i = P_t - A_{t-1}$ and $A_i = A_t - A_{t-1}$. (Granger and Newbold, 1977, argue that all evaluation statistics should be computed in terms of the differences.) If the value of u falls between zero and one, the forecast is better than the one obtained from a naive model; if $u = 1$, this is equivalent to the forecasting ability of a naive model; and if u is greater than one, then the forecasting equation is performing worse than the naive model. In other words, the larger the value of u, the poorer the equation's ability to forecast.

The Economic Consequences of Forecasts

The payoff to an individual firm from making an accurate forecast can be high if the manager has sufficient time to alter decisions in response to the forecast. The public also may gain through improved resource allocation if accurate forecasts are made of long-run equilibrium prices. Costs associated with variable production and the variable use of marketing facilities can be quite high, and accurate price forecasts may help to smooth production. The government also needs to have accurate forecasts of how producers and consumers are likely to react to alternative price or subsidy programs if rational decisions are to be made.

Short-run public forecasting of prices, however, presents a serious dilemma. If the forecast is made sufficiently far in advance to enable producers to alter production plans, it may turn out to be inaccurate. For example, if the government forecasts a rise in hog prices over the next eighteen months, prices may begin to fall before the expiration of that period because a sufficient number of producers have taken the forecast seriously and have increased production. Forecasts of prices made after the time production decisions can be altered are likely to be more accurate, but less useful to producers. By then it is too late for producers to use the information generated by forecasts; however, such forecasts may still be useful to those involved in processing and marketing or price determination.

The longer forecasts are made into the future, the more important it is to take account of the "feedback" effect of the forecast on subsequent decisions. This again emphasizes the need to develop recursive or sequential models in agriculture which make it possible to take account of the effects of decisions made in one period on outcomes in another. These, in turn, affect future decisions. Forecasting can be improved by making such relationships explicit and quantifiable.

References

Dhrymes, Phoebus, *et al.* 1975. "Criteria for Evaluation of Econometric Models," in *The Brookings Model: Perspective and Recent Developments.* Eds. Garry Fromm and Lawrence Klein. Amsterdam: North-Holland. Pp. 477–520.

Feldstein, Martin S. 1971. "The Error of Forecast in Econometric Models when the Forecast-Period Exogenous Variables are Stochastic," *Econometrica,* 39:55–60.

Foote, Richard J. 1958. *Analytical Tools for Studying Demand and Price Structures.* USDA Ag. Hb. 146.

Freund, R. J., and D. L. Debertin. 1975. "Variable Selection and Statistical Significance: A Sampling Experiment," *Am. J. Ag. Econ.,* 57:721–722.

Friedman, Joan, and Richard J. Foote. 1957. *Computational Methods for Handling Systems of Simultaneous Equations.* USDA Ag. Hb. 94.

Granger, C. W. J., and Paul Newbold. 1977. *Forecasting Economic Time Series.* New York: Academic Press. Pp. 202–214.

Johnston, J. 1972. *Econometric Methods.* 2d ed. New York: McGraw-Hill.

Leuthold, Raymond M. 1975. "On the Use of Theil's Inequality Coefficients," *Am. J. Ag. Econ.,* 57:344–346.

Maddala, G. S. 1977. *Econometrics.* New York: McGraw-Hill.

Manderscheid, Lester V. 1965. "Significance Level—0.05, 0.01, or ?," *J. Farm Econ.,* 47:1381–1385.

Theil, H. 1965. *Economic Forecasts and Policy.* 2d rev. ed. Amsterdam: North-Holland.

———. 1966. *Applied Economic Forecasting.* Chicago: Rand-McNally.

Tomek, William G. 1972. "Distributed Lag Models of Cotton Acreage Response: A Further Result," *Am. J. Ag. Econ.*, 54:108–110.

Wallace, T. Dudley. 1977. "Pretest Estimation in Regression: A Survey," *Am. J. Ag. Econ.*, 59:431–443.

Walters, Forrest. 1965. "Predicting the Beef Cattle Inventory," *Ag. Econ. Res.*, 17:10–18.

Author Index

361

Author Index

Subject Index

Subject Index

Monopoly, *see* Price determination; Price discrimination

Multicollinearity, 320–321, 342, 345–346

Negotiating prices:
group bargaining, 220–222
individuals, 216

Opportunity cost, 75
Organized markets, 216–219, 229–231

Parity prices, 282–283
Parity ratio, 203
Price analysis:
data sources, 309–310
defined, 299
demand equations, 317–319
models, general, 302–309
objectives of, 299
supply equations, 314–317
techniques of, 300–302
see also Regression analysis
Price determination:
monopolistic competition, 112–113
monopoly, 103–106
oligopoly, 113–114
perfect and pure competition, 95–103
see also Price discrimination
Price discrimination:
analytics of, 110–112
applications in agriculture, 109–110
definition and conditions for, 106–109
Price discovery, *see* Pricing mechanisms
Price instability:
reasons for, 18–19, 189–190, 199–200
reducing of, 276–281
see also Annual price variation; Cycles
Price level, in aggregate, 194–196
Price policy objectives, 274–276
Price supports:
costs of, 287–288, 292–293
methods, 283–293
programs in United States, 281–283
Pricing mechanisms:
alternatives, 214–216
changes in, 224
performance of, 225–227
Pure competition:
definition, 93–94
price determination, 95–97
short run, 100–103
very short run, 97–100

Quality, *see* Grades for farm products
Quotas, *see* International commodity agreements; Supply control programs

Random walk, price changes as, 241, 243, 249
Recursive model, 313–314
see also Cobweb model
Regional price differentials:
boundary between supply areas, 155–158
observed versus theoretical differences, 153–155
principles of, 151
see also Spatial price equilibrium models
Regression analysis:
appraising results, 337–342
interpreting coefficients, 331–336
model, 302
residuals, analysis of, 340–342
Risk premium, 263–264
Risk, shifting of, 252–253, 255–256
Role of prices, 19–21

Scatter diagrams, 309
Seasonality in prices, 170–176
see also Futures markets
Serially correlated residuals, 341
Simultaneous equations model, 304–306
Slutsky (symmetry) condition, 55–56
Spatial differences in prices, *see* Regional price differentials
Spatial price equilibrium models:
assumptions, 162
concept, 158–161
two region illustrations, 158–159, 165–166
uses, 162, 164
Specification error, 342–345
Speculators, 232
see also Demand, speculative; Futures markets, role of speculators
Stabilization fund, 281
Stabilization:
gains to producers, 274, 277–279
of prices, 276–279
Stabilization programs, *see* Price instability
Standard error:
of estimate, 333–334
of forecast, 354
of regression coefficients, 334
Storage programs, 286–288
see also Buffer stocks
Structural changes:
demand, 33
quantitative analysis of, 315–316, 346–347
supply, 81

Library of Congress Cataloging in Publication Data

Tomek, William G.   1932–
   Agricultural product prices.

   Includes bibliographical references and indexes.
   1. Agricultural prices—United States.   I.   Robinson, Kenneth Leon, 1921–
joint author.   II.   Title.
HD9004.T65   1980   338.1'3'0973   80-16085
ISBN 0-8014-1337-0